D1083106

JAPAN'S PSEUDO-DEMOCRACY

JAPAN'S PSEUDO-DEMOCRACY

PETER J. HERZOG

NEW YORK UNIVERSITY PRESS
Washington Square, New York

JAPAN'S PSEUDO-DEMOCRACY

First published in the U.S.A. in 1993 by
NEW YORK UNIVERSITY PRESS
Washington Square
New York, N.Y. 10003

Library of Congress Cataloging-in-Publication Data

Hoshii, Iwao, 1905–
Japan's pseudo-democracy/Peter J. Herzog.
p. cm.
Includes index.
ISBN 0-8147-3497-9
1. Japan—Politics and government—1945– 2. Democracy—Japan.
I. Title.
JQ1681.H68 1993
320.952—dc20

93-918
CIP

Printed and bound in England by BPCC Wheatons Ltd., Exeter

Contents

Introduction

A conspicuous development since the end of the Second World War has been Japan's political and economic integration into the West. The post-war Occupation provided the initial impetus for this transformation which found a practical as well as symbolic expression in the adoption of the present constitution. The defeat had totally discredited the pre-war and wartime ideology, yet the attempt to fill the void resulting from the demise of the old order by the creation of a Western-style democracy has been unsuccessful. The reforms initiated by the Occupation and the implementation of the post-war constitution have created a number of democratic institutions but these alone do not necessarily impart the convictions and attitudes from which they originated.

The pattern in which Western democracies have organised public order shows a considerable variety and it is impossible to consider a particular form as definitive. There are, however, some fundamental ideas essential to democracy. As a kind of political creed, democracy admits of a wide latitude in detail but contains some core requirements without which it becomes a sham.

A characteristic of modern democracy is the demarcation of a sphere of individual inviolability and circumscription of the possible interference by the state in people's private affairs. The 'Bill of Rights' not only defines the prerogatives of the individual but also ensures him or her membership in a political society based on the idea of free cooperation between equal members. The liberal conception of democracy demands freedom and equality for all members as an indispensable condition. It would be wrong to consider these rights merely in relation to the individual; they represent a necessary element of that form of political existence which the constitution is meant to organise. The recognition of these rights is just as essential to the state as it is to the individual citizen.

In Western countries with a strong democratic tradition, democracy is not just a political system but a way of life. The people are familiar with the institutions, values and preferences peculiar to a democratic system. Japan is not without democratic traditions but these never affected the political life of the nation as a whole. The Japanese state under the Tokugawa and Emperor Meiji was a highly centralised, bureaucratic, omnicompetent government state whereas Japan's democratic traditions never transcended the sphere of local use. What is often referred to as the 'Taisho democracy' (Taisho era: 1912-1926) was the short-lived ascendancy of bourgeois politicians under a system of restricted male suffrage. The leading *zaibatsu*, Mitsui and Mitsubishi, greatly strengthened by the prosperity resulting from the First World War, manipulated the political parties to promote their business interests. The Taisho period also brought the awakening of the working classes and the first attempts (forcefully suppressed by the police) to organise labour unions and proletarian parties. These movements had little connection with Anglo-American democracy, and of the parties organised after the Second World War, only the Socialists and Communists had some tenuous personal and ideological links with the Taisho movements.

Japan's democratisation as envisioned by the Occupation constituted a radically new beginning - and the new order had to be imposed on a society completely unfamiliar with the values, ideologies and institutions enshrined in the constitution. Japan differed from Germany in that the national and local bureaucracies remained largely intact after the war so the new dispensation had to be implemented by an administration educated in an entirely different environment and at least partly hostile to the new order. The constitution and the legal and organisational measures based thereon were applied and interpreted by a judiciary unfamiliar with the origin, intent and meaning of the constitutional provisions. The disparity between the old and new dispensation was too acute to allow a smooth transition. It would have been overly sanguine to expect a thorough understanding of the new order to emerge at once. There was some opposition to the changes involved in the country's democratisation (e.g. the position of the Emperor, the family system, the renunciation of military forces) but no large-scale obstructionism.

It can hardly be maintained that at present democracy is flourishing in Japan. The most appalling lack of democratic consciousness and deplorable manifestations of undemocratic behaviour can be seen among politicians, while the bureaucracy must be blamed for preventing a more democratic ambience in Japan's national and international relations.

Lack of understanding has been an important factor affecting the progress of democracy. The judiciary has been called upon to document its comprehension of democracy in many cases involving the interpretation of the constitution. On a number of controversial issues, the courts have taken positions which I consider incompatible with democratic principles and their interpretation of the constitution has not always conformed to democratic values and convictions.

The present volume discusses some of the discrepancies with the Western understanding of democracy found in Japan. An examination of economic democracy is beyond the scope of this enquiry.

Chapter 1

How democratic is Japan's constitution?

The enactment of the 'Constitution of Japan' (*Nihon-koku Kempō*), promulgated on 3 November 1946 and effective six months later, formed an essential step in the process of democratisation, one of the key projects of the post-war Occupation. It has often been pointed out that expressions such as 'democracy', 'democratic' or 'democratisation' do not appear in the text of the document. The preamble asserts that 'sovereign power resides with the people' and proclaims as a 'universal principle of mankind' that 'Government is a sacred trust of the people, the authority for which is derived from the people, the powers of which are exercised by the representatives of the people, and the benefits of which are enjoyed by the people.' This sentence states the basic tenets of a representative democracy which leaves no doubt that Japan's constitution was meant to be the charter of a democratic state.

The question I want to explore is not the merits of the constitution in itself but whether its construction and interpretation conform to democratic principles. I base my discussion on the premise that, according to Abraham Lincoln's famous dictum 'government of the people, by the people, for the people', self-government constitutes the fundamental requirement of democracy.

'Government of the people' implies popular sovereignty, the principle that government is established by the people: 'Government by the people' - the principle that the people are the subject of government and that the government must be maintained and controlled by the people: 'Government for the people' - the principle that government exists for the good of the people, that the common weal, the common good is the purpose of government. 'Government of the people' therefore requires that the people participate in the adoption of the constitution. The form of the government as a political institution must be fixed by the people, and it must operate according to the principles and rules established by the people. Because the government is based on the constitution, it cannot be called a government of the people unless the people frame and adopt the constitution. If, therefore, the people do not participate in some way or another in the making of the constitution, the government based on such a constitution cannot be called democratic.

GOVERNMENT OF THE PEOPLE

The constitution of Japan can in no sense whatever be called a constitution of the people. The people did not draft the constitution, the people did not sanction it, the people did not establish it. Naturally, it is hardly feasible for the people to draw up a constitution directly, and in many cases, a constitution is composed by an assembly elected for this particular purpose. A constitutional convention undertakes the work of framing a constitution in accordance with the intention of the people, and if such a convention organises committees to discuss the contents and to prepare a draft, the people are at least indirectly involved in its composition.

In the case of Japan's present constitution, the initiative did not come from the people but from General Douglas MacArthur, Supreme Commander of the Allied Powers (SCAP). The actual framers of the constitution had no connection whatever with the Japanese people, nor were they members of an assembly entrusted by the people with the task of creating one for their country. Indeed, there may have been strong reasons for drafting and adopting the constitution in a way which excluded any influence on the part of the people. In 1967 Yasuhiro Nakasone (Prime Minister from November 1982 to November 1987) proposed that the constitution should be put to a national referendum to test its 'legitimacy'. He contended that the constitution could not be called democratic and did not reflect the free will of the people in a true sense because of the circumstances under which it had been established.

On 17 October 1946, shortly before the promulgation of the constitution, the Far Eastern Commission adopted a resolution to the effect that it could call for a popular referendum or some other appropriate measure to determine whether the constitution was an expression of the free will of the Japanese people but no such demand was made.

Even the most favourable interpretation must consider the constitution as some kind of grant (constitution *octroyée*). Instead of being granted by the Emperor, as was the Meiji constitution, it was bestowed by the Occupation authorities and the politicians and bureaucrats who made up Japan's leadership at the time. It is no wonder that the people's understanding of the constitution is far from adequate. Not only were the people excluded from any participation in its adoption, the resulting changes in the government and the political situation following its implementation were unfavourable for carrying out a sustained programme of familiarisation. Moreover, apart from Article 9 (Renunciation of War), few features of the constitution aroused popular interest and the occasional polemics involving constitutional problems usually generate more heat than light. The habit of appealing to the constitution in environmental disputes or claims for compensation has converted it into a kind of insurance covenant invoked by anybody who wants the state to pay for real or imagined losses. Despite the lawyers' use or abuse of the constitution as a possible legal loophole, it has not penetrated the public consciousness which allows the government to flout constitutional provisions openly.

GOVERNMENT BY THE PEOPLE

In the political system established by the constitution, direct democracy has no place. Japan pretends to be a representative democracy in which the representatives chosen by the people are supposed to work for the interest of the people. The representative system developed at a time when social homogeneity and cohesion were strong and the means of communication and transportation rather poor. The system is hardly appropriate for today's fractionalised and pluralistic society and completely unnecessary for a society with modern communication and transportation systems.

The constitution did not lay down basic rules for ensuring fair elections. Under the present Public Office Election Law, a minority of the voters can elect the majority of the representatives, and until now, attempts to rectify the flagrant inequities in the value of votes by appealing to the courts have been futile. There is little chance that a reform of the election system will ensure a fair representation in any case, since the voters have no influence on the nomination of candidates (there is nothing corresponding to the American primaries). Many candidates are not representatives of the people but agents or advocates of special interests or pressure groups. As a result, the Diet, supposed to be an assembly of representatives of the people, has become the gathering of delegates of organisations or cliques pushing the interests of their clients and disregarding the good of the people. Since the representatives care only about their own constituencies, they are not true representatives of the people.

A serious shortcoming of the present constitution is the total lack of direct participation of the people in the political process. Since any change in the constitution must be initiated by the politicians, this failure will not be corrected. Article 95 requires the consent of the majority of the voters of a local public entity in case the Diet enacts a special law applicable only to one local entity. Article 96 requires the affirmative vote of the majority of all votes cast at a special referendum or some other election for amendments to the constitution adopted by the concurring vote of two-thirds of all the members of each House. Particularly regrettable is the absence of provisions for a popular initiative. It was by this method that California voters, by the memorable Proposition 13, enforced tax reductions and limits on government spending.

A similar mistrust of the people prevailed in the adoption of the Fundamental Law of the German Federal Republic. It was not submitted to a popular vote and it limits the participation of the people in government to the election of the legislature (in addition to the legislature of the Federal Republic, each state has its own legislature). There are no provisions for a popular referendum or initiative and, unlike Japan, the Fundamental Law can be changed without the participation of the people (which has greatly facilitated the many changes in the Law). Referenda, however, are required for changes affecting territories of the federated states.

In the US and to a certain extent in some European countries, initiatives and referenda have been abused by so-called one-issue groups to press their demands, but in most cases, these groups are very small minorities and even an apathetic majority usually foils attempts to force minority views or values on the people by direct democratic processes. I harbour no illusions about the effectiveness of referenda or popular initiatives, nevertheless, they can be used to rectify flagrant abuses or oppose idiotic proposals. In Japan, the people cannot prevent excesses of the government and since recall is limited to the review of judges of the Supreme Court (Art. 79, par. 2), undesirable politicians or officials cannot be turned out.

The seemingly comprehensive regulations on matters for which everybody has the right of petition (Art. 16) is made practically useless by the prescription in the Petition Law whereby petitions must be submitted to the government office in charge of the matter (Art. 3). The Local Autonomy Law contains numerous provisions for petitions. The most important are: petitions for the enactment or abolition of ordinances addressed to the chief of an ordinary local body (Art. 74), petitions for the dissolution of a local assembly (Art. 76), petition for the discharge of a member of an assembly (Art. 80), petition for the dismissal of the chief of a local entity (Art. 81), petitions of auditing by the inhabitants (Art. 242), and inhabitants suits (Art. 242-2). Such matters are seldom of national significance and there are no legal provisions for corresponding issues on a national level. Suits for compensation (Art. 17) have generally been related to environmental issues (e.g. pollution, airport noise) or damage caused by natural disasters.

The present constitution protects the 'establishment' (politicians, bureaucrats and business leaders) against any influence from the outside. Individuals as well as the people as a whole are powerless against this establishment. Complaints about administrative matters must be submitted to the appropriate agency, which makes it very unlikely that they will have any effect. An appeal to the courts will usually be too late because law suits take time and money. The judiciary is not concerned with the issues of right or wrong but with the observance of rules and regulations. A superficial amendment of the constitution would hardly improve the situation.

The basic policy of Japan's conservative administration has been to shut out the people from exercising any influence and to prevent the 'obstruction' of the doings of politicians and bureaucrats. An illustrative example was the transfer of the election of the chiefs of the so-called special wards (the wards in Tokyo) from the voters of the wards to the Ward Assembly with the consent of the governor (Local Autonomy Law, Art. 281-3, par. 1. Art. 271, par 2, which provided for the election of the chiefs of the wards by the voters was abrogated in 1956 when Articles 264 to 280 were eliminated). The official reason for the change was that the special wards were not local public entities to which the prescription of Article 93, par. 2 of the constitution (which stipulates the election of the chief executive officer of all local public entities by direct popular vote) applied. The real reason was that opposition candidates were often successful in capturing these posts. Numerous commissions, councils and boards of inquiry are appointed by the 'competent minister' or other government organs and the voters have no influence whatever on the composition of these bodies. On the other hand, local organs often adopt the one-sided views of unrepresentative groups under the pretext of 'participatory' politics.

Today's democratic consciousness attaches great importance to equality. People are no longer satisfied with purely formal equality of opportunity and demand to see the practical results of this equality in their daily lives. In view of the natural differences between men, to make actual equality of all people the goal of politics is a chimera. The attempt of the Pol Pot regime in Cambodia to abolish all differences and to build a new society by reducing all people and all things to the same point of departure has only produced one of the worst cases of genocide in history. But the scheme to regard only a select minority as 'the people' is also unacceptable. For Aristotle, a citizen was a free man who, because of his leisure and economic security, could devote his whole time to politics. Women, slaves and the foreigners residing in the city were without political rights as were artisans and tradesmen. When John Locke asserted that government was based on the consent of the governed, he meant a small fraction of the English people, the gentlemen who on the basis of their wealth represented the establishment of their time. For many years Americans did not acknowledge the contradiction between the assertion that 'all men are created equal' in the Declaration of Independence and the system of slavery and the disenfranchisement of women.

GOVERNMENT FOR THE PEOPLE

The most serious shortcoming of the present constitution is its failure to ensure that government is conducted for the people. The common good is disregarded and all government organs operate for the benefit of special interests. The system seems to assume that the common good is the sum of all particular concerns. This way of thinking is basically wrong. The common good refers to the welfare of the people as a whole and is not the addition of the interests of various regions or of agriculture, manufacturing and trade, of producers and consumers or of pedestrians and drivers. The government's acknowledgement of the particular claims of a special group can only be justified if the recognition of these are required for the common good or at least not opposed to it. This requirement is usually disregarded in the measures which the Ministry of International Trade and Industry (MITI), the Ministry of Agriculture, Forestry and Fisheries or other government agencies sponsor for their clientèle.

Japan is a pluralistic society, and the diversification of values naturally influences the demands on government and the political system. It seems inevitable that the values guaranteed by the constitution will be interpreted differently and it becomes difficult to achieve a consensus on national values or goals. In such a situation, it is the task of the Diet to achieve an integration of the people's value-judgments and coordinate public policies. But Japan's law-makers have been unable to free themselves from their ties to special interests.

The problems arising from the peculiarities of Japanese society affect not only the implementation of the constitution and legislation but also politics, administration and the work of the judiciary. Japanese society is based on status and human relations; the consciousness of universal principles which should guide social relations and social conduct belongs to a sphere alien to the traditional way of thinking which directs people's conduct in everyday life. Hence the abstract knowledge of democratic values and principles does not guarantee their observance in real life.

THE PEOPLE'S REPRESENTATIVES

One of the basic problems of Japan's representative democracy is the character of the representatives themselves. In ancient times the representatives of the people (or the persons qualified to vote) did not consider their office as a job but as an honorary service. Today's representatives not only draw a salary and are entitled to a pension but receive high remuneration regardless of other qualifications or the results of their activities. The most important difference from other government officials is the limitation of their tenure to a finite term which makes their continuation in office dependent on re-election. In carrying out their work, therefore, dietmen approach everything from the point of view of re-election, and it is not surprising that they attach greater importance to cultivating their constituency than to the promotion of the common good. Their main concern is for the things that make their re-election possible: the party that must endorse their candidacy, the organisation that secures the votes and the donations that provide the necessary funds. An illustration of this was Japan's refusal to liberalise the importation of rice, which was prompted by the fear of politicians that such a measure would cost them the farm vote. The talk of food security and self-sufficiency was pure hogwash.

Another result of the influence, prestige and high income connected with the position of a dietman are the predominant high age levels within the Diet. The old age of the leadership group has strengthened the tendency to maintain the status quo. Dietmen are reluctant to retire and the incumbent can usually secure his nomination as a candidate in the next election. In the election to the House of Representatives in February 1990, for example, 353 of the newly-elected 512 representatives had been members of the House when it was dissolved, 26 were former dietmen and 133 were elected for the first time. This election was rather atypical on account of the major changes resulting from the increase in the number of Socialist representatives (60 of the 133 elected for the first time were members of the Japan Socialist Party); in the July 1986 election, 404 of the incumbents at the time of the dissolution of the House were re-elected and only 65 were newcomers. Only three of Japan's post-war prime ministers were in their fifties when they assumed office (Tetsu Katayama, Kakuei Tanaka and Toshiki Kaifu), twelve were in their sixties and five in their seventies. A related phenomenon is the increase in second-generation politicians and the appearance of third-generation dietmen. Measures and policies to cope with changes in the country's political, economic and social structure are being delayed, and entrenched interests are favoured at the expense of the common good.

Since dietmen are busy with personal or party affairs, the preparation of bills has largely been taken over by the bureaucracy which also makes most of the decisions. There is little scrutiny on the part of the nominal legislators and hardly any effort to protect the common people against the preferential treatment of special groups. The Diet's initiatives are generally limited to matters in which dietmen are personally involved or of importance to the party. Party polemics dominate all deliberations. Dietmen not only lack interest but also competence to pass on the substance of policy decisions. Even committees are more occupied with party politics than with the contents of the measures under consideration. The result has been that each ministry is preoccupied with protecting and promoting the interests of its clientele, or rather the party and the causes of its clientele favoured by the Liberal-Democratic Party.

In Japan's democratic system, legal equality has been more or less established for Japanese (foreigners and particularly Koreans are subject to official harassment). Government policy, however, is far from equitable: the consumer is Japan's forgotten man. The taxation system in particular is unjust, although the Ministry of Finance is the only government agency that sometimes tries to show some semblance of fiscal responsibility. But its efforts have been unable to stop the country's growing indebtedness. It began with the decision of the Sato cabinet in 1965 to throw out the principle of budgetary balance, a basic plank of the Shoup tax reform, and to issue so-called construction bonds. At the end of fiscal 1991 Japan's public debt amounted to ¥ 16 trillion, about half the value of the GNP and 2.4 times the amount of the fiscal 1991 budget.

A result of the disregard of public welfare has been the unfair distribution of public benefits and burdens and the violation of distributive justice by government policies and measures. The present taxation system is a notable example of such inequity and there are many cases in which the protectionist policies of the government have created unfair prices, tariffs and public charges. In some cases, the unwillingness of the government to deal with protest movements by people aggrieved by government projects has led to the suspension or delay of such projects and an enormous waste of taxpayers' money.

In short, under the present constitution, the basic aim of democracy, government of the people, by the people, for the people, has not been accomplished. Japan's experience demonstrates the insufficiency of equating democracy with the formal or nominal presence of certain institutions. The country is not a democracy in the Western sense. Although democratic institutions and proceedings were introduced by the post-war constitution, the country remains a paternalistic society dominated by an élite, the politicians, the bureaucracy and the business leadership, working inside and through their groups, the Liberal Democratic Party, the ministries and Keidanren (Federation of Economic Organisations, ie. commercial corporations). The people are conformist, disciplined and compliant, with only rare outbursts of opposition to the leadership.

Behind these shortcomings lies the incomprehension of the philosophical basis of democracy. The underlying ideas: the replacement of force by reason, of arbitrariness by right, of despotism by freedom, and of law dictated by an authoritarian government by law in conformity with human nature, remain alien to Japan. Democracy postulates the end of political, social and economic tutelage and the assertion of independence by the self-determination and self-government of the people, free from manipulation by special interests and outside influence. It is impossible to find this democratic spirit in today's Japan.

THE FRAMING OF THE CONSTITUTION

A constitution is not absolute, eternal or unchangeable. If the contents of the constitution no longer correspond to the actual political, social, economic or cultural reality of the country and have become outdated or unworkable, it must be amended. From the beginning, Japan's present constitution was not intended to be a lasting and definitive dispensation. On the contrary, in order to ward off the danger of having a constitution abolishing the Emperor system imposed by members of the Far Eastern Commission, it was prepared in great haste as something of an emergency measure under the direction of Brigadier Courtney C. Whitney, chief of GHQ's Government Section.

Many studies on the revision of the constitution attach great importance to the way in which the document was created. Formally, it was enacted by the procedure laid down in the Meiji Constitution for amendments, and the Emperor said so in ratifying the new constitution: 'I rejoice that the foundation for the construction of a new Japan has been laid according to the will of the Japanese people, and hereby sanction and promulgate the amendments of the Imperial Japanese Constitution effected following the consultation with the Privy Council and the decision of the Imperial Diet made in accordance with Article 73 of the said Constitution.' (The official title of the Meiji Constitution, '*Dai-Nippon Teikoku Kempō*' was avoided.)

Accordingly, in the immediate post-war years, the views of constitutional scholars were divided. Because the procedure of adopting the new constitution complied throughout with the Meiji Constitution, Dr. Sōichi Sasaki held that legally, the new constitution was merely an amendment of the former. Dr Tatsukichi Minobe, however, contended that the observance of the amendment procedure of the Meiji Constitution was a mere formality and that actually the new constitution was based on the general will of the Japanese people expressed in this procedure. In his view, the Imperial sanction had a completely different meaning from what it would have had in the case of an amendment of the Meiji Constitution. According to Dr Minobe, the acceptance of the Potsdam Declaration which implied the recognition of the sovereignty of the people, constituted a 'revolution'.

As Dr Eiichi Makino has pointed out, the opening phrase of the constitution's preamble: 'We, the Japanese people, acting through our duly-elected representatives in the National Diet (*kokkai*)'... is not literally true. It was not the National Diet of the new constitution, but the Imperial Diet (*Teikoku Gikai*) of the Meiji Constitution which enacted it, and in the Imperial Diet, only the members of the Lower House were 'duly-elected representatives'; moreover, the validity of the Diet's legislative actions depended finally on the sanction of the Emperor.

The combination of continuity and evolution in the procedure is closely related to the question of whether the *kokutai*, the structure of the state, underwent a change or not. The legal and political basis of the Meiji Constitution was the absolute sovereignty of the Emperor who was the bearer of national sovereignty (*tōchiken no sōransha*). The constitution assumed this premise but did not make the slightest attempt to justify it. The new constitution indirectly denied the conception of constitutionality embodied in the Meiji Constitution that the Emperor, in the plenitude of his power, lays down the constitution and uses his power only according to the constitution ('The Emperor, as sovereign [*kuni no genshu*: head of the country] controls the government and exercises it on the basis of the regulations of this constitution' - Art. 4).

In the theoretical justification of the position of the Emperor in the Meiji dispensation, an unbridgeable chasm obtained between the opinion of the 'orthodox' school which considered Japanese mythology as the ultimate foundation of the national polity and the views of the 'heretics' who interpreted the constitution on the basis of Western theory. The chief protagonist of the orthodox view was Yatsuka Hozumi, Professor of Constitutional Law at Tokyo's Imperial University. He distinguished between the 'structure of the state' (*kokutai*) which is immutable and the 'structure of the government' (*seitai*) which can be changed. The essence of the *kokutai* was the sovereignty of the Emperor, and the only legitimate source of the Emperor's authority was his descent from the Sun Goddess 'in an unbroken line for ages' (*bansei ikkei no tennō*).

The main exponent of the heretical view was Tatsukichi Minobe who had studied in Germany under Georg Jellinek and propounded the view that sovereignty resided in the state as a juridical person. The Emperor, Minobe taught, was an organ of the state, the highest organ but not the ultimate source of state power. His 'organ theory' did not deny that Japan was an absolute monarchy, but his academic controversy with Shinkichi Uesugi, Hozumi's successor at the university, spilled over into politics and with the ascendancy of Japanese militarism, Minobe was forced to resign his seat in the House of Peers and some of his works were banned. The government issued what was called a 'clarification of the structure of the state' (*kokutai meichō*) which affirmed the mythological foundation of the Emperor's sovereignty.

Nevertheless, Japan was considered a 'constitutional monarchy' and in this sense, mindful of the will of the people. But this had nothing to do with the theory of popular sovereignty. The Potsdam Declaration did not use the expression 'popular sovereignty' but it implied that sovereignty resided with the people. 'The revival and strengthening of democratic tendencies among the Japanese people' and 'freedom of speech, of religion and of thought as well as respect for the fundamental human rights' were enumerated among the objectives to be accomplished by the Occupation and the establishment of a 'peacefully-inclined and responsible government... in accordance with the freely-expressed will of the Japanese people' was to be achieved. The opinion that the Potsdam Declaration did not necessitate a revision of the Meiji Constitution and a restructuring of the Japanese polity was certainly erroneous.

'Constitution' first and foremost means the fundamental structure in which the political community exists. A constitution does not create the political reality but is a statement of its salient features and the institutionalisation of the political order by organs and procedures. By proclaiming the sovereignty of the people, the post-war constitution denied the existence of the political and legal order of the Meiji Constitution. Only the people have the right (and the duty) to establish for themselves the public order for which the constitution should determine the appropriate institutional forms.

In a policy decision adopted on 13 May 1946, the Far Eastern Commission demanded complete legal continuity between the constitution of 1889 and the new constitution. It may be argued that the old order remained valid until the new constitution came into effect and this is precisely what the champions of legal continuity intended. But it was not the new constitution which made the people sovereign. The new constitution was adopted because the people were sovereign and the political and legal forms of the Meiji dispensation no longer corresponded to the political reality of post-war Japan.

The sovereignty of the people is an elementary political and legal fact and there is nothing in this sublunar world (I skip the problem of its metaphysical foundation) from which popular sovereignty can be deduced. As mentioned above, the political and legal foundation of the Meiji Constitution was the absolute power of the Emperor as the bearer of national sovereignty. The organisation of the political order sanctioned by the Meiji Constitution rested on the assumption that the Emperor was the fountainhead of the authority which he exercised through the organs and procedures laid down in that document. The termination of the war destroyed this order as a political reality. A legal fiction hypostatised the remaining governmental machinery into a state while the living substance of the state, the people, were treated as a nonentity. Although a legalistic mind may find satisfaction in the compliance with the formal requirements of a dead document, the procedure could not make the new constitution a decision of the Japanese people despite the official declarations. The Diet had neither been elected as a constituent assembly nor did it have the power of such a body; it was merely the last of the Imperial Diets convoked under the constitution of the Empire of Japan.

General MacArthur and the Far Eastern Commission urged a review of the constitution between the first and the second year of its effectiveness, and both favoured a referendum or some other appropriate procedure for ascertaining directly the will of the people. On 20 March 1946 the Far Eastern Commission reacted sharply against General MacArthur's announcement that the draft of the constitution had his personal approval and demanded (3 May 1946) that the new constitution be adopted in such a manner as to demonstrate that it positively expressed the will of the Japanese people. In a letter to Prime Minister Yoshida urging reconsideration of the new constitution, General MacArthur wrote: 'As the bulwark of future Japanese freedom, the Allied Powers feel that there should be no future doubt that the constitution expresses both the free and considered will of the Japanese people.'

The above comments are not meant to impugn the validity of the present constitution but to show that the new order lacked the convincingness of a national decision which its adoption by national referendum or by a specially elected constitutional assembly would have provided. Short-sighted political considerations may have influenced the course of events but an important factor was the existence of a functioning government. Unlike Germany where public order had collapsed completely, Japan retained a reasonably efficient administrative machinery which the Occupation authorities used for their own purposes. Apart from the presence of foreign troops and the end of the air raids, there was no dramatic change in the outward appearance of the country which,veiled the fact that a revolution had taken place and that the old order was irrevocably gone.

The ambiguity of the procedure followed in the adoption of the new constitution allowed the ridiculous contention that the Meiji Constitution continued to form the only valid foundation of Japan's political and legal order. But the problem lies deeper. The new constitution, not being a true political decision of the entire nation, remained alien to the spirit of the people. It symbolised no national ideas, aroused no common enthusiasm, excited no prophetic dreams and crystallised no primordial myths. It remained a document without soul, without life, without spirit and without patriotism. The aspirations expressed in the preamble proclaimed idealistic expectations of a brave new world for which neither institutional safeguards nor social forces were in existence. So the constitution remained a purely legal document, relied on when its use seemed convenient, misinterpreted to suit political expediency, and overruled when an obstacle to quick solutions for inadequately analysed problems.

The question of who drafted the constitution is one of the historical aspects which may be fascinating to the researcher, but which is irrelevant to the problem of its validity. Yasuzō Suzuki has spent years of painstaking study on elucidating the role played by Hermann Roesler in drafting the Meiji Constitution. He has shown that Kaoru Inouye and Hirobumi Itō relied a great deal on the German jurist. This does not make the Meiji document a Prussian constitution, just as little as the work of Emile Gustave Boissonade would have made the civil code of 1890 French law. Catch phrases like 'Constitution made in USA' may be effective demagoguery but are of no help in evaluating the constitution.

The Potsdam Declaration did not contain an explicit statement calling for the abolition of the Meiji Constitution and nobody in the government of Prince Higashikuni (August-October 1945) seems to have thought a revision necessary. The problem surfaced when Prince Fumimaro Konoe met George Atcheson, political adviser to General MacArthur, on 8 October 1945, and was given a 12-point memorandum regarding constitutional revisions. This communication led to three independent, uncoordinated and partly secret Japanese undertakings to write a new constitution. On the order of the Emperor, Prince Konoe and Dr Sōichi Sasaki started work on a revision of the constitution at a special agency within the office of the Keeper of the Privy Seal. Prince Konoe submitted the draft of a constitutional revision on 22 November 1945. According to Dr Toshiyoshi Miyazawa, Prince Higashikuni interpreted the memorandum given to Prince Konoe as an official communication which led to the immediate resignation of the cabinet. Kijūrō Shidehara, the next prime minister (October 1945-May 1946) established a committee which, under state minister Jōji Matsumoto, included Professors

Toshiyoshi Miyazawa, Matasuke Kawamura and Shirō Shimizu while some of the luminaries in the field of constitutional law such a Tatsukichi Minobe, Kiyoshi Shimizu and Junji Nomura served as advisers. It is not clear whether Shidehara established the committee on the order of the Emperor but there seems to have been no connection whatever between the Emperor's committee and that of the government.

Foreign Ministry officials began to work on a revision of the constitution immediately after the signing of Japan's surrender on 2 September 1945. The group worked under the direction of Keiichi Tatsuke, then director of the ministry's second Treaty Division, and completed an outline of an amended constitution and a report on the circumstances that made it necessary to revise the constitution. These documents, dated 11 October 1946, were kept secret by the ministry and not submitted to the government. Not even the foreign minister, Shigeru Yoshida, knew about them. A group of scholars including Iwasaburō Takano and Tatsuo Morita formed a Constitution Study Club and published *An Outline of a Draft of a Constitution* on 27 December 1945.

The Matsumoto draft was the only one presented by the Japanese government to the Occupation authorities. Matsumoto was not only stubborn but also a dyed-in-the-wool reactionary and the draft merely contained cosmetic changes of the Meiji Constitution. It retained the principle that the Emperor was the bearer of national sovereignty (*tōchiken wo sōran-shi*); the words 'sacred and inviolable' of the Meiji text were replaced by 'supreme and inviolable'. Article 5 of the Matsumoto draft said: 'The Emperor shall be the commander-in-chief of the armed forces.' Article 6 read: 'The organisation and total strength of the standing army shall be determined by law.' The competence of parliament was enlarged but instead of including a bill of rights, the draft curtailed some of the rights mentioned in the Meiji document. No wonder that General Whitney and Col Charles L. Kades, the deputy chief of the Government Section, were furious. The draft completely disregarded the intentions of General MacArthur. In SCAP's opinion, the draft would be approved neither by the American government nor by the Far Eastern Commission.

When General MacArthur met with Kijūrō Shidehara on 11 October, he demanded that the constitutional reform should include five measures: the liberation of women, recognition of labour unions, democratisation of education, establishment of an open and democratic judicial system and democratisation of the economy.

Although called unconditional, Japan's surrender did not give the Allies *carte blanche* to do what they pleased in Japan. Since the surrender was based on the Potsdam Declaration, the terms laid down in the declaration were binding on the Allies. They provided for, *inter alia* the establishment of basic human rights, a certain level of economic activity, access to raw materials and withdrawal of the Occupation forces after accomplishment of the objectives stated in the declaration.

Negotiations by which the Japanese attemped to secure a guarantee that the Emperor system would be preserved delayed the agreement to end the war. Even though the authority of the Emperor and the Japanese government to rule the country were subject to the Supreme Commander of the Allied Powers, the Emperor and the government continued to function. The Hague Convention of 1928 prohibited interference in the political system of an occupied country.

The compilation of a new constitution was not among the instructions given to General MacArthur; on the contrary, under the Moscow agreement of December 1945 the United States had to consult the Far Eastern Commission on constitutional reforms. Since the Soviet Union was represented on the commission, MacArthur foresaw trouble with his policy of retaining the Emperor if the commission got involved in the issue. MacArthur was under severe pressure to pursue a harsher policy in the administration of the Occupation and some of the Allies, notably the Soviet Union and Australia, demanded the abolition of the Emperor system and the trial of Emperor Hirohito as a war criminal. MacArthur considered the retention of the Emperor system essential for the successful implementation of the Occupation policies. In addition, he gained a very favourable personal opinion of the Emperor in their historic meeting on 27 September 1945. MacArthur resolved to confront the Far Eastern Commission with a *fait accompli*.

The situation required two things: first, whatever was done had to be done as quickly as possible. The first meeting of the Far Eastern Commission was to be held in Washington on 26 February 1946; the process of revising the constitution, therefore, had to be well on its way before that date. Secondly, the impression had to be created that the initiative came from the Japanese government and that the new constitution was a Japanese product. The General ordered the Government Section to prepare an outline which could serve as a model for the revision to be undertaken by the Japanese. He gave General Courtney Whitney full discretion but insisted that three points had to be included in the draft. They were, according to General MacArthur's own notes: 'The Emperor is the head of the State'; 'War as a sovereign right of the nation is abolished'; and 'The feudal system of Japan will cease'. These principles do not seem to have been formed in reaction to the Japanese proposal because they were given to General Whitney on 3 February 1946, whereas the Matsumoto draft was presented to GHQ on 8 February.

The Government Section formed nine working groups for different subject matters and a committee of three officers, Charles Kades, Alfred Hussey and Milo Rowell to supervise and coordinate the work. None of these men was an expert in constitutional law, and besides General MacArthur's instructions, the Potsdam Declaration and SWNCC 228 (State-War-Navy Department Coordinating Committee policy statement on the reform of the Japanese government system sent to General MacArthur on 11 January 1946) constituted their frame of reference.

The Constitutional Research Council (a body created by the Japanese government in 1956) never elucidated the actual process by which the draft of the constitution had been elaborated. In its 16th general meeting on 3 September 1958 the Council decided to send a three-man delegation made up of chairman Kenzō Takayanagi, Liberal representative Osamu Inaba, and Motosaburō Tanaka, president of the Japan-American News Agency, to the United States to obtain from the Americans connected with the framing of the constitution information concerning the origin of the document. Quite a sensation was created when General MacArthur curtly refused to be subjected to an interrogation by inquisitive researchers, and even an explanation of the 'fact-finding' nature of their mission did not move the old proconsul to invite them to a cup of tea.

General Whitney personally presented the American draft to a surprised Foreign Minister Yoshida at the minister's official residence on 13 February 1946. There followed spirited discussions inside the Japanese government as well as between the Japanese and the Americans. According to the Ashida Diary, Prime Minister Kijūrō Shidehara reported on a three-hour meeting he had with General MacArthur on 21 February at a cabinet meeting on the following day. MacArthur had stressed that he was sincerely working for the best interest of Japan. Since his meeting with the Emperor, he was doing everything to save him, but the atmosphere in the Far Eastern Commission was not good. The demand to bring the Emperor to trial as a war criminal was still strong and the Soviet Union and Australia were afraid that Japan was planning revenge. There was no unbridgeable gap between the Japanese and the American drafts but all provisions concerning armed forces had to be completely removed. Japan had to take into consideration the sentiment abroad. If such provisions were retained, other countries would naturally think that Japan was bent on revenge. In its own interest, Japan should take the lead in renouncing war as an instrument of national policy. To this exhortation, Shidehara had replied: 'You talk about Japan taking the lead. But probably no other country will follow suit.' MacArthur remarked that a constitution like the Matsumoto draft would cast doubt on Japan's sincerity. It would make it imposible to ensure Japan's safety. It was important to think of the reaction abroad. If the American proposal was not adopted, Japan would lose an excellent chance. When General Whitney presented the American draft to Foreign Minister Yoshida, he intimated that its speedy acceptance would be the last chance of saving the Emperor system.

The Japanese politicians and bureaucrats did not realise the depth of anti-Japanese sentiment in the countries which had fought Japan, and the apparent smooth running of the Occupation (despite many ugly incidents not reported in the press) obscured the still hostile attitude abroad. The ideology behind the official war aims of the Allies spelled out in the Atlantic Charter and the Potsdam Declaration was incomprehensible to most Japanese politicians. While the Atlantic Charter was no treaty but a unilateral declaration of the Allies, the acceptance of the Potsdam Declaration resulted in a kind of armistice and created particular international law. But the Japanese government did not understand the historic meaning of the Potsdam Declaration and was unable to produce a constitution which corresponded to the intentions of the declaration. Actually, the acceptance of the declaration implied a revolution (the expression '15 August revolution' gained considerable currency) because it recognised the transfer of sovereignty from the Emperor to the people. Such a measure was impossible on the basis of the Meiji constitution since it implied a change (or even a denial) of the *kokutai*. This episode offers an example of the 'normative power of facts'. In view of Japan's situation, a legally unimpeachable solution was not the most important condition; a politically smooth transition from the emergency situation of the Occupation to peace and independence was the most pressing task in framing a new constitution.

In the course of the cabinet discussions of the American draft, Dr Matsumoto seems to have become very excited. It would be impossible to adapt the American draft to a form that could be presented to the Diet. It might be accepted by the Lower House but would never pass the House of Peers. As the examples of Germany and Latin America showed, constitutions imposed by outside influence cannot be observed. Minister of Education Yoshinari Abe observed that the principles might be the same but that there were great differences between the Matsumoto and the American drafts, such as the provisions on sovereignty and the armed forces.

The Constitutional Research Council mentioned above was created by the Diet in 1956 and charged with investigating the enactment, operation and possible revision of the post-war constitution. The Council was composed of 50 members of whom 30 were dietmen of both houses and the rest scholars and 'men of learning and experience'. The Japan Socialist Party strongly opposed the formation of the Council as a violation of the constitutional provisions for amending the constitution and boycotted the Council. The declassification of key documents relevant to the formation of the constitution has shed new light on some phases of the procedure but has not necessitated a basic revision of the issues.

The role played by the Occupation authorities in drafting the constitution naturally formed a central point of discussion. The most extreme view propounded before the Council by Liberal-Democratic representative Kenji Tomita maintained that the constitution, imposed upon Japan by the Occupation, was invalid and that theoretically, the Meiji constitution was still in force. According to Ichirō Hatoyama (three times prime minister, 1954-56), the mere fact that the constitution was forced upon Japan (the expression '*ochitsuki kempō*' became a standard term) was reason enough to change it and this position found many adherents. A more moderate view admitted that pressure had been exerted in bringing about the constitutional change but stressed that the question of revision should be judged upon the merits of the constitution.

The main arguments adduced to demonstrate the invalidity of the constitution were as follows. Firstly, under the Occupation, Japan's independence was limited and no expression of the free will of the people was possible. Secondly, the constitution was accepted under pressure from the Occupation. Thirdly, formally and legally, the constitution was adopted as a revision of the Meiji Constitution which it actually abolished. Fourthly, the constitution was a violation of international law which prohibits a change in the political system of an occupied territory.

The majority of the witnesses who appeared before the Constitutional Research Council confirmed that the initiative in drafting the constitution had come from SCAP but at the same time maintained that there was no necessity for an early or thorough-going revision. This view was presented most forcefully by former Prime Minister Yoshida who excused himself from appearing before the Council for reasons of health but stated his opinion in a lengthy communication dated 17 December 1957. In this memorandum, he gave a brief account of the negotiations between the government and SCAP concerning the draft of the constitution and summed up the development by the appraisal that the cabinet had been largely passive but agreed to the draft because, on the whole, it made sense and seemed for the best of the people.

Because the amendment process of the Meiji Constitution was used for the adoption of the constitution, the procedure involved a frequent use of the authority of the Emperor. For drafting the Constitution Revision Bill, the government negotiated with SCAP's Government Section on a text based on the American draft but incorporating certain changes desired by the Japanese. These negotiations were largely in the hands of Tatsuo Sato, then department chief in the Cabinet Legislative Bureau. In addition to adding a second chamber to the legislature, the final draft omitted a clause providing for the nationalisation of land and deleted another giving the Diet the right to override decisions of the Supreme Court, a provision probably put in by the Americans in view of the fight between President Roosevelt and the US Supreme Court over the New Deal legislation.

In conformity with established practice under the Meiji Constitution, the bill was first submitted to the Privy Council and approved by this body without amendment on 3 June 1946. Then it was introduced in the House of Representatives at its extra-ordinary session convened on 20 June (the House had been elected under the procedure of the Meiji Constitution on 10 April). The House deliberated on the bill from April to 24 August and passed it with certain amendments by a vote of 421 to 8. Then the bill went before the House of Peers which had been largely reconstituted by the appointment of new members to replace those purged by the Occupation. It was approved again with some amendments on 6 October and returned to the Privy Council for final examination.

The legislative process which had been set in motion by an Imperial rescript (*chokugo*) on 5 March 1946 was terminated by an Imperial edict (*jōyu*). The constitution was promulgated by another Imperial rescript on 3 November 1946, and went into effect on 3 May 1947.

Given the situation under the Occupation, it is not surprising that the Japanese were unable to draft a constitution in accordance with the demands of the time. Although the military and most of the nationalist leaders ('exponents of chauvinism') had left the scene, the bureaucracy remained largely unchanged and the influence of the older generation was very strong. At the beginning of the Occupation, Foreign Minister Mamoru Shigemitsu had succeeded in persuading the American authorities not to put Japan under 'direct control'. But there were occasions when the Occupation authorities complained about the 'uncooperative attitude' of the Japanese government and considered the possibility of putting Japan under direct control.

Chapter 2

The political role of the Judiciary

One of the most radical changes in the pattern of Japan's polity was the adoption of the system of judicial review. In hindsight, it appears that the Occupation authorities underestimated the impact which this innovation was to have on Japan's legal and political thinking, and neglected to organise the kind of instruction which would have been necessary to familiarise Japan's judiciary with the juridical principles and the political philosophy underlying this system. The judges, trained in an establishment based on a jurisprudence incorporating a different ideology, could hardly be expected to conform automatically to the way of thinking proper to the new dispensation. Japan's pre-war judicial thinking was largely modelled on continental Europe's jurisprudence.

Enormous efforts were made in the middle of the Meiji era to adapt Japan's public institutions and regulations to what was considered most progressive and fashionable to the extent compatible with the power of the ruling oligarchy. French and German scholars were the main collaborators of the Japanese officials entrusted with the modernisation of the legal system and the judiciary. The hasty modernisation was primarily motivated by the desire to facilitate a revision of the unequal treaties forced upon Japan and especially a modification of the provisions of extra-territoriality. The clearly-defined patterns of the continental codes looked far more rational than the amorphous mass of Anglo-American case law grafted onto the common law.

Another important change effected by the 1946 constitution was the liberation of the judiciary from the dominance of the Ministry of Justice. In the pre-war system the minister of justice had unrestricted authority over the appointment and removal of judges, and his approval was required for judgements in criminal cases involving political crimes. Supervision of trials of serious crimes was reserved for the cabinet.

In the new dispensation, the courts have become completely independent, although the nomination of the justices of the Supreme Court by the cabinet is an unsatisfactory solution to a difficult problem. The procuracy, however, remains under the control of the Minister of Justice which includes the highly controversial right of the minister to issue directives to the Procurator-General.

As one of the reforms of the judicial system, the Constitutional Research Council proposed the organisation of a constitutional court.

The reason for this proposal was the restrictive interpretation by the Supreme Court of its functions. In the Tomabechi case (see below), the court declared that it was not a constitutional but a judicial court and could only rule on matters within the limits of the judicial power. This meant that the courts were incompetent to pass on the constitutionality of the acts of state organs unless there had been a direct violation of personal or property rights of individuals or corporations. In its decision on the constitutionality of the police reserve on 8 October 1952, the Supreme Court stated: 'Under the present system, the judgement of the court can only be demanded in case there is a dispute concerning the concrete legal relations of particular persons. The opinion that a court possesses the authority to decide the constitutionality of a law or order abstractly apart from such a concrete case has no foundation in the constitution or in law.'

The question whether a law or an administrative disposition is constitutional or not can hardly be said to be necessarily abstract. It concerns the very concrete question of whether the act of the legislature enacting a law or the act of an administrative organ making a certain disposition is in conformity with the constitution. There are jurists who support the self-denying interpretation of the Supreme Court but their arguments distort the text of the constitution and are juridically and politically illogical.

The constitution states: 'The whole judicial power is vested in a Supreme Court and in such inferior courts as shall be established by law' (Art. 76, par. 1). Article 81 makes it clear that the question of constitutionality of any law, order, regulation or official act falls under the competence of the Supreme Court. If there were a constitutional court, it would undoubtedly be a judicial organ and its jurisdiction would come under the judicial power. (Germany's Fundamental Law says in Article 92: 'The judicial power is entrusted to the judges; it is exercised by the federal constitutional court, the federal courts provided for in the Fundamental Law and the courts of the states.') Since the Japanese constitution and laws do not attribute the competence or function of a constitutional court to any other court, the Supreme Court in which the 'whole judicial power is vested' undoubtedly possesses this competence and has the duty of using it.

Article 76 of the Japanese constitution and Article 3 of the American constitution are basically different. The American constitution deals with the judicial power of the US, i.e., the Union as distinct from the individual states, and defines the 'cases' and 'controversies' to which the judicial power of the Union extends. Japan, on the contrary, is a unitary state with a single judicial system.

THE TOMABECHI CASE

An analysis of Article 81 confirms the comprehensive jurisdiction of the Supreme Court. The Article reads: 'The Supreme Court is the court of last resort with power to determine the constitutionality of any law, order, regulation or official act.' In the Tomabechi case the Supreme Court made a distinction between ordinary administrative acts and 'acts of state of a highly political nature' (*kokka no kōdo tōji kōi*) and asserted that the court's jurisdiction did not extend to acts of state of a highly political nature. To justify its interpretation, the court said: 'On the basis of the separation of powers and in view of the highly political nature of the respective act of state, the nature of the courts as judicial organs and the procedural limitations necessarily accompanying judicial decisions, although there is no regulation based on a special express provision, it must be understood as a limitation inherent in the constitutional essence of the judicial power.'

In the decision on the Sunakawa case (see Chapter 9), the Supreme Court applied the same distinction, stating that the right of review of the Supreme Court did not extend to the conclusion of the Japan-US Security Treaty because it constituted a 'highly political act' (the decision in this case did not depend on this distinction). The prosecution had argued that the court was incompetent to pass on the constitutionality of the treaty. In its ruling, the court remarked on highly political acts of government: 'unless the unconstitutionality and nullity is evident, review is impossible.' There is not the slightest foundation for the assertion of the prosecution and the conclusion that a highly political act is evidently unconstitutional supposes that the court examines this act.

The most deplorable application of the Supreme Court's interpretation of the right of judicial review was its decision in the Tomabechi case. On 26 August 1952 Prime Minister Shigeru Yoshida dissolved the House of Representatives. He based his action on Article 7 of the constitution which, among the acts in matters of state which the Emperor can perform with the advice and approval of thc cabinet lists the dissolution of the House of Representatives (no. 3). In order to parry Yoshida's snap dissolution of the House, Gizō Tomabechi, at that time a member of the Progressive Party, filed a suit for the payment of his salary as a representative (because the courts do not entertain suits questioning the legality of government acts not involving an alleged injury). Tomabechi demanded payment of his salary on the premise that the dissolution of the House was invalid. The Tokyo District Court recognised the government's claim that the House could be dissolved not only on the basis of Article 69 of the constitution but also in accordance with Article 7 but rejected the assertion that the court could not entertain the suit because the dissolution of the House was a highly political problem over which the court lacked jurisdiction.

The court held the dissolution invalid because the decision had not been made at a cabinet meeting. The dissolution, the court found, had been the personal decision of Prime Minister Yoshida and not the collective decision of the cabinet. The cabinet had not been assembled and the signature of each cabinet minister had been obtained separately.

Because a newspaper, the *Mainichi Shimbun*, had heard in advance of the impending dissolution, the matter was urgent,and on the day in question the signatures of only six cabinet members could be secured (Takeshi Yamazaki, Hayato Ikeda, Eisaku Sato, Katsuo Okazaki, Tokutaro Kimura and Giichi Murakami).

According to the testimony of the Chief of the General Affairs Section of the Cabinet Secretariat, Yoshida certainly collected the signatures of Yamazaki, Ikeda and Sato, but probably did not have the signatures of Okazaki, Kimura and Murakami, when, in the evening of the 26 August, he went to Nasu (the location of an Imperial villa, about 150 km north of Tokyo) and at 11.30 p.m. had the Emperor sign his name on *torinoko* paper (Japanese vellum), left Nasu on the following morning and received the Imperial seal at the Imperial Household Agency at about 9.00 a.m. Originally, Yoshida had planned to dissolve the House on the 27 August but because not all cabinet ministers had given their signatures, the procedure was completed in the morning of 28 August. The testimony of the Chief of the General Affairs Section seemed to indicate that Yoshida had informed the Emperor of his intention to dissolve the House on 25 August. Corporations rather frequently expedite resolutions of the board of directors by collecting the signatures of the individual directors which, of course, does not constitute the collegiate decision envisaged by the law but may have no serious effect on the management of the corporation.

Upon the appeal of the government, the Tokyo High Court[1] reversed the decision of the District Court and ruled that the decision of the cabinet had been reached in a legal and appropriate manner so that the dissolution of the House had been valid and Tomabechi was not entitled to his salary as a member of the Diet. The court rejected the contention that on account of the highly political nature of the matter, the courts had no jurisdiction and affirmed that in order to ascertain whether a right had been violated, the courts could inquire into the validity of actions of the cabinet. The court reiterated the claim of the District Court that the dissolution was possible on the basis of Article 7.

To prove this point, the court inquired where the right to dissolve was located. The Diet, the court reasoned, was the 'highest organ of state power' and the position of the House of Representatives was superior to that of the House of Councillors. Theoretically, only the people as a whole,with whom the sovereign power resided, should have the right to dissolve the House. In Article 7, the dissolution of the House is enumerated among the actions the Emperor is to perform 'with the advice and approval of the cabinet... on behalf of the people'. Article 1 says that the Emperor derives his position as symbol of the state and of the unity of the people from the will of the people so that

1 In Japan's judicial system an appeal (Kōso) from a court of first instance (District Court) to a court of second instance (High Court) can concern facts as well as law whereas an appeal (jō-koku) from the court of second instance to the Supreme Court lies only for questions of law.

theoretically the right of the people as a whole to dissolve the House should formally belong to the Emperor who, however, must exercise this right with the consent and approval of the cabinet which bears the political responsibility.

DISSOLUTION OF THE HOUSE OF REPRESENTATIVES

Concerning the requirements for the dissolution of the House of Representatives, Article 69 says nothing about the location of this right or the requirements for its exercise. It only provides that the cabinet must resign within ten days after a vote of no confidence but does not say that the House can only be dissolved in accordance with this article. The dissolution is to be made according to a political judgement based on the changing political situation. To restrict the exercise of this right by a legal rule would be inappropriate. The present constitution contains no provisions whatever concerning the requirements for the dissolution of the House and the decision in which cases the dissolution should be carried out is to be left entirely to political discretion. Whether the dissolution was appropriate or not is completely outside the purview of a judicial decision. Therefore it cannot be said that in the present case it was a violation of the constitution because there was no vote of no confidence or rejection of a vote of confidence. The court further concluded that the cabinet approved the dissolution.

The decision is a conspicuous example of obfuscation, ignorance of constitutional theory and disregard of the facts. The statement that the dissolution of the House of Representatives should theoretically be carried out by the people is pure fabrication, supported by nothing in the constitution or in political theory. It is only used as a device to bring in the Emperor and to obscure the fact that the actions of the Emperor listed in Article 7 are purely formal functions. According to Article 4, the Emperor can only perform 'acts in matters of state' and has no 'powers related to government'. The dissolution of the House of Representatives is an act based on powers of government and therefore beyond the competence of the Emperor.

The constitution says nothing about the right to dissolve the House because the right to dissolve the House is an invention of the politicians. The constitution conceives it as a duty: in case of a vote of no confidence or rejection of a vote of confidence, the cabinet has the duty to resign or to dissolve the House. Naturally, it has the right to perform this duty but the dissolution of the House is not the object of a right. The court completely misrepresents the issue in the treatment of this problem because it disregards the connection between the no confidence vote and the dissolution. In the construction of the constitution, the resignation of the cabinet is the first and ordinary result of a vote of no confidence and the dissolution of the House is an alternative. The court made the dissolution of the House the main issue in Article 69 which is a misinterpretation. If that were the object of the article, it should be in Chapter IV (The Diet) and not in Chapter V (The Cabinet).

There is not the slightest foundation for the assertion of the court that the dissolution of the House should be a matter of political judgement and of the political discretion of the cabinet. Such a construction is incompatible with the basic concept of the parliamentary system set up by the constitution and the position of the Diet as 'the highest organ of state power'.

It is true that the courts are incompetent to decide whether the dissolution of the House is appropriate or not, but it is the business of the courts to judge whether the procedure laid down in the constitution has been observed or not. It was flagrantly disregarded by Prime Minister Yoshida in the arbitrary dissolution of 27 August 1952, and the courts are responsible for having condoned this act of capricious authoritarianism which has permanently destabilised Japan's parliamentary system.

Even more atrocious than the ruling of the High Court was the decision of the Supreme Court announced on 8 June 1960 (almost eight years after the event). The court stated that an inquiry whether there had been a flaw in the procedure laid down in the constitution was beyond the reach of judicial review. Because of the separation of powers, judicial review does not extend to all state actions. State actions of a highly political nature directly concerning the basis of national policy are beyond judicial review even if there is the legal possibility of an invalid decision. This decision is left to the government or the Diet which are politically responsible to the people and therefore the decision is ultimately left to the people.

Although there are no express provisions, because of the highly political nature of state acts and the nature and procedural limitations of the judiciary, they must be understood as limitations inherent in the constitutional nature of the judicial power. The dissolution of the House of Representatives is not only legally important but also of high political importance. It is an action related to the basis of national policy of an extremely high political nature and therefore beyond the power of the judicial courts to pass on their legal validity.

There is a very simple answer to this blatant evasion of the court's responsibility dictated by political expediency. It is the duty of the courts to judge whether the constitutional process was violated. No degree of political importance can dispense the government from the duty to observe the constitution and no degree of political influence should deter the courts from determining whether or not an act of government was unconstitutional. The whole affair was a disgrace to the judiciary and its effects are beyond repair.

There are three internal reasons and the authority of a precedent for the position that, according to the constitution, the dissolution of the House of Representatives is only possible on the basis of Article 69.

First, as stated above, Article 7 does not define the powers of the cabinet but enumerates the actions the Emperor can perform on behalf of the people with the advice and approval of the cabinet. These actions are merely formal (adjective) actions related to ceremonial functions while the substantive constitutional or legal authority depends on the advice and approval of the cabinet. Article 7 does not lay down under which conditions the cabinet can advise the Emperor to dissolve the House. The only place in the constitution where this case is provided for is Article 69. Nobody has ever asserted that the cabinet can revise the constitution or enact laws on the basis of Article 7 but this would be just as logical (or illogical) as to assert that the cabinet can dissolve the House on the basis of Article 7.

Secondly, the alternatives provided for in Article 69 gives the cabinet the choice to resign in case of a vote of no confidence or the rejection of a vote of confidence or to dissolve the House. Because the House must pass a vote of no confidence or reject a vote of confidence, it remains master of its own existence because a dissolution can only occur in response to its action. It depends on the House whether there will be an appeal to the electorate to settle a conflict between the executive and the legislature. In the present interpretation of the constitution, the House of Representatives exists at the discretion of the Prime Minister. Even a superficial acquaintance with the history of political institutions will teach that such a situation is incompatible with the Diet's theoretical position as 'the highest organ of state power'. To appeal to the electorate not for solving an unsolvable discord between the executive and the legislature but for the convenience of the Prime Minister is a political absurdity.

Thirdly, the present practice gives the cabinet (actually the Prime Minister) unlimited power to dissolve the House of Representatives and thereby annuls the provision in the constitution fixing the term of representatives at four years. The mass media and the politicians always refer to the 'right' or 'privilege' of the Prime Minister to dissolve the House as if the position of the Japanese Prime Minister were the same as that of Britain's Prime Minister. There is nothing in the constitution to support such an interpretation which makes it possible to deprive the members of the House of their constitutional right to represent the people.

THE 1948 DISSOLUTION

An external confirmation of the unconstitutionality of the dissolution of the House of Representatives on the basis of Article 7 is furnished by the events in connection with a former dissolution on 23 December 1948. In a conference between Prime Minister Yoshida (then leader of the Democratic Liberal Party), Tetsu Katayama (leader of the Socialist Party), Gizō Tomabechi (leader of the Democratic Party) and Brigadier General Courtney Whitney (chief of SCAP's Government Section), it was agreed that the only basis on which the cabinet could dissolve the

House was Article 69.

In order to play down the importance of this agreement between the party leaders, the expression 'government and opposition party collusion dissolution' was later fabricated. But among the materials of the Occupation era made public on 1 December 1979, is a document showing that General MacArthur transmitted to Prime Minister Yoshida his sharp disapproval of Yoshida's plan to dissolve the House by using the Emperor (i.e., on the basis of Article 7). He told Yoshida that the constitution does not give the Prime Minister the right to dissolution, which can only be carried out in conformity with Article 69.

From the point of view of constitutional law and political theory, the proposition that the Prime Minister can dissolve the House of Representatives at will is so absurd that its acceptance by the courts amounts to a major imbecility but its persistency shows how little the constitution is understood. The Constitutional Research Council not even once touched upon this problem and the restoration of the original interpretation has never been urged. It shows the lamentable failure of so-called experts to grasp the basic principles of democratic government. It is sad that the 'highest organ of state power' has become a mere tool for political expediency and the arbitrary decisions of the bureaucracy but it is even sadder to see the members of the House raising their hands like a bunch of schoolboys and shouting '*banzai*' when they are deprived of their authority.

Since the Supreme Court relied on Article 7 for its decision, I want to add a few words on the jurisprudential value of this article. The amateurishness of the drafters of the constitution, apparent throughout the document, is particularly obvious in Chapter 1. The requirement laid down in Article 3 (and repeated in Article 7) for the functions of the Emperor ('The advice and approval of the cabinet shall be required for all acts of the Emperor in matters of state, and the cabinet shall be responsible thereof') cannot be complied with in the appointment of the Prime Minister and is inconsistent with the constitutional procedure for legislation and the amendment of the constitution.

When the Diet designates the Prime Minister (Art. 67, par. 1 and 6), no cabinet exists and it is therefore incongruous that the cabinet should be responsible for his appointment. (The procedure corresponding to the constitutional system would be for the Speaker of the House of Representatives and the President of the House of Councillors - in the case of Article 67, par. 2, the Speaker alone - to inform the Emperor of the designation of the Prime Minister and request his appointment.) In practice, the constitutional procedure is ignored and the Prime Minister countersigns his own appointment.

Since the Prime Minister can appoint and remove ministers of state at will, the advice and approval of the cabinet for the appointment and dismissal of ministers of state is a strange requirement and simply impossible when a new cabinet is formed. The cabinet as such is not involved in legislation (Art. 59) and the amendment of the constitution

(Art. 96); all laws and cabinet orders must be signed by the competent minister and countersigned by the prime minister, and it is strange that the advice and approval of the cabinet should be required for their promulgation. Finally, the words 'on behalf of the people' (Art. 7) have no meaning whatever and are an empty formula.

EFFECTS OF THE TOMABECHI DECISION

As a result of the Tomabechi decision, the members of the House of Representatives have served the four-year term of office only once. At the time of Prime Minister Takeo Miki (December 1974-December 1976), the term of the House members elected on 10 December 1972, was to expire on 9 December 1976, and the 34th general election was held on 5 December 1976. But the average term of office of the members of the House, starting with the election held on 25 April 1947, and including the members elected in the 38th general election on 6 June 1986, has been about two years and six months (the shortest term was 150 days).

The misinterpretation of the constitution has become part of Japan's political folklore. When in his ruling on the unconstitutionality of the 1983 election to the House of Representatives Judge Shigenobu Suzuki of the Tokyo High Court remarked that the unconstitutionality could limit the Prime Minister's right to dissolve the House, then Chief Cabinet Secretary Takao Fujinami emphatically stated that the Prime Minister's right would not be limited by the court's ruling or any other factor because it was an independent constitutional right.

Even within the Liberal-Democratic Party, the possibility that the House can be dissolved at the discretion of the Prime Minister has caused some concern. When the late Shigeru Hori was Speaker of the House, he wrote in what has been called the Hori Memorandum that dissolution on the basis of Article 7 was undesirable because it diminished the authority and dignity of the Diet. But Hori's concern was not prompted by the distortion of the constitutional system and the disregard of democratic principles but by the abuse of the dissolution for the factional power struggle within the Liberal-Democratic Party. Successive prime ministers have used the dissolution for strengthening the influence of their factions. As leaders of the party, they can nominate their followers as official party candidates which assures them of party funds and logistic support for the election campaign. None of the dissolutions in the post-war period had anything to do with the welfare of the people or important shifts in policy, they were only dictated by the political ambitions of the Prime Minister. There is a constant tug-of-war among the various factions of the Liberal-Democratic Party. The faction in power can secure most ministerial posts for its members (the hope of becoming minister is one of the strongest motives for joining a faction). Because no single faction can secure the two-thirds majority necessary for the election of party president (which assures the election as Prime Minister), the cooperation of other factions must be bought by appointing certain of their members to ministerial posts. Every member of the Liberal-Democratic Party who has been elected to the Diet five times expects to be nominated a minister before he retires. The lure of ministerial posts enticed Komeito ('Clean Government Party') to forsake the opposition and support the Liberal-Democratic Party.

To reward as many as possible with such appointments, changes in the cabinet are frequent. Since the end of the war (1945-1989) Japan has had 38 cabinets (including five different cabinets headed by Yoshida, three by Hatoyama, two by Kishi, three by Ikeda, three by Sato, two by Tanaka, two by Ohira, three by Nakasone, two by Takeshita and three by Kaifu). The instability of political leadership has been a major factor in the ascendency of the bureaucracy in controlling the course of the nation.

The impairment of the position of the Diet by the Prime Minister's arrogation of the right of dissolution may appear trivial compared with the actual working of that institution which makes a mockery of the constitutional provision that the Diet is the 'highest organ of state power'. Most decisions are made by the factional leaders or other influential politicians meeting in Japanese restaurants or result from negotiations of the political with the business leadership. Debates in the plenum as well as in committees are irrelevant to the actual conduct of the state's business. Legislative measures are prepared by the competent ministries and often enacted without study or debate.

Actual political power has nothing to do with constitutional or legal arrangements. Political power is not in the hands of the party but is wielded by the leaders of the major factions of the Liberal-Democratic Party (at present five). But the country's policies are shaped by the bureaucracy, particularly the Ministry of Finance and MITI. The higher echelons of the Ministry of Finance are almost exclusively occupied by graduates of the University of Tokyo, notably graduates of the Faculty of Law. Among the pressure groups influencing government policies, the most powerful are Keidanren (*Keizai Dantai Rengōkai*; Federation of Economic Organisations) and Nokyo (*Nōgyō Kyōdō Kumiai Rengōkai*; Federation of Agricultural Cooperatives).

THE COURTS AND POLITICS

The decision in the Tomabechi case was a patently political decision. In order to reach a politically desirable result (from the point of view of the party in power), the courts discarded juridical logic and neglected to fulfill their constitutional duty. In this case, four justices of the Supreme Court opposed the position of the majority that judicial review did not extend to highly political actions and in the Sunakawa case, three justices, in a dissenting opinion, branded the denial of the court's right to review 'a regrettable disregard of the constitution'. It is incomprehensible that in a so-called democracy, the highest court of the land recognises a claim that goes back to the darkest days of eighteenth century absolutism and how so-called scholars can try to justify this throwback to capricious government.

Under the pretext of not interfering with politics, the Supreme Court condoned Mr Yoshida's autocratic manœuvre. It seems that the majority of the Supreme Court trembled at the thought of what would happen if it declared Mr Yoshida's arbitrary dissolution unconstitutional but in allowing this lawlessness, they not only supported an assertion that has been used in the past to justify atrocities but also upset the constitutional balance between the executive and the legislature in Japan's political system.

People who contend that, notwithstanding Article 81 of the constitution, there are political acts not subject to judicial review fear that the courts would become entangled in politics if the right of review were to apply to the entire spectrum of government activities. But the constitution is a political document and its interpretation must also take into account political science. On the basis of the separation of powers, the legislature as well as the executive can define autonomously the limits of their respective powers but this definition must be based on the constitution and the decision whether their definition is correct must be made by the courts. The Diet is the highest organ of state power but it has no absolute power and neither the cabinet nor administrative agencies can claim a sphere of power impervious to the scrutiny of constitutionality. 'The constitution is what the Supreme Court says it is' describes drastically but not erroneously the situation in the US. If the Diet or the legislature is dissatisfied with the interpretation of the courts, they must propose a constitutional amendment and submit it to the judgement of the people. Politics is a question of power, and one of the means to prevent power from becoming absolute is the system of checks and balances involved in the separation of powers. For the question of constitutionality, there can be no government action exempt from examination by the courts and no absolutely free discretion. Otherwise, the rule of law established by the constitution will crumble.

To protect the supremacy of the constitution is not only the right of the courts but their duty. This negates the theory of 'inherent limitations'. In a monograph refuting the theory that highly political acts of state are outside the purview of judicial review, Professor Tatsugoro Isosaki argued that the power to decide whether actions conform to the constitution extends to all state acts and that it is the duty of the courts to institute such a review. If the courts were to decline such a review, because it had no basis in the constitution, they would be negligent in their official duty and violate the constitution.

The argument of the Supreme Court in the Tomabechi case strongly reflects the continental system of administrative law and the Japanese system under the Meiji Constitution. The way of thinking of the majority was not in tune with the American system. The Japanese constitution, like the American system, incorporates a system of checks and balances although this is not expressly stated. Each power is independent but it is checked by the two other powers so as to maintain a balance between them. Each power can act freely within its own sphere but if its activities transcend the constitutional limits, it will be called back to its proper sphere by the courts. In other words, the legislature and the executive can assert the constitutionality of their activities on the basis of their understanding of the constitution but their interpretation of the constitution and the law is not definitive and can be challenged in the courts.

The Supreme Court has the final word on the interpretation of the constitution. This constitutes an important political function which the Supreme Court has to fulfill in the system of separation of powers. The court's excuse of incompetence is in conflict with the text of Article 81. Since the dissolution of the House was within the ambit described by 'any law, order, regulation or official act', it was the duty of the courts to declare whether the dissolution of the House of Representatives conformed to constitutional and legal requirements. By shirking their constitutional responsibility, the courts have avoided a temporary inconvenience but negated an important principle for the protection of Japan's constitutional equilibrium and of individual rights.

Judicial review is the main device by which the judiciary implements its political function in the system of checks and balances. Such a review can take two forms; formal or material. Formal review is limited to the examination of the question whether a law has been enacted in conformity with constitutional requirements or an administrative action has been taken according to existing regulations and with observance of all due formalities. Formal review can only protect the 'rule by law', i.e. that government action (or inaction) conforms to the existing legal norms. But totalitarian regimes can observe legality and Fascist as well as Communist dictatorships have suppressed individual liberty and violated human rights by clothing their despotic measures in the form of law.

Material review also inquires into the substantive compatibility of a law or order with the constitution or of an administrative act with the relevant laws; such an inquiry, therefore, addresses itself to the contents or subject matter of a law or disposition. The right of the courts to probe the compatibility of all laws with the constitution represents the main form of the control of the legislature by the judiciary whereas the legality of administrative actions can also be examined in other ways.

In Anglo-American law, the ordinary courts remain controllers of the executive although the function of the courts in checking the administration has been violently attacked and in some cases circumscribed. In his book *The New Despotism*, Lord Hewart of Bury, then Lord Chief Justice of England, denounced the tendency to supplant the courts and the rule of law in favour of efficiency through government by experts. He impugned particularly the attempt to make administrative findings conclusive and the delegation of law-making functions to administrative agencies. On the European continent, the system of administrative courts made it possible to control administrative action by independent organs but the sphere of controllability was often limited by devices such as the necessity of *autorisation préalable* in French administrative law prior to 1870 or the so-called *Konfliktserhebung* prescribed by the Prussian law of 1854. Another form of the control of the executive and the legislature is the state court competent to adjudicate questions of constitutionality (*Staatsgerichtshof* in Germany's Weimar Constitution and *Bundesverfassungsgericht* in the Fundamental Law of 1949).

With regard to substantive law, the idea of the rule of law led to the drafting of written constitutions and further to formulation of specially guaranteed rights. The Bill of Rights in the US constitution (contained in the first ten amendments), the Rights and Duties of the People in the Japanese constitution and the *Grundrechte* in Germany's Fundamental Law as well as the Convention for the Protection of Human Rights and Fundamental Freedoms contain substantive provisions protecting the individual's personal and economic interests which, therefore, cannot be impaired by legislative or executive action. But many constitutions recognise that in an emergency, fundamental human rights can be suspended and the practice of martial law often exposes the individual and the people to arbitrary force and even lawlessness.

POLITICAL DONATIONS OF CORPORATIONS

Among the politically motivated decisions, one of the most fateful has been the ruling justifying political donations by business corporations. In 1960 a stockholder of Yawata Iron and Steel Co. (which later merged with Fuji Iron and Steel Co. to form Nippon Steel Corporation) sued the President and Vice-President of the firm demanding reimbursement of ¥ 2.5 million the firm had given as a political donation to the Liberal-Democratic Party. The verdict of the Tokyo District Court (1963) was in favour of the plaintiff. 'Since the company is an association making the pursuit of profit its goal, all non-profit actions are actions outside the sphere of the business goal and a violation of the articles of incorporation. Political contributions to a particular political party such as the Liberal-Democratic Party are different from socially obligatory actions such as contributions to disaster relief or donations for educational activities to which nobody objects.' Judge Hidero Ito compared donations to a particular political party to donations to a particular religion which cannot be expected to be approved of by all stockholders. The decision caused consternation in political and business circles. It was overturned by the Tokyo High Court in 1966 and an appeal was rejected by the Supreme Court in June 1970.

In quashing the verdict of the District Court, the High Court reasoned: 'The success or failure of a democratic system depends on the activities of political parties. Contributions to those public activities are lawful in the same way as contributions to charitable activities'. In upholding the High Court's ruling, the Supreme Court repeated the same argument: 'Since political parties are an indispensable element supporting parliamentary democracy, the donation of political funds in order to cooperate with their sound development is allowable to the extent that it can be deemed to fulfill the social functions of the company.' Defining these limits, the court laid down two rules. First, the contribution should not aim at the interests of a particular person in the company to fulfill his political ambitions; secondly, the amount of the donation must be appropriate in view of the size of the company and the situation of the political party to which the donation is made.

The social obligations of business corporations have been the subject of many controversies. Their basic social obligation is to perform their economic function to provide goods and services necessary or useful for the community. Their responsibility for side effects of these activities (e.g., environmental pollution) has often been discussed as a problem of social responsibility and on principle their liability is determined by law. Obviously, these obligations have no relation whatever to charitable activities. In a certain sense, a company is also a member of the local community and to cultivate relations with the local residents contributes directly or indirectly to the business performance of the company. But expenditures for such purposes are quite different from political donations.

Although a company is a legal person, it is not a human person and is no citizen. It has no political rights and duties (the duty to pay taxes is based on income and/or the enjoyment of community services). As the District Court pointed out, the legal owners of a company are the stockholders and it can hardly be presumed that all stockholders support the same political party. Since 'aid for natural calamities or charitable contributions are actions for which the approval of the stockholders can be presumed, the responsibility of the directors does not become a problem. But donations to a particular political party cannot be said to be actions for which the agreement of the stockholders' meeting can be expected.' The High Court, however, contended: 'In the same way as charitable contributions, political donations are useful actions for society.' As in other instances, the decision relies on the assertion that the end justifies the means. The inference that something is lawful because it is useful is false. That a company can lawfully make political donations because political parties play an important role in a parliamentary system disregards logic. The assumption that everything contributing to the public welfare is in accordance with the legal order is a fallacy.

To my mind, this erroneous decision has been largely responsible for the rise of 'money politics' and the corruption of politicians. The numerous cases of bribery make it abundantly clear that the Supreme

Court's contention that political donations of business corporations contribute to the sound development of parliamentary democracy was an enormous miscalculation. Theoretically the distinction between political donations and bribes may be clear but in practice, political donations without expectation of some kind of return are pure theory. The decision which legalised the purchase of political favours has been one of the causes of Japan's 'money politics'. But there is not the slightest possibility that political contributions by business corporations (or labour unions) will be prohibited.

Chapter 3

Human Rights

INTERNATIONAL PROTECTION OF HUMAN RIGHTS

The old international law maintained the principle of freedom of international intercourse. The UN Charter advocates 'respect for human rights and for fundamental freedoms for all without distinction as to race, sex, language or religion' (Art. 1, par. 2; cf Art. 55; Art. 62, par. 2 adds 'observance of' to 'respect for' human rights and fundamental freedoms for all). But the Charter does not enumerate these rights and freedoms. It negates, however, the old rule that a state can treat its nationals according to its discretion and establishes the principle that the protection of human rights is a matter of international law.

The General Declaration of Human Rights adopted by the General Assembly on 10 December 1948, affirms that all human beings are born free and equal in dignity and rights. The fundamental human rights are based on the dignity and value of the human person so that all human beings without distinction of race, colour, sex, language, political persuasion, national or social origin, property or other circumstances possess the same inalienable rights to be recognised by all states. The right to life, liberty and personal security is particularised in the prohibition of slavery (Art. 4), of torture and the imposition of inhuman punishment (Art. 5), of arbitrary arrest and expulsion (Art. 9), of retroactive penal law (Art. 11, par. 2), of restrictions on the freedom of action and on leaving and returning to one's home country (Art. 13), of arbitrary deprivation of citizenship (Art. 15, par. 2) and arbitrary confiscation (Art. 17, par 2).

The Declaration further demands freedom of thought and religion (Art. 18), freedom of information and expression (Art. 19) and freedom of assembly and association (Art. 20). Positive action on the part of the state is demanded concerning judicial procedures and political and social rights. States are bound to give fair legal protection by independent tribunals (Art. 7, 8, 9 and 12), and to grant universal and equal franchise and participation in public affairs (Art. 21). Social rights include the right of the individual to acquire and possess property, the right to social security including the right to work, to choose one's occupation, the right to a fair wage, protection against unemployment and the right to recreation. The right to education should guarantee at least elementary instruction. Medical care, particularly assistance for mothers and children, is to be provided irrespective of marital status (Art. 22-25). Also mentioned are the right to a cultural life (Art. 26) and a public order in which the fundamental human rights can be realised (Art. 27). For the enforcement of these rights, every person should be entitled to invoke the competent courts (Art. 28) but the Declaration does not provide for complaints or petitions to international organs.

The General Declaration of Human Rights was accepted by a vote of 48 to 0 but eight states abstained. Six Communist states criticised the insufficient attention given to 'socialist rights'; Saudi Arabia found the Declaration incompatible with Islamic principles and South Africa objected to the 'equality of races'. Since the UN General Assembly has no legislative power, the Declaration is not law or a treaty binding governments, but it incorporates the principles containing the standards of the civilised world which should be upheld by the courts.

The Japanese government has ratified the International Convention on Civil and Political Rights which went into effect in September 1979. Japan did not accept some of the provisions of the first covenant (right to strike, holiday payments) and refused to sign the covenant giving individuals whose human rights have been violated the right to appeal to the United Nations. Rights protected by the covenant on civil and political rights include the right to life (Art. 6), prohibition of torture and cruelty (Art. 7), prohibition of slavery (Art. 8), prohibition of arbitrary arrest and detention (Art. 9), humane treatment of detainees (Art. 10), freedom of movement and residence, freedom to leave and re-enter one's home country (Art. 12), restrictions on the expulsion of foreigners (Art. 13), right to a fair trial (Art. 14), respect for privacy, honour and reputation (Art. 17), freedom of thought, conscience and religion (Art. 18), freedom of expression (Art. 19), freedom of peaceful assembly (Art. 21), freedom of association (Art. 22) and protection of the rights of minorities (Art. 27). Some provisions of Japan's existing laws, particularly the Alien Registration Law and the Emigration and Immigration Control Ordinance, are incompatible with the covenants.

Japan has not signed even one-third of the 23 UN treaties on human rights. The country does not grant political asylum. There were about 200 Iranians in Japan who had been denied refugee status; the category of political asylum does not exist in the Emigration and Immigration Control Ordinance and therefore the Immigration Bureau cannot legally recognise such a status. Since the Ministry of Justice is not inclined to change the law to allow political asylum and to recognise refugee status, the Diet does not act.

Vietnamese and other refugees are treated under special arrangements (based on the discretionary power of the Minister of Justice) with the UN High Commissioner for Refugees. Iranians could come to Japan without obtaining a visa in Iran and could be given a 90-day visa in Japan; but after this term, they became illegal aliens unless they obtained refugee status. All petitions of Iranians for refugee status were denied with the exception of Bahai and Kurdish refugees who could prove that their lives were in danger if they returned to Iran. No Iranians were deported but because they were illegal aliens, they could not get jobs.

After the June 1989 Tiananmen Square massacre in Beijing, Chinese students in Japan wanted to have their visas extended but the immigration authorities refused to take the situation into account. Students who had taken part in the pro-democracy demonstrations were told that things had returned to normal and that there was no reason to extend their visas. Requests for visa extension were denied for the most idiotic reasons. A Chinese student whose guarantor lived in Gumma Prefecture (which is adjacent to Tokyo) was told that he needed a guarantor living in Tokyo. When the student persisted, the immigration official retorted: 'In China, you may have a guarantor living far away, but not in Japan. If you don't like it here, you can go to a better country.' There is, of course, nothing in the law which says that the guarantor must live in the same prefecture.

The reservations which Japan made with regard to the covenants demonstrate the autocratic thinking of the Japanese bureaucracy. They do not want to have independent international agencies or representatives of third countries monitor Japan's performance in the field of human rights. When Japan ratified the two covenants on human rights, the press discussed some of the discriminatory measures against foreigners which would have to be corrected. Foreigners did not qualify for public housing and housing loans and were not eligible for state pensions (they could, however, participate in the health insurance systems). As long as state pensions are not internationally transferable, participation is of little interest to foreigners not permanently resident in Japan. It is, however, of great concern to the Korean and Chinese minorities and was probably limited to Japanese on purpose in order to exclude these minorities.

Another problem was the appointment of foreigners as professors at public universities. Foreigners were not employed at national and public universities because of the Personnel Authority's interpretation of the qualifications for these positions as equivalent to those of government employees. The Ministry of Education had drafted a bill with the title 'Law for Special Measures for the Appointment of Foreigners as Professors' which would have allowed the employment of foreigners as professors or assistant professors but barred them from assuming posts such as president or dean and from taking part in faculty meetings. But other government agencies were apprehensive that such a measure could lead to the appointment of foreigners at government research facilities or as government employees and the bill was not submitted to the Diet. In 1982, however, full-time positions at national universities were opened to foreigners by the 'Foreign University Teachers' Employment Law'.

JAPAN'S HUMAN RIGHTS SITUATION

According to a report of the Civil Liberties Bureau of the Ministry of Justice, confirmed cases of violations of human rights in 1990 amounted to 15,067 cases of which violations by public servants accounted for 214 cases, those by private individuals and organisations for 14,853 cases. Teachers were responsible for 146 infringements such as physical punishment or searches of students' bags or clothing. The largest number of violations by private individuals or organisations involved coercion and oppression such as forcing or hindering children to marry, requiring residents to make donations, abuse of workers by employers or forcing lessees to vacate their dwellings by damaging or destroying houses or apartments.

In an article on human rights, Ribō Hatano, a professor of law at Gakushuin University and Japanese representative on the UN Subcommission on Prevention of Discrimination and Protection of Minorities, wrote that Japan was an advanced country in terms of human rights compared with many other countries where human rights violations occurred frequently and on a massive scale. He defended the government's treatment of the Ainu and opposed the idea of appealing to the UN to have the Ex-Natives Protection Law repealed. From 1974 to 1988, he stated, the Hokkaido Prefectural Government spent over ¥ 33 billion on the welfare of the Ainu. A minority receiving such protection would look strange if it appealed to the UN for being discriminated against. He also observed that Asian female workers in Japan can be regarded not only as 'victims' but also as 'criminals' because some of them engage in prostitution. In discussing detention in police stations, he asserted that it was impossible to confirm that torture had actually been used in police cells.

Human rights activists disagreed with Hatano's views, accusing him of lacking even basic knowledge of human rights issues in Japan and demanded his resignation from the UN subcommission. Shigeki Miyazaki, Professor of Law at Meiji University, remarked that Japan, which has not yet ratified the Optional Protocol to the International Covenant on Civil and Political Rights giving individuals the right to appeal to the UN on human rights, could hardly be considered an 'advanced country' in this field.

Japanese human rights organisations submitted a counter report to refute the one on the human rights situation in Japan presented by the government to the UN Human Rights Committee in Geneva in July 1988. The intransigent attitude of the bureaucracy on the question of foreign workers contributed to numerous violations of the human rights of 'illegal aliens', the activists maintained. Japan has not ratified the International Convention for the Protection of the Rights of All Migrant Workers and Members of their Families (adopted by the UN in December 1991) because the Ministry of Justice does not want to revise conflicting domestic laws. The Ministries of Justice and Labour were only interested in detecting and deporting foreigners living in Japan in contravention of applicable laws and regulations. Because 'undocumented workers' were afraid of being deported, they remained silent and did not seek protection when their human rights were infringed. The counter-report protested against the plan of the government to use police stations as 'substitute detention houses' and explained that the questioning of suspects in custody at police stations was connected with serious human rights violations.

Asia Watch, a human rights organisation, accused the Japanese government of the forcible repatriation of Chinese despite their plea that they would face reprisals at home for supporting the democracy movement. The organisation sent a report to the Japanese government on the disregard of the human rights of Chinese dissidents staying in Japan but received no reply. The Japanese government, the report stated, has forcibly repatriated some Chinese claiming to be dissidents. It has obstructed the processing of requests for asylum, refugee status and visa extensions for Chinese afraid of returning to China and consistently disregarded evidence indicating that the returnees would suffer arrest and imprisonment. Not a single student, the report claimed, had been granted political asylum.

The immigration authorities disregard the situation of foreigners seeking asylum. In April 1990 the Chinese hijacker of an Air China jet who claimed he took part in the June 1989 Tiananmen demonstration was deported. In August 1991 a 24-year-old Chinese woman, Lin Guizhen, was put on a China Eastern Airline jet bound for Shanghai. She had filed suit against the immigration authorities in March 1990 for denying her claim for asylum and also challenged the deportation order in court. The Fukuoka Immigration Bureau, however, contended that she only came to Japan to seek work and decided that the pending legal procedures were no reason for deferring her deportation. She was sent back to China despite her assertion that she faced political prosecution because she had taken part in pro-democracy demonstrations in her native Fujian Province.

A Fukuoka TV station reported that according to Lin Guizhen's parents, she is serving a two-year prison sentence and is in poor health. An immigration official asserted that the woman never mentioned her political activities and was deported because she agreed with the immigration authorities - an unbelievable statement in view of Lin Guizhen's two lawsuits to stop the government from deporting her. In March 1992 the Fukuoka District Court announced its decision rejecting Lin Guizhen's demand to nullify her deportation order.

Asia Watch further blamed the Japanese government for failure to protest against the systematic harassment and intimidation of Chinese students participating in protest activities or belonging to dissident organisations by Chinese embassy officials. The report quoted Japanese and Chinese critics maintaining that the Japanese government was bowing to pressure of Japanese business circles eager to resume trade and industrial ties with China and immigration officials intent on stopping the influx of 'illegal' labourers.

In February 1991 the Japan Civil Liberties Union submitted a report to the government and the Supreme Court detailing violations of human rights, particularly of persons from less developed countries, by Japan's law enforcement agencies. Among the instances of physical abuse of suspects held in detention, the report mentioned as the most common forms of mistreatment grabbing a suspect by the hair and knocking his or her head against the wall, slapping the person in the face with a shoe or kicking over the chair on which the individual was sitting. Information on the basic rights of defendants is available only in Japanese and English, and court interpretation is generally limited to English, Korean and Chinese. Westerners from industrialised countries seem to be treated somewhat better than foreigners from Third World countries.

According to a 1991 poll by the Osaka Bar Association about 30 per cent of the foreigners who were indicted for crimes and tried in Japanese courts did not understand the court procedures. The rapid influx of foreigners has increased the difficulty of the police to cope with the law violations of people who do not understand Japanese. The authorities are unable to find enough competent interpreters, particularly for languages such as Tagalog, Urdu or Arabic, and few interpreters are familiar with Japan's legal system. In addition to the language difficulties, cultural differences create serious obstacles in the administration of justice involving foreigners, above all those from South East Asia.

The basic individual rights guaranteed in the constitution reflect the Anglo-American tradition of democratic liberalism but the constitution fails to make the realisation and protection of social justice a task of the Japanese polity. But no democratic state can disregard the social values of freedom, peace and justice. The social and economic rights mentioned in the constitution are conceived as interests of the individual entitled to protection by the state. Absent is the concept of a state responsible for social justice and social security.

The atrocious disregard of human rights by the authorities in pre-war and war-time Japan was notorious but respect of human rights is not perfect in post-war Japan. 'Economic growth cannot be bought at the expense of social justice', Norway's Prime Minister Gro Harlem Brundtland once said. The treatment of minorities involves a continuous disregard of human rights. Japanese politicians have caused protests in foreign countries because of their racial slurs. A former Prime Minister, Yasuhiro Nakasone, made derogatory remarks on the ethnic diversity in the United States in 1986 and Michio Watanabe, who has held four different portfolios, committed similar slips of the tongue in 1988.

In September 1990 Seiroku Kajiyama, who had just been appointed Minister of Justice, told reporters the day after he had observed a crackdown on foreign women loitering in the Shinjuku red-light district in quest of customers: 'It's like in America when neighbourhoods become mixed because blacks move in and whites are forced out. Prostitutes ruin the atmosphere in the same way.' Blacks in the US were furious and six members of the Congressional Black Caucus filed a protest with the Japanese Embassy in Washington demanding an apology and the dismissal of Kajiyama. He had already withdrawn his remarks and Prime Minister Kaifu had called them 'extremely inappropriate' but he did not dismiss Kajiyama. Nakasone blamed the considerable number of blacks, Puerto Ricans and Mexicans for America's relatively low literacy rate and Watanabe implied that American blacks were inclined to neglect the repayment of debts.

TREATMENT OF SUSPECTS

The treatment of suspected law violators by police and prosecutors is another area of fierce contention concerning human rights. The rule that 'a person is presumed innocent until he (or she) is proven guilty' seems to be disregarded not only in practice but also in existing regulations. The detention of suspects in police cells which allows police and investigators to use threatening tactics to extract confessions is provided for in the Prison Law (*Kangoku-hō*) enacted in 1908 and still in force. Police custody can be extended up to 23 days and prolonged if a new violation of the law by the suspect is proferred. Lawyers are barred from the investigation and suspects are entitled to a public attorney only after being indicted.

In 1982, 1989 and 1992 the government prepared a revision of the Prison Law which would have institutionalised the use of 'substitute detention houses', meaning detention cells in police stations. The Japan Federation of Bar Associations and human rights organisations opposed this revision, alleging that suspects held at police stations were more likely to be subjected to psychological and physical abuse because the suspects were in the custody of the investigators in charge of the case instead of wardens not involved in the inquest. The Ministry of Justice contended that the shortage of detention houses made the use of police cells necessary. But Futabe Igarashi, a member of the Japan Federation of Bar Associations, claimed that detention houses were used at little more than half their capacity. As the Ministry of Justice and the National Police Agency refused to disclose the capacity and utilisation rate of the detention facilities, Igarashi undertook his own research. In 1988 there were 154 detention houses run by the Ministry of Justice with a total capacity of 16,321 persons but the average number of detainees was about 9,000, a utilisation rate of about 55 per cent. In 1985 the police operated 1,242 detention facilities at police stations with a capacity of 16,406 persons. The daily average of their utilisation was 6,552 suspects, a rate of only 40 per cent.

Since the Japanese government maintains that the use of police cells for the investigation of crimes does not violate UN conventions and that no change is required unless the UN Commission on Human Rights adopts a formal resolution demanding abolition of the practice, Futabe Igarashi tried to have the UN take up the issue. In August 1991 he organised a delegation composed of lawyers and representatives of civic groups to appeal to a subcommittee of the UN Commission on Human Rights and call for prohibiting the use of police cells for the investigation of suspects. He cited the case of Iwao Hakamada, arrested on suspicion of having killed a family of four. He was held in a police cell for 50 days, interrogated an average of 12 hours a day, not given food or water nor permitted to use the toilet during questioning. He was kicked, punched and dragged by the hair and made a false confession in order to end the torture. He was convicted and sentenced to death on the basis of the extorted confession and is now on death row.

A UN human rights official who visited Japan in 1980 remarked that the police should hold a suspect for no longer than 24 hours without bringing him before a judge. Japanese law sets the duration of the initial police investigation at 48 hours and judges can permit detention up to 23 days before an indictment is made. Human rights activists contend that this period is used or misused by the investigators to extort confessions.

With typical bureaucratic stubbornness, the Ministry of Justice resuscitated two bills, the Criminal Detention Facilities Bill and the Police Custody Facilities Bill, and, in equally typical robot-like fashion, the cabinet approved them for submission to the Diet in March 1991. They were substantially identical with the bills previously rejected by the legislature and again contained provisions allowing police to detain suspects in police stations for longer than 48 hours instead of transferring them to the detention facilities of the public prosecutors. The Detention Facilities Bill, an amendment to the Prison Law, ordained some improvements in the treatment of detainees and prisoners but both measures failed to provide practical rules to protect the human rights of suspects and detainees.

Foreigners arrested by the police on suspicion of having committed a crime are often unaware of their right to remain silent or to contact a next of kin or consulate and the police are not eager to inform suspects of these rights (Japan has no Miranda decision). Interrogation of people who do not understand Japanese is sometimes conducted without competent interpreters, the protocol is drawn up in Japanese and suspects who do not even speak the language are urged to sign it. Once the prosecution has such a signed statement, the defence is in a very weak position to contest the facts alleged in the record and the judges' willingness to rely on these written statements can cause serious injustice. Once an accused has been jailed, conversations with visitors in any other language than Japanese are monitored by an interpreter.

In a decision announced in May 1991 the Supreme Court left the issue of the right to counsel in a very unsatisfactory state of ambiguity. The court upheld the ruling of the Nagoya High Court that a prosecutor had unlawfully denied a defence attorney access to his client and confirmed the order directing the state to pay ¥ 50,000 in compensation. But at the same time, the top court ruled that the investigating authorities can delay such access if they deem it necessary to question a suspect immediately.

The case arose from an incident in October 1973 when a lawyer, Tadashi Asai, tried to see a client arrested on suspicion of trespassing and held at the Uozu Police Station in Toyama Prefecture. Asai arrived at the police station 20 minutes before the authorities were to start questioning the suspect. The prosecutor had the police delay the consultation by ordering the lawyer to obtain a document from the public prosecutor's office, a one-hour trip from the police station. He also barred the lawyer from giving his client a compendium of laws and other items.

The Supreme Court decided that, on principle, investigating and prosecuting authorities should allow a lawyer access to a client at any time. The court, however, conceded that the authorities could delay consultations between an attorney and his client if they would severely hamper an investigation. In former decisions the court had sanctioned the refusal of consultations when a suspect was being questioned or taken to the scene of the alleged crime.

After the police investigation, people arrested on suspicion of having committed a crime in Tokyo are imprisoned (I use this word advertently) in the Kosuga Detention Centre. Treatment and conditions are barbaric. The detainees, stripped naked, have to squat on hands and legs and exhibit their backside to a guard who takes a sample for the examination of the feces. The detainees are kept in solitary confinement in cells with a floor space of less than three mats (about 5m^2), furnished with 15 articles specified in the Enforcement Ordinance of the Prison Law (bedding, table, broom, dust-pan, water jug, etc.). The cells are unheated in winter and suffocatingly hot in summer. The food consists of boiled barley with rice.

In 1971 the daily caloric value of the rice and barley ration was increased from 1,700 kilocalories to 2,400 kilocalories and the caloric content of side dishes was fixed at 800 kilocalories. In 1987 the composition of the staple food was improved to seven parts of white rice to three parts of barley. Detainees can have food brought in from outside but the kinds of food are strictly limited. No visitors are allowed and the detainee can see his lawyer only with the permission of the prosecutor. References to the case for which the detainee is incarcerated in newspapers and magazines are deleted.

In December 1991 the Japanese Federation of Bar Associations submitted a 162-page report on the violation of human rights of detainees to the Human Rights Committee in Geneva. It cited over 30 cases of mistreatment in the course of legal proceedings. A British suspect held in the Tokyo Detention House for over a year described conditions as 'living hell'. He charged that he had been treated like 'a brute animal', subjected to 'varying degrees of torture'. The Ministry of Justice contended that officials at the facility respected detainees' human rights and adhered to the Prison Law, but this law, drafted and enacted under an autocratic government, does not ensure respect for human rights.

In July 1988 a woman related her experience in police custody at a police station in Nerima Ward and the Metropolitan Police Department headquarters to the Active Women Association, a group for the protection of human rights. It was a tale of unbelievable arrogance and sadism. The woman, Ms Chisako Tezuka of Asaka, Saitama Prefecture, was arrested in July 1987 on the charge of having fraudulently obtained a bank loan. At the police station, a male detective asked her how many panties she was wearing. She wanted to know the reason for the question and was told that she had to undergo a physical examination by a male investigator.

A female investigator untied Ms Tezuka's long hair and ran her fingers through it as if searching for drugs or weapons. She was then forced to take off her clothes, including her underwear, and made to jump several times to check whether she was hiding something in her vagina or anus. While still nude, she had to spread her legs and shake her waist; then, the investigator examined her vagina and anus. Next, she was handcuffed, roped and led to a toilet where she had to urinate with the door open and the investigator watching. She was told that the urine examination was performed to check whether she was taking stimulant drugs.

A scar on her body from an appendectomy, a doctor's scratches for allergy tests and other marks on her body were noted in a drawing. When she asked why she was subjected to this examination, she was told: 'Shut up! that's the rule'. During her detention, Ms Tezuka was twice genitally searched and interrogated for eight to ten hours a day during the first ten days of her detention while handcuffed and tied to a chair.

An account of this case was published in the *Japan Times* of 13 July 1988, and the paper commented on this case in an editorial on 15 July 1988. The case was mentioned again in an article published in the same paper on 23 June 1990.

The denial of counsel is a direct violation of Article 34 of the constitution which reads: 'No person shall be arrested or detained without being at once informed of the charges against him or without the immediate privilege of counsel; nor shall he be detained without adequate cause; and upon demand of any person such cause must be immediately shown in open court in his presence and the presence of his counsel.' The entire procedure in the case of Ms Tezuka constituted psychological torture and offended against Article 36 of the constitution.

The reporter who wrote the first article, Takashi Ono, inquired about the case at the Metropolitan Police Department. A public relations officer stated that under the law, a male investigator is permitted to perform a physical examination of a female suspect as long as a female observer is present. Such physical examinations, he said, are daily routine in police stations. To the best of my knowledge, the law has not been changed. Ms Tezuka was released after twenty days when the police failed to find evidence of the fraud she had been charged with, and learned that she had repaid the loan two months prior to her arrest.

In November 1990 the Nagano District Court ordered the Nagano Prefectural government to pay Tokiko Take ¥ 350,000 for having been strip-searched without a warrant. The 38-year-old woman had been arrested in February 1990 for driving without a licence. She was forced to strip at the Nagano Minami Police Station and, according to her account, made to urinate in front of a police officer to test whether she was using stimulants. The police contended that she agreed to the urine test and the court accepted the police version of the drug test. Presiding Judge Kenji Yamazaki stated that, as a general rule, police can search a suspect in jail for weapons without a warrant but that in the Take case, there was no possibility that the woman was concealing a weapon.

To arrest a person for driving without a licence seems to me to be completely unnecessary unless there were highly exceptional circumstances. Judge Yamazaki's opinion that the police can search suspects without a warrant is in conflict with the constitutional requirement laid down in Article 35. It seems obvious that notwithstanding some amendments, a law enacted in 1908 does not provide what today is considered adequate protection of human rights. The Charter of Paris for a New Europe (therefore not immediately affecting Japan) affirmed today's concern for these rights by providing that no one will be subject to arbitrary arrest or detention, or subject to torture or other cruel, inhuman or degrading treatment or punishment.

Defendants indicted on the strength of their confessions often repudiate their depositions later, claiming that they were made under duress and that they confessed to the crime in order to end the torture. In recent years, six persons found guilty and condemned to death have been acquitted in re-trials and in two cases, ex-convicts have been cleared of the crimes of which they were convicted. In all these cases, the convictions were mainly based on confessions which the accused claimed were obtained by coercion. It seems that some judges share the opinion of the late Chief Justice Kōtarō Tanaka who once told me, 'Our prosecutors don't make mistakes'.

INVESTIGATION OF RAPE CASES

As in some Westerm countries, the handling of rape cases by the authorities has been the subject of bitter complaints. Women's rights advocates assert that the indifference, distrust and callousness that rape victims experience in the course of investigation aggravate their sufferings. Frequently the victim is treated as if she were the criminal. A woman lawyer reported that one of her clients, a 16-year-old girl who had been raped twice by the same man was subjected to 10 days of obtuse questioning. There are no special provisions for the examination of rape victims except that the victim has the right to have a relative, friend or lawyer present. Since women constitute only 2 per cent of the police force, rape investigations are almost always conducted by male officers and it is rare that a policewoman is present. Rape victims who went to the police had the impression that the police were more interested in prying into their sex life than in identifying the attacker. Foreign women, in particular, felt that they were on trial; their sexual past and practices were considered an open book by judges and lawyers.

The prosecution of rape cases is only undertaken if the victim submits a formal complaint (*kokuso*) which must be filed within six months after the victim knows the identity of the rapist. A complaint is not required if two or more assailants committed the rape. The common procedure in criminal investigations is to re-enact the crime which means that the rape victim is taken to the scene of the crime and forced to go in her mind through an experience which probably was the most traumatic event in her life. There is a tendency to assume that the woman provoked the attack or consented to a sexual encounter. The judiciary commonly adheres to the stereotype of rape as a crime between strangers involving violence and are reluctant to consider rape between people who know each other as a crime.

In April 1991 the Tokyo High Court acquitted Tetsuo Ono, a 54-year-old native of Ibaraki Prefecture, of the charge of rape and murder of a credit union employee and quashed the sentence of life imprisonment but sustained his conviction for theft and rape in another case. Ono had been in custody for six months following his arrest in September 1974 for theft and rape when he was charged with the killing of the 19-year-old woman and removal of her body. The Matsudo branch of the Chiba District Court found him guilty mainly on the strength of his confession and the material evidence (the victim's clothes, umbrella and commuter pass) allegedly found on the basis of the defendant's indications. Presiding Judge Shinichi Tateyama of the Tokyo High Court declared that the confession, the result of relentless questioning protracted over 164 days of detention during which the defendant was sequestered from all contacts and the investigators took over the guard duties, showed the marks of coercion and lacked consistency and credibility. The account of the killing in the confession conflicted with the findings of the autopsy. The discovery of the material evidence was questionable and although it could not be said that it was engineered by the investigators, it could not be ascribed to the information given by the defendant. The court confirmed the six-year prison sentence for theft and rape but ordered the defendant released from custody because he had already been confined much longer than the duration of his sentence.

The defence expressed severe concern regarding the tendency to keep suspects in solitary police cells in order to extract confessions and deplored the inclination of the judges to rely on confessions. The lawyers also complained of the inordinate length of criminal trials which had kept the defendant almost 17 years behind bars.

INTERROGATION/COVER-UPS

In a 1988 case, a janitor was accused of two cases of arson. He had argued with tenants who disregarded the house rules. The janitor confessed to the charges while in police custody but repudiated his confession in court. The Tokyo District Court ruled that the prosecution had failed to submit any evidence corroborating the charges. Judge Hiroshi Sorimachi severely chided the law-enforcing authorities for putting too much emphasis on confessions. The confession on which the prosecution had based its case was so ridiculous that nobody with common sense would believe it. As a member of the legal profession, the judge said, he was ashamed of the methods the police and the prosecution had used to extract the confession.

In 1989 the Supreme Court overturned the conviction of a truck driver found guilty by two lower courts in a hit and run case. In December 1975 a drunk construction worker who had fallen asleep on a highway was hit by a truck and died. The public prosecutors indicted a truck driver in 1977 on the ground that a stain on one of the truck's rear tyres was from the victim's blood and the confession extorted from the driver that he had felt the truck bounce near the place of the accident. The Niigata District Court sentenced the driver to six months imprisonment with two years probation in 1982 and the Tokyo High Court upheld the verdict in 1984. The Supreme Court ruled that the police had been careless in its investigation and that the lower courts had been mistaken in assessing the evidence.

A man angered by protracted and unreasonable police interrogation tore up a police blotter and was arrested on the charge of destroying an official document and obstructing the execution of police duties. Michio Toyoshima checked into a Kyoto motel with a woman who was a habitual stimulant drug user. An employee of the motel, suspicious of the two, alerted the police. Finding that the car Toyoshima was driving had been stolen, the police took him to the police station for questioning. By 4 pm the next day, the police were satisfied that Toyoshima had nothing to do with the car theft and had purchased the car in good faith from another man. Nevertheless, the police continued the interrogation. At 5 pm Toyoshima asked the interrogators to let him go because he was tired and when the police refused, an argument ensued. The police stopped the interrogation and began reading the record of the interrogation. Toyoshima grabbed the blotter and tore it up.

The Kyoto District Court sentenced Toyoshima to six months in jail but the Osaka High Court reversed the sentence ruling that the blotter resulted from an unlawful interrogation and did not qualify for protection under the law. In June 1987, however, the Supreme Court quashed the verdict of the High Court and sentenced Toyoshima to three months imprisonment with one year probation. Presiding Justice Shigemitsu Dando asserted that although the way the police had interrogated the defendant was illegal, the police blotter was an offical document. But considering the circumstances of the case, the six-month sentence was too severe.

There have been some cases in which the authorities refused to prosecute apparent violations of the law. When Kōkō Sato, former parliamentary vice minister of transportation, who was found guilty of having accepted a bribe in the Lockheed trial and sentenced to two years imprisonment with three years probation came to the Diet after the end of the period in July 1986,a reporter, Hiroto Muraoka, asked him why he had denied his involvement during the trial but was now admitting it. Sato shouted: 'Shut up!' and slapped him in the face. The reporter filed a complaint with the Tokyo District Prosecutor's Office but in July 1989, the Prosecutor's Office decided to stay the prosecution. Since numerous people had witnessed the incident, the fact of the assault was not in doubt. Said Muraoka: 'If the prosecution of a crime of a politician is suspended in consideration of extenuating circumstances, something is fishy.' In 1991 Sato became chairman of the Executive Council of the LDP.

Yasuo Ogata, chief of the International Affairs Department of the Japan Communist Party, complained in November 1986 that his residence in Machida (Tokyo Prefecture) had been wire-tapped. An investigation by the public prosecutors found that five officers of the Kanagawa Prefectural Police Headquarters were involved in the illegal operation and indicted two of the policemen for suspected violations of the Telecommunications Enterprise Law and abuse of authority. But after a few months, the prosecutors decided to suspend the prosecution of the two officers and not to indict two others. The fifth officer had died.

Dissatisfied, Ogata filed a special request with the Tokyo District Court demanding that the four officers be put on trial on charges of abuse of authority but the court rejected the request. Ogata's appeal to the Tokyo High Court was likewise turned down. In March 1989, the Supreme Court denied Ogata's petition to reopen the case,ruling that there had been no abuse of authority by the four officers. Unless officials rely on their position, the court said, there can be no abuse of authority. In the present case, the officers acted not as policemen but as private individuals.

It is possible that the court would have reached the same conclusion if there had been a regular trial but the decision not to prosecute seems highly arbitrary. Ogata has filed a civil suit for damages in order to force a trial that will give him an opportunity to state his charges.

ADMISSIBILITY OF EVIDENCE

Among the complaints about the violation of individual rights in legal procedures are the cases of unlawfully obtained evidence. The blanket provisions of the constitution concerning entries and searches are routinely disregarded. Checks are carried out on the approaches to airports, and searches of aeroplane passengers and their luggage are considered normal procedure. Police often set up checkpoints and stop vehicles that might be used for illegal activities. The public's complaints about police interference can partly be attributed to the survival of police methods that were widely used in pre-war times but have no legal basis and constitute an arbitrary use of police power. The blind enforcement of rules without regard to the burden imposed on individuals creates unnecessary friction. Before the war, windows in the upper floors of the houses lining the roads through which the Emperor passed had to be closed and nobody was allowed to look out of the windows. Even now, when cars are stopped to let the Imperial limousine pass, drivers have to close the car windows, also in summer. There is no legal foundation for such a measure.

The most flagrant disregard of the public occurred on the occasion of Emperor Hirohito's funeral in February 1989. In order to protect the representatives of 165 countries coming to Tokyo for the ritual, the police mobilised a force of 32,000 officers, adding 6,000 officers from other prefectures to the 26,000-men strong metropolitan police. The centre of Tokyo looked like city under martial law. Police not only stopped motorists and had them open the trunks of their cars but also inspected houses along the road of the funeral procession and searched the belongings of pedestrians walking with some kind of luggage in the restricted areas.

The Supreme Court has ruled that a defect in the gathering of evidence does not necessarily impair its admissibility. Police questioning a man searched his belongings without his agreement and without a warrant. Because drugs were found, the man was indicted for violation of the Stimulant Drugs Control Law. The District Court and the High Court found him not guilty because the evidence had been illegally obtained. But in September 1978 the Supreme Court reversed the lower courts verdict, ruling that the illegality of the seizure did not necessarily invalidate the admissibility of the evidence. Unless there had been a serious violation of the principal that a warrant must be obtained for searches and seizures laid down in the constitution and the Code of Criminal Procedure, the evidence can be used. The court followed an earlier precedent in which it had held that real evidence may be admissible although illegally obtained because the substance of the illegal evidence is not changed by the illegal seizure. In a 1961 drug case, six justices expressed the view that illegally obtained real evidence should be excluded if basic human rights had been violated.

In a case involving the constitutional guarantee against self-incrimination (Art. 38, par. 1), the Supreme Court held that the provisions making refusal to cooperate with the tax authorities punishable (Income Tax Law - *Shotokuzei-hō* - Art. 234, par. 1; Art. 242, No. 8; National Tax General Rules Law - *Kokuzei Tsūsoku-hō* Art. 126) were not unconstitutional although the investigation, including the inspection of books, is carried out without a court order or warrant and the procedure compels the delinquent taxpayer to avow his infraction of the law. The Supreme Court argued that the investigation by the tax office personnel was a procedure aimed at equity in taxation and that the enforcement of cooperation by penal provisions did not directly physically coerce the free will of the individual. It could not be called an unequal and unreasonable system and there was no ground to hold it unconstitutional.

The ruling is an example of the tendency of the courts to negate the (erroneous) principle that the end justifies the means theoretically but to follow it in practice. The guarantee against self-incrimination applies to a compulsory investigation involving criminal liability but the investigation by the tax office is considered non-criminal. Cooperation is voluntary but refusal is punishable. Paragraph 2 of Article 234 of the Income Tax Law says that the right to question and search of the tax authorities laid down in Paragraph 1 cannot be interpreted as sanctioning a criminal investigation. This provision seems to be based on the childish assumption that the say-so of the legislature can change the nature of an act but the Supreme Court accepted it. The prevailing opinion at the time of the decision (November 1972) considered the system as incompatible with Articles 35 and 38 of the constitution.

FREEDOM OF EXPRESSION

In order to prevent 'fishing expeditions' by the law-enforcing agencies, articles 33 and 35 require that for arrests, entries, searches and seizures, the warrant must 'specify the offence with which the person is charged..., the place to be searched and things to be seized'. In a case involving a labour union, the Supreme Court, in a decision announced on 29 July 1958, held that the description of the 'adequate cause' as 'violation of the Local Public Service Law', and the things to be seized as 'minutes of meetings, struggle diaries, orders, communications, circulars, reports, memos and all other documents and materials considered relevant to the present case' met the requirements of the constitution. The meaning of 'all other documents and materials' could be understood from the enumeration preceding that expression.

Freedom of speech has often been a 'law and order' issue. How freedom of expression and other fundamental human rights of individuals and groups can be reconciled with the requirements of the public order and particularly of public safety can pose difficult problems. Freedom of expression includes the right to hold demonstrations, parades, processions and marches. In pre-war Japan, the Peace Preservation Law and the Police Regulations of Public Meetings constituted the main basis of police oppression. These laws were abrogated in 1945 at the order of the Occupation authorities and attempts to replace them by a new law met fierce opposition.

In the turbulent years immediately following the end of the war and in the period of student unrest in the 1960s and 1970s, demonstrations often resulted in fierce clashes between demonstrators and the police. In 1948 the Occupation authorities were greatly concerned about leftist-instigated anti-government movements. Because of the reluctance of the national government to take unpopular measures, SCAP proposed to have local governments enact public safety ordinances under which the police could curb wild demonstrations. A prototype prepared by the Americans was distributed to the military government teams. These teams, usually headed by a colonel and staffed by military personnel and army civilians, were headquartered in all prefectural capitals in order to supervise the activities of Japanese officials and advise them on the implementation of SCAP directives.

There were two types of public safety ordinances. Some required organisers merely to report in advance demonstrations and similar activities while others made it obligatory to obtain a licence. The courts have held ordinances which unduly restricted the freedom of expression unconstitutional.

In the so-called Enterprise case, which involved violent demonstrations by about 500 radical students against the docking of the nuclear-powered aircraft carrier *Enterprise* in Sasebo, the demonstrators were charged with violation of the Road Traffic Law, obstruction of police duties, assault and battery and violation of the special criminal law protecting American military installations in Japan because Nagasaki Prefecture had no public safety ordinance. In the course of the lengthy trial, 11 of the defendants accepted the lower court's ruling of guilty but five took the case up to the Supreme Court. In November 1982 the court decided that disorderly street demonstrations could be prosecuted under the Road Traffic Law and that the police action in quelling the rioters' attacks with rocks, bottles and staves did not violate freedom of expression.

At the time of the student demonstrations in the 1960s, the Japan Lawyers' Federation set up a special committee to inquire into the unlawful checking by the police and cautioned that there had been many cases of police excesses. On the other hand, violent protest actions such as the demonstrations against the Security Treaty in 1960, the anti-Vietnam demonstrations in 1968, particularly the riots at Shinjuku Station, and the clash between police and students at Haneda Airport cannot by any stretch of imagination be considered as lawful expressions of political convictions.

The disruptions at several Tokyo universities in 1968 and 1969, above all the epic battle carried live on TV in January 1969 when 8,000 police tried to dislodge riotous students from the Yasuda Auditorium on the campus of Tokyo University, cannot be justified as assertions of the freedom of expression. Ever since the construction of the Narita Airport began in 1968, there have been vicious attacks by radicals which have so far claimed the lives of five policemen, three of them murdered in cold blood by the rioters, two demonstrators and two uninvolved civilians. On 26 March 1978, four days before the scheduled opening of the airport, members of the Japan Revolutionary Communist League destroyed the equipment of the control tower. The obvious idiocy of the project was no excuse for the violence.

Freedom of speech was a major issue in the prosecution of two former leaders of Chūkakuha (Middle Core Faction), one of the radical student groups responsible for many of the riots. The two were indicted under the Subversive Activities Prevention Law (*Hakai Katsudō Bōshi hō*) of 1952, a law seldom used because of the difficulty of proving the crimes punishable under the law. In a campaign for the return of Okinawa without American bases and nuclear arms, the defendants organised rallies in April 1969 and urged their Chukakuha followers to take over the Prime Minister's official residence and paralyse the government and Tokyo metropolis. On 28 April about 10,000 students attacked the Prime Minister's residence and police boxes and invaded railway stations, disrupting rail service in the Tokyo area. The two leaders were indicted on sedition charges and found guilty by the Tokyo District Court in March 1985. The Tokyo High Court upheld the ruling of the lower court in March 1987. The defence argued that the sedition charge was unconstitutional because it applied to speeches for political purposes, not to actions, and therefore violated freedom of thought and expression.

The defendants contended that their speeches were mere recitals of slogans and did not constitute an attempt to revolt. The court held that the sedition charge applied not only to the action but also to the intent to commit such actions and that the inflammatory speeches were not just political sloganeering but specific appeals to carry out a plan for putting the metropolitan area under siege. The judicial proceedings, the court declared, concerned the activities of the defendants, not their political convictions. The court noted that freedom of speech can be restricted for the sake of the public welfare and concluded that the sedition charge under the Subversive Activities Prevention Law was constitutional. The defendants appealed to the Supreme Court.

The Supreme Court considered their appeals together with that of a third defendant, a former chairman of Chukakuha, who had been found guilty by the Tokyo District Court and the Tokyo High Court of having violated the Subversive Activities Prevention Law by advocating violence in order to prevent an agreement allowing US armed forces to stay on Okinawa. In October 1990 the Supreme Court, affirming (for the first time) the constitutionality of the law, rejected the appeals. Although, as the lower court had said, the law applied to objective, external activities and not to thoughts and principles, the defendants' actions were definitely instigation to riots and sedition.

Prior to the return of Okinawa to Japanese sovereignty on 27 May 1972, demonstrations were held to demand that the Self-Defence Forces (SDF) should not be deployed on the island. Six members of the SDF read a statement to that effect at the gates of the Self-Defence Agency in Tokyo on 27 April and at a rally in Shiba Park on the following day. Two of the soldiers who had been discharged from the army in May 1972 filed suit for reinstatement in November 1974 claiming that soldiers were guaranteed the right of expression and that their discharge was unconstitutional. In the first ruling on the suit on 27 September 1989(!), presiding Judge Yutaka Oka of the Tokyo District Court declared that the members of the SDF belonged to a team that required strict discipline and order in carrying out its duties, which restricted their freedom of opposing SDF policies. Because the two plaintiffs had volunteered for the SDF, they had accepted the limitations on their rights and freedoms to the extent necessary to carry out the duties of the force and this limitation did not contradict Article 21 of the constitution. The plaintiffs' behaviour, the judge said in dismissing their demand, took advantage of their position in the SDF and their uniform for propaganda purposes.

There are no reasons to deprive soldiers of their rights as citizens and the reasons adduced by Judge Oka to justify the court's decision are unconvincing. In Germany, for example, soldiers enjoy the rights of assembly and association and can form labour unions. Purely verbal opposition to government policies off duty does not impair the effectiveness of an army.

Prompted by the escalating violence of the clashes between underworld groups, the Diet passed a law making assembly with weapons a crime. In 1974 at a time of frequent brawls between the rival radical student groups Chūkakuha and Kakumaruha (Revolutionary Marxist Faction), police raided the Tokyo stronghold of Chukakuha and found six members of the group with weapons such as steel pipes, iron bars and bricks in their possession. The Tokyo District Court found the six guilty of assembling with weapons, adopting the view that they were prepared not only to defend themselves but also to attack other people. When the Tokyo High Court rejected their appeal, their leader, Yutaka Moriguchi alone appealed to the Supreme Court. The point of contention was whether the crime of assembly with weapons was committed even if there was no possibility of the weapons being used. In its ruling announced on 23 June 1983, the Supreme Court held that the law was intended not only to protect the life and property of individuals but also to safeguard peace and security of society. Even if objectively the possibility of an assault does not exist, an assembly with weapons in a way endangering the peace of society constitutes a crime under the law.

A law which went into effect in March 1992 gives the police new power to control underworld syndicates. Based on public hearings and screening by prefectural Public Safety Commissions, the National Public Safety Commission can designate groups meeting certain criteria as crime syndicates (*bōryoku-dan*). A group or organisation can be declared a crime syndicate if its membership includes a certain number of people with criminal records, the group has exacted money from ordinary citizens under pressure, and if relations inside the group involve an *oyabunkobun* (boss-henchmen) pattern. According to some critics, the law could also be used to suppress legitimate activities.

Restrictions on the freedom of expression imposed by general law are very numerous. Limitations are implied in the provisions of Japan's Penal Code on libel (Art. 230), insult (Art. 231), calumny (Art. 172), coercion (Art. 222-3), blackmail (Art. 249), perjury (Art. 169-171), forgery of documents (Art. 157-161), forgery of securities (Art. 162-3), forgery of seal (Art. 164-8), fraud (Art. 246-8) and interference in business through injury of credit (Art. 233). Moreover, the Public Office Election Law imposes restraints on electioneering and other limitations are contained in the Subversive Activities Prevention Law. Besides the restraints based on written law, the principle formulated by Justice Oliver W. Holmes that freedom of speech does not extend to utterances that would create 'clear and present danger' imposes curbs on public behaviour. Explaining the meaning of this restriction, Justice Holmes observed that the guarantee of freedom of expression does not protect a man shouting 'fire' in a crowded theatre when there is no fire.

FREEDOM OF THE PRESS

In connection with freedom of expression, the constitution explicitly mentions freedom of speech and the press. Freedom of the press is not a human right in the sense of concerning immediately man's existence as a person (such as personal freedom, freedom of thought and conscience, freedom of religion and the secrecy of communications), but an institutional guarantee, as are the freedom of gathering news and the protection of the secrecy of news sources. But it is generally held that in the interest of crime prevention and investigation, it is lawful to listen to and tape telephone and other conversations with the permission of one of the parties. Disregarding human relations and considering only the legal aspect, it is lawful to record a telephone or other conversation without informing or asking the permission of the interlocutor.

The Japanese press has been accused of servility and opportunism. Reporters attached to a certain agency, ministry or association form a club and only club members have direct access to information concerning the organisation while outsiders are barred. The clubs try to remain on good terms with the organisation and their inclination to protect their special relationship allows officials to closely monitor press coverage and slant the news.

During Emperor Hirohito's last illness, people generally felt sympathy for the ailing Emperor but some groups revived the question of his responsibility for the war. The Mayor of Nagasaki, Hiroshi Motojima, stated in the city assembly on 18 December 1988 that the Emperor bore some responsibility for the war. If the war had ended earlier, there would have been no fighting on Okinawa and no atomic bombs would have been dropped on Hiroshima and Nagasaki. Despite heavy pressure from the Liberal-Democratic Party, Motojima refused to retract his remarks. He was seriously wounded in an assassination attempt and rightist groups attacked his statement. One of those groups was Shokijuku which wanted to publish an opinion advertisement asserting that the Emperor was not responsible for the war in a Nagasaki newspaper. When the newspaper refused to carry the advertisement, the organisation filed suit. In February 1991 the Nagasaki District Court rejected the complaint. A publication, the court ruled, cannot be forced to run an advertisement it considers unacceptable.

In connection with the freedom of expression, the constitution stipulates: 'No censorship will be maintained, nor shall the security of any means of communications be violated' (Art. 21, par. 2). The constitution does not define censorship, and the courts have interpreted the constitution in a way which makes a mockery of common sense. In addition to the Ministry of Education's censorship of textbooks, censorship has been a controversial issue in connection with pornography. A special aspect of this problem, the censorship of books and other materials by the Japanese customs, has frequently been criticised.

CENSORSHIP AND PORNOGRAPHY

The Customs Tariff Law of 1911 (Art. 21, par. 3, No. 3) gives the chief customs inspector the right to prohibit the importation of 'Books, pictures, carvings and other articles impairing the public order and good morals.' Generally speaking, censorship means the previous examination of publications for the purpose of suppressing what is deemed objectionable on military, political, moral or other grounds, but there is no reason to suggest that the constitutional prohibition of censorship does not extend to subsequent censorship (i.e., after publication). The examination and confiscation of material imported from abroad certainly interferes with freedom of information, and the remedy provided by the Customs Tariff Law, the filing of a complaint with the administrative agency which decreed the prohibition (Art. 4) is by its very nature ineffective. No official will admit that he has been wrong and still less that he has been stupid.

The constitutionality of the prohibition of imported publications deemed harmful to public morals by the Customs inspectors has been contested in the courts but the results have only shown the absolute incomprehension of the higher courts of individual rights and their blind support of the government bureaucracy.

In its decision on two cases on 12 December 1984, the Supreme Court affirmed the constitutionality of the Customs censorship. In order to arrive at the conclusion that censorship by the Customs officials is not censorship, the court adopted a restrictive definition of censorship ('an act of an administrative authority having as its object the expression of an ideological content aiming at the prohibition of all or part'). The court did not give the slightest reason why the constitutional prohibition of censorship should be restricted to preceding censorship and the expression of an ideological content. Since foreign publications deemed obscene by the Customs inspectors are barred from entering Japan, the ban on obscene literature may appear as previous censorship, infringing on the right to know, the court said, but because these publications previously appear abroad, the ban does not mean all-out previous prohibition of publication and the Customs censorship does not constitute an antecedent restraint. The court seems to have a very low opinion of the intellectual abilities of the people whom it expects to swallow this sophism.

The court reaffirmed its position that the prohibition of obscene literature does not clash with the constitutional guarantee of freedom of expression because this guarantee is not absolute and can be curtailed in order to protect the common welfare which also justifies the curb on the influx of obscenity from abroad.

In view of the actual situation in Japan, the regulations of the Customs Tariff Law are ludicrous. The readily available comics, particularly the so-called adult comics, contain a wide assortment of obscene material, with particular emphasis on sexual violence. The rationale of the courts that obscene publications imported from abroad could endanger the public order and that Customs inspection is necessary for protecting Japan's morality is unrelated to the real Japan.

In May 1991 the Tokyo Customs Office impounded 600 copies of the American magazine *ARTnews* because an advertisement contained the photo of a nude woman showing pubic hair. The advertisement announced the New York exhibition of the works of Joel-Peter Witkin. *ARTnews* argued that Witkin was a recognised artist whose works were exhibited in museums around the world, including the Tokyo Metropolitan Museum of Photography. The photo had artistic value, the magazine contended, which distinguished it from pornography. Customs officials, however, refused to release the shipment nor did they explain their refusal. According to the magazine's editor, it has not been seized in any of the 92 other countries in which the magazine is sold for this advertisement nor for any other reason.

In a decision announced on 13 July 1992 the Tokyo High Court overturned a decision of the Tokyo District Court and ruled that the importation of obscene objects by individuals for private use was not punishable. The Chief Customs Inspector at Haneda Airport, Tokyo, had declared seven magazines and five video tapes which Ken Togo had bought at San Francisco airport a violation of Article 21 of the Customs Tariff Law. Togo was fined ¥ 84,000 and when he refused to pay the fine, was indicted and found guilty by the Tokyo District Court. In overruling the District Court sentence, presiding Judge Kyōichi Hanya declared that Article 109, paragraph 1 of the Customs Law which fixes the punishment for Article 21 of the Customs Tariff

Law had to be interpreted restrictively. The importation of obscene objects for the sole purpose of individual appreciation could not be regarded as punishable. Offences related to obscene materials, the judge observed, belonged to the sphere of morality and individual actions were only punishable if they transcended the sphere of privacy and were in conflict with the sound social order.

The provisions of the Penal Code regarding obscene objects extended only to possession for the purpose of selling and not to possession for individual appreciation, which pertained to the order left to individual freedom; its punishment would therefore transcend the limits of the sphere to be regulated by law. This consideration also applied to the importation of obscene objects by individuals not for the purpose of trafficking or with other unlawful intent. Its prohibition would invade the sphere of morality which belonged to individual freedom. In order to avoid a conflict with Article 13 of the constitution, the penal provisions of the Customs Law must be interpreted not to apply to importation for individual appreciation.

It cannot be denied, the judge said, that the occasions on which the people will be exposed to obscene objects will increase if their importation is not checked but since Japan cannot stop contact with foreign countries in which the diffusion and sale of obscene materials are lawful, a certain degree of tolerance is unavoidable.

As expected, the prosecution appealed to the Supreme Court, citing two grounds for the appeal. The first, that Judge Hanya's ruling misinterpreted the constitution, is nonsense; it is the Customs censorship that is unconstitutional. The second, the disregard of precedents, raises an interesting problem. There have been plenty of decisions on pornography but none, as far as I know, on the question of punishment and the interpretation of Article 109 of the Customs Law on which Judge Hanya based his decision. It remains to be seen how the Supreme Court deals with this issue. Customs inspectors at Narita Airport declared that they would continue impounding obscene objects brought into the country by individuals as long as the ruling was not final.

Pornography is a field in which it is difficult to draw a line between the legitimate requirements of the public order and oppressive regulations. The protection of minors and the suppression of child pornography constitute important concerns demanding appropriate measures by the authorities, and the production, distribution and showing of films and other audio-visual material involving degrading and dangerous performances must be banned.

Japan's approach to pornography has been flawed by equating nudity with obscenity. Nudity is the most natural human condition. It is morally indifferent, artistically legitimate and socially acceptable in some societies. Courts and legislatures have laboured hard to find an unimpeachable definition of pornography which would allow them to separate smut from ethically and socially acceptable treatment of sex.

They have failed and have also been unable to answer challenges such as 'what has obscene literature to do with public welfare?' or 'why is pornography bad?' Nagisa Oshima, the producer of the film *Ai no Corrida* (Empire of the Senses) maintained that the portrayal of feminine eroticism and sexual pleasure was a Japanese tradition lost with Japan's modernisation. His position was supported by Ronald V. Bell who pointed out that Japan's police, prosecutors and judges were not defending Japan's traditional moral values but the standards of nineteenth-century prudery accepted by the Meiji oligarchs so as not to be looked upon as barbarians by Westerners. Basically, Japan clings to the 'non-publicity of sex' in order to prevent the moral decay of society. As a matter of fact, sex had nothing to do with the moral decay of Japanese society which was brought about by the quest for money by men driven by greed and the lust for power.

FREEDOM OF INFORMATION

Japan has no freedom of information law, and although 32 prefectures and major cities and 128 towns (as of September 1989) have ordinances providing for access to data held by public agencies, in practice use is hampered by restrictive conditions, red tape and uncooperative officials. The central government's basic policy is to hide anything potentially embarrassing to the government, the ruling party and the business establishment. Scholars and human rights activists have had recourse to the US Freedom of Information Act to obtain data related to Japanese conditions and occurrences.

Based on Osaka's freedom of information ordinance, a group calling itself Citizen Ombudsman requested information on the governor's expense account. The prefectural government refused to comply with the request alleging that it would be detrimental to the governor's performance of his duties and infringe on the privacy of the people concerned. When the Osaka District Court ordered the prefectural government to disclose the information, the prefecture appealed. In November 1990 the Osaka High Court upheld the ruling of the District Court. Although the governor can decide how to allocate the expenses, the court said, the accounts belong to the prefectural government and should not be made confidential. Disclosing the information would not cause the governor any difficulties in carrying out his duties. Since the expense accounts did not refer to private engagements, the privacy of people meeting the governor would not be jeopardised. Even secret meetings should be disclosed once the relevant projects were completed because there would no longer be any need for secrecy.

The Nagoya High Court agreed with the District Court's ruling that a doctor is not obliged to reveal the results of his diagnosis to a patient or his/her family. Four relatives of a deceased woman sued the Japan Red Cross Society claiming that they had been unable to save the woman's life because a doctor at the Red Cross Hospital had failed to inform the patient or her family that she had cancer. The woman went to the hospital because she felt a sharp pain in her abdomen. The diagnosis revealed that the woman had cancer of the gallbladder but the doctor in charge of the examination told her that she had a serious gallstone condition requiring urgent surgery. The woman, a former nurse, decided that she did not want a gallstone operation and left the hospital. She collapsed eighteen months later and died despite emergency surgery.

The Nagoya District Court ruled in favour of the Red Cross Society and the Nagoya High Court upheld the verdict. Presiding Judge Shigeo Ito declared that the deceased and her doctor did not share a relationship of mutual trust that would have enabled him to disclose the true condition to the patient or her family and that it was common for doctors not to reveal their diagnosis to their patients.

These decisions are wrong. Although there are cases in which the disclosure of the true state of health would only add to the anxiety of the patient or his family, he has a right to be informed of his condition. The duty of the doctor to tell the truth is not based on a relationship of mutual trust but on the doctor's professional obligation which he assumes when he agrees to treat a patient. A physician may be bound by professional secrecy not to reveal to third parties what he knows on the basis of his professional activities.

The Code of Civil Procedure (Art. 281) as well as the Code of Criminal Procedure (Art. 149) recognises the right of physicians, dentists, lawyers, etc. to refuse testimony on secrets of which they have professional knowledge but a patient who seeks the professional services of a doctor has a right to be told the truth and unless, as mentioned above, special circumstances would create an additional danger to the patient's physical or mental health without helping him if apprised of the truth, the physician has no right to withhold the result of his diagnosis. Christian moralists emphasise that if a patient is facing certain or even possible death, the doctor is obliged to reveal this condition to the patient and/or his family so that the patient can prepare himself for his death.

Under a Fukuoka freedom of information ordinance, Masatoshi Haraguchi, a teacher at Nishi Nippon Junior High School, requested information on the number of students who quit high school or repeated the same class. The prefectural Board of Education refused to publish this information claiming that publication was contrary to administrative practice and entailed the danger of violating privacy. When a prefectural panel ruled that the board should release the information, the board provided figures based on district-wide statistics but rejected the request for a breakdown by individual high schools.

Haraguchi thereupon filed suit with the Fukuoka District Court which nullified the board's decision to withhold the information. In April 1991 the Fukuoka High Court turned down the board's appeal and upheld the lower court's ruling. Presiding Judge Tsuneo Oga declared that the statistical data did not violate the students's privacy since individuals could not be identified on the basis of purely numerical information and the freedom of information ordinance protected important constitutional guarantees.

Mikita Morimoto, a 15-year-old junior high school student, demanded to be given access to her school records before they were sent to senior high schools in the course of the admission procedure. The Takatsuki (Osaka Prefecture) Board of Education rejected the request although it had been supported by the city's committee for the protection of information on individuals. Disclosure of the records, the board said, would deter teachers from a fair and objective assessment of the students. The board, however, conceded that students should have access to the part of the records known a *naishinsho*. Morimoto, who was admitted to a prefectural senior high school, filed suit demanding ¥ 50,000 in compensation for the board's delay in responding to her request and retraction of its decision.

Demands for disclosure of information often involve a clash of interests. A resident of Zushi (Kanagawa Prefecture) tried to gain access to plans for a privately-owned condominium building claiming that the information was necessary for assessing the building's environmental impact. The Kanagawa prefectural governor rejected the request and the Yokohama District Court as well as the Tokyo High Court sided with the governor. The High Court's presiding judge, Shigeru Yamaguchi, ruled that the preliminary design drawings which were open to public inspection were sufficient to assess the impact of the building on the environment. Publication of the plans, the judge said, would infringe on the architect's copyright and violate the freedom of information ordinance which prohibits the disclosure of personal information.

Chapter 4
Minorities

AINU

Japan has the reputation of being a homogeneous country and Japanese often emphasise the ethnic, linguistic and cultural unity of their country. In its 1980 report to the Commission on Human Rights, the Japanese government stated that there were no ethnic minorities in Japan. This view was immediately attacked by the Ainu and termed erroneous by Japanese anthropologists and sociologists. Nevertheless, while trying to explain his racist remarks on minorities in the United States, the then Prime Minister Yasuhiro Nakasone told a Diet committee in October 1986 that Japan was an ethnically homogeneous country and declared before the House of Representatives that there was no member of an ethnic minority group with Japanese nationality in Japan that was subject to discrimination.

Actually, there are minorities in Japan and their existence involves numerous difficult problems. The Ainu, who are basically different from the Japanese, are often referred to as the original inhabitants of Japan. They were called *ebisu* (barbarians) until the Meiji era and may once have occupied the largest part of Japan but had been pushed back to the northern part of Honshu, Hokkaido, Sakhalin, the Kuriles and Kamchatka by the close of the seventh century. They are of paleoasiatic origin and differ from today's Japanese particularly by their heavy beards and hairy chests. They may have numbered about 50,000 at the beginning of the seventeenth century, but their number has steadily declined.

During the Edo era the Ainu were decimated by internal struggles as well as by the oppressive rule of the Matsumae clan and were exploited by unscrupulous Japanese merchants. The Ainu complain that from 1868 the government secluded them in deserted areas and forced them to work as slaves for colonists who came from the mainland. Under the policy of assimilation, Ainu children were prohibited from using their language in school and were taught to become subjects of the Emperor like other Japanese. Before the war, children had to learn by heart the names of Japan's 124 Emperors.

In 1899 the government enacted a protection law which attempted to transform the Ainu, who were hunters and fishermen, into farmers and forced them to adopt a completely alien life-style. The law, called Hokkaido Ex-Natives Protection Law (the Japanese title, *Hokkaido Kyū Dojin Hogo-hō*, is derogatory), is still on the books. Ninety years later in December 1989 the government, recognising that the law was discriminatory, organised a committee made up of officials of the Hokkaido Development Agency and three ministries involved in the issue, to prepare a new law for the Ainu. At present, the Ainu need the approval of the Hokkaido government to sell or purchase land. Under the assimilation policy, the Ainu were forced to abandon their culture, religion and language. The government treated Hokkaido as no-man's land and distributed most of the habitable areas to aristocrats, bureaucrats, settlers from the mainland and soldiers called *tondenhei* (soldier-colonists).

A survey carried out by the prefectural government in 1986 put the Ainu population at 24,331, living in 70 towns and cities. Of the Ainu in Hokkaido, 42.3 per cent are engaged in farming and fishing, compared with 8.6 per cent of the non-Ainu population of the island. A survey undertaken by Professor Jiro Suzuki in 1988-9 found that 35.6 per cent of Ainu households in Tokyo have annual incomes of between ¥ 2 to 3 million while over 40 per cent of Tokyo households have annual incomes of ¥ 5 million. Most of the Ainu men living in Tokyo are blue-collar workers while many women are bar hostesses. Since Ainu face discrimination in employment, their average income is only about half of the national average and nearly 60 out of 1,000 receive welfare assistance. Recipients of welfare assistance account for 2.3 per cent of Tokyo Ainu residents while the percentage is 1.8 per cent for all Tokyo households. The ratio of unmarried people between the ages of 35 and 40 is 26.9 per cent among Ainu but only 15.9 per cent for the general population.

Serious discrimination also exists in education. Ainu children are often teased on account of their physical appearance (e.g., they are called 'gorilla' because of their thick hair on arms and legs). While most Ainu now in their 50s and 60s taught their children to hide their ethnic identity, today's Ainu are more aware of their roots,and associations such as the Hokkaido Utari (Ainu for 'fellow men') Society fight against discrimination. Roughly 70 per cent of the Ainu covered in a 1986 survey had experienced some kind of discrimination, 43 per cent in the form of opposition to marriage and about the same percentage had suffered insults in society. At the seventh UN Human Rights Commission working session for minorities in August 1989, the Ainu Association of Hokkaido criticised the Japanese government's unwillingness to adopt the UN human rights declaration for aborigines and to preserve indigenous Ainu culture.

OKINAWA

Another ethnic minority almost completely assimilated into the predominant Japanese mainland culture is the indigenous population of Okinawa. In the fifteenth century, the rulers of Shuri claimed authority over the Ryukyu islands and in 1451 the first embassy came to Kyoto and was received by the Shogun Yoshimasa. From that time on, embassies were sent periodically to Japan but at the same time, the Ryukyuans paid tribute to China which asserted suzerainty over the islands. In 1609 Iehisa Shimazu, daimyō of Satsuma, sent a force to the island which took the king's son and 100 of his nobles as prisoners to Kagoshima. The Ryukyuans had to pay a yearly tribute to Satsuma; moreover, a merciless exploitation impoverished the islands. In 1873 the king of the Ryukyus came to Tokyo and received the investiture of his domains but in 1879 the islands were annexed and made into a prefecture. In spite of China's protests, ex-President Ulyssus S. Grant, who acted as arbitrator, ruled in favour of Japan.

Okinawa is the only part of Japan which directly experienced the horrors of war. Many Okinawans committed suicide when the island became a battlefield, others were executed as spies by the Japanese Army. The islands remained under American control until 15 May 1972, but even thereafter, the American bases continued to play an important role in the life of Okinawa. While the American presence has made a considerable contribution to the island's economy, problems such as the lease of land for the American bases, the environmental impact of the airfields and military exercises, and the unanswered question of the presence of nuclear weapons have caused the Okinawans to complain that they are being victimised for objectives unrelated to their own lives. Although there is no discrimination in the usual sense of the word, Okinawa is the poorest of all prefectures and has been left behind in the country's economic development.

The Ryukyuan language is different from Japanese. It comprises several different dialects: spoken on Amami Oshima, the northern part of Okinawa, the southern part of this island, on Miyakojima and on the Yaeyama islands. At school, however, children learn only standard Japanese. Ryukyuan is widely considered a Japanese dialect, not an independent language.

BURAKUMIN

Numerous problems are presented by a minority usually referred to as *burakumin*, (literally 'village people'). They are the descendants of people outside the four classes of the Tokugawa society (warriors, farmers, artisans and merchants) called *hinin* (non-men) or *eta* (outcast, pariah) engaged in occupations deemed unclean (by Shinto standards) such a flayers, tanners and curriers. In August 1871 a decree of the *Dajōkan* (*mibun kaihō-rei* - social position emancipation order) abolished the designation *hinin* or *eta* and prescribed that they were to be considered equal to commoners (*heimin*). But the decree could not abolish the social discrimination. The new commoners, (*shin-heimin*), as they were sometimes called, continued to live in separate communities (hence the designation *burakumin*; '*buraku*' were the traditional villages whereas '*mura*' were the villages set up as administrative units by the government). Some of the *buraku* were Japan's worst slums, with narrow, unpaved roads, and substandard housing without sewers.

A survey of the Management and Coordination Agency carried out in 1985 counted 4,603 *buraku* communities with a population of 1.7 million but *buraku* activists claim that there are 5,365 communities with 3 million people. About 80 per cent of the *burakumin* live in agricultural communities but only a few can engage in farming; most men work as day labourers. Those living in fishing villages are usually excluded from fishing grounds and do not own large boats or advanced equipment.

In the cities, *burakumin* often depend on piecework, simple manufacturing or assembling for cottage industries and other intermediates. Leatherwork and braiding used to be the main types of work. They are deprived of job opportunities and form the lowest rank of labour, working on construction sites or hired as auxiliary labour and for odd jobs. Other typical occupations are the reclamation of waste material or peddling. The unemployment rate among *buraku* people is high, sometimes over 20 per cent. The number of people living on welfare is 6 or 8 times the national average.

Discrimination is rampant in education, employment and marriage. According to a survey by a *burakumin* organisation, 60 per cent of all *buraku* marriages are with other *burakumin*; even then the families often oppose the marriage. The custom of engaging enquiry or detective agencies to check the families of prospective marriage partners is mainly to prevent marriage with somebody of *buraku* background. Discrimination followed the *burakumin* even beyond death. Some old graves in northern Kanto bear derogatory posthumous names (*kaimy–o*) and temple registers contain the remark '*eta*'.

Some years ago the number of publications listing *buraku* communities (e.g. *Buraku Chimei Sōkan*, Register of Buraku Place Names) increased. They are bought by enquiry agencies and large enterprises. Usually, a copy of the family register must be attached to a job application; if the applicant comes from a *buraku* community, his job application will not be considered. In March 1985 Osaka Prefecture passed an ordinance for private enquiry or detective agencies. They were required to notify the prefecture of their business and prohibited to carry out discriminatory investigations and prepare reports related to marriage and employment in *buraku* districts. Osaka has the largest concentration of *buraku* people.

In education, *buraku* children are handicapped by their living conditions and are often victims of harassment. The percentage of *buraku* children advancing to high school or university is below the national average. Graffiti such as '*buraku* people are not human beings' are scribbled on school walls. Crimes such as robbery or murder are blamed on *buraku* people without any proof. On the other hand, the Japanese try to conceal the existence of *buraku* not only from the outside world but also from the general public. The Japanese translation of Professor Reischauer's book *The Japanese* omitted all passages referring to *buraku*. James Clavel's novel *Shogun* contained some derogatory remarks on *eta* and the Japanese translation prepared by TBS Britannica had to be withdrawn.

According to a 1984 survey of the Buraku Research Institute, 16 per cent of the *burakumin* covered by the survey were 'completely illiterate' or 'hardly literate', and 30 per cent were 'slightly illiterate'. Women constituted the largest part of the illiterate. Of the 6 per cent of the respondents who did not attend or finish elementary school and were deemed 'completely illiterate', 68 per cent were women. Of the respondents, 66 per cent finished elementary school only, while of Japan's entire population, only 0.3 per cent did not attend or finish elementary school and 39 per cent did not advance beyond elementary school.

The first organised attempt of the *burakumin* to fight discrimination and attain equality was the Suihei Undō (Horizontal Movement) starting with the foundation of the Suiheisha (Horizontal Society) in Kyoto in 1922. The movement was reconstituted in 1946 with the establishment of the Buraku Kaihō Zenkoku Iinkai (National Buraku Emancipation Committee) which was transformed in 1955 into the Buraku Kaihō Dōmei (Buraku Emancipation League). Since this organisation was closly linked to the Socialist Party, the Liberal-Democratic Party started a rival organisation Zen-Nippon Dōwa-kai (All Japan Dōwa Association; *dōwa* [integration] is a euphemism now used for *buraku*) in 1960. The Communist Party launched a third organisation in 1970: Buraku Kaihō Dōmei Seijōka Zenkoku Renraku Kaigi (Buraku Emancipation League Normalisation National Liaison Conference).

In 1984 the Buraku Kaihō Dōmei had about 170,000 registered members, the Communist-affiliated organisation 80,000 and Dōwa-kai 35,000. The combined membership accounted for about 30 to 40 per cent of the *burakumin*. The activities of these organisations have been hurt by poor leadership and internal squabbles. Dōwa-kai was dissolved in 1986 because of internal dissensions. Members accused the leaders of bureaucratic and overbearing behaviour, misuse of their positions for personal gain and disregard of the members' interests. Basically, all three groups professed to work for the same goals: the guarantee of occupational and educational equality, equality in agricultural communities, social security and the improvement of the environment.

For a long time the government ignored the problems of the *burakumin* but in 1969 a law (*Dōwa Taisaku Jigyō Tokubetsu Sochi-hō* Law for Special Measures for Dōwa Countermeasure Activities) aimed at improving the social and environmental conditions of the *buraku*. The law was first limited to a period of ten years but was subsequently extended several times. Since money was made available for the improvement of roads, housing and other facilities, educational grants and support of cultural activities, to secure money became the main purpose of the *buraku* organisations. Some of these organisations resorted to strong-arm tactics to obtain what they wanted and soon the name *dōwa* became associated with intimidation and violence.

This gave rise to a special type of Japanese gangster organisation called '*ese dōwa*' (pseudo-*dōwa*) which used the name of *dōwa* for a large variety of money-making schemes. They secured licences for land use which they sold for large sums to real-estate companies. They acted as mediators for obtaining loans from financial institutions, secured government funds for *buraku* projects and demanded rebates or commissions from the enterprises executing the projects. They sought orders from government agencies or enterprises, e.g., for studies on *dōwa* problems, for which they pocketed exorbitant 'research' fees. They squeezed money out of individuals and corporations by ferreting out mistakes or scandals, collected contributions to fictitious social causes, had people buy a variety of goods, subscribe to publications or buy advertising space. They even used the courts to make money by obtaining preliminary injunctions (such as *tachi-iri kinshi*, prohibition to enter, or *shōmu bōgai kinshi*, prohibition to obstruct business) which they only withdrew against outrageous payments.

They helped tax frauds by arranging fictitious debts which could be deducted from the inheritance, they took charge of negotiations for compensation in traffic accidents, bribed officials in charge of public works or of *buraku* projects. Two officials involved in such briberies committed suicide. Some years ago, about 270 sham *dōwa* groups were active. A survey of the Ministry of Justice covering 5,700 enterprises found that one in three firms had been victimised by sham *dōwa* groups. Insurance, finance and construction companies suffered most damage. The situation was worst in Osaka, but conditions were also bad in Tokyo, Fukuoka, Nagoya, Sendai, Takamatsu and Sapporo.

The most notorious case of discrimination in which, according to *buraku* organisations, one of their people became the victim of police prejudice involved the rape-murder of a 16-year-old senior high school student, Yoshie Nakada, of Sayama (Saitama Prefecture). A note demanded a ransom of ¥ 200,000 but the police failed to apprehend the criminal who came to collect the ransom. Since the case occurred shortly after the abduction of a boy in Tokyo, there was considerable pressure to solve the case. The police botched the investigation and in a fishing expedition, 23-year-old Kazuo Ishikawa was arrested on a charge of violence and theft.

The case had been settled by the parties involved and Ishikawa was released, but he was rearrested as a suspect in the Nakada case. Ishikawa's education had ended with the second grade at elementary school; he could hardly write and had no knowledge whatever of the law. He had been taught to see in his lawyer his enemy and declined to talk to him. While in police custody he confessed to the murder and repeated his confession in the trial by the Urawa District Court.

The defence pointed out numerous discrepancies between the confession and the material evidence in the case. Ishikawa could not have written the threatening letter demanding ransom, and the belongings of the murdered girl discovered on the basis of the confession (bag, wrist watch and fountain pen) had been arranged in a completely unnatural way. The court acknowledged that there were inconsistencies but attributed them to the shortcomings of the investigation. The confession was a mixture of truth and falsehood.

Ishikawa was found guilty and condemned to death in March 1964. The Buraku Emancipation League called the verdict an expression of discrimination and the defence appealed. The proceedings lasted ten years; the Tokyo High Court held 80 sessions and the presiding judge changed five times during the trial. Ishikawa pleaded innocent and claimed that he had been deceived by the police. If he confessed, he had been told, he would be set free in ten years; if he did not, he would be hanged. The High Court ruled that the confession was essentially true but reduced the punishment to life imprisonment. The defence contended that the sentence was based on prejudice and appealed to the Supreme Court. In August 1977 the court rejected the appeal and upheld the life sentence. Although some details of the evidence remained doubtful, Ishikawa was the murderer, the court said.

The verdict provoked violent protests by *burakumin*, involving attacks on police boxes with Molotov cocktails. The lawyers appealed to the Tokyo High Court asking the court to reopen the case because they could prove that the confession was a put-up job. The court denied the petition in February 1980. The lawyers then protested to the Supreme Court demanding to be allowed to submit new evidence and asking the court to examine the facts (which the Supreme Court usually does not do). In May 1985 the court rejected the petition stating that there was no clear evidence necessitating a not guilty verdict. The lawyers called the court's ruling an unjust, highly political sentence.

KOREANS

According to the Ministry of Justice, officially registered foreigners living in Japan at the end of 1990 numbered 1.07 million, accounting for 0.87 per cent of the country's total population (123.6 million). Koreans represented the largest group with 687,940, of whom 610,924 were officially recognised as first generation, i.e., Koreans having lived in Japan before the end of the Second World War and their children. Most of the genealogically second and third generation Koreans, born and raised in Japan, speak Japanese as their first and often their only language. Osaka has the largest concentration of Koreans; of the 200,000 inhabitants of Ikuno Ward, 40,000 are Koreans. Chinese constituted the second largest group with 150,339, followed by Brazilians with 56,429.

The Russo-Japanese War led to a growing infiltration of Japan into Korea and the Treaty of Portsmouth, which ended the war, formally recognised Korea as a Japanese sphere of influence. The forced abdication of the Korean Emperor in favour of his son in 1907 brought a renewal of the armed uprisings against the Japanese occupation which were brutally suppressed. The assassination of Prince Ito by a Korean in 1909 led to the annexation of Korea in 1910.

Through the annexation, Korea became an integral part of the Japanese Empire. The name of Seoul was changed to Keijō, and Pyongyan became Heijō. Japanese was made the official language. All important administrative posts were filled by Japanese; in some cities the elected mayors were dismissed and Japanese mayors were installed. All judges were Japanese and Japanese police were not only very numerous but also entrusted with broad powers: they could make arrests without a warrant, detain suspects for an unlimited period and frequently used torture. Schools had to have Japanese principals and at least three Japanese teachers. Korean history books were destroyed and new textbooks introduced. Instruction was in Japanese in all schools and Korean teachers were sometimes even stricter than Japanese teachers in enforcing the ban on Korean. Pupils using Korean were punished.

According to a 1988 survey covering 1,106 first-generation Koreans who came to Japan between 1910 and the end of the war, Koreans were forced to change both their given and family names and three-quarters complied. Japanese *bonzes* and *kannushi* were sent to Korea to offset the influence of the Christian missionaries. The government commanded worship at Shinto shrines although 70 per cent of the interviewees said that they did not comply. When boarding the ship to Japan, people were made to sing '*Kimi ga yo*', the Japanese national anthem, and those who did not know the song were forced to board the ship on hands and knees.

On of the most traumatic events in the experience of Koreans in Japan was the massacre of Koreans at the time of the Great Kanto Earthquake in 1929. Rumours spread by the government blamed the Koreans for fictitious atrocities. Vigilante groups slaughtered about 6,000 Koreans in the days following the earthquake.

Of the two million young Korean men brought to Japan between 1938 and 1945, 60,000 were sent to Sakhalin, then Japanese territory named Karafuto. Shortly before the end of the war, 20,000 men were moved to Hokkaido, but 43,000 remained on Sakhalin. Some later became Soviet citizens but others became stateless. Their wives, who had remained in Japan, were left without support because neither the Japanese nor the Korean government cared for them. About 35,000 Koreans are still living on Sakhalin (47,000 Japanese were repatriated after the end of the war).

Since South Korea had no diplomatic relations with the Soviet Union, the Koreans were left without protection or support. Japan declared that the Koreans were no longer Japanese subjects, did nothing to help these people and failed to pay any compensation for their treatment. Instead of wasting billions of yen on prestige projects in far-away developing countries, the Japanese government should have honoured its moral obligation to people deported from their home country by

Japan. In 1963 a 'Russianisation' programme enforced under Nikita Kruschev closed all Korean schools and theatres. Since *perestroika*, however, Korean language classes have been provided in high schools and the local university at Yuzhno Sakhalinsk.

Taking advantage of the Occupation's repatriation programme,over one million Koreans returned to their homeland after the war. Many chose to stay in Japan and others, disillusioned with conditions in Korea, tried to return to Japan illegally. When the San Francisco Peace Treaty came into effect, the Koreans who had remained in Japan, together with Taiwanese, were automatically deprived of their Japanese citizenship by an administrative notice issued on 19 April 1952, in the name of the chief of the Civil Affairs Bureau of the Ministry of Justice. They were henceforth treated as foreigners. The measure was particularly arbitrary since these people had declined repatriation and opted to stay in Japan. The change was made without any kind of hearing and without giving the people involved any opportunity of contesting the order.

Under an agreement between the Japanese government and the Republic of Korea which went into effect in January 1966, Koreans could apply for permanent residence status. The agreement applied to first- and second-generation Koreans (legally, first generation are those who came to Japan before the end of the Second World War and their offspring born prior to 16 January 1971; second generation are those born after that date).

Under a Japan-South Korea Treaty signed in 1965, neither government is liable to compensate Koreans who were forced to fight for Japan in the Second World War. In October 1990, 22 Koreans living in South Korea filed suit in the Tokyo District Court demanding compensation from the Japanese government. In January 1991 Chong Sang Gun, a Korean living in Japan, who had served in the Japanese navy and lost his right arm while fighting in the Marshall Islands sued the government for ¥10 million in compensation for his injury and mental suffering. Chong had applied for compensation after the war but his claim was rejected. The law limits compensation for injuries and allowances to surviving families to Japanese nationals.

Six Koreans who had been drafted into the Japanese Imperial Army and convicted of war crimes by the Allies and the family of another conscript executed for war crimes filed suit demanding ¥ 130 million in compensation and a formal apology by the Prime Minister. A total of 148 Korean conscripts were tried after the war for Class B and C war crimes. Of these, 23 were executed and 125 sentenced to prison. They were accused of having violated the Geneva Convention by forcing prisoners of war to work, abusing prisoners and mistreating them by failing to provide food and medicine. The Japanese government has maintained that it has no obligation to compensate the former soldiers whom it deprived of their Japanese citizenship.

'COMFORT' GIRLS

During the war about 870,000 Koreans were brought to Japan where they were mainly used for heavy work - Koreans constituted 32 per cent of the workforce in the coal mines. In the course of the war 142,000 Koreans were drafted into the Japanese army and 101,000 into the navy. 22,000 Korean conscripts were killed in action. Between 80,000 and 200,000 Korean women were conscripted by the Japanese army to serve as 'comfort women' (*ianfu*) for the troops (the officers were furnished with Japanese prostitutes). A large number of these women were teenagers who did not know what they would be forced to do until they arrived at their destination. Sometimes they had to serve 70 to 80 soldiers a day each. Many of them were killed at the end of the war because the Japanese army sought to destroy the evidence of the infamous treatment of these women. Those who survived were reluctant to return to their homeland because they were ashamed to meet relatives and friends.

Among the many claims for compensation by Koreans, Taiwanese, Indonesians and Chinese against the Japanese government for backpay, mistreatment, injuries and other wrongs was also a demand that Japan pay damages and issue an apology to the women forced into prostitution. In addition to women from Asian countries, the military also forced at least 35 Dutch women living in the former Dutch East Indies to serve as prostitutes in military brothels. In June 1990 the Japanese government denied any responsibility asserting that the women were recruited by private brokers and not conscripted under the National Mobilization Law of 1938. In November 1990 the Korean Council for Women Drafted Under Japanese Rule issued an open letter to the Japanese government seeking compensation and an apology but the government again denied its responsibility.

Strict military rules regulated all aspects of what the army called 'houses of relaxation', including hours of operation, prices and hygienic conditions. The regulations for a facility in Manila stipulated that the 'geisha and hostesses' had to turn over half of their income to the Japanese manager of the brothel. In the period from August to October 1944, the cost of a 40-minute session was set at ¥ 1.50 for enlisted men, ¥ 2.50 for non-commissioned officers and ¥ 4 for civilian employees. In the Shanghai area prices varied according to the nationality of the prostitutes. Officers and warrant officers paid ¥ 3 for a one-hour session with a Japanese or Korean prostitute and ¥ 2.50 for a Chinese. Regulations provided that association with hostesses was forbidden to those who refused to use condoms and that the women were not to be kissed. An army document dated 1938 called for the speedy installation of brothels in order to stop the widespread rape of local women in China by Japanese soldiers. Korea was divided into a number of districts which each had to furnish a fixed number of women.

When a volunteer group set up a telephone hotline in Tokyo in

February 1992, veterans, doctors and nurses called in to confirm Japan's official involvement in the operation. According to a Japanese who was involved in the procurement of 'comfort girls', the government's contention that these women were recruited by private brokers is a shameless lie. Sometimes an entire village was surrounded by troops or police, all women were herded together and the young women put on a truck and carried away.

Wartime documents found in January 1992 confirmed that the Imperial Japanese Army had been involved in the kidnapping and forced prostitution of women from Korea and other Asian countries. A confidential war-time directive of the Ministry of the Army stated that the military should control the recruitment process and ensure that no mistakes were committed so as not to cause social repercussions and protect the reputation of the army. Foreign Minister Michio Watanabe's acknowledgement of the participation of the army in the forced prostitution of foreign women was the first time that the Japanese government recognised the country's responsibility for the misdeeds and brought official apologies - half a century after the atrocities - but left the issue of compensation unsettled.

Further investigations revealed that primary schoolgirls aged 11 or 12 years were drafted into a corps that included prostitutes for Japanese troops. During his visit to Seoul in January 1992 Prime Minister Kiichi Miyazawa expressed regret at Japan's actions while occupying Korea but failed to make any commitment on the question of compensation. The chairman of the Social Democratic Party urged the government to stop its insistence that legal claims had been met and to recognise its moral obligations to the victims of Japan's aggression by paying compensation to individual claimants.

In December 1991 35 Koreans filed a lawsuit in the Tokyo District Court demanding ¥ 700 million (¥ 20 million per person) in wartime damages from the Japanese government. The plaintiffs included former soldiers who served in the Japanese army, three 'comfort girls' and the families of soldiers killed in action. The plaintiffs based their claims on the assertion that they were victims of crimes against humanity which, they contended, had been established as justifiable by the war-crime trials.

One of the 'comfort girls', Kim Huk Sun, was 17 when the Japanese came along in a truck, beat a number of women and dragged them into the truck. She was raped the first day, sent to China and attached to a military brothel. For the next three months, she had to accommodate dozens of soldiers every single day. Kim tried to escape three times; twice she was caught and severely beaten; she succeeded on her third try with the help of a Korean man whom she later married. Her experience left an emotional trauma. 'I feel sick when I am close to a man', she said, and even her husband, now dead, made her feel that way.

There were, however, Japanese who opposed the payment of compensation to former 'comfort girls' on the ground that the 1965 normalisation treaty with South Korea settled all claims. The understanding of human rights prior to the Second World War was very different from today's recognition of human rights. The opponents also contend that at the time of the war, Korea formed part of Japan so that there was no question of national discrimination.

DISCRIMINATION

During Japan's occupation of what was then the Dutch East Indies, the army and navy employed about 45,000 Indonesians. Of the 23,000 who served as *heiho* (auxiliary soldiers), about 3,000 were killed and some 7,000 have died since the end of the war. An organisation of former Indonesian soldiers and survivors claim that Japan owes them about $ 650 million because the soldiers were forced to deposit one-third of their salaries at military posts and were not paid their outstanding stipends when the war ended. The organisation used the visit of the Imperial couple to Indonesia in 1991 to press their claim against Japan. Unlike Japan, the Netherlands still pays military pensions to the Indonesians who served with the Dutch forces.

Koreans are plagued by numerous social antagonisms. First, there is the animosity of the Japanese against Koreans. Secondly, the Koreans are divided between those adhering to the Republic of Korea (organised in the Korean Residents Union in Japan – Mindan) and those supporting the North (who belong to the General Association of Korean Residents in Japan – Chongryon). Thirdly, relations between Koreans living in Japan and in the peninsula are not always harmonious. Lastly, the regional antagonisms of the homeland also affect Koreans living abroad (e.g., the discord between the provinces of Kyeongsando and Cheollada, the native provinces respectively of President Roh Tae Woo and opposition leader Kim Dae Jung).

Koreans in Japan experience some of the worst forms of discrimination and harassment. Education and employment are the areas in which Koreans encounter the most unfair treatment but they are also disadvantaged in marriage, social security, housing and generally in daily life. Schools established by Korean organisations for Korean children were not recognised by the Ministry of Education as ordinary schools but were classified as 'special schools' (*tokushu gakkō*), a category which applies to vocational schools. Students of Korean high schools were not allowed to participate in prefectural or national sports events; only recently have some prefectures allowed Korean high school students to take part in prefectural athletic meets.

In a show of solidarity, the student council of Hiroshima's Nishi High School sent a petition with 9,253 signatures of students from 62 high schools to the Hiroshima High School Athletic Association asking to grant membership to Hiroshima Senior High School for Children of Korean Descent. The school, which has ties to North Korea, is not recognised as a regular high school by the Ministry of Education and the students are barred from taking part in prefectural sports events organised by the association. The students at Nishi High School have held cultural and sports exchanges with the students at the Korean school for eight years. They called on other high schools in the prefecture to join in the efforts to overturn the 'unfair and discriminatory' policy against schools for foreign residents. The Japan High School Baseball Federation allowed high schools affiliated with North Korea in Kanagawa and Hiroshima prefectures and Kobe to participate in regional competitions for the August national championship games and later extended this permission to high schools in Tokyo, Aichi and Ibaraki Prefectures.

Of about 430,000 students graduating from Japanese universities each year, around 15,000 are ethnic Koreans. They seldom succeed in finding employment in large corporations but due to the labour shortage which developed in the latter part of the 1980s even large companies began to take on non-Japanese employees. Some of the worst cases of discrimination occur in public employment. Japanese nationality is considered a requirement for teaching in public schools. On principle, no legal restrictions prevent employment of non-Japanese by local governments but,based on the theory that administration is an exercise of sovereignty, the Cabinet Legislative Bureau and the Home Ministry maintain that posts executing public authority must be held by Japanese and that this rule applies to teaching. In June 1983 the Home Ministry notified local governments that the restriction no longer applied to nurses. As of November 1986 22 prefectures had foreigners on their payrolls; most were doctors and nurses serving in remote areas. Many prefectural and municipal governments retain restrictions on administrative positions when they open jobs to foreign nationals. As a result, 30 prefectures had regulations containing the nationality clause and 25 prefectures did not employ any foreigners.

Some Korean residents have demanded to be given the right to vote in local elections. In a lawsuit filed with the Fukui District Court in May 1991 by four Koreans who have lived in Japan for over 40 years, the plaintiffs contended that the provisions in the Public Office Election Law and the Local Government Law concerning the qualification to vote were unconstitutional. They asserted that the constitution gives the right to elect the members of local assemblies to all residents (*jūmin*) whereas the Public Office Election Law restricts the right to Japanese nationals.

In Article 93 (paragraph 2) the constitution regulates the election of the chief executive officers of all local public bodies, the members of their assemblies and other local officials. The English text says that these persons shall be elected by direct popular vote but the Japanese text stipulates that the *residents* of these local public bodies shall directly elect them (*sono chihō kōkyō dantai no jūmin ga chokusetsu kore wo senkyo suru*). The same difference between the English and Japanese texts is found in Article 95 which concerns special laws applicable to only one public entity. According to the English text, such laws need the consent of the 'majority of the voters of the local public entity concerned'. The Japanese text says that the Diet cannot make such laws 'unless it obtains the consent of the majority in the voting of the residents of this public body' (*sono chihō kōkyō dantai no jūmin no tōhyō ni oite kahansū no dōi wo enakereba*).

The Public Office Election Law (*Kōshoku Senkyo-hō*) provides that the right to vote in local elections is given to persons who are Japanese nationals (*Nihon kokumin-taru mono*) of at least 20 years of age who have possessed a residence (*jūsho*) in the local public body uninterruptedly for at least three months (Art. 9, par. 2). The plaintiffs claimed that this legal requirement was contrary to the provision that the *residents* of the local public body were entitled to vote.

Prime Minister Masayoshi Ohira was of the opinion that local governments should be allowed to devise means of creating employment opportunities for non-Japanese residents in their regions. The Osaka municipal government had considered a plan which was to open more jobs to Koreans and other foreigners who had lived a long time in Japan. But due to pressure from the Home Ministry, which is opposed to foreigners serving as public employees, the municipal government dropped its plan of removing the restrictions barring foreigners from municipal employment. When the city abandoned its plan, it counted, besides school teachers and nurses, 54 foreigners among its 46,000 employees.

The Kawasaki Local Administration Research Centre drafted a report calling for corrective measures in municipal employment. Discriminatory practices against foreigners, notably Koreans, without legal grounds should be abolished, notwithstanding the central government's uniform policy of not allowing non-Japanese employment in public posts. The report supported the system adopted by Machida (a Tokyo suburban city) under which non-Japanese were hired but not promoted to section chiefs exercising public authority.

In May 1991 an association of 70 municipal governments in Hyogo Prefecture decided to abolish the regulation barring foreign nationals from taking examinations for public jobs. A third-generation Korean whose application for taking the examination required for teaching at public schools had been rejected by the Fukuoka Prefectural Board of Education three times was finally allowed to take the test. But in accordance with the instruction of the Ministry of Education, he will only be hired as a 'full-time lecturer'.

Teachers at Korean schools asked Transport Minister Kanezo Muraoka to have commuter tickets for Korean students priced the same as those for Japanese students. Private railroad companies apply the same rate to Japanese and Korean students but the JR companies continued the practice of the Japan National Railways and priced commuter tickets for Korean students 43 per cent higher than those for Japanese students. The reason is that the Ministry of Education classifies Korean schools as special schools to which the student discount for ordinary schools does not apply.

A Korean paid the contributions for the national insurance (old age pension) system and applied for a pension when he reached the age of 65. But he was told that he was ineligible because the system applied only to Japanese and he should not have been admitted in the first place. The man sued but lost in the District Court. The Tokyo High Court, however, reversed the decision explaining that the expectation and reliance on the receipt of a pension should be given legal protection. The law has been amended and the requirement of Japanese nationality for the national pension system and child allowances abolished.

Another Korean, a victim of the atomic bomb, secretly returned to Japan for treatment. He applied for a certificate entitling him to treatment but the Fukuoka prefectural government refused to give him the document. The Fukuoka District Court rejected his demand to quash the refusal of the prefecture but the Fukuoka High Court ordered the district court to nullify the prefecture's rejection and the Supreme Court upheld the decision of the High Court. Being a victim of the bomb, the court declared, is the result of the war which was an action of the state. The Law for the Medical Treatment of the Atomic Bomb Victims was partly enacted for the humanitarian purpose of helping the victims because the state itself was responsible. The law should apply without distinction to all living victims of the bomb.

Koreans experience difficulty in taking out loans from Japanese banks or obtaining credit cards. In localities with a large Korean population, apartment owners mean Koreans when they put up signs reading 'No foreigners allowed'. The most serious difficulty facing Koreans in Japan is the traditional Japanese dislike of foreigners. In June 1981 seven Koreans applied for positions at public schools in Aichi Prefecture and four in Nagoya city but all applicants were turned down because they did not possess Japanese citizenship. One of each group filed suit in Nagoya District Court asking for cancellation of the rejection but the suits were dismissed on a technicality without discussing the merits of the case. The Nagoya High Court upheld the ruling of the District Court.

A Korean high school student was recommended by her school for employment by the Kawasaki Agricultural Credit Cooperative and in August 1989 went to the cooperative's office for an interview. She had been asked to bring a copy of the family register to the interview and in the afternoon the cooperative contacted the school's placement officer and explained that they would not let the girl take the employment test because of her nationality. It would be better for the girl to look for a job with a different enterprise than to be failed in the examination. The school replied that the refusal obviously constituted discrimination on account of nationality which was contrary to the Labour Ministry's guidelines. The cooperative, however, refused to reconsider its decision saying that it was the policy of the cooperative not to employ non-Japanese. The prefecture's Labour Bureau declared that the cooperative's action was regrettable but it could do nothing more than demand a change in policy.

The harassment of Koreans became worse after the bombing of a Korean airliner. Particularly girls wearing the *chima chogori* became victims of verbal and physical abuse. In Hamamatsu (Shizuoka Prefecture), about ten Japanese high school students surrounded a Korean girl riding a bicycle and wearing a Korean dress, poked at her and shouted 'What did you come to Japan for? Go to your own country!' A middle-aged man on a bus hurled obscenities at six elementary school children returning home from school. Another man grabbed a female student by the neck and threw her on the ground on a station platform. Koreans have been spat at and schools run by Chongryon have received threatening telephone calls. The Pachinko scandal had a similar effect. Korean residents received anonymous phone calls and Korean schools were threatened with arson.

In a sharply-worded statement distributed to reporters at the Foreign Correspondents Club, Pak Jae Ro, vice-chairman of Chongryon's Central Committee, accused the Liberal-Democratic Party of racial harassment of Koreans. He rejected the allegations by LDP politicians that the Korean Pachinko operators had made donations to members of the Socialist Party to gain political favours as groundless and slanderous and denied that Chongryon had been involved in attempts to interfere in Japan's internal affairs. He said that he had documented 50 cases of violence against Korean residents, including children.

A glaring example of the arrogance and stupidity of Japanese politicians and bureaucrats in handling Koreans was the treatment of a North Korean table-tennis team taking part in the Asian Table Tennis Championship games held at Niigata in May 1988. The Japanese government had imposed so-called sanctions on North Korea for the destruction of a South Korean aircraft allegedly by North Korean agents. Under these sanctions, North Korean officials were not allowed to enter Japan and no North Korean could come to Japan for political activities. The table-tennis team was allowed to participate in the game on condition that no government official would accompany the players and that the team would not attend meetings of a political nature.

While the championship games were still going on, the 18 players and officials were invited to a reception at the Okura Hotel, Niigata, sponsored by the General Association of Korean residents in Japan (Chongryon) and a Japanese group. About 150 people, including the mayor of Niigata, Genki Wakasugi, and Chongryon chairman Han Dok Su attended the reception. At 1 p.m., while dinner was being served, the Ministry of Justice telephoned the organisers of the reception and informed them of the decision of the Entry Division of the Immigration Bureau that the North Koreans were not permitted to attend the function. Complying with the government's instructions, the organisers made the North Koreans leave the hotel without finishing dinner.

Li Jong Ho, the leader of the team, told a press conference that they had withdrawn from the competition, were going home immediately and would never again take part in any event held in Japan. A spokesman for the Physical Education Association of Korean Residents in Japan expressed the common sentiment of the North Koreans shared by many Japanese: 'We can't understand why eating dinner with the North Korean delegates and Japanese constitutes a political activity.' Minister of Justice Yukio Hayashida, trying to justify the action of his bureaucrats, remarked that although the reception itself may not have been a political activity, it was undesirable that the North Korean team had contacts with members of Chongryon. An official of the Foreign Ministry defended the action of the Immigration Bureau stating that the North Koreans should have observed the conditions of their entry into Japan. This is difficult if the conditions are interpreted by an arrogant bureaucracy to mean whatever they want them to mean.

KOREAN NAMES & 'NATIONALITY'

Prior to the war Koreans were often forced to assume Japanese names and even today, many Koreans use Japanese names in elementary, junior and senior high school which is what the prefectural Boards of Education want. A growing number of students change to their Korean name when they go to college. Many Koreans, however, keep their Japanese name for business use.

The pronunciation of Korean names has been a source of irritation. Since the names are written in Chinese characters (ideographs), the Japanese usually pronounce them according to the *on* reading of the characters (i.e., a pronunciation derived from the Chinese reading) which is quite different from the Korean pronunciation (e.g., Roh Tae Woo becomes Ro Tai Gu; Chinese names are pronounced in the same way, e.g., Den Xiaoping becomes Tō Shō Hei). In a broadcast, NHK, the public broadcasting system, pronounced the name of a Korean clergyman living in Japan in the Japanese way. The clergyman complained that he had been treated as a colonial and demanded an apology. Since NHK demurred, the clergyman sued demanding ¥ 1 and an apology.

The Fukuoka District Court turned down his demand in 1977 and when the Fukuoka High Court rejected his appeal, he took the case to the Supreme Court. (The clergyman's name is Choi Chan Hwa; NHK pronounced it Sai Shō Ka. The pronunciation based on the Japanese *on* reading was the rule when Korea was a Japanese colony, hence the clergyman's complaint.) In 1983 the Japanese government changed its regulation and decreed that names written in Chinese characters had to be pronounced in accordance with their reading in the original language.

A 34-year-old teacher born of a Japanese mother and a Korean father asked the Family Court to be permitted to use her Korean name (Yun Cho Ja) instead of her Japanese name (Oshima Teruko). When she was born her mother had had to register her as an illegitimate child so that she could obtain Japanese nationality. The court denied her request. Devotion to her father's place of origin, the judge said, was no reason for changing the name in the family register. But three years later, the Kawasaki branch of the Yokohama Family Court allowed her to change her Japanese name for the Korean name she had been using for over a decade. She wanted the change, she told the court, because her volunteer work for Korean children in Kawasaki and Osaka had made her aware of the discrimination suffered by Korean residents in Japan.

When she submitted her application for registration to the ward office, she wrote her name in Chinese characters with the phonetic transcription in *kana* at the side of the characters. The ward office delayed accepting her application until it had consulted the Ministry of Justice, stating the most peremptory reason of the bureaucracy for refusing to act: 'It has never been done before. There are no precedents for putting a pronunciation beside a surname in the register.'

Under the 1985 revision of the Nationality Law, children with one Japanese parent born after 1 January 1985 can have dual nationality until the age of 22 (the usual age when young people graduate from university). A second-generation Korean, Pak Yong Bok, married to a Japanese, Akiko Takahashi, wanted his daughter, born 7 March 1989, to have Japanese nationality but a Korean name, Pak Sa Lee. The Shibuya Ward Office officials refused to accept the registration. Under a notice issued by the Ministry of Justice, they said, those who want Japanese nationality must register under a Japanese name. Pak did not fill out the registration form but when he visited the office again in May, he discovered that his daughter had been registered under the name of Sara Takahashi.

Pak pointed out that the Nationality Law did not stipulate that a child must have a Japanese name in order to get Japanese nationality and that the local or national government did not have the right to determine the name of his child. Minoru Tagawa, head of the Family Registration Section, apologised, admitting that he had ordered the registration but insisted that he could not disregard the Ministry of Justice's directive. The notice of the ministry again shows its authoritarian attitude and its tendency to claim legal validity for its usurpation of authority.

For many years the Ministry of Justice required applicants for naturalisation to adopt a Japanese name. This requirement had no basis in law; it was enforced, the ministry said, to facilitate the assimilation into Japanese society. This policy was the direct outcome of the pre-war efforts to amalgamate the colonies and it was continued after the war because the administration found it convenient. With the growing national consciousness of the Koreans living in Japan, the practical necessity of retaining or adopting a Japanese name kept many Koreans from applying for naturalisation despite the obvious benefits they would gain from such a step.

A second-generation Korean, Cho Geon Chi, filed suit with the Shimonoseki branch of the Yamaguchi District Court demanding restoration of his Japanese nationality, a solatium of ¥ 300 million and an apology by the Prime Minister for the discriminatory treatment of Koreans. Cho was born in February 1944 in Yukahashi (Fukuoka Prefecture) and automatically became a Japanese citizen. But, as mentioned above, with the conclusion of the San Francisco Peace Treaty in September 1951, people from Japan's former colonies residing in Japan were deprived of their Japanese nationality by an administrative decision. Cho contended that under the Japanese Nationality Law, Japanese nationality is only lost when a person voluntarily acquires another nationality.

The Yamaguchi District Court rejected Cho's claim, siding with the government's contention that, when Japan gave up sovereignty over Korea as a result of the peace treaty, it also gave up sovereignty over the people. The flaw in this argument is that the Koreans living in Japan at that time were not Korean but Japanese nationals and that the renunciation of sovereignty over Korea did not affect the Koreans living in Japan. There have been many cases of general deprivation of citizenship after the First World War but Paragraph 2 of Article 15 of the Declaration of Human Rights states: 'No one shall be arbitrarily deprived of his nationality.' According to international law, a state can determine *by legislation* who are its nationals but no state can determine how a foreign nationality can be acquired or lost (The Hague Convention on the Conflict of Nationality Laws). Koreans born after the annexation of Korea by Japan and particularly second-generation Koreans born in Japan never possessed Korean nationality.

In January 1989 the Fukuoka High Court rejected an appeal by Kim Chon Kap and upheld a District Court decision denying Kim's demand to have his Japanese nationality restored and to be paid ¥ 30 million for having been forcibly brought to Japan during the war. The court relied on a 1961 decision of the Supreme Court holding that the Peace Treaty of San Francisco resulted in the loss of Japanese nationality by Koreans living in Japan. Under the Peace Treaty, the High Court said, Japan gave up its sovereignty over Korean territory and thereby also over the Korean people. Moreover, the court said, even if the deprivation of Japanese nationality had involved an unlawful act, the statute of limitation applied.

The plaintiff had argued that the Peace Treaty concerned territorial matters and did not affect the nationality of Koreans residing in Japan. The Japanese government violated international law because it did not allow Korean residents to choose either Japanese or Korean nationality. While the statute of limitations may apply to the claim for damages, it is irrelevant to the question of nationality. The court's reasoning that people who ought to belong to Korea lost their Japanese nationality when Japan renounced sovereignty over Korea is wrong. When North and South Korea became sovereign states, ethnic Koreans did not become *ipso facto* Korean nationals. That Koreans living in Japan 'ought to belong to Korea' is an assumption of the Japanese bureaucracy and judiciary without foundation in law and is only an attempt to mask an arbitrary and illegal measure.

Japan has no official relations with North Korea and the antipathy has been mutual. The North Korean government jailed the captain of a Japanese boat and his mate because Japan refused to extradite a Korean soldier who had smuggled himself to Japan on this boat. In the latter half of 1990, however, both sides probed the possibility of finding a less antagonistic *modus vivendi*.

FINGERPRINTING & THE ALIEN REGISTRATION LAW

A major confrontation between foreigners living in Japan and the Japanese bureaucracy arose from the fingerprinting regulations in the Alien Registration Law. Prior to the revision of the law in 1985, foreigners over the age of 14 intending to stay in Japan for a period of one year or longer had to register at the city office and obtain a registration certificate which they had to carry with them at all times and produce whenever requested by the police. At registration, they had to be fingerprinted, and this was repeated whenever they had to renew their registration (which depended on their residence status and varied from one to five years). At the time of the initial registration, foreigners had to put their fingerprints on three official documents: the original register for storage with the local authorities, the registration certificate for personal use, and the fingerprint register for storage by the central government. In a notice issued in April 1974 the Ministry of Justice permitted the local authorities to dispense with the fingerprinting for the original fingerprint register at the renewal of registration but this simplification was cancelled in August 1982. On account of the protests against the fingerprinting, black ink for fingerprinting was replaced by a colourless fluid and the left forefinger need no longer be rolled in the ink but only pressed.

Originally, the Alien Registration Ordinance contained no provision for fingerprinting but in 1952 fingerprinting was made obligatory in the Alien Registration Law. The authorities considered it necessary for dealing with the practice of some Koreans to obtain several registration certificates and sell the surplus certificates to Koreans who smuggled themselves into Japan. The Ministry of Justice maintains that the system remains necessary because there are about 500 illegal entrants annually from the Korean peninsula. It is also true that in the immediate post-war period, many Koreans engaged in black-marketeering but so did many Japanese; often Koreans worked for Japanese bosses.

A further revision of the Alien Registration Law which took effect on 1 June 1988 provided that fingerprinting would only be required once, at the time of the first registration. A laminated card replaced the registration certificate to which the fingerprint taken at the initial registration is transferred. The fingerprints are now translated into computer signals which means that they can be reproduced many times without the slightest deterioration and that the police can have immediate access to the prints. Local government employees do not use the fingerprints for identification but usually rely on the photos on the registration certificates. The Ministry of Justice wants to keep the fingerprinting system because it is the most efficient way of identifying criminals. Because 99 per cent of the foreign residents are not criminals it means that the system is enforced for the one per cent who might be. Critics of the fingerprinting system did not fail to point out the government's inconsistency. Until the 1988 revision, the government had maintained that fingerprinting at each renewal was necessary for identification; in June 1988 this was no longer the case.

The enforcement of the Immigration Law required an ever-growing number of staff. In 1987 about 600,000 visa renewals were processed, more than half of which were handled by the Tokyo Immigration Bureau. In the first half of 1988, the Tokyo bureau examined over 180,000 applications for renewal. Since the bureau is chronically short of manpower and office space, foreign residents often have to wait several hours; on some days, it can be as long as seven hours. The number of officials has been increased every year, from 61 in 1984 to 79 in 1988, and though they sometimes put in four to five hours overtime, they cannot cope with the growing amount of work.

Since local governments are charged with the administration of the registration procedure, they also have to deal with the opposition to the fingerprinting requirement. Some municipalities issued registration certificates to foreigners who refused to be fingerprinted or failed to notify the police of the refusal. At one time in 1985 only three of the 23 Tokyo wards followed the instructions of the Ministry of Justice on the handling of refusers. Mayor Saburo Ito of Kawasaki announced that he would not ask the police to investigate foreigners who refused to be fingerprinted. The municipality, Ito said, arrived at this decision for humanitarian reasons. Japanese, as members of the world community, should respect the human rights of other people. Ito's decision infuriated the Ministry of Justice and Justice Minister Hitoshi Shimasaki made the Kanagawa Prefectural Office warn the mayor and admonish him to obey the law.

Resolutions calling for a revision of the Alien Registration Law were adopted by 702 municipal assemblies and in 1983 the National Council of Mayors asked the government to discontinue fingerprinting and abolish the requirement to carry the certificate at all times. The Ministry of Justice exerted great pressure on the municipalities to execute the law, and the revisions in the registration procedures were mainly intended to alleviate the burden on the municipalities. The demand to abolish the system was reiterated by individual local governments such as the mayors of Kyoto's 11 wards. The mayors supported the refusers' argument that they were treated as criminals and that the compulsory fingerprinting violated their human rights.

While in the past the number of refusers has risen to several thousands (1985: 14,000), there have been relatively few arrests. Arrests and criminal prosecutions have occurred in Okayama, Kobe, Tokyo, Yokohama, Nagoya and Fukuoka. One of the first to be arrested was Kim Myong Kwan, a lecturer at Seika Junior College in Kyoto. He had refused to be fingerprinted in 1981 and was taken into custody when he failed to comply with several summonses to appear voluntarily for questioning by the police. The Korean government expressed concern because the arrest came at a time when negotiations on reforming the fingerprinting system were pending. In May 1985 Lee Sang Ho, a leader of the Kawasaki Korean community, was arrested for having refused to be fingerprinted since May 1983. His arrest drew violent protests.

Arrests have not been confined to Koreans. The first American to be arrested was Robert Ricketts, a freelance translator. He stated in court that his refusal was a form of civil disobedience to protest the 'institutionalised racial discrimination' in Japan's immigration system. Ricketts complained that his arm was injured when five police officers at the Shibuya Police Station forcibly took his fingerprints. In December 1988 the Tokyo District Court imposed a fine of ¥ 10,000 on Ricketts who said that the court should consider the origin of the fingerprinting. He said that it was introduced after the war with the collaboration of the Occupation authorities for the surveillance of Korean and Chinese residents whom the authorities suspected of being Communists. At present, Ricketts asserted, the system is irrational.

Judge Yoshifusa Nakayama repeated the government's old assertion that the system was rational and a necessary method of confirming the identity of foreigners. To treat foreigners differently from Japanese, the judge said, was natural since they had no inherent right to stay in Japan. The attitude of the bureaucracy may have been influenced by the inclination to consider the admission of foreigners into the country as granting a privilege and to expect them to behave like guests. Although every state can regulate the entry and sojourn of foreigners, the UN Convention on Human Rights guarantees these rights also for persons living abroad or travelling in foreign countries.

Actually, Japan's use of fingerprinting as a control mechanism for people other than criminals goes back to pre-war times. The South Manchurian Railway Co. used to fingerprint Chinese labourers forced by the Kwangtun Army to work in the company's coal mines. After Japan's occupation of Manchuria in 1931 Koreans settled in the so-called 'strategic hamlets' were fingerprinted and had to present an identification card when entering or leaving the camps. Controls by fingerprinting and identification documents were extended after the outbreak of the war with China in 1937. From 1939 Koreans living in Japan had to register with an organisation called Kyōwakai and carry a Kyōwakai passbook. The organisation was under direct police control.

In the post-war era the Occupation initiated a registration and passbook system for the Koreans who had refused repatriation by having the Japanese government issue an Alien Registration Ordinance in 1947. To prevent the entry of Communist agents, a revision of the ordinance in 1949 required Koreans to have a Korean registration certificate which was to be renewed periodically. Criminal sanctions were imposed for failure to carry the certificate on one's person. The Korean War prompted the Occupation authorities to insist that the Japanese government take further measures, including fingerprinting, based on the US Alien Registration Act of 1940 and the Internal Security Act of 1950. The purpose of the legislation was strictly political, the prevention and suppression of subversion and espionage, and had nothing to do with ordinary administrative regulations. The Alien Registration Law which came into effect with the Peace Treaty is tainted by this pedigree.

Because fingerprinting affects mainly Koreans, the Korean government has repeatedly expressed its concern over the situation and requested that Koreans should be treated like Japanese by upgrading their legal status and promoting welfare and education. When Prime Minister Nakasone visited Seoul, he promised to work for an improvement of the registration system. The improvement was a farce. At the same time as changing the method of fingerprinting (billed as an improvement) the government strengthened the enforcement of the fingerprinting. In October 1982 the Ministry of Justice adopted the policy of disqualifying refusers from living in Japan and denying re-entry permits. The ministry issued an order to all mayors instructing them not to issue registration certificates to foreigners refusing to be fingerprinted. Local governments should try to persuade the refusers to comply with the law during a three-month grace period but after the expiration of that time, the local authorities should inform the police for further legal action.

The Seoul government also wanted the Japanese to abolish the deportation system for Korean residents convicted of crimes. This system was instituted in 1965 on the basis of a Japan-South Korea agreement but for a number of years, Seoul refused to accept deportees.

The South Korean government had often urged the Japanese authorities to abolish fingerprinting for first- and second-generation Koreans but the Japanese government maintained that the system could not be scrapped until a suitable substitute for fingerprinting was found. In November 1990, however, Japan promised the South Korean government that fingerprinting would be discontinued for Koreans residing in Japan. The Ministry of Justice was preparing a revision of the Immigration Law which would give the same legal status to South and North Koreans and Taiwanese who were deprived of their Japanese nationality in 1952, and their descendants, regarding deportation and re-entry.

Concerning the government's revision of the Alien Registration Law, Koreans pointed out that the law treats foreigners in Japan basically as a law-and-order problem. It takes the view that they are all potential criminals and the purpose of registration is to control them. The revision which replaces fingerprinting by registration of signature, photograph and family records and retains the obligation to carry the alien registration card at all times remains a system of control.

THE FINGERPRINTING CONTROVERSY

Basically, Japanese legal thinking and political practice lack a philosophical foundation and the idea of justice, in particular, has been replaced by ingeniousness in interpreting legal norms to reach a desired conclusion. The government is just as much bound to the common good as the people. The arbitrary exercise of authority not respecting the common good cannot impose moral obligations. The reason why the government does not discontinue the fingerprinting requirement for the registration of foreigners was stated clearly by Shunji Kobayashi, former Director-General of the Immigration Bureau of the Ministry of Justice, 'There is no example in the world', he said, 'where a law was changed because a movement violated the law.'

The crusade against fingerprinting has been supported by foreign missionaries, both Catholic and Protestant. A Protestant missionary, Ronald Susumu Fujiyoshi, first refused to be fingerprinted in 1981. He was prosecuted and found guilty by the Kobe District Court in 1986 and fined ¥ 10,000. Although his registration certificate was without a fingerprint, he was given a three-year extension in 1984 but was refused an extension in 1987. Jesse Jackson, a friend of Fujiyoshi's since his days at a theological college in Chicago, interceded for him with the Japanese Embassy in Washington, but he was ordered to leave Japan and went to Hawaii in February 1988.

Etienne de Guchteneere, who came to Japan as a Catholic missionary in 1956 and also taught French at the Miyagi University of Education in Sendai, refused to be fingerprinted in 1984. He was given a three-month extension in 1985 but told he would be deported at the end of this period if he did not comply with the fingerprinting requirement. The Catholic Bishops' Conference asked the government for an explanation of the threatened deportation order but in the end, Father de Guchteneere agreed to be fingerprinted. However, he was given only a one-year extension instead of the usual three years.

Another missionary, Father Jules Rand, who had lived in Japan for 29 years, refused to be fingerprinted because he considered the system a symbol of the discrimination against Koreans. The Shiraishi Ward Office (Sapporo) renewed his certificate without the three-month delay. It would be useless, an official of the ward office said, to try to persuade Father Rand to change his mind. Another French missionary, Father Edward Brgostowski, who had refused to be fingerprinted in order to protest the arrest of Lee Sang Ho, agreed to the procedure in order to obtain a re-entry permit so he could go home to attend the funeral of his father. But Father Constantin Louis who had been working in Tokyo since 1956 gave up his plan to go home for the funeral of his mother rather than comply with the fingerprinting law to get a re-entry permit. He commented that one-third of the residents in his neighbourhood were Koreans and he refused to be fingerprinted to protest against the racial discrimination from which they suffered.

Minister of Justice Yukio Hayashida announced a more flexible policy regarding re-entry permits for fingerprint refusers in March 1988. The first person to receive a re-entry permit under the new policy was Pak Hong Kyu, a teacher at a junior high school in Higashi, Osaka. She had applied for a re-entry permit in order to take the ashes of her deceased father to Cheju Island. In October 1988 the Ministry of Justice, in a noteworthy departure from past practice, granted re-entry permits to senior members of Chongryon, the association supporting North Korea, for attending an international conference. Until then, the ministry had refused the issue of re-entry permits to Chongryon members for trips with political implications.

Confirming an earlier decision of the Japanese government to abolish the fingerprinting system for foreigners, the foreign ministers of Japan and the Republic of Korea signed a memorandum on the occasion of Prime Minister Kaifu's visit to Seoul in January 1991 in which the Japanese government pledged to end fingerprinting and to open jobs in local governments to Koreans and allow teaching in public schools. The government planned to introduce a system similar to the Japanese family register consisting of photos, signatures and the names of parents and grandparents. Japan also promised to reduce the crimes for which Koreans can be deported.

The government prepared a revision of the Alien Registration Law to exempt Koreans and Taiwanese who had been deprived of their Japanese citizenship in 1952 from the obligation to submit to fingerprinting. The exemption was to be extended to their descendants and to other foreign nationals with permanent residence status. The Foreign Office and the Ministry of Justice intended to abolish fingerprinting for all foreign residents but the National Police Agency opposed this measure claiming that the increase in the number of foreigners involved in crimes or working without proper visas required the continuation of fingerprinting.

In the same way as the Koreans, the Taiwanese residing in Japan were deprived of Japanese nationality when the San Francisco Peace Treaty came into effect; they were considered as Chinese nationals. An estimated 210,000 Taiwanese who had served in the Japanese army thereby were stripped of their right to pensions. It was only in 1988 that the Diet passed a law stipulating payment of ¥ 2 million to Taiwanese who were wounded in the Second World War or to the surviving relatives of those who were killed. Compounding the injustice of the long delay, the ungenerous terms of the payments was a further blow. Payments were to be made in bonds redeemable at the end of

March 1993. Actually, payments were made earlier and by the middle of 1991, the equivalent of $ 389 million had been paid to 27,491 of the roughly 28,000 former soldiers or their families who had applied for compensation. At about the same time, the government decided to pay ¥ 100,000 to each of the 260,000 Japanese soldiers detained in Siberia after the war or to the families of those who had died.

The Liberal-Democratic Party and the government used the demise of Emperor Hirohito to declare a general amnesty. About 10,000 foreigners, most of them Koreans, were pardoned. But some violators of the Alien Registration Law claimed to reject the amnesty. All 34 fingerprint refusers on trial at the beginning of February 1989 released a statement expressing their intention to reject the pardon. The government, they claimed, was going to use the amnesty to avoid the issue of the violation of human rights raised by the lawsuits. Cho Geon Chi, a resident of Shimonoseki, who was being prosecuted on charges of refusing to be fingerprinted, destroyed the registration certificate given to him when the Hiroshima High Court dismissed the charges against him. The amnesty, he said, had deprived him of an opportunity to challenge the government's unjust attitude towards Korean residents. He hoped he would again be put on trial.

In June 1989,13 Chinese, Korean and American fingerprint refusers filed a lawsuit againt the state and seven prefectural and municipal governments complaining that the amnesty had deprived them of their right to a trial in which they could have attacked the constitutionality of the fingerprinting regulations. They demanded ¥ 13 million in compensation for the mental distress caused by the amnesty.

In order to stem the influx of foreigners seeking work in Japan without proper visas, the Immigration Bureau initiated a revision of the Immigration Control Law making it illegal for employers to hire foreigners without working status certificates. There are about 50,000 to 100,000 South Koreans in Japan who were repatriated after the war but drifted back to Japan before the normalisation of relations between Japan and the Republic of Korea in 1965. Moreover, there is a large number of Koreans who came recently to Japan attracted by better living conditions. Under the revised law, legal Korean residents will have to apply for the new certificate in addition to their alien registration certificate.

Under the new law passed by the Diet in November 1989, certificates are issued to legitimate workers whose visa status entitles them to work in Japan. Employers who hire workers without proper working status can be fined ¥ 2 million; in case of repeated infractions, employers can be imprisoned for up to three years. Employment agencies must obey the same regulations and violations of the law entail the same penalties. The authorities claim that the law does not impose new burdens but only clarifies the working status of the foreigner. Actually, in its tenacity to drive all 'illegal' aliens out of Japan, the government resorted to a new form of harassment.

The law is a new demonstration of the xenophobia of the bureaucracy and its efforts to make Japan a closed society. The trend towards an open society which started in the Meiji era and was furthered by such different individuals as Yukichi Fukuzawa, Eiichi Shibuzawa and Shigenobu Okuma was stopped by the nationalism of the Taisho era because the liberalism of the monied classes was not channelled into organisational forms capable of gaining the support of the masses.

In April 1988 a private US human rights fact-finding mission organised by the US National Council of the Churches of Christ called Japan's Alien Registration Law an 'instrument of institutionalised racism' giving legal sanction to political, economic and social discrimination against Koreans in Japan.

A meeting of the UN Commission on Human Rights in July 1988 discussed Japan's Alien Registration Law and particularly the fingerprinting requirement. The Japanese officials attending the meeting explained that fingerprinting had been useful in preventing false registrations, the forging of passports and other crimes, but their answers were evasive and even discriminatory.

A revision of the Immigration Control and Refugee Recognition Law in June 1990 aimed at encouraging the entry of foreign nationals with special skills while shutting out unskilled workers. At a time when many Japanese enterprises, especially small outfits, go bankrupt on account of the labour shortage, the Justice and Labour Ministries devote their main efforts to finding and deporting every one of the estimated 100,000 so-called illegal workers staying in the country. Because they have no proper visas, many of these workers are in desperate circumstances, without any guaranteed rights to life, employment, welfare and educational benefits which affects not only the workers themselves but also their families.

Illegal workers have to pay their medical bills in full because they are not covered by health insurance and the Health and Welfare Ministry has instructed local governments not to pay for medical expenses out of welfare funds. Foreign workers, therefore, hesitate to go to a hospital when they become sick and hospitals sometimes refuse to handle emergency cases because of the uncertainty of payment. If foreigners without proper visas are involved in labour accidents, they are allowed to stay in the country until the investigation and procedures for accident insurance are completed but they are not allowed to stay for the purpose of recovering their outstanding wages. There are no provisions for amnesty or relief measures to protect the basic human rights of illegal workers. A group calling itself Lawyers for Foreign Labourers' Rights demanded an amnesty for foreigners working without proper visas as a way of protecting their basic human rights. The 1965 International Convention on the Elimination of All Forms of Racial Discrimination is one of about a dozen international treaties, conventions or protocols signed by Japan but not ratified because the bureaucracy does not want to change relevant laws (which would limit their arbitrariness).

In December 1990 the UN General Assembly adopted a 93-article treaty called the International Convention on the Protection of the Rights of All Migrant Workers and Members of Their Families. The convention guarantees human and labour rights, whether workers are legally documented or not, including basic human rights such as freedom of thought, expression and religion and the right to form labour unions. It also protects the right to receive the same medical services, social welfare and unemployment insurance as the citizens of the host country and stipulates that free language assistance is to be given if migrant workers become involved in legal procedures.

The treaty requires the signatory governments to institute appropriate court procedures in case of forced deportation. Other provisions concern invitations to visit or live with resident families, to change jobs or make temporary home visits. Documented workers are entitled to placement services and job training. Workers are guaranteed the use of their mother tongue and their children have the right to educational services and to acquire the nationality of the parents' country of employment (in states where nationality is determined by the place of birth).

The convention was backed by developing countries but opposed by industrialised nations such as Germany, Britain and Japan, who did not sign the convention. An official of Japan's Foreign Ministry said: 'The convention was written by labour-exporting countries in line with their own interests. Many of the articles of the convention do not suit Japan.'

There are no laws prohibiting discrimination in housing. Real estate companies and individuals can get long-term, low-interest loans from the government's Housing Loan Corporation or buy apartments under very favourable conditions from the Housing and Urban Development Corporation. The contract with the HUDC prohibits selling during a certain period of time and the exaction of 'key money' (usually two months rent, not refundable) from tenants. Otherwise, the owners are free to choose their tenants and they do not let their apartments to foreigners, not even foreigners married to Japanese. The usual reason given for this sort of discrimination is that foreigners do not take good care of the apartments or that they may leave without paying the rent.

Koreans and other Asians are not the only foreigners experiencing racial discrimination in Japan. Blacks have been the victims of racial prejudice in various ways. In localities where American servicemen are stationed, restaurants and bars have sometimes shut out all foreigners because they wanted to keep out blacks. Landlords have often refused to accept them as tenants. Japanese firms have frequently used caricatures of black people in their advertising and 'Little Black Sambo' featured on toys and in books has drawn sharp criticism from the US.

Blacks have encountered racial prejudice in employment. Under the government-sponsored Japan Exchange Teaching Programme, Americans come to Japan to serve as Assistant English Teachers (AET). Although Japanese racism is different from the discrimination practised in the US, it is just as cruel. An American accepted as an AET by a high school in Hamamatsu was refused a renewal of her one-year contract although there never had been any questions regarding her academic credentials or her teaching performance. The teacher had a master's degree in English literature, had studied French at the Sorbonne and had grown up speaking Spanish with her Latin-American-born mother.

At her first visit to the school, the head of the high school's English department greeted her with the exclamation 'Hey, are you big' and then asked her whether she would teach the 'black dialect'. Later, she would regularly hear 'Can you speak standard English?' A group of male colleagues asked 'At what age do women begin to have sex in your country?' followed by 'What about blacks? Do they usually get married first?' After having been told that the high school did not want her to stay on, she tried to find employment at other schools but the colour of her skin proved to be an insurmountable obstacle.

She related an episode exemplifying the prejudice against blacks. A friend of hers, a third-generation American of Japanese descent, applied for a credit card at a department store and was issued one immediately, no questions asked. She found the card convenient and suggested to her black friend that she should get one. To her amazement, the black woman was told that she needed a sponsor and documents proving her solvency.

The popular Japanese stereotype that Americans are white, blond, with blue eyes is reinforced by the selection of AETs. Apart from Japanese-Americans, a disproportionally large number are middle-class Caucasians which perpetuates the biased picture of foreigners held by the Japanese.

Chapter 5
Freedom of Religion

Among the fundamental human rights guaranteed by the constitution is freedom of religion, a typical tenet of Western liberalism. The Meiji Constitution severely restricted freedom of religion: Article 28 said 'Japanese subjects possess freedom of religion to the extent not contrary to the duties as subjects.' In the present constitution, a number of articles relate to religion (Art. 14, 19, 20, 89). 'Freedom of conscience' protected by Article 19 concerns man's convictions and beliefs which imply man's inner, spiritual independence. Negatively, although the protection of freedom of conscience means that no man can be forced to act contrary to his conscience, it does not give everybody the unrestrained right to act in accordance with his beliefs. 'Freedom of thought and conscience' (Art. 19) protects the right of every individual to embrace whatever ideas he likes and reject what he finds unacceptable but in his external conduct, he must conform to the rules of public order, i.e., the law.

Article 20 involves six different rights. (1) The freedom of belief of every individual. Every person has the right to belong (or not to belong) to a religious body, to follow his religion, and to live in accordance with the spirit and the commandments of his religion. He has the right to the outward manifestion of his religion, to worship in private and in public, to attend meetings and services, and to establish or adhere to religious organisations. But the individual can also remain silent on religion, change or renounce his faith or church and choose not to practice any religion. (2) Religious organisations are prohibited from being given any privileges. No religious body can be treated more favourably than any others. (3) Religious organisations are prohibited from exercising any political power. (4) No individual can be forced to take part in any religious act, rite, ceremony or performance. (5) The state and its organs are prohibited from engaging in religious education or activities. (6) The state cannot establish a state church or make adherence to any religion compulsory.

SEPARATION OF STATE AND RELIGION

The intent of Article 20 of the constitution is often summarised by the expression 'separation of state and religion' (*saisei bunri*). This is a tendentious and biased interpretation although many Japanese are unaware of this. The state (and its organs) must be neutral in the sense that it cannot perform religious activities, order or direct religious actions,but it does not say that the state must be irreligious. The First Amendment to the American Constitution on which this article is modelled was construed to mean separation of state and religion by judicial decisions in the nineteenth century when a flood of Catholic immigrants (mainly from Ireland) prompted American states to adopt a constitutional or statutory prohibition of using public funds for private educational establishments (parochial schools). The original meaning of the First Amendment was to prohibit Congress (the federal legislature) from establishing a church, i.e., from making a certain religion the state religion or from enacting laws prohibiting the free exercise of religion (in short, to establish a church similar to the Church of England to which all people would be forced to belong). The amendment did not intend to create an atheistic state. The interpretation of the amendment to mean that private education could not be subsidised because it involved the teaching of religion or that religious instruction (including prayer) was not to be tolerated in public schools was the creation of the virulent anti-clericalism of the upper classes. Article 89 of the Japanese constitution is an expression of the same bigotry.

The reverse of the prohibition of an established church is the freedom of religious organisations. Under the present system, religious bodies can obtain legal status as religious corporations under the Religious Corporation Law (Shūkyō Hōjin-hō). The main purpose of the incorporation is the regulation of the ownership and management of assets. The law treats religious organisations as some kind of company, and many provisions of the law resuscitated the regulations enforced during the war when religious bodies were considered as based solely on Japanese law and only subject to Japanese jurisdiction without any ties abroad or to international or supranational organisations. Fortunately, the real situation is quite different.

Nevertheless, the present legislation does not recognise churches and religious organisations as entities existing prior to and independent of official recognition by the state as religious corporations. In other words, the state claims an unlimited exclusive right over the public order of the country and does not recognise any rights of other organisations independent of their reception by national law. This conception of the public order is the natural consequence of the positivistic legal thinking prevalent in Japan and in the US and is in conflict with the reality of a pluralistic society.

In the US, not only prayer, the Bible and the singing of hymns are prohibited in public schools but all other manifestations of religion. In many cases, this situation is the result of lawsuits by aggressive militant atheists. A completely different situation prevails in Germany where the Fundamental Law also guarantees freedom of conscience and religion. (Art. 4, par. 1) but also makes religion a regular subject of instruction in public schools except in those expressly designated as non-religious (Art. 7, par. 3). The parents have the right to decide whether their children should receive religious instruction (*ibid.*, par.

2). Germany's Federal Constitutional Court upheld the principle of toleration and ruled that school prayer was constitutional. The religious beliefs of adherents of religion have just as much right to toleration as the atheists' claim for their anti-religious views. Although a pupil or his parents may object to prayer, there is no constitutional principle against school prayer. If participation in school prayer is voluntary and there is no coercion, the fundamental right of the freedom of disbelief is not injured. Also in public schools which are not denominational, religious activities (e.g., prayer before and after classes) are constitutional if they are conducted freely and not at the order of the authorities.

The right of a free decision on religious activities laid down in Article 4 of the Fundamental Law means the right to the free exercise of religion also in public as well as the right to abstain from religious activities (and not to belong to a church or religious organisation). Both rights, the freedom of positive adherence to religion and the freedom of negative repudiation of religion, must observe the principle of toleration.

The decision of the Constitutional Court overruled the State Court of Hessen which, in 1965, had decided that school prayer was not allowed if even only one pupil objected. The reasoning of the Hessen Court was that a pupil who did not want to participate in prayer would have to reveal his opposition (by his non-participation) which would violate the right to the free development of personality guaranteed in Germany's Fundamental Law (Art. 2, par. 1). (Hessen had been under the control of the Social-Democratic Party until the elections in May 1982.) The decision maintained the absurd position that the right of one person to remain uncommitted about his religious convictions prevailed over the right of the majority to manifest their convictions.

THE FUNERAL OF EMPEROR HIROHITO AND THE ACCESSION OF EMPEROR AKIHITO

The funeral of Emperor Hirohito in February 1989 drew attention to the ambiguities in the status of the Emperor who, traditionally, is also the high priest of Shinto. The controversy on the constitutionality of the activities connected with the Emperor became acrimonious with regard to the enthronement ceremonies for Emperor Akihito.

The palace compound in the centre of Tokyo contains three Shinto shrines, *kashikodokoro*, where the sacred mirror is preserved, *kōreiden*, the shrine of the Imperial ancestors, and *shinden*, the sanctuary of Shinto deities. One of the rituals the Emperor performs is *niinami-sai*, the harvest festival. For this observance, the Emperor personally plants rice in the palace grounds, and after the rice harvest, offers the new rice to the gods of heaven and earth and then partakes of it himself. The Japanese gloss over the problems involved in this position of the Emperor by calling the solemnities 'cultural activities'. Although culture certainly includes religion, religion is not identical with culture. The

Shinto establishment connected with the Imperial household forms an area of murky constitutionality since it is supported and financed by the state.

Emperor Hirohito's funeral comprised two ceremonies. The first was a Shinto ritual called *sōdōden* (ritual of the funeral hall) attended by the Imperial family, the other a state funeral called *tsuitō no rei* (mourning ceremony) attended by public officials, foreign dignitaries and the representatives of foreign governments. The government had planned to erect a partition between the shrine erected for the Shinto ceremony and the area of the state funeral but decided to mark the separation only by some token barrier when Prime Minister Noboru Takeshita and other members of the Liberal-Democratic Party and some foreign delegations wanted to be present at the Shinto ceremony.

Under the Meiji constitution, the rituals related to the Emperor's accession to the throne (*senso no shiki*) comprised a ceremony at the *kashikodokoro*, ceremonies announcing the accession at the *kōreiden* and the *shinden*, and the ceremony transferring sword and seal (*kenji togyo*). The Emperor receives the Imperial and the state seals as well as replicas of two of the three sacred treasures of the Imperial House (*sanshu no shinki*: the curved jewel, sword and mirror) said to have been bestowed by Amaterasu-ō-mikami on her grandson, Ninigi-no-mikoto, when he landed in Hyūga. Three days after the enthronement, the Emperor received the highest officials of the country. In November 1990 *sokui no rei*, the public announcement of the succession to the throne, took place. For this ceremony, a 6-metre tall 7-ton structure called *takamikura* (High Palace) was repaired and flown from Kyoto to Tokyo at a cost of ¥ 420 million.

Finally, the Emperor officiated at the *daijōsai* (Great Food Festival) which is the first *niinami-sai* in his reign. For this ritual, two rice paddies, one in Akita and the other in Oita prefectures, were selected from which the rice for the ritual was taken. The *daijōsai* is performed in honour of the Imperial ancestors, the *tenjin*, the seven generations of heavenly spirits before Amaterasu-ō-mikami, and the *chigi*, the five generations of terrestrial spirits preceding Jimmu Tennō. The festival entails an intricate array of Shinto ceremonies: the announcement of the date of the ritual at the three shrines in the palace compound; the dispatch of messengers reporting the dates of the *sokui no rei* and the *daijōsai* to the Grand Shrine at Ise, to the mausoleum of Jimmu Tennō and those of the last four Emperors preceding Emperor Akihito; the designation of the rice fields; the purification of the building site of the hall for the *daijōsai*, the messengers and the people harvesting the rice; the ceremony of harvesting the rice and of its delivery; dispatch of messengers to the Ise Grand Shrine reporting the conduct of the *daijōsai*; the purification of the Emperor, the Empress and other members of the Imperial household for ensuring heavenly protection of those involved in the ritual; the report of the performance of the ritual to the *kashikodokoro*, the *kōreiden* and the *shinden*. In the ceremony, the

Emperor offers food and rice wine prepared from the new rice. After the offering, the Emperor reads a dedicatory address to the Imperial ancestors and then partakes of the offerings of rice and saké. After the dismantling of the shrines built for the ritual, the site is purified. The Emperor then visits the *kashikodokoro*, the *kōreiden* and the *shinden*.

In addition to the Shinto rites, several banquets, a parade and a tea ceremony at the Imperial Palace at Kyoto were held. The festivities, conducted in accordance with the pre-war regulations, were patently inconsonant with the constitutional position of the Emperor.

How to pay for the ceremonies - the total costs were estimated at ¥ 12.3 billion - became the subject of fierce debate. The government established a special committee headed by the Chief Cabinet Secretary and composed of 14 scholars and a lawyer. Many observers asserted that the *sokui no rei* was a strictly Shinto ceremony and that the *daijōsai* also was a Shinto ritual. These ceremonies were prescribed by the Regulation Governing the Accession to the Throne Law enacted in 1907 but the post-war Imperial House Law of 1946 merely stipulates that a ceremony marking the accession to the throne will be performed (Art. 24). The cabinet regarded the first two of the four functions as secular activities but thought that the last two were religious. The Imperial Household Agency wanted the government to pay half of the ¥ 2 billion required for building the shrines used for the *daijōsai*. They proposed that the government should shoulder the cost of constructing the shrines (built of freshly felled Japanese cypress trees) while the cost of the ceremony itself would be borne by the Emperor's personal allowance. The Agency had originally planned to have the entire costs of the ritual paid by the state, but the government's legal advisers thought that such an arrangement would cause problems. Of the ¥ 12.3 billion the state spent on the enthronement rituals about one-third was for security, ¥ 5.55 billion was for the enthronement ceremony itself and ¥ 2.57 billion was for the *daijōsai*. Together with the ¥ 9.8 billion the government paid for the funeral of Emperor Hirohito in February 1989, the Imperial succession cost the taxpayers ¥ 22.1 billion.

In an address given in February 1989 the former Prime Minister, Yasuhiro Nakasone, argued that the state should provide for the *daijōsai* in the budget and bear the entire expenses. The *daijōsai*, he asserted, was a traditional and cultural event rather than a religious ritual. In the United States, he said, the President puts his hand on the Bible when he is sworn in, and the Archbishop of Canterbury plays an active role in the enthronement of the sovereign in Britain. Nationalists are unhappy with the constitutional provisions concerning the Emperor because they seem to make him subordinate to the cabinet. The spiritual influence of the Emperor, Shinto loyalists believe, should make the Emperor system the core of the national community.

Because of the ritual's pronounced Shintoist character, the government termed the *daijōsai* an event of the Imperial family. Chief Cabinet Secretary Misoji Sakamoto defended the government's financing of the ritual on the ground that the *daijōsai* was part of the enthronement tradition and served the public because the Emperor prayed on behalf of the Japanese people. While the enthronement ceremony (conducted on 12 November) was attended by 2,500 guests from Japan and abroad, only Japanese were invited to the partly secret *daijōsai* celebrated from the evening of 22 November to the following morning. Only 733 of the 900 invited to 'observe' the ritual attended because the Diet members of the Socialist and Communist parties, Komeito and Shaminren as well as 16 prefectural governors declined the invitation since they considered the government's involvement unconstitutional.

In some cases the number of people who declined to attend the event to which they were invited was embarrassingly high. Of the 2,422 invited to one of the five banquets for Japanese, 362 turned down the invitation. All Diet members of the Communist Party and some Socialists did not attend the banquet for the legislators. Speaking in the name of the Communist members of the Upper House, Shinnosuke Kamitani declared that according to the *Official Gazette* of 1928, *sokui no rei* conferred sovereignty (*shuken*) on the Emperor and the *daijōsai* made him a *kami*. The government should have designed a ceremony more in conformity with the constitution. The revival of the old rituals was an attempt to prepare the restoration of the pre-war Emperor system.

The protest actions of radical groups, above all Chūkakuha, opposing the ritual were more violent. They set fire to some railway stations and to numerous Shinto shrines all over the country, tried to disturb the Imperial parade and caused explosions near the Katsura Palace in Kyoto. They had built mortars to lob shells on sites related to the ceremonies. Christian and Buddhist organisations as well as a number of scholars denounced the government's violation of the constitution but the mobilisation of a police force of about 37,000 men prevented any counter-demonstration.

YASUKUNI SHRINE

The two main topics in the controversies surrounding Yasukuni Shrine in recent years have been the attempts to restore the status of Yasukuni as a state-supported shrine and the so-called 'official' visits of the Emperor and government personnel, above all the Prime Minister and members of the cabinet, to the shrine. In pre-war times, Shinto shrines were divided into two classes, religious shrines and state shrines. The religious shrines were those belonging to Shinto sects (*shūho Shintō*; there were 13 sects) while the state shrines had a special status. Officially, state Shinto (*kokka Shintō, jinja Shintō*) was not a religion but the national creed of Japan.

The shrines of state Shinto were divided into *kanpeisha* (government shrines) and *kokuheisha* (national shrines), and each category was subdivided (*kanpei taisha, kanpei chūsha, kanpei shōsha, bekkaku kanpeisha; kokuhei taisha, kokuhei chūsha, kokuhei shōsha*). At the pinnacle of the state shrines stood *Ise Daijingū*, dedicated to Amaterasu-ō-mikami, the ancestress of the Imperial family, which guarded the three Imperial emblems, mirror, sword and jewel (*sanshu no shinki*, also called after the Japanese reading of the ideographs *mi-kusa no kan-dakara*). Yasukuni Shrine was founded by Emperor Meiji in June 1869 as Tokyo *Shōkonsha* (shrine dedicated to the spirits of the war dead) and enshrined those who had died for the cause of the Meiji Restoration. It was renamed Yasukuni Jinja (*Yasukuni* may be translated as 'country at peace'; *Jinja* means shrine) in 1879 and given the status of *bekkan kanpeisha* entitled to subsidies by the Imperial household as well as the government.

As has often been pointed out, Yasukuni Shrine is entirely different from a 'Tomb of the Unknown Soldier'. The war dead are 'enshrined' individually and each entry is documented. Only those who can be identified by name and whose deaths can be verified with some certainty are listed in the records deposited in the inner chamber of the main sanctuary. The shrine is in no way a tomb; there are no remains, ashes, fingernails or strands of hair preserved in the sanctuary or in any of the buildings in the shrine precinct. To keep a corpse in a Shinto shrine is entirely incompatible with Shinto beliefs. To enshrine means to add the individual to the roll of those venerated as '*kami*'. In 1968 the shrine completed procedures to add about 2 million persons killed in the Second World War, including high school girls killed on Okinawa, to the roster which brought the total number of enshrined spirits to about 2.46 million. Despite protests by minority groups, 27,800 Taiwanese and 22,000 Koreans who had been drafted in the Japanese armed forces were also enshrined at Yasukuni.

In the autumn of 1945 the shrine conducted a mass festival enshrining those who had died in the war up to September of that year without listing them individually. But after the end of the Occupation, the shrine set out to enshrine the dead of the Second World War individually. The way in which this enshrinement was accomplished shows the government's astonishing disregard of the religious nature of the 'enshrinement'. The Ministry of Health and Welfare took the initiative in recommending who should be enshrined at Yasukuni. (All records of the former War Ministry had been destroyed but because the Ministry of Health and Welfare administers the pensions paid to the bereaved families, it was in a position to gather the relevant data.) The ministry also bore the expenses for the administrative procedures of the enshrinement. The ministry's Relief Bureau of Repatriates and Victims issued instructions entitled 'On Cooperation for Enshrinement at Yasukuni Shrine' in April 1956. When a revision of the Pension Law made families of war criminals who were either executed or died in prison eligible for government pensions, the ministry, in 1959, began to include class B and class C war criminals in the list of recommendations. On 8 February 1965 the ministry presented its list of class A war criminals for enshrinement (they were enshrined in October 1978). The ministry said it ended its cooperation with the shrine in 1971 because it could be interpreted as unconstitutional.

In pre-war times, Buddhism, Christianity, sect Shinto and other religions were under the jurisdiction of the Ministry of Education but the shrines of state Shinto were under the control of the Shrine Bureau of the Home Ministry. Jingū Kōgakkō, a *senmon gakkō* (special school), established in 1882, under the direct control of the Home Ministry, trained Shinto priests. It was made a *daigaku* (university) in 1941 and placed under the Ministry of Education but was later closed by the Occupation. About 20 per cent of the graduates of the school actually became Shinto priests; most of the others became teachers.

Before the war Yasukuni Shrine was placed under the joint supervision of the War and Navy Ministries and served to prepare the population morally and ideologically for what was termed 'the sacred war against the Anglo-American devils'. The Army and Navy Ministers served as chief ritualists for the spring and autumn festivals of the shrine.

The pre-war rationale for reconciling the official policy of considering Shinto as Japan's state religion and the constitutional provision of freedom of religion (Article 28 of the Meiji Constitution) held that Shinto was not a religion but patriotism and that obeisance at Yasukuni and other state shrines was a demonstration of loyal citizenship. The situation became particularly oppressive under pre-war militarism and during the war when Yasukuni was used to foster the chauvinism of the military. The Meiji Constitution was based on the unity of state and religion (*saisei itchi*). The Emperor was the bearer of national sovereignty (*tōchiken no sōransha*) because of his descent from the Sun Goddess Amaterasu-ō-mikami in an unbroken line (*bansei-ikkei no tennō*) and thus 'manifest god' (*akitsu mi-kami*). The real meaning of the provision in the Meiji Constitution that religious freedom was given 'to the extent compatible with the duties as subjects' was that religion had to be reconcilable with the Japanese version of the 'divine right of kings', i.e., with the belief in the divinity of the Emperor and state Shinto ('*kami nagara no michi*'). The government denied any infringement of the freedom of religion by insisting that the state shrines had nothing to do with religion and that the ceremonies at these shrines were only rites for the veneration of the ancestors. Shinto, the government declared, was not a religion in the sense of the constitution.

An order of the Ministry of Education issued in 1899 prohibited religious instruction at all schools except for Shinto rituals which were promoted because they were not religious. The people were forced to worship at Shinto shrines and officials as well as soldiers were obliged to attend Shinto rites. State Shinto was an institution of public law, all Japanese were required to adhere to Shinto, all other religions were heretical. Shinto was the religion of the Emperor, a religion which worshipped the Imperial ancestors as gods. Emperor worship was the spiritual foundation of the 'structure of the state' (*kokutai*). Public business was '*matsurigoto*', i.e., the business of conducting worshipping ceremonies. People who refused to participate in the rites at Shinto shrines were branded '*hikokumin*' (unpatriotic, traitors). When a sixth-grade boy whose mother was a student at a Protestant bible school refused to go to Ise shrine with his class, the case became a national issue and the boy and two other Christian children were expelled.

The attempts at legislating the transformation of Yasukuni shrine into a state shrine show three things. First, obtuseness to the pre-war role of Yasukuni and the complete disregard of its symbolic significance as an expression of chauvinistic militarism. People may feel compassion for the fate of the individual soldiers but the cause for which they died or were forced to die was anything but glorious. To make Yasukuni a state-supported institution would legitimate the 'holy war' of the 'Imperial Army'. Secondly, the infantile assumption that legislative fiat could change the nature of the shrine and create a new identity. Thirdly, the 'enshrinement' of the souls of the war dead is a distinctly Shinto concept and this would remain the same if Yasukuni became a state shrine.

An important factor in the interpretation of the constitutional prohibition of religious activities by the state is the traditional Japanese tolerance (with many exceptions) in religious affairs which is sustained by the absence of the concept of any absolute truth. Because of the historic syncretism and the age-old coexistence of Shinto and Buddhism, an unaccommodating exclusiveness seems strange. Article 1 of the proposed bill to nationalise Yasukuni said: 'In order to manifest the sense of veneration of the people for the heroic souls of the war dead and those who sacrificed themselves for national affairs, Yasukuni Shrine has for its objective to remember the benefits derived from their virtues, console them and conduct ceremonies and functions extolling their exploits and thus eternally transmit their achievements.'

On 12 April 1974 the House of Representatives Cabinet Committee, in a surprise move, cleared the bill placing Yasukuni under state control for presentation to the House whereupon the opposition parties boycotted the Diet proceedings. Not only Christian religious groups, but also Buddhists, labour unions and other organisations joined the protest movement against the bill. The Association of Christian Survivors (Christo-shū Izoku no kai) branded the bill as a 'war-related measure' and made preparations to go to court if the bill were enacted. They manifested their opposition by hunger strikes, sit-ins in front of the prime minister's official residence and protest meetings attended by 1,100 Catholics and Protestants. *Jōdo Shinshū* (Nishi Honganji) and the Otani sect of *Shinshū* (Higashi Honganji) sent telegrams to the prime minister protesting against the legislation and the youth section of Soka Gakkai distributed leaflets in all major cities. Organisations for the defence of the constitution joined with the Japan Teachers' Union and Sōhyō in the protest and 15 women's organisations handed resolutions demanding the retraction of the bill to the Speaker of the House.

In February 1975 the government abandoned its effort to have the Yasukuni bill passed by the House and prepared a law calling for the official participation of the Emperor in the rites performed at the shrine (*Irei Hyōkei-hō*, Law for Expressing Reverence to the Heroic Souls) although the enactment of the Yasukuni bill remained its goal. On the other hand, Christian organisations continued to campaign against the nationalisation of Yasukuni. A poll carried out by religious broadcasting stations showed that 82 per cent of those polled favoured official visits by the Emperor to the shrine and 64 per cent supported state protection for Yasukuni. In 1979 Jinja Honchō organised a drive for promoting official visits to Yasukuni Jinja and intended to collect a million signatures but the effort suffered a setback when Prime Minister Masayoshi Ohira failed to back up the initiative.

In August 1980 the Jōdo Shinshū sect appealed to 98 dietmen who were adherents of the sect to stop the legislation for giving state protection to Yasukuni; and the head of another Buddhist organisation, Risshō Kōsei-kai, asked Prime Minister Zenkō Suzuki personally not to make Yasukuni a state shrine. In September of the same year, the Socialist Party demanded that the government clarify its stand on the Yasukuni issue but the government was unable to arrive at a 'unified' view. A month later, the government conceded that state support would make it necessary to divest Yasukuni shrine of its religious character but gave no indication how this could be accomplished. The statement said nothing on the question of 'official' visits.

WORSHIP AT YASUKUNI SHRINE

The problem has never been clearly analysed, largely because the Japanese expressions used in the debate do not allow the necessary distinctions to be made. In English, the expression 'to attend a religious service' does not imply anything about the inner attitude of the people who are in attendance - an atheist can attend a religious marriage ceremony or a funeral without compromising his convictions. '*Sanpai*' (pronounced *sampai*), the term used for going to a shrine or temple, means to go to worship, and thus *sanpai* to Yasukuni Jinja is not just a visit but an affirmation of the mythology embodied in the place. It means to worship the 'heroic souls' 'enshrined' in Yasukuni and therefore implies an affirmation of the ideology involved in the enshrinement. The government showed that it was not unaware of the special shade of meaning in *sanpai*. Reacting to a complaint by foreigners about President Reagan's visit to Yasukuni Jinja during his stay in Japan (November 1983), the Foreign Ministry stated that the original announcement had used the word '*hōmon*' (visit), not '*sanpai*'.

At the shrine, the Hall of Worship (*sanpaidō*) is open to all visitors but for entering the Main Hall (*hondō*) which enshrines the 'heroic souls', visitors must apply at the reception office and sign the register; then, led by a shrine priest, they ascend to the hall observing the ritual prescribed in the 'Formal Worship Service'. Somebody attending a funeral in a Catholic church by no means identifies himself with the Catholic Church in doing so, but if he worships at Yasukuni Jinja, he declares his solidarity with the Shintoist conception of *kami* enshrined at this place.

'OFFICIAL' VISITS

'Official' visits of the Prime Minister or members of the cabinet are a misnomer, because an 'official' visit would be a public act performed by virtue of the office or mandate of the official. The conduct of religious rites does not belong to the official functions of the Prime Minister or the members of the cabinet. Contrary to the mere attendance at religious ceremonies, '*sanpai*' constitutes the active performance of a religious rite and is further objectionable because it means an endorsement of the nationalistic militarism symbolised by Yasukuni Shrine.

Japanese courts have never investigated the nature of *sanpai* and until the Sendai High Court decision did not understand that an 'official' visit by a state official contravenes the constitutional prohibition of religious activities by the state and its organs. To visit Yasukuni Jinja does not belong to the official functions of any public employee. An official visit to Yasukuni Shrine is incompatible with any public office. When the bill for giving state protection to Yasukuni failed to be passed by the Diet in 1974, some 50 groups, including Nippon Izoku-kai, Gunonren (Federation of Recipients of Veterans' Pensions) and Jinja Honchō formed 'Eirei ni Kotaeru Kai' (Association Responding to the Heroic Souls) and started another movement to make Yasukuni Jinja a state supported shrine. The organisation campaigned to have cabinet members make official visits to Yasukuni, which was regarded as a stepping stone to the nationalisation of the shrine. It asked local assemblies to pass resolutions urging such visits and as of July 1980, 20 prefectural assemblies and 364 assemblies of cities, towns and villages had adopted such resolutions.

For many years, visits by the Emperor, Prime Ministers or cabinet members stirred little controversy. Emperor Hirohito visited the shrine about eight times after the end of the war, and with the exception of Prime Minister Tanzan Ishibashi, all Prime Ministers have paid homage at Yasukuni. The Cabinet Legislative Bureau held that a Prime Minister's visit to Yasukuni as a 'private individual' did not violate the constitution but that no official car was to be used, the offering was not to be paid out of state funds and no cabinet member ought to accompany the Prime Minister.

When Takeo Miki (Prime Minister 1974-1976) visited the shrine, he did not use the official limousine but the car for the President of the Liberal-Democratic Party. He signed the visitors' book without adding his official title in order to stress that he went as a private individual. His successor, Takeo Fukuda (Prime Minister 1976-1978) caused an uproar by his first visit to Yasukuni in April 1977 because he was accompanied by Sunao Sonoda, the Chief Cabinet Secretary. But Fukuda insisted that he was there as a private person. On 15 August 1978 Fukuda went together with his new Chief Cabinet Secretary, Shintaro Abe, and five state ministers visited the shrine on the same day. Fukuda used an official car and he and three other ministers signed their names with their official titles. After Fukuda's visit, the cabinet revised its position and stated as its 'unified' view that the use of an official car was unavoidable for security reasons and that affixing the individual's official title was a social custom.

Another complication arose when Masayoshi Ohira (Prime Minister 1978-1980) paid his first visit to the shrine as premier in April 1979. Only a few days before his visit, it transpired that the souls of 14 class A war criminals, including General Tōjō, had been enshrined at Yasukuni during the autumn festival in the preceding year. Ohira, who was supposed to be a Christian, thought that there was no constitutional problem because he went of his own free will and the Chief Cabinet Secretary announced that 'according to precedent, the Prime Minister's visit will be paid as a private affair'. After attending an official ceremony remembering the war dead, Ohira's successor, Zenkō Suzuki (Prime Minister 1980-1982) went to worship at Yasukuni Shrine together with 17 of his ministers. If a minister who visited Yasukuni on the preceding day is counted in, 18 of the 21 members of the cabinet joined in this demonstration of nationalistic patriotism. It was seen as the implementation of the exhortation of Tatsuo Tanaka (then Minister of Education) in a cabinet meeting in July of that year in which he said: 'All cabinet ministers and the Prime Minister should go and worship,' and was advertised as an 'official' visit.

Yoshio Sakurauchi, then Secretary-General of the Liberal-Democratic Party, pressed for making Yasukuni a state shrine and asserted that the party had publicly pledged this before the 'double election' (the elections to both houses of the Diet in June 1980). 197 dietmen, including some state ministers, attended the opening of the shrine's spring festival as a group (*shūdan sanpai*) in April 1981. The cabinet's official view was that it could not be denied that the official worship of state ministers (*kōshiki sanpai*) was constitutionally doubtful. At his last visit to Yasukuni as Prime Minister in April 1988, Suzuki declined to answer whether his visit was that of a public or a private person.

The government and the executives of the Liberal-Democratic Party agreed in July 1981 to entrust a panel with the study of a proposal to designate 15 August as a memorial day for the war dead. The executives also asked the government to permit cabinet members to visit Yasukuni 'in their official capacity'. The Soviet news agency Tass criticised these proposals and called the views of the Liberal-Democratic Party 'chauvinistic, militant ideology' and wrote: 'In militaristic Japan, the Yasukuni Shrine was the hotbed of the notorious samurai spirit, of the lunatic ideas about the superiority of the Japanese nation over all others.'

Nationalistic causes received a fresh impetus with the nomination of Yasuhiro Nakasone as Prime Minister in November 1982. During the war, Nakasone served in the navy and was a great admirer of Adolf Hitler. He remained a fervent nationalist who believed in the superiority of Japanese spirituality and morality and was a supporter of the monoethnic policies of the International Research Centre for Japanese Studies funded by the Japanese government. When Nakasone and 14 cabinet ministers visited Yasukuni in August 1983, they avoided clarifying whether they went in an official capacity or as private citizens. The Cabinet Legislative Bureau stuck to its position that the constitutionality of the visits was doubtful and that the Prime Minister and cabinet ministers should refrain from worshipping in that capacity. The Liberal-Democratic Party formed a subcommittee headed by a former Minister of Justice, Seisuke Okuno, to study the Yasukuni question. The conclusions of the subcommittee were: (1) the worship for consoling the heroic souls and reverence shown by public agents does not constitute a religious activity prohibited by the constitution; (2) occasional visits to Yasukuni Jinja by the Prime Minister as a public figure are natural. Worship (*sanpai*) by the Prime Minister and cabinet members at Yasukuni is in accordance with the constitution (*gōken*).

Nakasone visited the shrine regularly and used the phrase that he worshipped as 'Yasuhiro Nakasone who is Prime Minister' (*naikaku sōri daijin-taru Nakasone Yasuhiro to shite*). In August 1984, another subcommittee called 'Round Table Conference Concerning the Question of the Visits of Cabinet Members to Yasukuni Shrine' was formed which stated in its report that in accordance with the feelings of a large part of the population and the sentiments of the bereaved families, the Prime Minister and cabinet ministers should visit Yasukuni Shrine but the visits should be carried out in a form which did not contravene the constitutional principle of separation of state and religion.

In its second report, submitted in August 1985, the subcommittee declared: 'It is natural that as representatives of the people, the government remembers the war dead. A large part of the people and the bereaved families recognise Yasukuni Shrine as the central establishment for commemorating the war dead and desire official worship by the Prime Minister and the cabinet. Official visits by the Prime Minister and the cabinet do not require a resolution of the cabinet in order to be official and no definite form of worship, e.g., Shinto, is required.' The report relies on the 1977 decision of the Supreme Court on the Tsu case for the claim that religious activities by the state and its agencies which are not prohibited by the constitution are possible (actually, the majority opinion in the Tsu case did not hold that there are religious activities the state and its organs may perform but that there is no complete rift between the state and religion and that there are activities of a religious nature that have become purely social acts). The report contained six views which ranged from the affirmation of 'official' visits as constitutional to their rejection as unconstitutional.

In August 1985 the entire cabinet (with the exception of two ministers who were on trips abroad, worshipped at the shrine in what was called an official visit, the first 'official' visit of a Prime Minister since the end of the war. In September, a spokesman of the Chinese foreign ministry declared that the official visits to Yasukuni Shrine injured the feelings of the Chinese people, and similar remonstrances came from other countries in the region. The Chinese were particularly upset because General Tōjō and other war criminals were among the heroic souls venerated by the cabinet. In demonstrations all over China, one of the slogans was 'Down with Japanese militarism'. China's ambassador to Japan, Zhang Shu, told a press luncheon: 'Sensitive issues still remain between China and Japan 40 years after the last war due to their unhappy history in the past and the Yasukuni issue is a matter of this nature.' In order to remove the main irritant of Japan's neighbours, the League of Liberal-Democratic Party Diet Members for Making an Independent Constitution headed by a former Prime Minister, Nobusuke Kishi covertly approached Yasukuni and proposed to establish a new shrine dedicated solely to the class A war criminals or let another shrine or other shrines 'take care of them'. The shrine rejected the request.

Mindful of the international repercussions, Nakasone thereafter refrained from visiting Yasukuni but said that he had not changed his view on the constitutionality of the visits. In answering the Chinese complaint, the Ministry of Foreign Affairs explained that worship at Yasukuni Shrine would not be transformed into a system. The right wing proclaimed its discontent with the Prime Minister's caution and in October 1985 a group of 143 Liberal-Democratic dietmen visited Yasukuni. Although Prime Minister Nakasone did not visit Yasukuni in August 1986 and 1987, most of the cabinet members did. On 15 August 1987 16 out of 20 ministers and the Chief Cabinet Secretary, Masaharu Gotoda, went to the shrine and five of them expressly stated that their visit was in their official capacity. They were joined by numerous members of the Diet. The Chinese press promptly denounced the visits as 'impudent' and connected them with Japan's increase in defence expenditure and the country's participation in the US Strategic Defence Initiative.

Yasukuni's spring festival in 1989 was held at a time when the unresolved Recruit scandal had plunged the cabinet of Prime Minister Noboru Takeshita into deep trouble. The conservative law-makers seemed to have felt the need of help. On 21 April 1989, 147 members of the Lower House and 59 members of the Upper House or their substitutes followed the call of the 'Association of Diet Members Worshipping Collectively at Yasukuni Shrine', and joined in the ritual, the largest number of dietmen to participate in the festival. They included ten members of the cabinet. Prime Minister Takeshita did not visit the shrime while in office and Sōsuke Uno, the first politician who succeeeded him, only remained in office until the middle of August.

On 15 August 1989 the newly-installed Prime Minister, Toshiki Kaifu, the Foreign Minister, Taro Nakayama and the Chief Cabinet Secretary, Tokuo Yamashita, refrained from visiting Yasukuni in order to avoid giving offence to South Korea, China and other Asian countries but about 200 dietmen, including members of the cabinet and top party officials, paid respect to the war dead. For the autumn rites in 1989, five members of the cabinet and 200 Liberal-Democratic politicians made the pilgrimage to Yasukuni. About 120 people belonging to the Peace Association of Bereaved Families marched through Tokyo carrying banners calling for peace and asking cabinet members to stop making 'official' visits to Yasukuni Shrine. In a street corner speech, Takako Doi, chairwoman of the Socialist Party, said that 15 August was an occasion for Japan to reaffirm its renunciation of military force and called for less spending on defence and more on welfare and education.

On 15 August 1990, the 45th anniversary of the end of the Pacific War, 18 cabinet ministers and 191 other members of the Liberal-Democratic Party worshipped at Yasukuni Shrine. Again the Prime Minister Toshiki Kaifu, the Foreign Minister, Taro Nakayama, and the Chief Cabinet Secretary, Misoji Sakamoto, refrained from visiting the shrine in order to avoid adverse reaction from neighbouring Asian countries. Kaifu, Nakayama and Sakamoto did not worship at the shrine the following August either, which drew criticism from nationalistic organisations. While 12 members of the cabinet visited Yasukuni, the Emperor, the Empress and the Prime Minister attended an official memorial service at Tokyo's *Budōkan*.

Buddhist and Christian organisations of bereaved families demanded that the enshrinement of their relatives be rescinded. In 1972, when the Church of Christ in Japan requested Yasukuni to remove the names of four of its pastors from the rolls, the shrine refused. The deputy chief priest of the shrine explained the shrine's attitude: 'Yasukuni Shrine is not a religion. It is a kind of national morality. There are adorers, but no believers. We do not make supplications or pray. The shrine is the object of adoration, but it is not a place to which people entrust their spirituality.' A poll conducted by the *Yomiuri* newspaper after Nakasone's visit to Yasukuni in October 1985 found that 51 per cent approved of Nakasone's 'official' visit, 25 per cent opposed it and 23 per cent gave no answer. According to an *Asahi* newspaper poll carried out at the same time, more than 60 per cent of those aged 50 and over supported Nakasone's visit but fewer than 35 per cent of those under 30 expressed this view.

Masayuki Fujio, newly-installed as Minister of Education, blamed the Occupation for the 'Yasukuni allergy' and asserted that the Occupation's educational policies gave the Japanese people the impression that 'official visits to Yasukuni Jinja would be wrong'. This was not his only silly utterance. He got into hot water when, soon after assuming his post in July 1986, he attacked, without naming them, China and South Korea. These countries had been incensed by the attempts in a history book to gloss over the wartime atrocities committed by the Japanese army. Fujio was quoted as saying: 'Those who complain should look back to see if they didn't commit similar acts themselves in world history.' He further angered South Korea when a magazine reported his remarks about Japan's annexation of Korea in 1910: 'Formally as well as actually, it was established by the agreement of the two countries. Korea also had a certain responsibility.' This was too much for the Prime Minister and he sacked Fujio. Bungei Shunju Ltd., publisher of the monthly *Bungei Shunjū*, filed a protest with Prime Minister Nakasone and Chief Cabinet Secretary Gotoda claiming that Gotoda had pleaded with the editor of the magazine to delete parts of an article based on an interview with Fujio.

Heeding the urgings of an association of dietmen for promoting visits to Yasukuni Shrine, about 200 members of the Liberal-Democratic Party went to the shrine for the Grand Spring Festival in April 1988. Seizing the occasion to display the haughtiness and fatuity of Japanese nationalists, Seisuke Okuno, then Director of the National Land Agency (and therefore a member of the cabinet) defended Japan's military actions against Asian countries in the Second World War. 'Asia was colonised by Caucasians at that time', he said. 'Japan was by no means an aggressive nation.' Japan fought the war, he asserted, in order to secure its safety. He maintained that the outbreak of Japan's war with China (the Marco Polo Bridge incident, 7 July 1934) was 'accidental' and said that this was also the opinion of Edwin O. Reischauer, former US ambassador to Japan. Okuno asserted that the Pacific War liberated the Asian peoples from the domination of the white race and that the independence gained by China, Indochina, Burma, Indonesia and the Philippines betokens the historic significance of Japan's struggle.

Okuno also attacked China's leader Deng Xiaoping. The Japanese people, he said, had been 'twisted around' by Deng's remark that he regretted the existence of a few Japanese opposing the improvement of Sino-Japanese relations. The People's Republic of China and South Korea lodged official protests. China's official news agency termed Okuno's statement completely preposterous, contrary to historic truth and intolerable to the Chinese people. South Korea also voiced anger at the denial of Japan's aggressiveness. In an editorial entitled 'Selective Amnesia', the *Straits Times* called Okuno's diatribe a blatant attempt to whitewash his country's wartime misdeeds. Okuno and some of his countrymen, the paper said, have become quite good at glossing over the details of the last war because for many years they have practised what is called selective amnesia, remembering only what they want to remember.

Masayuki Fujio had been forced to resign for a similar 'slip of the tongue,' but this time, neither the government nor the Liberal-

Democratic Party reprimanded Okuno for his imbecilic arrogance. On the contrary, Chief Cabinet Secretary Keizō Obuchi defended Okuno saying that Okuno did not intend to slander other nations - which was not the real issue. And Prime Minister Takeshita showed his inability or unwillingness to understand the real issue when he said that Okuno had only set forth a certain view of history. The misrepresentation of the war began with the Emperor's rescript accepting the Potsdam Declaration. The document avoids the words 'surrender' or 'defeat' (which is quite understandable) and the rescript's euphemistic circumlocution '...the war situation has developed not necessarily to Japan's advantage' has become a classic. It embellishes Japan's war aims ('... We declared war on America and Britain out of Our sincere desire to ensure Japan's self-preservation and the stabilisation of East Asia, it being far from Our thought either to infringe upon the sovereignty of other nations or to embark upon territorial aggrandizement'). While mentioning the sufferings of Japan, the rescript fails to acknowledge the havoc wrought by Japan on other nations or to apologise for the war. The vernacular press was even more self-righteous, calling the conflict 'a war of justice as well as a war of self-defence and self-preservation' and asserting that it was waged for 'the liberation of East Asia and intended to contribute to peace in the world and the progress of mankind'.

Okuno refused to resign his post or to retract his remarks. Obuchi's negotiations with Okuno produced no solution and the opposition parties prepared a motion demanding his dismissal. After three weeks of wrangling, Okuno tendered his resignation, but even then he repeated his offensive statement that Japan's attack on China had not been an aggressive war and that Japan should not be told what to do by Deng Xiaoping. In the heated cabinet debate prior to Okuno's resignation, Eiichi Nakao, Director-General of the Economic Planning Agency, defended Okuno's position and a group of like-minded members of the Liberal-Democratic Party criticised Takeshita for his failure to settle the incident without Okuno's resignation. A statement issued by a group comprising 41 right-wing parliamentarians led by Shizuka Kamei backed Okuno and denied that Japan was the aggressor in the Pacific War. In informal talks after a cabinet meeting in April 1988, Posts and Telecommunications Minister, Masaaki Nakayama, criticised the film *The Last Emperor*, saying that it was not faithful to historical fact and might be yet another form of Japan-bashing.

A few days before the representatives of practically the entire world assembled in Tokyo for the state funeral of Emperor Hirohito, Prime Minister Takeshita demonstrated again the unreconstructed nationalism of the right wing. Speaking during the session of the Budget Committee of the Lower House on 18 February 1989, he remarked that scholars held different views about Japan's wartime conduct. Whether or not Japan committed aggression was a problem which could only be judged by future historians. He added that it was also difficult to decide whether the war started by Adolf Hitler in Europe was a war of aggression. His remarks were severely criticised not only in China and South Korea but also by Tass, Hong Kong and Italian newspapers. He worsened the situation by refusing to withdraw his remarks and having his ministers confirm that there had been no change in the government's official position.

An unfortunate display of the knack of Japanese politicians to make unpolitic remarks infuriating foreigners occurred at the beginning of 1992. Just a few days after President Bush,accompanied by a delegation of American businessmen,had come to Japan, Yoshio Sakurauchi, the speaker of the House of Representatives, called American workers lazy and illiterate and predicted that the United States would become Japan's subcontractor. Shortly thereafter, Prime Minister Kiichi Miyazawa asserted that American workers were poorly motivated, lazy, greedy and without any work ethic. Surprised by the fury these slurs unleashed in the US, the government declared that the Prime Minister's words did not mean what they appeared to mean and that no insult was intended.

CONSTITUTIONALITY OF OFFICIAL SUPPORT OF YASUKUNI SHRINE

'Official' visits to Yasukuni were declared unconstitutional in 1991. A suit filed with the Morioka District Court in 1981 was decided in 1987. The suit was brought by three Morioka residents who demanded that 40 Iwate prefectural assemblymen refund the expenses (about ¥ 70,000) used for delivering an assembly resolution calling on the Emperor and the Prime Minister to pay official visits to Yasukuni Shrine to the central government. A second suit was brought in June 1982 by ten complainants against the prefectural governor and other officials seeking repayment of ¥ 21,000 given to Yasukuni Shrine in 1981. The two suits were combined in August 1983. The court held that it was impossible to separate the character of a public official (*kōjin*) from that of a private citizen (*shijin*). A public official enjoys the constitutional rights of freedom of thought, conscience and religion and he can act according to his beliefs also as a public official. Hence, worship in an official capacity does not violate the constitution.

The offerings to the shrine are gifts presented as a social etiquette in order to console the souls of the war dead and do not constitute a religious activity. In view of the purpose, objective and amount of the expenditures, they cannot be said to give Yasukuni Shrine a privilege or to have provided support and maintenance. Quoting the Tsu case, the court said that some relation between the state and religion was possible and that acts constituting such a relation would not be allowed if, in view of their purpose and effects, they exceeded a certain limit. The ruling of the court on the responsibility of the defendants is irrelevant to the Yasukuni controversy. Although, as the court said, cabinet members need not be 'politically neutral', the assertion that they can act in accordance with their beliefs is erroneous. Nobody can be obliged to act against his conscience, but nobody has an absolute right to do whatever he thinks is right. External conduct is subject to the restrictions of law and this is exactly the question in the visits of public officials to Yasukuni: What is the law?

In January 1991 the Sendai High Court overturned the decision of the Morioka District Court and ruled that official visits to Yasukuni Shrine by cabinet members as well as offerings to the shrine from public funds were unconstitutional. Presiding Judge Tadao Kasuya declared that visits to the shrine by cabinet members in their official capacity constituted religious acts violating the principle of separation of state and religion. A visit by the Emperor to the shrine as requested in the assembly resolution would have an enormous impact on society and promote a particular religion.

A few days after this ruling on the Yasukuni case, Judge Kasuya resigned from the bench although he had still three years left until his mandatory retirement age. He said that he had decided to quit when he was writing his ruling on the case. At a news conference following his verdict, Judge Kasuya observed: 'The post-war constitution is incomparably superior to the pre-war constitution. We can be proud of it. Judges have the duty to respect it.' Although the High Court ruled that the offerings of public funds were unconstitutional, the court did not order these sums to be repaid. The prefectural assembly and the governor appealed to the High Court asking for a review of the ruling but the court refused; there was no reason to appeal the decision, the court said. But in March 1991 the prefectural assembly and the governor filed a special appeal to the Supreme Court contending that the refusal of the High Court to accept the request for an appeal was unlawful. On 25 September of the same year, the second Petit Bench of the Supreme Court (presiding Judge Akira Fujishima) turned down the special appeal, stating that the appeal was contrary to law because it lacked legal reasons.

The question of official visits of members of the cabinet to Yasukuni is primarily a political and ideological issue, but it is also a legal and constitutional problem. The verdict of the Morioka court was basically flawed. As pointed out above, the nature of the worship at Yasukuni Shrine is different from mere attendance at a religious service and constitutes the performance of a Shinto ritual and a profession of the ideology underlying the enshrinement of the 'heroic souls'. To rely on the Tsu case (see below) for justifying these visits amounts to a misinterpretation of the Tsu decision.

The Matsuyama District Court reached a verdict which was completely contrary to the Morioka decision. Ehime Prefecture had a long-standing reputation for supporting Yasukuni Shrine. In 1982 the Home Ministry issued a warning to prefectural governments against contributing public funds to shrines and other religious organisations.

Responding to a complaint by Komeito, Ehime Prefecture stopped making offerings to Yasukuni and *gokoku* shrines out of public funds which Komeito had called unconstitutional. The governor was to make these offerings out of his own funds. Ehime also was to discontinue sponsoring memorial services for the war dead at the *gokoku* shrine in Matsuyama.

The Matsuyama suit was filed by 24 residents of Ehime Prefecture led by Kenji Anzai, chief priest of the Buddhist temple Sennenji in Matsuyama. They demanded that Governor Haruki Shiraishi and six other prefectural leaders refund ¥ 160,000 paid on 22 occasions over a period of six years as *tamagushiryō* (fee for a Sasaki sprig offered to the gods) to Yasukuni Shrine and offerings paid to the associations of bereaved families for rites at the prefectural *gokoku* shrine.

In his ruling in March 1989 presiding Judge Kazuaki Yamashita relied on the criteria of religious activities developed by the Supreme Court in the Tsu case, analysing 'purpose' and 'effect' of the actions under scrutiny. He found that Shiraishi (who at that time was no longer governor) had violated the constitutional ban against the support of a particular religion by the state. The other defendants were acquitted because they had not acted against their official duties. Judge Yamashita urgued that the donations to Yasukuni Shrine had a religious purpose and gave support and encouragement to religious activities. The donations formally given to the prefectural association of bereaved families were actually for conducting religious activities (*saishi*) at the *gokoku* shrine of Ehime Prefecture. They not only had a religious purpose but also promoted and encouraged the religious activities of the shrine. The court found that the relations of the prefecture with Yasukuni Shrine as well as with the *gokoku* shrine exceeded the proper level of cultural and social relations appropriate for Japan. The decision was widely perceived as a critical response of the democratic wing of the judiciary to the nationalistic challenges.

In May 1992 the Takamatsu High Court overturned the decision of the Matsuyama District Court and ruled that the donations of Ehime Prefecture were constitutional. Presiding Judge Kazuo Takagi declared that the donations were meant to show respect to the war dead and their families and remained within the ambit of social etiquette. They did not support or promote religion and each donation was so small that it could not be considered as assistance to the shrines. Judge Takagi obviously relied on the spurious maxim that the end justifies the means. Donations to Shinto shrines do not cease to be contributions to religious organisations because they are meant to honour the war dead and the quantitative plus or minus does not change their character.

An administrative suit seeking repayment of the treasury costs for the use of government cars by cabinet members visiting Yasukuni Shrine was turned down by the Tokyo District Court. In February 1988 the Fukuoka District Court ruled that private individuals could not collect damages from former Prime Minister Nakasone for his 'official' visit to Yasukuni Shrine on 15 August 1985. The plaintiffs, 43 Buddhists, Christians and members of families of war dead enshrined at Yasukuni had charged that Nakasone's action violated the constitutional guarantee of freedom of religion, the separation of religion and state, and the prohibition of spending public funds on religious institutions. Nakasone's action, they argued, had conferred official status on the shrine which was only one of many religious entities in Japan. The visit gave official sanction to the belief in the souls of the dead war heroes which caused mental anguish to the plaintiffs. The lawsuit was filed against both the state and the former prime minister on the premise that Nakasone had used his position to further his ambition. Despite the protest of the plaintiffs, Judge Hiroshi Tanimizu had separated the issues and the decision concerned only the former prime minister. State or municipal governments are responsible for illegal acts by a public servant acting in his legal capacity but the government employee is not liable as an individual. The state's compensation system, the court said, covered property damages caused by unlawful acts of government officials but not the kind of damages claimed by the plaintiffs. The court rejected an appeal in February 1992.

Other civil actions demanding damages for mental suffering caused by the official visits to Yasukuni were filed in Himeji and Osaka. In November 1989 the Osaka District Court rejected the demand for compensation of six Kansai residents whose relatives had died in the war and had been enshrined at Yasukuni. They claimed that their religious feelings had been hurt by then Prime Minister Nakasone's 'official' visit to the shrine on 15 August 1985, which, they contended, was a religious activity prohibited by the constitution. Presiding Judge Masayuki Matsuo held that Nakasone's visit did not lead to any disadvantageous treatment of the plaintiffs in matters of faith or impose any religious belief on them. Their argument that people have the right to remember their dead without interference from the state was not relevant to the case. The discomfort or irritation the plaintiffs felt on account of the 'official' visit was not an injury capable of being decided by legal proceedings, the court said. Neither could Mr Nakasone be held personally responsible for actions performed in his official capacity. The claim for damages, the court held, was groundless. A similar ruling was announced by the Himeji branch of the Kobe District Court in March 1990. The court rejected a damage suit by residents of Hyogo Prefecture claiming damages for mental anguish from the 1985 visit of then Prime Minister Nakasone to Yasukuni Shrine.

ENSHRINEMENT: THE NAKAYA CASE

As mentioned above, all soldiers who died on the battlefield were enshrined as 'heroic souls' in Yasukuni Shrine. Since the religious beliefs of many Japanese were rather vague, the custom of 'inviting' the souls of national heroes to the shrines dedicated to the spirits of the war dead (*shōkonsha*) found little opposition. To the adherents of monotheistic religions (Jews, Christians and Muslims), the enshrinement of men as *kami* meant their deification which amounted to blasphemy. This point was never mentioned in the three decisions discussed below, rendered by the Yamaguchi District Court, the Hiroshima High Court, and the Supreme Court.

In January 1988, Takafumi Nakaya, a lieutenant in the Ground Self-Defence Force, died in a traffic accident while on a recruiting mission for the Kamaishi branch of the SDF Iwate Local Recruiting Office. In March and April 1972 officials of the SDF Yamaguchi Local Recruiting Office visited the late lieutenant's widow, Mrs Yasuko Nakaya who lived in Yamaguchi. They asked her to submit a copy of her family register and a certificate of her late husband because they were going to enshrine the spirits of him and 26 other deceased members of the SDF in the prefectural shrine dedicated to the war dead (*gokuku jinja*). Mrs Nakaya turned down the request saying that she was a Christian and could not agree to the enshrinement. On 5 July, however, the shrine informed her that her husband had been enshrined.

The addition of members of the SDF who die in the line of duty to the roll of 'heroic souls' (*eirei*) venerated as *kami* at the shrine is called *aidono hōsai*, but the enshrinement of two or more spirits at the same time is commonly referred to as *gōshi*. The reading of the names of the spirits at the festival celebrated each year signifies that they have become 'enshrined kami' (*saishin*). The custom of 'inviting' the souls of national heroes to the shrines dedicated to the war dead (called *shōkonsha* in the early Meiji era; the name was later changed to *gokoku jinja*) found little opposition.

Mrs Nakaya asked the Yamaguchi Local Recruiting Office to withdraw the enshrinement of her husband and when her repeated requests were refused, she filed suit in January 1973 against the Yamaguchi Regional SDF Liaison Office and the prefectural chapter of the SDF Friendship Association (veterans' association), demanding the cancellation of the enshrinement and compensation of ¥ 1 million. Since the plaintiff alleged that the application for enshrinement constituted an unlawful religious activity of a state agency, the defence invoked the Supreme Court's decision in the Tsu case for the assertion that the separation of state and religion represented an 'institutional guarantee' and that there was no legal ground for the plaintiff's suit. Furthermore, the defence contended, as a private organisation, the veterans' association also had a 'right to worship'. In his decision on 22 March 1979 Judge Norio Yokobatake of the Yamaguchi District Court affirmed Mrs Nakaya's right to institute the suit. Freedom of religion is a basic human right and its protection by an appeal to the courts against its unlawful violation constitutes a legal interest. A surviving widow has the right to pray for her deceased husband without interference by outsiders in a quiet religious atmosphere.

The court epitomised the opposing viewpoints of the defendants and the plaintiff as 'freedom to worship' and 'freedom not to be worshipped' (*matsuru jiyū - matsurare-nai jiyū*). Acting upon the request of the defendants, the prefectural shrine made the deceased an enshrined deity so that he became the object of public worship. The deceased's widow was under no obligation or coercion to worship but her remembrance of her late husband was disturbed by the thought of the enshrinement which was incompatible with her religious beliefs. There was a clash between the freedom of religion which the veterans' association claims and that of the widow. Although the action of one party may injure the inner peace of the other party, its action could not be termed unlawful as long as no coercion or violation of the public order was involved. There was no legal foundation for the claim that the freedom of religion of the widow should be given preference over that of the association. (The deceased himself had been a Buddhist. It is strange that the court places the relationship of the widow of the deceased on the same level as that of the veterans' association to which the lieutenant never belonged.)

The court, however, ruled that the request for enshrinement filed jointly by the SDF and the veterans' association constituted a religious activity prohibited to the state and its organs by Article 20, paragraph 3 of the constitution and that this action infringed on the religious beliefs of the plaintiff who had the right to pray for her deceased husband in an atmosphere of quiet. The court recognised the defendants' assertion that the freedom of religion also extends to associations but maintained that it could only be exercised within the limits of the public order. The state (SDF) appealed the decision but the Hiroshima High Court upheld the lower court in June 1982. Presiding Judge Isao Ebisuda rejected the state's argument that interference with a person's belief did not constitute a violation of the freedom of religion unless coercion were involved. The court negated Mrs Nakaya's demand that the enshrinement be cancelled on the ground that the prefectural chapter of the SDF Friendship Association had already applied to the shrine for retraction.

Because the courts failed to address Mrs Nakaya's basic objection to the enshrinement of her late husband, they reduced the violation of freedom of religion to its merely subjective and psychological effects. While the injury to Mrs Nakaya's religious feelings constituted an important aspect of the case, it was secondary to the objective situation into which Mrs Nakaya was placed, i.e., that she, a Christian, was associated with the veneration of her husband as a Shinto deity. The concept of *kami* is very vague, nevertheless, to monotheists, 'enshrined *kami*' blurs the distinction between Creator and created beings. A *kami* becomes part of the Shinto pantheon of the myriads of gods (*yaoyorozu kamigami*) and some Christians consider the enshrinement as a symptom of the movement towards the restoration of the pre-war mythology.

On appeal by the state, the Supreme Court, on 1 June 1988, overturned the lower courts. In a 14 to 1 decision, the justices denied that the principle of separation of state and religion had been compromised and that Mrs Nakaya had suffered a violation of her rights liable to trial by a court of law. Actually, the court split into five parties. The majority opinion was supported by seven justices, including Chief Justice Kōichi Yaguchi; there was one dissenting and three concurring opinions. The majority opinion stated that the enshrinement was performed by the chief priest of the shrine at the request of the Yamaguchi chapter of the SDF Friendship Association. Religious considerations are of little interest to the SDF in the enshrinement of military personnel; their intention is to enhance the position and aid the morale of the soldiers. The enshrinement was based on the independent judgement of the shrine and performed by the chief priest at the request of the veterans' association; the cooperation of the SDF Regional Office was merely auxiliary (thus rejecting the position of the lower courts that the application was made jointly by the SDF and the veterans' association).

The action of the SDF did not create interest in or help, assist or promote a particular religion nor oppress or interfere with other religions. According to the standards set out in the Tsu case, the actions did not constitute religious activities. The request was merely the premise of the enshrinement and had no legally binding force; it did not violate any rights of the appellee (Mrs Nakaya) and the only question was whether the enshrinement as such constituted an infringement of a legal interest of the appellee - a question of civil law.

As long as the freedom of one's own religion was not impaired, the court maintained, freedom of religion demands tolerance, a mutually generous attitude of the believers of various religions based on mutual respect. Just as the widow has the right to cherish the memory of her late husband, so everybody else's freedom to perform religious acts for remembering and honouring the dead is guaranteed. The appellee's claim to the right to live a religious life in a quiet atmosphere without interference does not necessarily constitute a legal interest. The enshrinement of Takafumi, which the shrine is free to perform under the guarantee of freedom of religion, in no way injured any legal interest of the appellee. Since there was no ground for the appellee's claim, it was rejected.

The decision attempted to vindicate the government's position and reached its conclusion by misrepresenting the facts and misinterpreting the law. The court repeated the assertion that paragraph 3 of Article 20 contains an institutional guarantee and that its violation does not give a private citizen the right to sue. It is true that this paragraph involves an institutional guarantee but it is also undeniable that its violation can impair the freedom of religion of individuals. In the court's interpretation, the government could 'nationalise' Yasukuni Shrine and make Shinto a state religion and no private person or organisation could do anything about it unless somebody were forced to embrace Shintoism.

The court's interpretation of freedom of religion is unacceptable. In a pluralistic society, tolerance is an indispensable collateral to religious freedom, but that does not mean that religious activities cannot violate the rights of other people. In the present case, the assertion that the enshrinement of her husband should be of no concern to Mrs Nakaya is absurd. If the deceased has given no instructions for his funeral, the family has, as a rule, the right to determine the way in which the funeral should be held and his memory observed. The shrine has the right to perform religious ceremonies and the veterans' association may request such ceremonies as long as they do not involve other people. But who gave the veterans' association the right to request the enshrinement of third parties? And who gave the shrine the right to deify people who had nothing to do with the shrine and any wish to be enshrined? These are questions the court should have addressed. The assertion that a Shinto ceremony offensive to the widow is protected by the constitutional guarantee of freedom of religion is so much against common sense that no jurist should have made it. Behind this position lies the government's desire to be able to enshrine military personnel regardless of the wishes of the relatives. The assertion that Mrs Nakaya's only legally relevant relation was with the chief priest of the shrine is simply erroneous. The parties that acted against her express wishes were the veterans' association and the SDF Liaison Office.

In a concurring opinion, three justices (Masao Takashima, Iwao Yotsuya, and Hikiyuki Okuno) found that religious neutrality might have been jeopardised by members of the SDF Liaison Office when they asserted that Takafumi's enshrinement was a matter of course since he had died in the line of duty, that the prefectural shrine for the war dead (*gokohu jinja*) was Japan's public religion (*kō no shukyo*) different from the religion cultivated by the family and that this kind of public worship was proper. These justices, however, maintained that a religious human right (*shūkyō-jō no jinkakuken*) or religious privacy was not a legally valid interest. In another concurring opinion, two justices (Rokuro Shimatani and Tetsuro Sato) came to the conclusion that the request for enshrinement was the joint action of the veterans' association and the SDF Liaison Office but that a violation of the principle of the separation of state and religion did not constitute an unlawful act against an individual if it did not infringe on his or her rights or legal interests and that a religious human right or religious privacy could not be recognised as a legal interest.

In his lone dissent, Justice Masami Ito maintained that the decisions of the lower courts had been right. The enshrinement of her husband against the wishes of Mrs Nakaya and his veneration by Shinto rites disturbed her peace of mind and constituted a legally valid interest. Justice Ito remarked that in the protection of basic human rights and particularly of spiritual freedom, the point of view of minorities had to be taken into consideration, especially by the judiciary. In the realm of thought and religion, this protection was important for minorities. Religious feelings were not sufficiently protected but it could not be denied that they constituted legal interests.

In the present case, it was improper to separate the chain of events leading to the request for enshrinement from the enshrinement itself. In a comprehensive view, the relationship of cause and effect between the application and the enshrinement was incontrovertible. The cooperation of the SDF Liaison Office may be called merely secretarial but in fact the office had been deeply involved in the matter from beginning to end. The cooperation between the SDF Liaison Office and the veterans' association had been extremely close and in view of the purpose of the enshrinement, which was the enhancement of the social position and morale of the SDF, it was appropriate to regard the request as a joint action. Although a violation of the separation of state and religion is not *eo ipso* an illegal act against individuals, the action in this case amounted to a serious disturbance of the constitutional order and the state is not in a position to demand that individuals should acquiesce in this action.

Justice Ito's conclusions were as follows: first, the request for enshrinement was inseparably connected with the enshrinement itself; secondly, the direct objective was to have the spirit of a member of the SDF venerated as *kami* in accordance with Shinto which was different from the ground-breaking ceremony of the Tsu case, which was a ceremony conducted in accordance with social custom; thirdly, the effect of the activities of the SDF Liaison Office was the special treatment of Shinto, giving help and assistance to a particular religion. Justice Ito, therefore, held that the state was responsible for unlawful actions and that Mrs Nakaya's claim should be recognised. Incidentally, Justice Ito is an Emeritus Professor of Tokyo University and his fields of specialisation are constitutional and Anglo-American law. A lawyer, Tsuguo Imamura, and the National Liaison Council to Support Yasuko Nakaya planned to bring the ruling of the Supreme Court to the attention of the UN Commission on Human Rights.

RELIGIOUS CEREMONIES: THE TSU CASE

The Supreme Court's decision on the ground-breaking ceremony of the city of Tsu, announced on 13 July 1977, was the court's first decision concerning freedom of religion. The facts of the case were as follows. In January 1965 the city of Tsu (Mie Prefecture) arranged for the ground-breaking ceremony for a city gymnasium. This ceremony, called *jichinsai*, is common in all construction projects and is usually a Shinto rite for the pacification of the earth spirits. The city paid ¥ 7,663 for the ceremony and Seiichi Sekiguchi, who attended the ceremony as a city councillor, brought suit claiming that the ceremony was a religious rite performed by a Shinto sect and thus the city's sponsorship of the rite violated the principle of separation of state and religion and the payment for the ceremony by the city was against Article 89 of the constitution. Sekiguchi demanded that the mayor reimburse the city for the expenses and pay him compensation of ¥ 50,000 because he had been made to attend a religious ceremony in which he did not believe.

The Tsu District Court held that the ground-breaking ceremony was a conventional performance so that the city's action did not offend against Article 20, paragraph 3 of the constitution and that the city's payment was not unlawful. The Nagoya High Court reversed the decision of the first instance. In the light of the meaning and the history of the ceremony, the court said, the *jichinsai* was a religious rite proper to shrine (religious) Shinto. Since it was impossible to discern whether it was just a social formality, a mere conventional observance or a quasi-religious function, the city was not allowed to sponsor the event and the action offended against the principle of the separation of state and religion. However, the court turned down the councillor's demand for compensation.

The Supreme Court split on the case ten to five. The majority held that the principle of separation did not mean that there should be no relation whatever between the state and religion. When the state regulated social life or implemented policies for the support and encouragement of education, welfare, culture, etc., there necessarily arose connections with religion. 'A complete separation of state and religion is near to impossible and would result in irrational situations. The separation, therefore, is of itself within certain limits and depending on the social and cultural conditions of each country, these limits become problematic. Hence, although the principle of separation of state and religion demands that the state be neutral in matters of religion, it does not mean that the state can have no relations whatever with religion. Depending on the purpose and effect of the action establishing a relation with religion, in case this relation exceeds the limits deemed appropriate in the light of the above conditions, it must be considered unallowable.'

As criteria for deciding whether the ground-breaking ceremony constituted a religious action forbidden by the constitution, the majority of the court examined the following points: the principle of the action; the religious evaluation by the ordinary man of the action; the intention of the performers, purpose, presence or absence and degree of a religious consciousness; effect and influence of the action on the ordinary man. Among religious ceremonies are many such as the pine trees (nowadays only twigs) put up at the gate for New Year, the bean-scattering ceremony at the end of winter (according to the old calendar) or the Christmas tree that, although initially of religious origin, over the years have lost their religious character and have become secular seasonal customs. The court conceded that the Shinto ground-breaking ceremony was connected with religion but that its purpose was to perform a formality following a general social custom which was entirely secular. Its effect was neither encouragement nor support of Shinto nor oppression of other religions and it did not constitute violation of Article 20, paragraph 3.

The decision further mentioned Japan's plurality of religions and the generally minimal interest of the Japanese in religion. Shrine Shinto is mainly concerned with festivals and ceremonies and hardly engages in the propaganda or proselytising often found in other religions. Noting that the ground-breaking ceremony was commonly regarded as a secular observance, the court said that it was unthinkable that the ceremony could result in a special relationship between the state and Shinto, let alone that Shinto would again acquire a privileged position and become a threat to the freedom of religion.

The minority opinion which was supported by Chief Justice Ekizō Fujibayashi contended that 'the constitutional principle of separation of state and religion must be interpreted to mean the complete separation between state and religion, i.e., the non-religious nature (*hishūkyōsei*) of the state. From this point of view, the religious activity mentioned in Article 20, paragraph 3 must be interpreted to include as a matter of course activities such as the propagation of religious doctrines or the religious instruction of the faithful but naturally also the performance of religious celebrations, ceremonies or functions. Religious functions which may have been secularised but may still be recognised as of a religious nature are also included in religious activities. In this regard, the ground-breaking ceremony involved in the present case retains a very strong religious colour, and evidently constitutes a religious activity in the meaning of Article 20, paragraph 3.'

I agree with the minority that in view of its history, meaning and ritual, the *jichinsai* constitutes without doubt a religious activity. The factors cited by the majority as criteria are legally irrelevant (what people think is of no concern to the law). But I do not accept the assertion that Article 20 demands the complete separation of state and religion and that the state should be non-religious. It is strange that the courts, instead of relying on the text of the constitution, base their arguments on the 'principle of separation of state and religion' which is not what the constitution says. The state (and its organs) cannot perform religious activities, order or direct them. But there is no basis for the assertion that it is unconstitutional if the state requests a religious ceremony (e.g., a Buddhist or Christian funeral service). In such a case, the state does not conduct a religious rite but the ministers of the religion in question perform the ceremony and are paid for their services. There is nothing in such an arrangement which would be in conflict with Article 89 of the constitution.

As mentioned above, the question was hotly debated in connection with the funeral of Emperor Hirohito (posthumously called Emperor Showa which was the name given to his reign). The funeral was divided into a religious part, conducted under the auspices and at the expense of the Imperial family and performed as a Shinto ritual,and a secular part sponsored and paid for by the government. It has been pointed out that on former occasions, the government saw no problem in shouldering the expenses of religious funerals. Empress Dowager

Teimei, the mother of Emperor Hirohito, was buried with Shinto ceremonies in 1951 and all expenses were borne by the state. In the same year, Kijūrō Shidehara, former Prime Minister and Speaker of the House of Representatives, was given a Buddhist funeral, while in 1949, Tsuneo Matsudaira, President of the House of Councillors, was buried with Shinto rites. In both cases, the respective legislative body paid the expenses.

WAR MEMORIALS

In March 1982 the Osaka District Court ruled that the municipal government of Minoo (Osaka Prefecture) acted unconstitutionally when it contributed land as a site for a momument dedicated to the war dead and financed its relocation. The monument was one of the numerous cenotaphs called *chūkonhi* (monument for loyal souls) found all over Japan. Until 1945 they were dedicated to the soldiers and sailors killed in the Sino-Japanese and Russo-Japanese wars and usually located in conspicuous public places. Between 1939 and the end of the war, the military tried to have a monument built in every locality. Because these memorials were regarded as symbols of militarism, the Occupation ordered their demolition. The *chūkonhi* of Minoo had been built in 1916 by the local branch of the veterans' association in commemoration of the 298 local men who had died in war. When the Occupation ended, the monument was retrieved from the place where it had been buried and restored to its old site in the grounds of a primary school.

In 1975 the city planned to build a swimming pool which necessitated the removal of the monument. The city bought a plot of land and financed the transfer of the memorial to the new site,spending a total of ¥ 86 million. In 1976 nine citizens brought suit against the mayor, the chairman of the Board of Education and other city officials demanding the reimbursement of ¥ 35 million on the basis of Articles 242-2 of the Local Autonomy Law (*Chihō Jichi-hō*) which allows citizens' suits against officials of local entities. The plaintiffs argued that the municipal government had violated Articles 20 and 89 of the constitution by preserving a symbol of militarism. The monument, they claimed, 'worshipped as heroic souls men who had looked up to the Emperor as a god and died in loyal devotion to the militaristic state. From every point of view, it is in conflict with the peace constitution.'

The court ruled that the *chūkonhi*, which have the nature of a memorial by displaying the word '*chūkon*', also function as objects of worship in the sense of worshipping the souls of the war dead by intimating the existence of the 'loyal souls'. The *chūkonhi* in question was also an object of worship based on a religious concept and constituted a religious institution serving for religious activities. By relocating the cenotaph on a plot owned by the city and giving the Association of Bereaved Families the free use of its property, the city became overly involved with religious institutions and violated Articles 20 and 89. According to Article 2, paragraph 16 of the Local Autonomy Law, the lease was invalid. The court ordered the mayor to make the Association of Bereaved Families remove the monument, return the land to the city's land development corporation and reimburse ¥ 78 million the city spent on the removal. The mayor and the chairman of the Board of Education were each ordered to pay ¥ 4.96 million of the expenses.

The Liberal-Democratic Party issued a statement criticising the decision and denied that the city's action had violated the constitution. 'To remember our compatriots who gave their lives for society and the state represents a natural and universal human feeling. The District Court's judgement, which totally negates this natural sentiment of the Japanese people challenges our traditional spiritual culture.' The party was obviously annoyed because the decision was a setback for its plans to nationalise Yasukuni Shrine.

The decision of the Osaka District Court was reversed by the Osaka High Court in July 1987. Presiding judge Shigeru Imatomi ruled that it was not unconstitutional for a local government to extend financial support for the relocation of the cenotaph and the Shinto ceremonies held by the Association of Bereaved Families. The cenotaph should be regarded as a simple monument dedicated to the war dead and not as an object of worship. Although the ceremonies performed were Shintoist, they were not necessarily purely religious activities because they were in accord with the social custom of consoling and praising the souls of the war dead. The participation of city officials did not constitute a violation of the constitutional principle of separation of state and religion.

The decision traced the development of the *chūkonhi* and explained that from the middle of the Meiji era these memorials served to foster patriotism and loyalty and that worship was enforced from the point of view of military education. Thus, these memorials provided support to state Shinto. But after the war, neither the Occupation nor the government regarded them as religious establishments. (The judge did not mention that the Occupation had ordered the removal of the monuments and that the cenotaph in question had been buried to avoid the ban by the Occupation.) Cenotaphs had been erected or restored all over the country (there are about 4,000 such cenotaphs). They had no connection with any religion and no relation with the militaristic ideology of the past. In honouring the war dead, they expressed a moral human attitude. The connection between Yasukuni Shrine, the prefectural shrine for the war dead (*gokoku jinja*) and the local cenotaph asserted by the plaintiffs did not exist, the judge stated, but did not mention that the 298 war dead whose names were inscribed on the cenotaph were enshrined at Yasukuni Shrine, one of the facts on which the plaintiffs relied for asserting the religious character of the monument.

The Association of Bereaved Families, the decision declared, was not a religious body and the Buddhist and Shinto ceremonies organised did not intend to promote a certain religion. The movement to have Yasukuni Shrine converted into a state shrine which the association supports intended only to honour the war dead and not to propagate Shinto. The constitutionality of the participation of city officials, the court explained, should be judged on the basis of the Tsu decision which has been interpreted to mean that a ceremony is not religious if its purpose has no religious meaning and its effects do not provide help to religion. The aim of the ceremonies in front of the cenotaph, the court held, was to console and honour the heroic souls but they were just a social custom and a civil rite. The participation of public personalities in these ceremonies was an act of social etiquette. There was no mention in the decision of the money spent by the city on the acquisition of the land and the removal of the cenotaph.

The decision contained nothing to disprove that the memorial and the rites performed in connection with it were expressions of Shinto beliefs. What Judge Imatomi called social customs were actually religious rituals. The bereaved families have an unquestionable right to console and praise the souls of the war dead in any way they like (within the limits of the law) but the state and its organs have no business to support activities such as those carried out at Minoo. The Minoo memorial was involved in another lawsuit in which citizens charged that the mayor and the superintendent of education had taken part in religious ceremonies in front of the war memorial organised by the Association of Bereaved Families. The Osaka District Court avoided blaming the officials for unconstitutional conduct. Since the ceremony was held with Buddhist and Shinto rites, the participation of the superintendent of education was not in an official capacity which would be against the constitution. 'To force a public official to participate in a religious rite by an official order is prohibited by constitutional regulation,' the court said. Therefore, he attended the ceremonies as a private citizen and must reimburse the city for the time that he attended in 1976 and 1977.

The string of decisions in favour of Shinto was continued by the verdict of Judge Norio Yamamoto of the Osaka District Court in October 1988 dismissing a suit of seven residents of Minoo city demanding that Mayor Buhei Nakai repay a subsidy of ¥445,000 granted to the Minoo Association of Bereaved Families for organising memorial services for the war dead and likewise indemnify the city for the services of city employees performed for the association. The association is affiliated with the Japan Association of Bereaved Families which has a cooperative agreement with the Association for Worshipping the Heroic Souls. The group promotes official visits to Yasukuni Jinja and supports efforts to have the state take over the shrine in order to enhance its public position.

Judge Yamamoto devoted the better part of his sentence to proving that the Association of Bereaved Families was not a religious organisation by showing that the elements of the courts' definitions of a religious body did not apply. The pre-war Yasukuni Shrine, the judge said, cultivated the worship of the Emperor and enshrined the spirits of those who died in war. Today, enshrinement (*eirei to shite gōshi sareru*) did not necessarily involve a relation to the Emperor but worshipped those who have died for the state. Judge Yamamoto contended that the religious meaning was slight and that the term 'heroic souls' (*eirei*) had assumed the general meaning of a laudatory expression. The foundation of the activities of the Japan Association of Bereaved Families was the religious idea of worshipping the souls of the war dead as *kami* in the Yasukuni Shrine. It promoted state support for the shrine and cooperated with the religious activities of this and other shrines for the war dead. In this sense, the work of honouring the heroic spirits possesses an affinity with the religious thought of Yasukuni Shrine and the propensity of easily tying up with it. Since Yasukuni Shrine has lost its pre-war character of being a state shrine and state Shinto has disappeared, the connection had lost some of its strength. Because the relatives (ie., the war dead) were worshipped by the state irrespective of the wishes of the bereaved families, it transcended the consciousness of worshipping and it was difficult to judge to what extent the bereaved families believed in the doctrines of Yasukuni Shrine and positively desired the development of the shrine.

In a comprehensive consideration, the judge wrote, it was impossible to say that the Japan Association of Bereaved Families was a group of believers in Yasukuni Shrine and it was not a religious institution or association in the sense of the first part of Article 89 or a religious organisation in the sense of Article 20, paragraph 1. Neither could the Minoo Association of Bereaved Families, the judge stated, be considered a group for the purpose of religious activities or an organisation united by the same religious views. There was no reason, therefore, for the assertion of the plaintiffs that the actions considered in the case contravened constitutional provisions. It could not be denied that the actions dealt with in this case supported and promoted the activities of the city Association of Bereaved Families (organisation of meetings for worshipping the heroic spirits and the arrangement of trips for paying homage at Yasukuni Shrine) which were related to religion. But the purpose of these activities was the purely secular effort of support provided from the point of view of promoting the welfare of the bereaved families. Although these activities constituted an important part of the work of the association, it was for the secular purpose of the spiritual consolation of the bereaved families. The assistance given to the religious activities of the association was only indirect. The actions cannot be considered to transcend the appropriate degree.

It is difficult to understand why it took the Osaka District Court 11 years to produce this decision. The court avoided giving a straight answer to the question of whether Shinto rites performed in front of the war memorial mentioned in the earlier case and based on Shinto ideology constitute religious activities. Many religious activities provide consolation. This may be called a secular effect but it does not divest the activities of their religious character.

The pre-war tradition of supporting Shinto because of its relation with patriotism (or nationalism) dies very hard. In Tokushima, the prefectural shrine for the war dead (*shōkonsha*) was built in 1938 on 2,900m^2 of land owned by the city and made available for the construction of the shrine at no cost. The shrine was renamed *gokokuji* in 1939 and 34,354 natives of the prefecture who died in war (including the Second World War) are enshrined there. A government circular issued after the promulgation of the constitution asked local governments to sell the land occupied by shrines and temples at half of the market value but Tokushima took no action. In recent years, the Tokushima municipal authorities have come under fire for letting the shrine use public property free of charge.

Eleven members of the Japan Mothers' Convention instituted a suit to have a monument,erected at the site of the former Sugamo prison (where General Hideki Tōjō and the other defendants in the Tokyo War Crime Trials were held),removed. The plaintiffs were later joined by another group of twelve women. The monument was built in a specially designed park at a cost of ¥ 250 million by a firm which bought the site for Ikebukuro Sunshine City and donated the park and monument to Toshima Ward. The suit alleged that the monument violated the constitution by venerating the death of war criminals and contravened the provisions of the Public Park Law. The plaintiffs demanded that the payment of public funds to maintain the memorial be stopped.

On 23 June 1989 the Tokyo District Court rejected the group's demand to have the monument removed. Presiding Judge Tatsunori Shishido declared that the monument did not censure the execution of the war criminals as unfair or treat the class A war criminals as victims of the war. He ruled that the removal of the monument could not be the objective of a financial suit by the residents. The monument, the judge declared, implied neither a positive nor a negative value judgement on the war crime trials. Its purpose and social effect was merely to record the historic fact and did not raise any constitutional problems.

Chapter 6

Japan's Election System: An Unequal Equation

DISTRIBUTION OF DIET SEATS

On account of their strength in the Diet, the conservatives have been in charge of Japan's government since the formation of the Ashida cabinet in 1948. They lost their majority in the House of Councillors in July 1989 but retained a majority in the House of Representatives in the February 1990 election. One of the factors facilitating the ascendancy of the conservative parties is the election system, which favours the rural voters at the expense of the urban population. As mentioned above, the election system is different for the House of Councillors and the House of Representatives. Representatives are elected from multi-member election districts. There is one constituency which elects only one representative and another which elects six; all others elect between two and five representatives (total House membership 512). For the House of Councillors, 100 members are chosen by the country at large while the prefectures serve as election districts for 152 Upper House members. As laid down in Article 46 of the constitution, the term of office for Upper House members is six years, and the election of half of the members takes place every three years. In each election, therefore, 50 members are chosen from the country as a whole - a system of proportional representation is now used - and 76 are elected in the prefectures. From one to four seats are allocated to each prefecture depending on the size of the population.

For local elections (prefectural and municipal assemblies), the Public Office Election Law explicitly requires that the representatives are allocated 'in proportion to the population' (Art. 15, par. 7), but there is no equivalent provision for national elections and the courts have only reluctantly conceded that the principle of equality laid down in Article 14 of the constitution applies to elections. The disparity between the number of seats allocated to an election district and the number of voters has been the point of contention in numerous lawsuits in which the performance of the courts, especially the Supreme Court, has been far from admirable.

POLITICIANS

The failure of the Diet to adjust the distribution of seats in accordance with demographic changes results from the inclination of individual politicians as well as political parties and their factions to protect their own vested interests. According to the route by which individuals enter national politics, three types may be distinguished: local politicians aspiring after a more influential job or recruited by the party bureaucracy to run for office, high-ranking bureaucrats, and officials of large organisations such as trade unions or women's associations. The last two classes are more common in the Upper House. The usual way in which politicians build up their reputation and acquire a following is by organising a supporters' group (called *kōenkai*). Many politicians who start out as representatives in local assemblies come from small towns or rural communities, and cultivating personal relations with their constituents is indispensable to their success. This includes attending weddings and funerals, or at least having an aide present a suitable gift, sending greetings for New Year or Mid-year which must be accompanied by appropriate gifts for important supporters, helping their children to be admitted to 'good' schools, offering congratulations on their graduation and finding employment in a 'good' company.

For many politicians from rural areas, the core of their supporters is the *buraku* community, the traditional village dating from feudal times. As a social unit, the *buraku* was usually controlled by the large land-owning families and the interests of the *buraku* continued to dominate local politics long after their legal abolition in 1947. The opposition of politicians to the liberalisation of rice imports had nothing to do with what the government called 'food security' but was simply dictated by the concern for the farm vote.

POLITICIANS AND MONEY

A politician's influence does not depend on his convictions or programmes nor on his or her personality but on the amount of money he or she can dispense. The Political Funds Control Law requires reports on revenues, donations and borrowings by political parties and organisations as well as expenditure. Funds raised in 1990 amounted to ¥ 184,490 million, up 6.4 per cent over the preceding year. The election to the House of Representatives in February 1990 and the gubernatorial, prefectural and municipal elections in April stimulated fund-raising activities. Party income reported to prefectural election administrative committees in 1989 amounted to ¥ 150.87 billion, bringing the total of reported political funds for that year to ¥ 324.2 billion.

For 1990 the total of political funds raised by all parties amounted to ¥ 337.38 billion. Party headquarters and nation-wide organisations collected ¥ 184.49 billion, local organisations raised ¥ 151.64 billion. Experts think that actual amounts raised and spent are about three or four times the reported amounts. While the sources of funds must be itemised, no strict accounting of the expenditures is required. Moreover, political parties must report only donations exceeding ¥ 10,000 and individual politicians only those exceeding ¥ 1 million. These stipulations are often abused by splitting up large sums. Donations from one company are limited to ¥ 1.5 million a year but this regulation is easily circumvented.

For many years the Communist Party has topped the list of the funds raised by political parties because, unlike other parties, all revenues are channelled exclusively to the party. In 1990 the party collected ¥ 32.05 billion, mostly from membership dues and sales of publications. The Liberal-Democratic Party was second with revenues of ¥ 30.84 billion which included ¥ 10.62 billion in donations from corporations and ¥ 15 billion borrowed from nine banks. In addition to the funds collected by the party as a whole, the five major LDP factions received a total of ¥ 7.4 billion in donations.

Altogether, 158 corporations and business groups made donations exceeding ¥ 30 million. Among the 20 largest donors were 16 banks. Fund-raising parties were held by 130 groups bringing in a net total of ¥ 2.31 billion. Funds spent for election campaigns detailed in the reports were ¥ 1.18 billion disbursed by the Abe faction, ¥ 330 million by the Miyazawa faction, ¥ 930 million by the Watanabe faction and ¥ 560 million by the Komoto faction. Members of the Abe faction contesting the election received between ¥ 10 million and ¥ 20 million, those of the Watanabe faction between ¥ 5 million and ¥ 20 million.

In August 1988 Takako Doi, then Chairwoman of the Japan Socialist Party, received a salary of ¥ 1,065,000 (in July 1989 the monthly salary of the members of the House of Representatives was ¥ 1,094,000). Mrs Doi received a tax-exempt allowance of ¥ 750,000 for correspondence and communications expenses. All members of the Diet are given free passes by Japan's railway companies and coupons worth ¥ 65,000 a month for domestic airlines. They are also entitled to have two secretaries whose salaries (¥ 671,770 a month) are paid directly by the state. Mrs Doi's take-home pay after taxes and contributions to the party came to ¥ 381,195. She earned additional income from lecture fees and was helped by political donations from supporters.

Politicians have improved on Japan's customary semi-annual bonuses and voted themselves three bonuses each fiscal year (in 1989: ¥ 1,835,150 in June, ¥ 2,491,375 in December, and ¥ 655,625 in March). A pension system for Diet members was established in 1958. The annual premium of ¥ 93,993 has not been changed since the adoption of the pension plan. A Diet member retiring after ten years of service is entitled to a yearly pension of ¥ 3,876,000 (¥ 323,000 a month); after twenty years of service, the yearly pension rises to ¥ 4,651,200 (¥ 387,600 a month); after thirty years, he receives ¥ 5,426,600 (¥ 452,200 a month); after forty years, ¥ 6,201,600 (¥ 516,400 a month). Should his career span half a century, his pension would amount to ¥ 6,976,800 (¥ 581,400 a month). This scheme should encourage politicians to serve as long as possible. If a member of the Diet dies, his surviving spouse receives half the pension. Since the premium payments are insufficient to fund the pension payments, the deficiency is made up by the government, i.e. from taxes.

A study group of 19 junior dietmen belonging to the Liberal-Democratic Party published an analysis of the 1987 revenues and expenditures of its members. Revenues averaged ¥ 126 million of which political donations accounted for ¥ 54 million, fund-raising parties for ¥ 20 million and support from party factions for ¥ 10 million. The average spending for political activities came to ¥ 116 million. Personnel expenses required ¥ 39 million, cash gifts for weddings and funerals ¥ 16 million and the management of support groups ¥ 18 million. The highest expenditure of a member of the group amounted to ¥ 109 million, the lowest was ¥ 63 million.

Typically, a politician from outside Tokyo employs 13 secretaries (eight in his constituency and five in Tokyo) at a yearly cost of ¥ 30 million. He spends ¥ 5-6 million on ten telephone lines, ¥ 15 million on petrol, ¥ 7-8 million on New Year cards to his supporters and about the same amount on newsletters. If he attends the wedding party of a member of his *kōenkai*, he is expected to make a gift of about ¥ 30,000; if he functions as *nakōdō* (matchmaker), his gift will be ¥ 70,000. For weddings other than those of his supporters, he must donate ¥ 20,000; for funerals, his condolence money will be ¥ 10,000. Mid-year and New Year gifts will cost about ¥ 6 million and get-well gifts for elderly patients about ¥ 700,000 a year. Politicians from outside the capital often invite their constituents on sightseeing tours in Tokyo, including a visit to the Diet building. With one overnight stay, such invitations cost at least ¥ 40,000 per person.

In his 1988 political fund report to the Home Ministry, Shizuka Kamei, a representative from Hiroshima, listed among the expenditure categories gloves for baseball tournaments, lunch boxes and prizes for marathon and other sports meetings, and paper lanterns for the *O-bon* festival. Because a politician has to create and maintain the image of a benefactor and patron of his home constituency, he must contribute to local causes, festivals, sports and other entertainment. The possibilities for collecting money within the constituency are rather limited outside the large cities, which leads to a heavy concentration of fund-raising activities in the metropolitan areas.

Members of the Diet cannot hold any other public office (except those connected with the cabinet), but they can engage in other remunerative activities. Gifts to government officials for favours received are only bribes if the favour was an act within the competence of the official. Members of the Diet who are not members of the cabinet or committee chairmen can use their influence without the risk of breaking the law. A politician performing a favour for a businessman will receive a money gift in return. If the deal is of some importance, the gift may amount to ¥ 300,000 - ¥ 500,000. The situation is more or less the same for local assemblies. Activities are on a smaller scale but local politicians are under the same pressure to cultivate relations with their constituencies as the members of the Diet. The issues involved in local politics often relate to everyday living conditions and present problems on which the views of the local population may be divided. Environmental pollution has given rise to many local disputes. The construction of garbage incinerators or sewage treatment plants is invariably opposed by the residents of the neighbourhood where such facilities are to be built. Zoning ordinances or plans for new roads often cause dissent. Road construction has been delayed for over ten years because people refused to vacate just a small piece of land. The construction of power plants, particularly of nuclear power stations, has been accompanied by drawn-out conflicts between local communities and the authorities. The most ferocious battles have been fought over the construction of Narita Airport.

The remuneration of the members of local councils (assemblies) is less generous than that the Diet members have voted for themselves but it is by no means insignificant. In 1988 the national average monthly salary of local assembly members amounted to ¥ 315,700, but the remuneration in the large cities was much higher. The highest salary was paid in Nagoya, ¥ 810,000; others were Kyoto ¥ 790,000, Osaka ¥ 780,000, Kobe ¥ 770,000, Tokyo ¥ 718,000, Yokohama ¥ 710,000, Sapporo ¥ 680,000, Kitakyushu and Kawasaki ¥ 640,000 (these cities have over a million inhabitants). Assemblymen in Ryotsu (Niigata Prefecture) received the lowest salary of ¥ 167,000. For cities with less than 50,000 inhabitants the average pay was ¥ 245,000, for those with 400,000 inhabitants, ¥ 497,500, and for cities with over 500,000 inhabitants, the average was ¥ 532,000.

SECOND-GENERATION POLITICIANS

A phenomenon characteristic of the generational change in the post-war period is the appearance of second-generation personalities in various segments of Japanese society. The most prominent field in which sons (very seldom daughters but occasionally sons-in-law) succeed their fathers is medicine. Physicians want their sons to become doctors because they have made a major investment in their clinics and hope that they can pass on their practice to them. Also numerous are second-generation politicians. At the end of 1988, 128 of the 501 members of the Lower House were the sons or adopted sons of legislators. Of the 297 members of the Liberal-Democratic Party, 115 belonged to the second generation. These politicians, who accounted for 39 per cent of all members of the Diet, enjoy a considerable advantage because they inherit a well-publicised name, loyal supporters and stable sources of money. As in the medical profession, it is difficult for politicians to recoup their investment in one generation.

Of the 390 or so candidates of the Liberal-Democratic Party in the February 1990 election, 135 were sons, sons-in-law or other relatives of members of the Diet or prefectural governors. The fathers of ten of the 44 candidates backed by the Democratic Socialist Party were former politicians and of the nearly 150 candidates of the Socialist Party, 11 were sons or sons-in-law of incumbent or former Diet members. In the United States voters dissatisfied with the performance of their elected representatives opposed the tendency of politicians to cling to their posts regardless of their records. Voters in Oklahoma approved an amendment to the state constitution limiting all future legislators to a maximum of 12 years in office. In California two proposals on term limitations were on the November 1990 ballot and a similar proposal was made in Washington State in 1991 although these proposals failed to be adopted. Veteran office-holders lost primaries to political newcomers.

Naturally, it is advantageous to the party if its members can retain their seats and this advantage will be put in jeopardy if there is a change in election districts. The aversion to redistribution of seats is strongest in the Liberal-Democratic Party because in most cases an adjustment would reduce the number of representatives from rural districts and increase those from the large cities. The opposition to change is particularly strong among party factions. The multi-member constituency system furthers the factionalism which was already rampant in the Meiji era and even small changes in numbers can upset the factional balance. Although the electorate has no influence on the distribution of seats, the districts which would be adversely affected by an adjustment of seats usually join Diet members in opposing corrective measures.

REFORM OF THE ELECTORAL SYSTEM

Prime Minister Toshiki Kaifu, who had made political reform a major goal of his administration, endorsed the plan of the Election System Council to introduce a system combining single-seat constituencies with proportional representation. The number of representatives was to be reduced from 512 to 471,of whom 300 were to be elected in single-seat constituencies and 171 in proportional representation. The new regulation would abolish the ban on house-to-house canvassing although limitations would be imposed on the number of canvassers and the length of the visits.

A subcommittee which drew up guidelines for the demarcation of the constituencies proposed that no constituency should be larger than twice the size of any other constituency. The population of all constituencies should fall within a range of 274,692 to 549,384. These figures represented deviations of one-third from the figure obtained by dividing the number of the total population by the number of seats to be allocated. Cities and wards with a population larger than 549,000 would be divided into an appropriate number of single-seat constituencies but otherwise, cities, wards, towns and villages would not be split. No constituency would comprise two separate areas, no

two-seat constituencies would be created and, further diluting the population principle, historical and social conditions might be taken into consideration.
Kochi Prefecture would be the smallest constituency, with about 250,000 inhabitants, and five other constituencies would have fewer than 274,000 inhabitants. Twenty-seven constituencies would have a population of more than twice the size of Kochi and a vote in the smallest constituency would have 2.15 times the value of a vote in the largest constituency. The opposition charged that the constituencies created in the districts which had to be divided were delineated in the subcommittee's proposal to coincide with the power bases of LDP politicians.

The proposal obviously failed to remedy the shortcomings in the present system and the opposition parties unanimously rejected the one-seat constituency system as a scheme to perpetuate the ascendancy of the Liberal-Democratic Party. A second proposal was meant to impose limits on the funds collected by politicians. A politician could procure no more than ¥ 1 million from an individual or company official through the sale of tickets to a fund-raising party. The ceiling would be ¥ 1.5 million if the event were organised by a political party. Opponents charged that the proposal was full of loopholes. As an example they pointed out that there was no limit on the number of officials of the same company who could make donations.

A third measure devised by the LDP committee provided that the government should shoulder part of the cost of elections by giving subsidies to political parties. The proposal mentioned a total of ¥ 30 billion, a figure obtained by multiplying the population by ¥ 250. Masaya Miyoshi, Executive Director of Keidanren, opined that elections and other political expenditures should be shared equally by the government, the parties and support groups. Independents would be allowed to run for the proportional representation seats but time on public television would be allotted to parties only, not to individuals. After a transition period of five years, business and labour organisations would be prohibited from making political donations to individuals. Each politician would be limited to two fund-raising support groups.

INEQUALITY IN THE VALUE OF VOTES

Controversies concerning the inequality in the distribution of Diet seats has occupied the courts many times in the post-war era. Of the earlier decisions, two rulings of the Supreme Court in 1964 should be mentioned. The first decision was handed down on 5 February 1964. The case concerned the election to the House of Councillors in July 1962 and rejected an appeal against the ruling of the Tokyo High Court which had refused to nullify the election results of the Tokyo electoral district. In the original complaint, the plaintiffs had argued that in the Tokyo electoral district, one seat in the Upper House was allocated to

740,000 electors whereas in Tottori Prefecture, the ration was 180,000 electors to one seat. One vote in Tokyo, therefore, was worth only a quarter of a vote in Tottori. Although strict arithmetical proportion might be impossible, the plaintiffs claimed, there was no reason for the unequal treatment of one part of the population which violated the principle of equality laid down in Article 14 of the constitution.

The Metropolitan Election Management Commission retorted that the allocation of seats was a highly political problem not subject to judicial review. The courts, therefore, were incompetent to judge the appropriateness of the distribution. Furthermore, the proportion to the population was not the only factor to be considered; the size of the election district and historical conditions had to be taken into account. The legislature should be free to make the appropriate arrangements.

The Tokyo High Court ruled that the matter was subject to judicial review but that Article 14 of the constitution forebade only discrimination because of race, creed, sex, social status or family origin and that Article 43 left all matters concerning electoral districts to the legislature. The allocation of seats, therefore, was a matter of legislative discretion and the constitution did not require an allocation of seats strictly proportional to the population. Naturally, there were limits and if the inequality were to be excessive, the election would be invalid. This, however, the court concluded, was not the case in the suit before the court. The Grand Bench of the Supreme Court turned down an appeal by the plaintiffs on two grounds. First, the distribution of seats was left to the discretion of the legislature and, second, the proportion to the electorate was not the decisive factor. Since the constitution had left the regulation of elections to the legislature, the Diet had the right to determine the modalities of the elections. The Diet, therefore, could by law introduce the distinction between the national constituency and local constituencies, circumscribe the local constituencies and fix the number of councillors to be elected in each constituency.

The allocation of seats in proportion to the population of the individual constituencies was desirable in view of the principle of equality before the law laid down in the constitution. Although it could not be denied that the proportion to the population was the main element to be considered in the allocation of seats, this did not prevent other factors being taken into account. One such factor was the provision in the constitution that half of the members of the Upper House should be elected every three years. This implied that each constituency should have at least two seats. It was, therefore, difficult to reduce the number of seats of constituencies which already had only two seats. Moreover, it was not unreasonable to consider the size of the constituency, the history of the region, and its relation to the administrative structure. Unless there were serious inequalities, the distribution of seats was inconsequential for the exercise of the right to vote, and the question of the ratio of the number of seats to the population of the constituency was for the legislature to decide. Even if, as in the present case, some inequalities occur, it is a question of the appropriateness of legislative policy and not of constitutionality.

I find the decision as well as the reasoning of the court open to question. Behind this decision are two erroneous assumptions. The first is the way of thinking of the division of powers. Before the war the so-called continental theory was dominant in Japanese legal thinking. It stresses the independence of each branch of the government and its own assessment of its competence. The Anglo-American concept of the division of powers implies the theory of checks and balances which is the foundation of the power of the Supreme Court to determine the constitutionality of any law, order, regulation or official act (Art. 81). In fact, in many cases, the Supreme Court has avoided forming its own judgement on the constitutionality of the policies and measures of the legislature or the government and has gone to unreasonable length to uphold the lawfulness of legislative or governmental action.

The determination of the election methods is the right of the legislature but it cannot disregard relevant constitutional or legal provisions. While the court maintains that the ratio to the number of electors constitutes a basic requirement for the distribution of seats, it does not give the slightest reason for its assertion that the case before the court did not involve extreme inequality in the enjoyment of the right to vote. This is the personal opinion of the judges without any foundation in fact. The second point to be noted in the case is the thought underlying the reasoning of the court that the members of the Diet are representatives of the constituency in which they are elected. What the decision refers to as other factors to be considered in determining the number of seats to be allocated to each constituency relies on the premise that the Diet members represent a particular constituency. The example used by the court, that no constituency should have fewer than two councillors is only meaningful on the assumption that they are delegates of the particular election district. On the supposition that all members of the Diet, no matter where and how they are elected, are representatives of the entire people (Article 43 of the constitution), the argument proves nothing.

The system of representative government undoubtedly originated from the arrangement that delegates or procurators acted as agents of a certain locality or even more often (particularly in the Church) of a body of people. But the principle that all members of the popular assembly are representatives of the entire people was expressly laid down in the 1791 French constitution adopted after the French Revolution, and the constitution of the German Empire of 1871 stated that the members of the Imperial Diet were representatives of the entire people and could not be bound by instructions or orders from their constituents. Germany's Weimar constitution contained a provision to the same effect. The Fundamental Law of the German Federal Republic says: 'They (i.e., the members of the German Federal Assembly) are representatives of the entire people, not bound to mandates and instructions and only subject to their consciences' (Art. 38, par. 1).

The decision of the Tokyo High Court must be faulted for much the same reasons. There are limits to the discretion of the legislature, and although the constitution does not state that seats must be allocated in proportion to the electorate in an election district, there can be no doubt that the election system should conform to the principle of equality before the law. It is not a question of 'extreme inequality' or what the people's sense of justice will tolerate but of respect for basic constitutional principles. The reluctance of the courts to enforce strict adherence to the principle of equality is all the more regrettable because elections are frequently marred by fraud, particularly by vote-buying. There are too many politicians who have a very cavalier attitude towards vote-buying and other illegal practices. One of the worst offenders, Eitaro Itoyama, who was ordered by the Kobe District Court to quit the Diet (he had been parliamentary Vice-Minister of Agriculture, Forestry and Fisheries), declared that he did not resign in order to take responsibility for the election law violations but to enable the LDP to win the next election. Itoyama married the step-daughter of Ryōhei Sasakawa, younger brother of Ryōichi Sasakawa, Chairman of the Japan Shipbuilding Industry Foundation which is financed by earnings from motor-boat races. The foundation's fiscal 1991 budget amounted to ¥ 136.09 billion. In his report on the elections to the House of Councillors in 1974, Itoyama stated that he spent ¥ 18 million (¥ 10 million from the LDP and ¥ 8 million from an association of supporters). He was said to have actually spent between ¥ 800 million and ¥ 1 billion.

THE SUPREME COURT'S 1974 DECISION

In an administrative suit against the Metropolitan Election Management Commission, a group of Tokyo electors charged that in the June 1971 election to the House of Councillors, the imbalance in the allocation of seats had made the election unconstitutional. On 31 July 1973 the Tokyo High Court found that, 'compared with the population, the Annexed Table 2 of the Public Office Election Law which determined the allocated number of dietmen for each local constituency, shows that an unequal distribution exists and unconstitutionality is suspected.' But the court rejected the demand for new elections which, the court said, were actually impossible.

The Election Management Commission had argued that the allocation of seats was the exclusive right of the legislature and that this action was beyond interference by the judiciary. To this, the court replied that the distribution of seats had a direct influence on the right to vote of the electors and constituted a serious, fundamental problem. If the inequality in the allocation of seats violated equality among the voters, the mere fact that the distribution of seats was the exclusive right of the legislature could not be allowed to place the issue beyond judicial review.

At the time of this decision, an official of the Metropolitan Election Management Commission recognised that the existing distribution of seats was irrational but on 25 April 1974 the Supreme Court rejected the demand to declare the election invalid. As long as there is no extreme inequality, the court declared, the distribution of seats is a question of the legislative policy of the Diet, and there had been no extreme inequality in the case before the court. There was no explanation on the grounds on which it had been decided that there had been no extreme inequality or why the suspicion of unconstitutionality voiced by the Tokyo High Court was unfounded. The insincerity of the Supreme Court in handling this case was appalling. A few days later, the Tokyo High Court turned down an administrative suit by a group of Tokyo voters claiming that the 1972 elections to the House of Representatives had been unconstitutional. As long as no extreme inequality arises, the election cannot be termed unconstitutional, the court ruled. The anger of the plaintiffs over these decisions is quite understandable. 'For goodness sake, what degree of inequality is unconstitutional? We want to be shown a standard for this!' Not even once in the ten years that the debate had been going on did the courts seriously consider this problem.

THE 1976 DECISION

The Supreme Court announced another decision on this issue on 14 April 1976. The suit concerned the December 1974 elections to the House of Representatives which voters from Chiba Prefecture wanted to have declared unconstitutional. In its ruling, the court stated that the Diet should have established a rational election system. 'Naturally, the equality of the ratio between the electors of the population of each election district and the allocated number of seats must be the most important and basic standard, but in addition, the prefectural division which forms the basis of the election district partition is an element that cannot be overlooked. In the further division of the prefectures, factors such as the results of earlier elections, the integrative power of the election district, cities, towns and villages and other administrative units, size (of the election district), density of population, type of inhabitants, transportation facilities, geographical conditions etc. are to be considered and the relation with the seats to be allocated is to be taken into account in making a concrete decision.

'Moreover, how the rapid changes in society, of which the urban conglomeration of the population is one phenomenon, should be taken into account and how it should be reflected in the division into election districts and the allocation of seats is one of the high policy factors to be considered in the Diet. Various elements, therefore, can be taken into consideration in the partition into election districts and the allocation of seats. Nevertheless, even if from this point of view allowance is made for all the elements which can be considered in the

Diet, if the inequality in the concrete value of votes has reached such a degree that it cannot possibly be regarded as generally possessing rationality, it must be inferred that the limit of the Diet's rational discretion has been transcended and unless a special reason is shown justifying this inequality, it must be judged to constitute a violation of the constitution.'

The court pointed out that despite a revision of the Election Law which brought the inequality in the ratio of the value of one vote in the most under-represented districts to the most over-represented districts to 1 : 2, the discrepancy from the national average of the number of votes necessary to elect one representative was 47.3 per cent for the most over-represented district and 162.87 per cent for the most under-represented constituency. The conclusion of the court was 'The inequality in the value of votes shown by this discrepancy was of such an extent that even if all factors mentioned above, particularly the necessity of coping with the rapid social changes, were included in a certain discretion in policy, it could not possibly be thought to generally possess rationality and was a condition contravening the equality of the right to vote required by the constitution.'

Since there had been no correction within the constitutionally required reasonable time, the determination of the election districts and the allocation of seats for the 10 December 1972 election to the House of Representatives violated the constitution. The inequality in the value of votes was not just a matter of some particular constituencies but vitiated the entire distribution schedule. Because the election was based on an unconstitutional distribution of seats, it was unlawful, but from the point of view of the public welfare, an unlawful administrative disposition need not necessarily be nullified. Pursuant to this legal principle as laid down in paragraph 1 of Article 31 of the Law of Administrative Procedure, the court did not invalidate the election but made its unlawfulness public.

The decision summarised above was the majority opinion supported by eight of the fifteen justices. Five justices held that the distribution schedule was divisible and that only the part concerning the Chiba 1 constituency should be called unconstitutional and the election invalidated. One of the justices thought that the allocation of seats to Chiba 1 was unconstitutional but that the election was valid while another justice wanted to have the suit rejected. Actually, the inequality was much greater than described by the court. The Osaka 3 constituency was allocated four seats for 1,590,783 voters, while the Hyogo 5 district had three seats for 238,209 voters. This gave Osaka 3 one seat for 397,696 voters and Hyogo 5 one seat for 73,770 voters, a ratio of 5.39 to 1. The national average was one seat for 150,245 voters. In actual voting, the candidate elected with the least votes in the Osaka 3 constituency needed 186,930 votes while the only candidate elected for the Amami Islands received 38,305 votes and the candidate elected with the lowest number of votes in the Niigata 3 constituency came in with

39,869 votes. This corresponded to a ratio of 4.88 to 1 or 4.69 to 1.

This situation shows that the Diet's exercise of discretion was far from reasonable and constituted a serious neglect of its duty to respect and uphold the constitution (Art. 99). Whereas in its 1964 decision, the Supreme Court expressed no opinion, it clearly stated in its 1976 decision that despite the absence of an express limitation, the Diet must exercise its discretion in a reasonable way and that its actions must be held unconstitutional if they transcend the limits of reasonable discretion. But the court did not indicate a standard of rationality and it is only the court's opinion which decides what is reasonable and unreasonable. The absence of an objective standard makes it impossible to determine whether the election system complies with the principle of equality laid down in the constitution.

REPRESENTATIVE PARLIAMENTARIANISM

There is no reason to assume that the system of representative parliamentarianism is no longer capable of evolution and improvement. As a matter of fact, the system now existing in Western democracies belongs to the horse-and-carriage times when transportation and communications had progressed little beyond the Middle Ages. In today's world, local constituencies are just as unnecessary as town criers and city gates. Modern technology would make it possible to allow any voter at any place to vote for any candidate. The main reason why such a system is not installed is the vested interest of the present office-holders who want to preserve their fiefs. The negative aspects of Japan's experience with the national constituency for the House of Councillors elections are not fatal. A better-educated, more sophisticated public will be less inclined to elect TV personalities who do not possess qualities required for political leadership, and the election of people supported by large national organisations has certain advantages. If electioneering were restricted to legally sanctioned activities and limits on election spending were strictly enforced, elections would not be exorbitantly expensive.

In December 1979 the Supreme Court dismissed appeals from two opposite decisions of the Tokyo High Court. Both cases concerned the December 1976 elections to the House of Representatives demanding the nullification of the elections because of the inequality in the allocation of seats. In a decision announced on 11 September 1978, the ninth chamber of the Tokyo High Court (Judge Satoru Ando presiding) rejected the demand of a group of voters from three election districts in Tokyo, Chiba and Kanagawa prefectures for the nullification of the elections. On 13 September the thirteenth chamber of the court (Judge Mitsuhiko Yasuoka presiding) recognised the claim of voters from ten election districts in Tokyo, Kanagawa, Saitama and Chiba that in order to ensure the equality of votes, the ratio of seats to the population was the most important factor and that in the election in December 1976, the discrepancy (one vote in the election district with the lowest number of voters per seat was equal to 3.5 votes in the election district with the highest number of voters per seat) exceeded the permissible disparity which made the entire allocation of seats, and consequently the election itself, unconstitutional. In nine constituencies, candidates who had received over 100,000 votes failed to be elected while in 89 constituencies all candidates were elected with less than 100,000 votes. In the Niigata 3 district, the candidate elected with the lowest number of votes needed only 37,107 votes.

Judge Ando recognised that the equality in the ratio of seats allocated to each constituency with the number of its voters was the primary consideration but contended that the problem could not be solved merely on the basis of a simple numerical ratio. By taking into account the importance of the local entities in the value of votes, it is possible to offset to a certain extent the difference between the urban conglomerates and the economically and culturally disadvantaged, sparsely populated regions. There is a great probability, Judge Ando reasoned, that the political power of the large metropolitan areas would be much stronger than that of rural districts. If perfect numerical equality in the right to vote were to be established, the political influence of the urban districts would become dominant and enable the urban population to enjoy political, economic and cultural advantages. Such a situation would not be desirable.

An allocation of seats merely proportional to the number of voters would severely diminish the political strength of the depopulated areas which greatly need strong political influence. Since human society is composed of people with different and multifarious qualities, simple arithmetic equality cannot possibly ensure fair representation. In view of the political function of local bodies, the Diet must have wide discretion in determining the election districts in relation to territorial limits, population and the number of representatives. Moreover, in determining the discrepancy in the value of votes, the comparison should not be made between the most over-represented and the most under-represented constituencies but with the national average. If the national average according to the 1970 census would be equal to 1, the ratio would be 1.04 for Chiba 4, 1.5 for Kanagawa and 1.08 for Tokyo 7. Such a discrepancy in the value of votes would be reasonable and within the limits of the discretion of the Diet.

Judge Ando made a respectable effort to buttress his decision but his arguments are not convincing. To take his last argument first; the basis is incorrect because the allocation of seats should be compared with the number of voters and not with the total population. But even assuming Judge Ando's premises, his arithmetic is faulty. According to the 1970 census, Japan's population came to 104,665,171 which, divided by 511 (the number of House seats at that time), gives 204,824. Judge Ando has used this figure for calculating the ratio for Kanagawa 3, but in calculating the ratios for Chiba 4 and Tokyo 7, he used the figure 304,824 (100,000 higher), so that the actual ratios according to Judge Ando's method should be: Chiba 4 1.51 and Tokyo 7, 1.6.

On the basis of the 1970 census, the Diet adjusted the distribution of seats in 1975, but the 1975 census showed that even with this adjustment, the discrepancies had increased. The results of this census were published in April 1976, but despite the considerable shift in population, the Diet made no adjustments and the December 1976 elections were carried out in accordance with the 1975 distribution. The plaintiffs, therefore, contended that the Diet failed in its constitutional duties in not correcting the distribution but Judge Ando retorted that even compared with the new national average, the ratio was 1.88 for Chiba 4, 1.83 for Kanagawa 3 and 1.68 for Tokyo 7. The national average does not influence the outcome of elections but voters in the actual constitutuencies do and the plaintiffs argued that it was unreasonable that one vote in the Hyogo 5 constituency should exercise the same influence as five voters in Chiba 4.

The basic errors in Judge Ando's decision are his misconception of the nature of legislative discretion and the functions of representatives. The Diet has no discretion whatever with regard to the essential purpose of the state which must be the common welfare and concerning the fundamental rights and duties laid down in the constitution. There can be various opinions on the requirements of the common good and conflicting views on the means by which the common good should be pursued. But no matter which means are chosen, they cannot negate the values and rights guaranteed by the constitution. Hence, in determining goals and means, the Diet cannot violate the constitutional values and the rights of all citizens and all people living in the country. It may well be that not all goals required by the common good can be achieved and that in order to protect important national interests constitutional rights have to be curtailed (strictly speaking, not the right but its use and enjoyment can be limited), but this can only be done if the interest to be protected is more important than the right to be curtailed and the result cannot be obtained in any other way.

Judge Ando asserted that the attractiveness of a stronger voice in elections was a suitable means of protecting sparsely populated areas. As a matter of fact, nobody would choose to live in a rural area because his vote would have more influence but the actual meaning of Judge Ando's argument is that a representative acts on behalf of his constituency and works for its interests which makes the Diet an assembly of agents for special interests, pressure groups and power brokers. This may be nearer to reality than the theoretical position (and constitutional requirement) that the Diet and all its members represent the entire people, and the distribution of seats may actually be more influenced by the desire of politicians to protect their turf than by considerations of equality. But the reasons why politicians oppose changes in the distribution of seats are certainly not reasons why the courts should condone the inequities of a skew election system, close their eyes to the real situation and invent fanciful arguments to justify unjust decisions.

Judge Yasuoka's ruling generally followed the Supreme Court's 1976 decision and held that a ratio of 3.5 to 1 in the number of voters for one Diet seat constituted a discrepancy which was intolerable and incompatible with the constitutional requirement of equality. He pronounced the 1976 election to the House of Representatives unconstitutional but turned down the demand to declare the elections invalid for reasons of national interest. The decision affirmed that, for the sake of the equality of votes, the ratio to the population was the most essential element in the distribution of seats but that, within reasonable limits, regional differences were acceptable. Differences exceeding a permissible limit would make the distribution of seats unconstitutional unless justified by extraordinary circumstances. The judge did not spell out what kind of extraordinary circumstances he meant but he found that the 3.5 to 1 ratio was unreasonable which was some progress compared to the Supreme Court's limit of 5 to 1. Judge Yasuoka pointed out that even if the apportionment had been based on the 1975 census, it would have failed to produce a desirable degree of equality. A distribution based on the 1975 national census would have left discrepancies of the order of 2.92 to 1 but at the time of the elections, these discrepancies had already increased to over 3 to 1. Such a development could have been foreseen but, the judge hinted, the bureaucracy did not regard the revision of the election law as a serious matter.

The Supreme Court dismissed appeals against the Ando and Yasuoka decisions because the dissolution of the House of Representatives and elections in September 1979 had made the issues obsolete.

JUDICIAL INDECISION

The Supreme Court has applied varying standards in its rulings on the inequality of votes. In a decision rendered on 7 November 1983 the Supreme Court, by an eight to seven vote, overturned verdicts of the Tokyo and Osaka High Courts which had held the June 1980 elections to the House of Representatives unconstitutional. The court acknowledged that the situation contravened the constitutional requirement of equality in the right to vote. When the Diet reapportioned the seats in 1975, the highest ratio of disparity was 1 to 2.92. At the time of the 1980 elections, the largest spread came to 1 to 3.94. Since five years had passed, the Diet had had reasonable time to adjust the distribution of seats, yet the majority of the court thought that the apportionment could not be considered unconstitutional. Of the seven dissenting justices, six shared the view of the High Courts that the election had been unconstitutional.

The following election to the Lower House took place in December 1983 and voters from 21 electoral districts demanded that the election be declared invalid because of the discrepancy in the value of votes. The number of voters entitled to elect one representative in the most under-represented and the most over-represented constituencies was as follows.

Constituency	*Number of voters*	*Constituency*	*Number of voters*
Chiba 4	*362,041*	*Hyogo 5*	*82,033*
Kanagawa 3	*333,312*	*Kagoshima 3*	*86,882*
Saitama 2	*321,901*	*Ishikawa 2*	*89,526*
Tokyo 11	*306,828*	*Ehime 3*	*91,904*
Hokkaido 1	*298,488*	*Akita 2*	*96,382*

The national average was 165,329 voters for one repre-sentative. The ratio of the constituency with the highest number of voters per representative (Chiba 4) to the constituency with the lowest number of voters per representative (Hyogo 5) was 4.41 to 1; the ratio of the former to the national average was 2.19 to 1, that of the latter 0.59 to 1.

In a series of decisions between September and December 1984, High Courts in Hiroshima, Tokyo, Osaka and Sapporo found the elections unconstitutional but refused to declare them invalid because such a decision would cause confusion (*jijō hanketsu,* i.e. a decision reflecting the situation). The Supreme Court, on 17 July 1985, upheld the decisions. The Diet, the court said, had recognised that the allocation offended against the equality guaranteed in the constitution but had let pass a reasonable time without taking action. The Chief Justice, Jiro Terada, supported by four other justices, expressed the view that if the next general election were held without revising the distribution of seats, the courts would have to nullify the election; and one justice, Masataka Taniguchi, wanted to have the election results invalidated in some constituencies.

UNSOLVED PROBLEMS

A survey by the Home Ministry conducted in September 1990 showed that the disparity in the value of votes had grown. In the Amami constituency, 105,577 voters were entitled to one representative in the Lower House while the number of voters per seat was 341,114 in Kanagawa 4, a ratio of 1 to 3.23, up from a ratio of 1 to 3.15 in 1989. The greatest discrepancy in the number of voters per seat in the Upper House was between Tottori Prefecture and Kanagawa Prefecture with a ratio of 1 to 6.43, up from 1 to 6.29 in 1989. In eight constituencies, the value of one vote was less than one-third of a Tottori vote.

Since the legislature has done nothing to correct the distortions in the election system, the situation was basically the same at the time of the Home Ministry's following survey in March 1991. For the elections to the House of Representatives, there were six constituencies in which one vote was worth less than one-third of a vote in the Tokyo 8 constituency (which comprises the inner-city Ghuo, Bunkyo and Taito wards). In the actual election to the Lower House in February 1990, 44,154 votes in Tokyo 8 elected one representative while in Hiroshima 1, the candidate elected with the least number of votes needed 127,635 votes, a ratio of 1 to 2.89. In the House of Councillors elections in July 1989, the successful candidate in Tottori was elected with 180,123 votes; in Tokyo, the candidate elected with the least number of votes needed 776,878, a ratio of 1 to 4.3.

Ten lawyers from Tokyo, Kanagawa, Chiba and Saitama prefectures filed suit with the Tokyo High Court demanding that the February 1990 election be declared unconstitutional. Six lawyers in Hiroshima Prefecture filed a similar suit with the Hiroshima High Court. Below are a few examples of the inequalities adduced in these suits. Keisuke Shiode, a Komeito candidate in the No. 1 constituency in Hiroshima Prefecture was a loser with 121,901 votes while Mitsuhiro Kaneko, a member of the Communist Party, was elected with 44,154 votes in the Tokyo 8 constituency. A vote in Miyazaki 2 was worth 3.18 times a vote in Kanagawa 4. The 890,000 registered voters in Hiroshima 1 were allocated three seats in the Lower House while the 660,000 voters in the prefecture's No. 3 electoral district were entitled to fill five house seats.

The Tokyo High Court rejected the suit brought by the lawyers from Tokyo and the three adjoining prefectures. Presiding Judge Taisuke Biwata ruled that in the light of the past decisions of the Supreme Court, the discrepancies did not exceed the Diet's discretionary authority. The Diet, the judge said, had revised the allocation of seats after the Supreme Court had declared the December 1983 election unconstitutional. Judge Biwata failed to say that the reallocation of seats was already unfair when it was made but he conceded that on the basis of the numerical discrepancy alone, the election would have to be declared unconstitutional.

In October 1991 the Hiroshima High Court turned down the demand of the six lawyers to declare the February 1990 election unconstitutional. Presiding Judge Chuji Yamada was of the opinion that there had not been sufficient time for the Diet to revise the allocation of seats and redress the disparity which had worsened after a revision of the distribution of seats.

On the basis of the 1990 national census, the Management and Coordination Agency calculated that in the Chiba 4 constituency, one seat was allocated to 464,170 voters while in the Tokyo 8 district, 137,420 voters were entitled to one seat in the House of Representatives. The discrepancy ratio was 1 to 3.38. Seven other constituencies had over more than three times more voters per representative than Tokyo 8. In the Upper House, the greatest disparity was between Tottori Prefecture whose 307,861 voters were allotted one seat, and Kanagawa where one seat was assigned to 1,995,098 voters, a ratio of 1 to 6.48. Even the Home Ministry was disturbed and called for corrective action.

A proposal drafted by the Liberal-Democratic Party's Political

Reform Headquarters advocated increasing the number of representatives in nine constituencies by one and decreasing their number by one in ten constituencies. The scheme would reduce the total number of representatives by one to 511 and would bring the highest ratio of discrepancy to 2.77, below the ratio of 3 to 1 held by the Supreme Court to be the largest constitutionally allowable ratio of disparity.

The courts have also upheld the principle of equality for local elections. In the election to the Tokyo Metropolitan Assembly in July 1981, the ratio of voters for one assemblyman in Chiyoda Ward to that in Edogawa Ward was 1 to 4.51, and the ratio of Chiyoda to the Nishitama district was 1 to 7.45. The Tokyo High Court held the election unconstitutional but did not invalidate the results. Equality requires that the representatives be allocated 'in proportion to the population' (Public Office Election Law, Article 15, paragraph 7), but the court allowed some latitude: 'If there are no special circumstances, population must generally be made the standard but the balance between districts can be taken into consideration.'

In response to the decision, the metropolitan assembly reapportioned the seats by decreasing their number by one in each three over-represented districts and increasing the seats in three under-represented districts. This reduced the ratio of the value of votes from 1 to 7.45 to 1 to 3.4 which the plaintiffs in the first suit found unsatisfactory. They therefore sought an injunction to prevent the Tokyo Metropolitan government from financing the assembly election scheduled for 7 July 1985. But the Tokyo District Court ruled that spending could only be frozen if the spending itself was unlawful. The court avoided passing on the constitutionality of the distribution of seats prior to the elections and declared that it was impossible to foretell whether the elections would be held unconstitutional. In a decision on a suit filed after the election, the Supreme Court held that despite the adjustment, the disparity remained unreasonable even if factors such as concern for preserving the power of sparsely populated agricultural or manufacturing districts were taken into account.

LOCAL CONDITIONS

A survey conducted by Kyodo News Service in view of the local assembly elections scheduled for April 1991 found that on the basis of the 1990 census, the value of the votes in 14 of the 47 prefectures was one-third of the value of the votes in the least populated electoral districts. In Chiba Prefecture, one assembly seat was allocated to 5.17 times the number of people in the most under-represented electoral district to the number of people given one seat in the most over-represented constituency. The ratio was 5.14 to 1 in Tokyo and 5.02 to 1 in Aichi Prefecture. In Osaka, where the ratio was 4.38 to 1, a readjustment was planned which was to bring the discrepancy to 2.37 to 1.

In a decision announced on 23 April 1991 the Supreme Court upheld the ruling of the Tokyo High Court which had declared the July 1988 elections to the Tokyo Metropolitan Assembly unconstitutional but did not invalidate the election results. Tokyo's inner city has largely been taken over by commercial buildings (shops and office buildings) while, due to the exorbitant land prices, the population has moved to the suburbs and the adjacent prefectures. Justice Hisao Sakagami found that the adjustment in the allocation of seats carried out by the assembly had been insufficient. On the basis of population, the 23 city wards (which had 96 seats) had been allocated six seats too many and the outlaying districts (which had 31 seats) had been given six seats too few. One vote in the least populated ward (Chiyoda) was worth 3.09 votes in Hino city. Such a discrepancy, Justice Sakagami declared, was unacceptable because it was contrary to the principle of proportion to population. The metropolitan assembly, the justice said, had been negligent in the reallocation of seats.

Voters who are listed on the local residents register are not qualified to vote in local elections unless they actually lived in the locality during the period of registration. In December 1983 the Supreme Court upheld a lower court ruling that the election management commission in Torahime, Shiga Prefecture, had erroneously registered people who did not live in the locality during the period of registry. The Supreme Court dealt a second time with the same election in a January 1985 decision when it overturned the ruling of the Osaka High Court which had rejected the demand to nullify the election. About 10 per cent of the voters had been falsely registered and the election management commission had failed to make an appropriate investigation. Because of the serious fault in the compilation of the register, the entire register was invalid and therewith the election.

Although the Public Office Election Law provides stiff penalties for infractions, the extreme slowness of the judicial procedure makes the law rather ineffective. In a case of unlawful electioneering and vote buying, the district manager of Eitarō Itoyama had been found guilty of having violated the law in elections to the House of Councillors in 1974. The law provides that a candidate loses his seat when his district manager is found guilty of vote buying (Art. 251-2, par. 1). When after eleven years of litigation, the sentence became final, Itoyama's mandate had long expired.

In the post-war era, two dietmen, both members of the LDP, have been convicted of vote-buying in elections to the House of Representatives. The first was Hisayuki Nishimura who was sentenced to one year in prison for violating the election law in the February 1955 election. The second was Tōru Uno who engaged in large-scale vote-buying in the October 1979 election to the Lower House (he came in fourth of four candidates elected in the Chiba 2 constituency). On 31 January 1984 the Supreme Court upheld the decisions of the lower courts and the sentence to a four-year prison term.

Chapter 7
Scandals

An inglorious feature of Japan's post-war development has been the rather frequent occurrence of cases of bribery involving politicians or government officials. Although official corruption constitutes a universal phenomenon, the scandals characteristic of the post-war era in Japan have been referred to as 'structural corruption'. This term is meant to indicate that many cases of corruption reflected the peculiar political and economic conditions prevailing in this period. The immediate post-war years were very chaotic and the shortages of daily necessities and materials for industrial production together with a weakened governmental authority encouraged not only the disregard of legal restrictions but also of moral duties. During the war the munitions industry had resorted to bribing the all-powerful military bureaucracy in order to stay afloat while after the war businessmen were anxious to improve their chances by bribing Japanese officials operating under the authority of the Occupation, issuing licences and awarding contracts. Civil servants were all the more susceptible to this kind of persuasion because inflation pushed prices up relentlessly while salaries failed to keep pace with the erosion of purchasing power.

Corruption received a boost with the ascendancy of party governments. Parties as well as individual politicians were constantly in need of funds and open to deals which promised handsome returns with little risk. The description of some of the major scandals outlined below may illustrate the synergism of politics and business in an economy operating under regulatory restraints.

SHOWA DENKO

The first of the large corruption cases in the post-war era was the Showa Denko scandal of 1948 which led to the resignation of the Ashida cabinet. Showa Denko, a leading chemical enterprise, was accused of having given bribes to Hitoshi Ashida (who was Prime Minister when the case surfaced) during his term as Foreign Minister in the Katayama cabinet. Among the four other politicians involved was Suehiro Nishio, who was Deputy Prime Minister under Ashida and had been Chief Cabinet Secretary under Katayama. Ashida, Nishio and over 30 politicians and businessmen were arrested. After a ten-year court battle, the Tokyo High Court found Ashida and other defendants not guilty because their actions did not constitute criminal offences.

THE SHIPBUILDING SCANDAL

The shipbuilding scandal which came to light in 1954 led to the arrest of 71 leading politicians, businessmen and officials and involved two politicians, Hayato Ikeda and Eisaku Sato, who were both to become Prime Ministers. The war had reduced Japan's merchant marine to less than a quarter of its pre-war tonnage and it included only 17 seagoing vessels. The government's indemnity payments for war losses had been cut off by order of the Occupation authorities which had made the position of the shipping companies extremely difficult. But in the 1950s the government drew up shipbuilding programmes through which loans were made available, and under a law passed in 1954 the government also subsidised the interest payments on these loans. The shipbuilding programmes paired a certain shipping company with a certain shipbuilder. In secret deals, the shipbuilding companies returned between 3 per cent and 5 per cent of the ship's price to the shipping companies and the funds thus created were used for donations to politicians and officials in a position to influence the allocation of ships to be built under the programmes.

The Tokyo Public Prosecutor's Office started investigations in 1953 and in January 1954 asked Foreign Minister Katsuo Okazaki, Secretary-General of the Liberal Party, Eisaku Sato and Hayato Ikeda, Chief of the Political Research Division of the party, to appear voluntarily for questioning. Some executives of Yamashita Steamship Co. were arrested and officials of the Ministry of Transport investigated. At the beginning of February three shipping companies were searched and their presidents arrested. The House of Representatives allowed the arrest of Jirō Arita, Deputy Secretary-General of the Liberal Party. On 19 February Shōkō Moriwaka, a financier (President of Edobashi Shōji) who had been involved in earlier bribery cases, gave a memorandum to the Lower House Budget Committee listing the names of politicians and government officials who had been entertained by business before and after the enactment of the Shipbuilding Interest Supplement Law. On the following day, Seiki Satake revealed the names of cabinet members and party officials involved in the affair. Yasuhiro Nakasone, then a member of the Diet belonging to the Progressive Party (which later became the Democratic Party) alleged in the Budget Committee that Transport Minister Mitsujirō Ishii and Bamboku Ohno (minister in charge of the Hokkaido Development Agency) had received money from business. A memo drawn up by the President of Yamashita Steamship Co. listed donations to politicians.

At the end of February Ikeda was interrogated by the prosecutor in charge of the shipbuilding case, Shintarō Kawai, who was known as the 'investigation demon'. In March and April several politicians were arrested. A vote of no confidence against Justice Minister Takeru Inukai was defeated. (Takeru Inukai was the son of Tsuyoshi Inukai, Prime Minister in the last pre-war 'party cabinet'. He was famous for his battles with the military in the Diet and was assassinated in the '15 May' affair in 1932.) The prosecution intended to indict Sato and Ikeda under Article 197-4 of the Penal Code, a charge called *daisansha shūwai* (acceptance of a bribe by a third party to have another official perform a certain action).

The crux of the prosecution for bribery is proof of what is usually referred to as entreaty (solicitation), the request of the giver of the bribe to the recipient for a certain favour. Sato maintained that the neglect of proper book-keeping procedures in accepting political donations from the Shipbuilders' Association and Shipowners' Association did not constitute bribery, and that he personally had not received a single yen. The prosecution asserted that the donations were intended to influence the revision of the Shipbuilding Interest Supplement Law and budgetary allocations.

When, on 17 April, the prosecution deliberated on the arrest of Eisaku Sato, Inukai told Taketora Ogata (who was Deputy Prime Minister) that he wanted to resign. On 19 April the prosecution decided to arrest Sato. Informed of the situation, Prime Minister Shigeru Yoshida returned from his home in Oiso to Tokyo. Inukai was relieved of his duties as Director of the National Police but remained Minister of Justice. On 20 April the Prosecutor-General conferred with Inukai who was unwilling to interfere with the investigation but was persuaded by Ogata that the political situation required Sato's protection from arrest when Inukai, accompanied by the Vice-Minister of Justice and the Director of the Criminal Bureau, visited Ogata. Representatives of the cabinet, the Ministry of Justice and the procurator's office agreed on invoking Article 14 of the Public Prosecutor Law. Inukai, therefore, instructed the Procurator-General on 21 April to postpone Sato's arrest and on the following day resigned as Minister of Justice.

His successor, Ryōgoro Kato, decided that the deferment of Sato's arrest would end with the end of the Diet session (19 June). A vote of no confidence against the cabinet failed. On 20 June Sato was indicted for violation of the Political Funds Control Law but the case was discontinued due to the general amnesty declared on the occasion of Japan's admission to the United Nations (December 1956). On 19 June Sato resigned, declaring that he had fulfilled his task. Over 100 individuals were investigated in connection with the shipbuilding affair but the political establishment survived with no lasting damage. Three of the four members of the Liberal Party arrested were convicted.

LOCAL CORRUPTION

Scandals were not limited to the national government. In local governments, bribery was particularly frequent in deals for securing offices such as speaker of prefectural or municipal assemblies or for obtaining public works contracts. Bribes took the form of gifts for foreign junkets labelled 'inspection tours', or of mid-year or year-end gifts. There have been numerous arrests for bribery, misappropriations and blackmail. Of the 196 corruption cases detected in 1980 involving local government, 85 per cent concerned bribery or embezzlement. The suspects included 262 officials serving in 123 local government units (bribery 66 cases involving 125 officials, embezzlement 59 cases involving 89 officials). Many of these cases were connected with construction projects.

In February 1983 the municipal assembly of Sakai (Osaka Prefecture) approved an ordinance providing for the expulsion of assemblymen and mayors convicted of taking bribes. The ordinance provides for annual financial reports on income and assets. Assemblymen and the mayor are required to disclose income exceeding ¥ 30,000 from any one source including salaries, interest, gifts in cash and other gifts worth more than ¥ 10,000 per item and entertainment costing more than ¥ 50,000, as well as the value of all property assets and securities transactions. The reports are made public and examined by a committee composed of six assemblymen and seven Sakai citizens. Other municipalities have followed Sakai's example.

The import restrictions, numerous in the post-war era, became a fertile ground for shady deals. Importers generally formed associations which were involved in the allocation of import quotas and the negotiations for fixing the quotas provided plenty of opportunities for politicians to act as brokers. A typical sector was the import of bananas which the government regulated in order to protect the *mikan* (mandarin orange) growers. The import of bananas from Taiwan had been under an allocation system but the system was abolished when Takeo Miki was Minister of International Trade and Industry. However, abuses became so rampant that the allocation system was reintroduced.

This did not mean that abuses disappeared; according to the Banana Import Association, only 10 per cent of its 653 members were genuine businesses. Most were paper companies set up to sell their import allocations. Groups which had nothing to do with the legitimate banana trade secured quotas and the imported lots were passed through a series of paper companies to be finally sold at exorbitant prices. A Socialist dietman charged that a member of the Diet had imported 200,000 crates of bananas. Import duties on bananas were kept high because the LDP wanted to protect the interests of their agricultural clientele. When import duties were liberalised in 1963, the nominal rate was 30 per cent but the actual rate was 110 per cent.

BLACK MIST

During the administration of Eisaku Sato (1964-1972) the term *kuroi kiri* (black mist) came into vogue for the shady transactions in which politicians and officials were rumoured to be involved. One of the affairs came to light through investigations in the United States. Reports published by the Securities and Exchange Commission in 1978 and

1979 stated that two American aircraft manufacturers, McDonnell-Douglas and Grumman Aircraft Engineering Corp., had bought the influence of Japanese officials in trying to sell their products. In a six-month investigation, the Tokyo Public Prosecutor's Office discovered that Nissho-Iwai, a leading trading company, had made payments to politicians in order to sell McDonnell-Douglas's F-4E Phantom jet fighter to the Defence Agency.

In 1965 Hachiro Kaifu, then Vice-President of Nissho-Iwai, had repeatedly visited Nobusuke Kishi, former Prime Minister and the elder brother of Prime Minister Eisaku Sato,to ask for his intervention in favour of McDonnell-Douglas. Through Nagayoshi Nakamura, Kishi's chief secretary, he arranged a meeting between Kishi and Charles Forsyth, Vice-President of McDonnell-Douglas at a San Francisco hotel in July 1965. According to Kaifu's recollection, Kishi said 'I will cooperate as much as possible'. It was reported that Kishi had been offered a $20,000 'initiation fee' for his services and that eventually Kishi was paid ¥ 7.2 million. Kishi met McDonnell-Douglas executives again in 1967 at the Ambassador Hotel in Los Angeles.

Kaifu also enlisted the help of Raizō Matsuno to whom he had been introduced a few years earlier and whom he visited in April or May 1965 just before Matsuno became Director-General of the Defence Agency (June 1965). Between 1967 and 1972, Nissho-Iwai paid a total of ¥ 500 million which Matsuno had asked for his efforts. Matsuno was not indicted because the statute of limitations on bribery had expired. The help given by Kishi and Matsuno also included the appointment to a key position of a Self-Defence Forces officer favourable to Nissho-Iwai instead of another officer close to Osamu Kaihara (later Secretary-General of the National Defence Council) who advocated the purchase of Northrop's F-5 jet fighter which C. Itoh & Co. was trying to sell.

Kaifu's trial, which started in the Tokyo District Court in May 1979 under Judge Kyōichi Hanya, led to his conviction for violation of the Foreign Exchange Law and for perjury (false testimony before the Diet). He was sentenced to two years hard labour with three years probation. Together with Kaifu, two other former executives of Nissho-Iwai were indicted: Shōichi Yamaoka, who had been a director and chief of the company's aircraft department, and Yūjirō Imamura, former deputy chief of the department. Both were accused of violating the Foreign Exchange Law and of forging official documents. They were alleged to have used part of the $2,380,000 commission the company received from McDonnell-Douglas for paying the ¥ 500 million to Matsuno and to have falsified accounting documents to cover up the payments.

Kaifu and Yamaoka were also accused of having received part of a secret commission paid by Boeing Corporation to Nissho-Iwai's American subsidiary around 1975 to promote the sale of Boeing's 747-SR jumbo jet to Japan Air Lines with the help of Japanese politicians.

Yamaoka was also accused of having embezzled $95,000 paid by two American airlines as commissions for arranging leases of their planes to All Nippon Airways. In case jumbo jets were sold to only one airline, Nissho-Iwai would pay ¥ 1 million to the prime minister. The Prime Minister mentioned in the memo was Kakuei Tanaka. When the scandal surfaced, Mitsuhiro Shimada committed suicide. Kaifu denied having known the memo but recognised the handwriting as Shimada's. In a separate trial, another Nissho-Iwai employee, Kunio Arimori, who had been Deputy Section Chief of the aircraft department, was sentenced to a five-month prison term with one year probation for having refused to testify before the Diet.

THE KDD AFFAIR

Until recently, KDD (Kokusai Denshin Denwa Kaisha) held a monopoly on Japan's international telecommunications. Irregularities involving KDD officials and the Ministry of Posts and Telecommunications came to light in October 1979 when KDD President Manabu Itano and Yōichi Sato, Chief of the President's Office Secretariat, returned from a visit to Moscow. Two employees who had accompanied them were held at the Narita customs office for violations of the Customs Law, involving about 130 items of jewellery and other articles. In the course of the investigation, it appeared that in addition to evading ¥ 384 million in customs duties and commodity taxes, KDD had spent billions of yen on gifts to 190 politicians and bureaucrats since 1975. The company's entertainment expenses had risen from ¥ 929 million in 1976 to ¥ 1,399 million in 1977 and ¥ 2,238 million in 1978. One of the objectives for which KDD sought the help of dietmen and other politicians was to keep out competition by foreign firms. Sato was charged with having embezzled about ¥ 1,377 million from the expense accounts of KDD's directors. KDD bought expensive foreign-made furniture from a firm in which Yasushi Hattori, a former Post and Telecommunications Minister, had invested, and invoices were falsified to conceal the transactions. Itano used some of the furniture as well as art objects bought by company funds for his private residence.

Two officials of the Ministry of Post and Telecommunications were indicted for having accepted bribes. KDD had paid the expenses of a two-week trip to Italy and Spain when they were sent to Europe as members of a delegation to attend a meeting in Geneva. Two KDD officials questioned by police on the irregularities committed suicide. Two former KDD employees charged that the company made donations to politicians connected with telecommunications. Three members of the Liberal-Democratic Party were said to have received ¥ 500,000 each and two members of the Japan Socialist Party to have received ¥ 200,000 each. All five denied the allegations as did two former ministers said to have been given ¥ 1 million each. No politicians were indicted in connection with this affair.

THE KYŌWA SEITŌ CASE

A 16-year-long court battle came to a close in 1983 when the Supreme Court dismissed an appeal filed by Sadato Kan, former President of Kyōwa Seitō. The case arose from a plan to build a large sugar refining complex to strengthen the domestic sugar industry in view of the liberalisation of crude sugar imports. Sadato Kan, a naturalised Japanese from Taiwan, who had founded a sugar refining company called Kyōwa Seitō Co. in 1959, borrowed a total of ¥ 2.6 billion from three government financial institutions. A loan from the Norinchukin Bank (Central Cooperative Bank for Agriculture and Forestry) was secured by a mortgage on forest land the company had acquired from the state. Kan forged documents to make the value of the land look higher.

When the Diet began to investigate questionable transactions of Norinchukin, Kan offered Shigeaki Aizawa, a Socialist member of the Audit Committee of the Upper House ¥ 1 million to stop the inquiry. Kyōwa Seitō had established a lobbying organisation through which it funnelled donations to politicians. Among the recipients was Seishi Shigemaru who received nearly ¥ 22 million through his support group. Shigemaru had been chairman of Kyōwa Seitō before being appointed Minister of Agriculture. Prosecutors discovered that a total of about ¥ 120 million had been disbursed to politicians. Although 50 members of the Diet were questioned in connection with this case, only Aizawa was indicted and sentenced to two years in jail for accepting a bribe, fraud and other law violations. Aizawa died in 1981 while his appeal to the Supreme Court was pending.

THE LOCKHEED SCANDAL

One of the most notorious scandals in post-war Japan was the Lockheed case. It concerned the attempt of Lockheed Aircraft Corporation to bribe Japanese politicians in order to promote the sale of its wide-bodied L-1011 TriStar jet to All Nippon Airways (ANA). The main facts of the case were as follows. Toshio Kodama, a 'fixer' with strong right-wing connections but also well acquainted with gangster organisations had been working for Lockheed as a 'consultant' since 1958. His first job concerned the sale of the F-104S fighter plane, and he received about ¥ 15-20 million annually over the next ten years. He was also involved in the sale of the P-3C Orion (anti-submarine patrol plane) to the Defence Agency. In 1969 Lockheed made a consultant contract with Kodama for the sale of the L-1011 TriStar jet then under development with a ¥ 50 million yearly fee.

Japanese airlines had not yet finalised their plans on which type of the new generation of aircraft they would adopt. For Lockheed, which was behind other manufacturers of wide-bodied jets, it was imperative to have the decision postponed as long as possible. Furthermore, ANA was inferior to Japan Air Lines (JAL) and wanted to limit the advantage JAL would gain from the introduction of new planes.

Tetsuo Oba, the President of ANA, was negotiating with Mitsui Corporation, the agent for Douglas Aircraft Co., on the acquisition of the DC-10. In October 1969 Yoshinari Tezuka, Chief of the Ministry of Transport's Aviation Bureau, announced the ministry's intention to use 'administrative guidance' for unifying the types of aircraft used by JAL and ANA. A few months later, ANA established a committee for selecting the new aircraft type. Tokuji Wakasa, then ANA's Vice-President, was appointed chairman of this committee. In February 1970 Wakasa met A. C. Kotchian, then Vice-President of Lockheed, but in March, Oba informed Douglas that ANA would take an option on the L-10 in September. In May, the Minister of Transport, Tomisaburo Hashimoto, hinted at a possible reorganisation of Japan's airlines and announced in June that ANA would be permitted to fly international routes (which had been the exclusive domain of JAL). In 1971 Hashimoto declared that the introduction of the new wide-bodied aircraft would be postponed. The circular making the 'administrative guidance' for postponing the introduction of the wide-bodied jets official was sent by the parliamentary Vice-Minister of Transport Takayuki Sato. In July 1972 the Minister of Transport declared that the new jets would be introduced after 1974.

In August 1972 A. C. Kotchian came to Japan and met Hiro Hiyama, President of Marubeni Corporation. He asked Hiyama to appeal to Prime Minister Kakuei Tanaka for help in selling the TriStar. He also asked Kodama to arrange a meeting with Kenji Osano, Chairman of Kokusai Kōgyō, whom Tanaka called his 'bosom friend'. Osano had made a fortune by the procurement of war supplies during the war. He later bought famous hotels and bus companies and also acquired hotels in Hawaii and on the mainland. Kotchian was not surprised when Kodama suggested that it would take ¥ 500 million to persuade Osano.

The crucial event of the scandal took place on 23 August 1972. Accompanied by Toshiharu Okubo, Managing Director of Marubeni, Hiyama visited Tanaka at his Meijiro residence. After introducing Okubo, Hiyama had a short conversation with Tanaka under four eyes in which Tanaka, upon hearing Hiyama's request, said '*yosha, yosha*'. In its decision, the Tokyo District Court noted that Tanaka had once been asked by Ishiguro, Managing Director of Mitsui Corporation, to recommend that ANA purchase the DC-105 and had been told of the competition between Douglas and Lockheed as well as of ANA's plans to buy large-size aircraft. This makes it plausible that Tanaka well understood the meaning of Hiyama's request.

On 22 August when Hiyama told Okubo that they were going to see Tanaka the following day, he remarked that they could not go without a suitable present. He therefore instructed Okubo to sound out Kotchian about a sum of ¥ 500 million. Okubo did as told and persuaded Kotchian that the money was essential for promoting Lockheed's sale. On their way back from the visit to Tanaka, Hiyama spread five fingers and said

'This'. Okubo asked 'You mean the large figure?' (meaning ¥ 500 million - five *oku* in Japanese) to which Hiyama replied 'How could it be otherwise?'

On the following day Hiroshi Ito, also Managing Director of Marubeni, telephoned Toshio Enomoto, Tanaka's secretary, on Hiyama's instruction and told him that he, Ito, would act as contact man for Tanaka while Okubo would be in charge of the liaison with Lockheed (Ito was Chief of the President's Office of Marubeni and Okubo was in charge of machinery imports). Enomoto answered that he had heard of the arrangement from Tanaka. On 25 August Ito entertained Enomoto at the restaurant Kinoshita. Ito repeated Marubeni's request to have Tanaka influence ANA in favour of the acquisition of TriStar. A few days later, Hiyama met Tanaka at the Japanese-style restaurant Chiyoshin where Tanaka's 'Monday Group' was having a meeting. Hiyama repeated his request for Tanaka's help in selling Lockheed's TriStar to ANA. He told Tanaka that TriStar's body was manufactured by Lockheed but that the aircraft was to be fitted with Rolls Royce engines so that the purchase of TriStar would also improve Britain's trade balance with Japan.

On 1 September 1972 Tanaka met with President Nixon in Hawaii and agreed to the 'emergency' import of American-made jets. During his trip to Hawaii, Tanaka stayed at the Surfside Hotel owned by Osano. After the meeting with Nixon, Tanaka told Osano that Nixon had said he would be much obliged if Japan favoured the TriStar. He asked Osano about ANA's policy of selecting aircraft. Osano took this as a request to influence ANA and informed Naoji Watanabe, ANA's Vice-President and chief of the company's aircraft selection committee, of Nixon's request. Watanabe later passed this on to Wakasa, then ANA's President.

In early October, Ito asked Enomoto how things were going for TriStar. Enomoto replied that TriStar had a chance of being chosen but that there were many other factors involved. It was still too early to say that it had been selected. He added that Tanaka was trying hard to keep his promise. Hiyama visited Tanaka's residence on the morning of 14 October. Everything was going smoothly, Tanaka said, and Marubeni had nothing to worry about. Wakasa met Tanaka at the Prime Minister's official residence on 24 October 1972. He was told that both President Nixon and British Prime Minister Edward Heath wanted ANA to buy the TriStar. Tanaka remarked that he had no authority over a private company and asked Wakasa just to keep it in mind.

In the course of October, Kotchian was assured that ANA would buy the TriStar. On 29 October Okubo contacted Kotchian and told him that TriStar would be chosen on the following day if Lockheed paid ¥ 120 million. On 30 October Kotchian handed Okubo ¥ 30 million in cash and ANA gave written notice that it intended to buy the TriStar. On 6 November John W. Clutter, Lockheed's former representative in Tokyo, sent Okubo ¥ 90 million. Receipts for '30 units' and '90 units' were signed by Okubo.

After the elections in December 1972 Tanaka formed his second cabinet. In January 1973 ANA and Lockheed signed a contract for the purchase of TriStar jets. Okubo telephoned Kotchian in June advising him that the ¥ 500 million promised to Tanaka should be paid. Between August 1973 and February 1974 Clutter delivered to Ito cardboard boxes stuffed with cash which Ito handed to Toshio Enomoto, Tanaka's secretary, at four different locations. Ito signed receipts for '100 peanuts' (9 August 1973), '150 peanuts' (12 October 1973), '125 peanuts' (21 January 1974), and '125 peanuts' (28 February 1974). Altogether, Lockheed seems to have spent ¥ 2,634 million on promoting the sale of TriStar in Japan. Of this sum, ¥ 1.8 billion went to Kodama for consulting fees, and Kenji Osano received ¥ 54 million. The rest was paid to politicians; ¥ 500 million to Tanaka through Marubeni and an additional ¥ 10 million through ANA which also funnelled money to other politicians.

On 28 October 1972 ANA decided to scrap the option for McDonnell-Douglas DC-10s. Wakasa told Kyōichi Fujihara, then Managing Director of ANA, that he wanted donations made to certain politicians. Marubeni agreed and paid ¥ 5 million each to Susumu Nikaido, LDP General Secretary, and Tomisaburo Hashimoto, Minister of Transport, ¥ 3 million each to Kazutomi Fukunaga (then Chairman of the Special LDP Committee on Aviation) and Hideyo Sasaki (former Minister of Transport), and ¥ 2 million each to Takayuki Sato (then parliamentary Vice-Minister of Transport) and Mutsuki Kato (former parliamentary Vice-Minister of Transport). The politicians suspected of illegal acts but not indicted were referred to as 'grey officials'.

THE EXPOSURE OF THE LOCKHEED SCANDAL

The Lockheed affair first surfaced in hearings of the subcommittee on multinational enterprises of the US Senate. A. C. Kotchian, Lockheed's Vice-President, and W. Finlay, the firm's auditor, mentioned that Lockheed had spent over $22 million on manoeuvres to sell the TriStar in Japan. On 6 February 1976 Kotchian told of his relations with Kenji Osano. A few days later Henry Kissinger, then Secretary of State, advised the subcommittee that the publication of names would destabilise a foreign government. Later in the same month the Japanese government asked the American authorities for the information brought to light in the Senate hearings. The Department of State as well as the Securities and Exchange Commission transmitted information on condition that it should not be made public until the persons named therein had been indicted. The Finlay testimony, however, became known in Japan and the Budget Committee of the House of Representatives called Kenji Osano, Hiro Hiyama, Hiroshi Ito, Toshiharu Okubo, Tokuji Wakasa and Naoji Watanabe to testify as witnesses (under oath). Toshio Kodama was sick and could not appear. They all denied any knowledge of the transactions in which they had been reported to have been involved. Hence, later in the trial, when the facts had been established, they were all charged with perjury.

Kakuei Tanaka had been forced to resign as Prime Minister in November 1974. The worldwide economic expansion which started in 1970 had reached a peak in 1973 when the energy crisis triggered by OPEC's oil policy (which quadrupled the price of oil) led to the combination of recession and inflation known as stagflation. Restrictive policies adopted by the leading industrial nations depressed world trade while oil dollars flooded the Eurodollar market and played an important role in the upward price spiral which was reinforced by the excessive liquidity. Speculation resulted in a large number of bankruptcies - the collapse of large banking institutions such as the Franklin National Bank in the United States and Herstatt in West Germany indicated the seriousness of the situation.

The increase in unemployment further contributed to the sense of uncertainty and the collusion between big business and the bureaucracy stymied effective countermeasures. Tanaka's pet project concerning the relocation of industry and new towns was published in English with the title 'Restructuring of the Japanese Archipelago', and directly contributed to the inflationary trend and caused a sharp rise in land prices (from which Tanaka profited). The elections to the Upper House in July 1974 brought a setback to the conservatives despite the large amounts of money distributed by the party. The mood in the LDP turned against Tanaka because its leading members thought that it would be impossible to overcome the crisis without popular support.

A crucial factor in Tanaka's downfall was the revelation of his money policy by Takashi Tachibana in the monthly *Bungei Shunjū* which furnished the Miki and Fukuda factions with ammunition for their attacks. Tachibana discussed Tanaka's career as a businessman and politician and set forth in considerable detail the way in which he had acquired his wealth and concealed his income. Tachibana estimated that dietmen and other politicians connected with the Diet needed an income of about ¥ 20 billion (in 1974 purchasing power) a year. The funds reported by politicians and political organisations are only a small part of the funds that actually move in Japanese politics. While donations, particularly by large enterprises, account for a considerable part of the funds collected by politicians, transactions in land and stocks were used to provide enormous additional funds. When Tanaka was Minister of Finance, sales of government-owned land skyrocketed. Land prices were artificially raised by having the same piece of land bought and sold by a number of dummy companies before it was sold to the ultimate buyer - in some cases, the government or local public bodies. (This practice, known as *tochi-korogashi*, was also responsible for the enormous increase in land prices during the time of the 'bubble economy', particularly in 1986-1987.)

In many transactions, Tanaka worked together with Kenji Osano. As Tachibana put it, it was not the fact that Tanaka made money that was reprehensible but the way in which he did it - sometimes, in the later years, by abuse of his official position (Minister of Postal Services, 1957-58, Finance Minister 1962-64, Minister of International Trade and Industry, 1971-72, Prime Minister, 1972-74). There were only two occasions when Tanaka's tax returns showed an income of over ¥ 50 million yet his investments many times exceeded his income. The capital of the companies he owned rose from ¥227 million to ¥ 2,345 million. He was once ordered to pay ¥ 150 million in additional taxes because his tax returns for three years had been incomplete. While the tax office publishes reported income, it refuses to divulge omissions or falsifications under the pretext of its duty not to reveal secrets.

On 18 February 1976 the Supreme Public Prosecutor's Office decided to start a criminal investigation. The Tokyo Prosecutor's Office with the help of the Metropolitan Police Department and the Tax Administration mobilised 380 officers and carried out searches at 27 locations. The first indictment, accusing Toshio Kodama of tax evasion, was hurried because of the statute of limitations.

The documents of the US Securities and Exchange Commission containing the secret testimony of Vice-President Kotchian named high-ranking Japanese officials who had been bribed. The opposition parties urged Prime Minister Takeo Miki to ask the American government for the documents, but in his answer to this request, President Gerald Ford declared that the documents would only be transmitted on condition that they would not be made public until the investigation had been completed. Prime Minister Miki agreed to the American conditions. The prosecutors concluded that it would be technically difficult to proceed on the basis of the secret American documents and wanted to interrogate Kotchian and other Lockheed officials but this became a lengthy process.

An agreement for cooperation between Japan and the United States for the interrogation of A. C. Kotchian and John W. Clutter was signed on 24 March 1976. The use of the information obtained through this arrangement was limited to investigation and judicial proceedings. The Japanese public prosecutor declared that the Americans would not be indicted in Japan for any statements made in the investigation. The prosecution asked the Los Angeles Federal Court for Kotchian and two other Lockheed executives to be interrogated by public prosecutors. Kotchian objected to the procedure and when the Los Angeles court overruled his objection, he took the case to the San Francisco Appeals Court. When his appeal was rejected, he went to the Supreme Court where he was also turned down. Kotchian's interrogation finished in July and he signed his deposition, which became evidence for the Japanese courts, on 4 August 1976. After a one-month delay, the Los Angeles court resumed the interrogation of John W. Clutter and A. H. Elliot. Their interrogation ended in September. The Japanese Supreme Court gave the Lockheed executives written assurances of immunity. In addition to the depositions, the prosecutors also obtained Clutter's notebook with entries on money paid in Japan.

THE LOCKHEED TRIAL

In June 1976, Toshiharu Okubo and three executives of ANA were arrested as were, in July, Hiroshi Ito, Tokuji Wakasa and Naoji Watanabe. The initial charges were perjury (false testimony before the Diet), violation of the Foreign Exchange Law and tax evasion. Toshio Kodama, who was not arrested because of his illness, was indicted for tax evasion and violation of the Foreign Exchange Law. Also arrested were Hiro Hiyama and, on 27 July, Kakuei Tanaka and Toshio Enomoto, on suspicion of violations of the Foreign Exchange Law. The Tokyo district prosecutor indicted Tanaka on 16 August for accepting a bribe and violating the Foreign Exchange Law, and Hiyama, Ito and Okubo for offering a bribe. On the following day, Tanaka was released on ¥ 200 million bail.

The prosecutors felt confident that they could obtain convictions of the main actors in the case. Their relentless interrogation broke the resistance of most of the accused, who confessed the charges although they repudiated their confessions during the trial, claiming that they had been fabricated by the prosecutors. Only Tanaka was consistent in his denial and disputed all the allegations of the prosecution. His disclaimer greatly embarrassed his defence attorneys since Enomoto admitted that he had received ¥ 500 million (although he denied that it was a bribe and called it a 'political donation') while Tanaka maintained that he had never heard of the money, let alone received it.

A victim of the prosecutors' thoroughness was Tanaka's chauffeur, Masanori Kasahara, who confessed that he had carried Enomoto and the cardboard boxes, and on the day following his confession committed suicide because he thought that he had betrayed his employer's trust. It was a modern version of the feudal *giri*, the loyalty binding the retainer to his lord. A similar incident happened in connection with the Recruit scandal (discussed below), when Ihei Aoki, long-time secretary of former Prime Minister Noboru Takeshita, committed suicide. In the same month of August 1976, Takayuki Sato and Tomisaburo Hashimoto were arrested on suspicion of bribery. The so-called 'grey officials' were not prosecuted for various reasons. They had received money but no connection with their official position could be shown; the statute of limitations had run out; there was no connection with the Lockheed case; they had received money from ANA in the form of political donations, travel expenses or year-end gifts.

Based on the prosecution's differentiation of three money routes, there were four different trials in the Tokyo District Court. The so-called Marubeni route (Judge Mitsunori Okada presiding) involved five defendants: Kakuei Tanaka, accused of accepting a bribe; Toshio Enomoto, former secretary of Tanaka, violation of the Foreign Exchange Law; Hiro Hiyama, former President of Marubeni Corporation, Hiroshi

Ito and Toshiharu Okubo, both former Managing Directors of Marubeni Corp., bribery, perjury, violation of the Foreign Exchange Law. In addition to the acceptance of money, the prosecution had to prove that Tanaka had official authority to make a decision regarding the acquisition of aircraft by ANA and that he acted in response to an entreaty.

At the beginning of the trial, Tanaka's lawyers moved to have the indictment dismissed. Tanaka maintained that he had done nothing to be ashamed of, and his lawyers asserted that even if all the facts alleged by the prosecution were true, Tanaka had done nothing wrong because he had no authority to influence the purchase of aircraft by a private company. Enomoto contended that he had done nothing unlawful and his lawyers argued that the immunity given to the Americans (Kotchian, Clutter and Elliot) offended against equality. The Marubeni defence made similar objections. Hiyama stated that in his meeting with Tanaka on 23 August 1974, he had merely transmitted a message from Kotchian. Okubo declared that, although he had accompanied Hiyama and had been introduced to Tanaka, he was not present at the conversation and had no idea what was discussed and was not party to a conspiracy. When he was informed by Clutter that the money had been prepared, he transmitted the message to Ito but had no part in the money transaction. Ito conceded that he had received cardboard boxes from Clutter four times but held that he had been unaware of their contents.

The prosecutors' initial statement ran to 110 pages with 40,000 characters. It discussed the evidential value of the American depositions and asserted that they had the same value as a deposition before a Japanese judge. The defence contended that the promise of immunity vitiated the depositions and cited a decision of the Supreme Court against the recognition of such evidence. The prosecution maintained that the promise of the chief prosecutor not to prosecute violated neither the constitution nor the Code of Criminal Procedure. For proving Tanaka's authority to influence the selection of aircraft, the prosecution relied not only on the position of the Prime Minister as the highest administrator but also on the actual handling of business and the decision-making process. In their depositions, Kotchian and Clutter did not use the word 'bribe' nor mention the TriStar sales saying only that Lockheed had been willing to make a ¥ 500 million donation.

In his interrogation as well as in his testimony in court, Okubo more or less confirmed the assertions of the prosecution. Hiyama, however, only admitted that Tanaka had asked to speed up the payment of the money in June 1976 and branded everything else in the report of his interrogation as fabrication. After the case had surfaced, Tanaka had tried to return the ¥ 500 million but in court, Tanaka and Enomoto repeated their denial of having received the money. Ito admitted that he had transmitted ¥ 500 million to Enomoto, that he had received a phone call from Enomoto urging the speedy fulfillment of the promise, that he had heard from Hiyama that Lockheed had promised a ¥ 500 million political donation, and that he received an encouraging phone call from Tanaka after the case had become known. He insisted that the ¥ 500 million had been a political donation and denied that there had been any conversation with Hiyama concerning a bribe for Tanaka. He stated that he did not remember the details of the transfer of the money. In addition to Tanaka's '*yosha, yosha*' to Hiyama, the prosecution also adduced the fact that on the return flight from Hawaii, Tanaka told Osano that President Nixon had thanked him for choosing the TriStar. The prosecution wanted to call Tanaka as a witness but he refused to take the stand. Enomoto, who also declined to testify in court, was upbraided by Judge Okada when he talked about the case in an interview with the monthly *Bungei Shunjū* on TV Asahi where he admitted his role in the case.

The defence started to present counter-evidence in April 1981. One of the attempts to destroy the case of the prosecution was the establishment of alibis for the four times which the prosecution had said Enomoto received money from Ito. The defence hoped to prove that the evidence was at least doubtful which, in accordance with the maxim *in dubio pro reo* (in doubt, the guilty is to be favoured) would have benefited Enomoto. The defence produced the record of Enomoto's driver (referred to as Shimizu's notebook) which, the defence said, showed that Enomoto had been at different places to those at which, according to the prosecution, he had received the money. The prosecution, however, succeeded in refuting the testimony of the witnesses as well as the assertion that the ¥ 500 million which Enomoto received between the fall of 1972 and the spring of 1975 were political donations and had no relation to Lockheed.

Enomoto's defence suffered a fatal blow when his former wife, Mieko Enomoto, testified that in a conversation after the disclosure of the scandal, Enomoto, avowing that he had handled the ¥ 500 million, said 'What shall I do?' whereupon she retorted 'As secretary of Tanaka Sensei, you have to say that nothing happened.' When the prosecution put Mrs Enomoto on the witness stand, Minister of Justice Seisuke Okuno said public prosecutors should be careful not to act contrary to ethics and morality. He denied any intention to declare Mrs Enomoto's testimony contrary to morality but it was clear that he supported Tanaka and Enomoto's defence counsel who opposed calling Mrs Enomoto as a witness on the ground that it was immoral to expose intimate relations, even those of divorced couples. Although Okuno did not belong to Tanaka's faction, he was a close friend. Under attack by the opposition, Prime Minister Suzuki had to express his regret over the remarks made by his Minister of Justice.

On 12 October 1983 Judge Mitsunori Okada found all five defendants guilty. Kakuei Tanaka was sentenced to four years hard labour and the forfeiture of ¥ 500 million; Toshio Enomoto to one year hard labour with three years probation; Hiro Hiyama to two years and six months hard labour; Hiroshi Ito to two years hard labour and Toshiharu Okubo to two years hard labour with four years probation. The guilty verdict for Tanaka was seen as a confirmation of the impartiality of the courts.

The decision refuted the defendants' claim that cabinet ministers were not authorised to perform illegal acts and that, therefore, the actions for which Tanaka was indicted, were not in his power by pointing out that the provisions on bribery in the Penal Code were intended to ensure the fair use of power by public servants and that illegal acts were to be regarded as part of their powers as far as the Penal Code was concerned.

According to the constitution and related laws, the Prime Minister directs and supervises all sectors of the administration. As the representative of the cabinet, he has the authority to control the administration. He can, therefore, intervene in matters within the competence of the various ministries. The Minister of Transport has authority to approve or disapprove changes in the business plans of the private airlines and his discretion to make decisions is clear from cases of administrative guidance in the past. The cabinet has made decisions concerning the importation of wide-bodied jets. Thus, the Prime Minister, although he has no legal authority to directly give orders to private airlines, can exercise a strong influence on the actions of the Minister of Transport. Tanaka's direct influence on ANA can be regarded as a para-official act of the Prime Minister.

All defendants appealed their sentences. Tanaka revamped his team and brought the number of his lawyers to 19. Their briefs, comprising 3,024 pages, followed three lines of attack, questioning first the facts, secondly the authority of the Prime Minister to influence the selection of the aircraft, and thirdly the admissibility of the American depositions. The defence put a new interpretation on the money paid by Lockheed, claiming that it was not for the TriStar but for the P3C anti-submarine plane, and that the money did not go to Tanaka but to other politicians. The defence also produced an alibi for Masanori Kasahara (Tanaka's chauffeur) asserting that on 10 August 1973, the day the prosecution said Enomoto received the first installment near the British Embassy, Kasahara had borrowed the car of an acquaintance and gone on a trip to Ito with his family. Kasahara's wife appeared as a witness for this event but the prosecution was able to demolish this alibi. It produced a photo taken by Kasahara's acquaintance which showed that the date of the trip was 13 August 1973, and proved that on 10 August the car of Kasahara's acquaintance was on the ferry from Kisarazu to Kawasaki.

Tanaka's defence produced a last summing-up of 852 pages for its appeal to the High Court but in its decision announced by presiding Judge Takeo Naito on 29 July 1987, the High Court turned down Tanaka's appeal as well as those of Enomoto, Hiyama and Okubo. Ito's sentence was reduced to two years hard labour with four years probation. In its written judgement of 780 pages (640,000 characters) distributed to the parties on 20 November 1987, the court called the assertion that the ¥ 500 million were paid for promoting the sale of the P3C pure speculation. The court also stated that of the sum of ¥ 30 million channelled through Marubeni to six 'grey officials', including Susumu Nikaido, Enomoto received ¥ 10 million. With the exception of Ito, all defendants appealed to the Supreme Court. Tanaka's lawyers again questioned the court's interpretation of the authority of the Prime Minister and the legality of the US depositions.

The trial connected with the ANA route involved eight defendants: Tomisaburo Hashimoto, former Minister of Transport, and Takayuki Sato, former parliamentary Vice-Minister of Transport, of accepting bribes, Tokuji Wakasa, former President of ANA, and Naoji Watanabe, former Vice-President of ANA, of violation of the Foreign Exchange Law and perjury, Katatsugi Sawa and Kyōichi Fujihara, former Managing Directors of ANA, Hisanori Aoki, former chief of ANA's accounting division, and Tadao Ueki, former chief of ANA's business division, of violation of the Foreign Exchange Law.

The trial, under presiding Judge Takashi Kon, began on 31 January 1977. Judge Kon died during the trial and was replaced by Judge Kazunobu Hanya in February 1981. Judge Hanya separated the trial of the two politicians (Hashimoto and Sato) from that of the ANA defendants.

The prosecution contended that Wakasa and Watanabe tried to delay the introduction of wide-bodied aircraft because ANA was not ready for the change and feared that ANA would fall further behind JAL. They therefore sought to delay the adoption of the new jets by administrative guidance and demanded money from Lockheed for this scheme.

Hashimoto (who was wounded by an assailant in March 1977) denied all allegations, while Sato argued that, although theoretically he had jurisdiction over the acquisition of aircraft, he actually exercised no influence. The ANA defendants conceded the receipt of funds from Lockheed but denied criminal intent and collusion and claimed that they thought the money had come from Lockheed's Tokyo office and that the Foreign Exchange Law was not involved.

The prosecution called the prosecutors who had conducted the investigation to establish the credibility of their reports (in Japanese practice, prosecutors who interrogate suspects form a different group from prosecutors who appear in court). It also had officials of the Ministry of Transport testify so as to establish the fact of administrative guidance of the airlines between 1969 and 1972. The court accepted the depositions of Kotchian and Clutter as evidence. The basic contention of the prosecution was that Wakasa made the request for administrative guidance to Hashimoto and, as remuneration, had ¥ 50 million in cash paid to Hashimoto through Marubeni. Hashimoto accepted the money.

The defence argued that the introduction of new aircraft was a decision reached in the course of ordinary administrative procedure and that there never was a situation in which ANA would have to ask Hashimoto to intervene. Hashimoto denied that Wakasa had made such a request and also denied that he had received ¥ 50 million. The request and the ¥ 50 million bribe appeared in the prosecutors' reports but in court, Wakasa and Fujihara denied these allegations and called them inventions of the prosecutors.

Wakasa had visited Sato three times between April and June 1972 and asked to give ANA favourable consideration. Sato prepared the notification of the Ministry of Transport postponing the introduction of wide-bodied jets on 1 July 1972. He received ¥ 2 million in cash in his room in the Diet members' office building after 11 am on 31 October 1972. Sato produced an alibi saying that on that morning, he went straight to Haneda Airport after a photo session for campaign posters, flew to Hakodate and was present at a meeting in Hakodate in the evening. The prosecution produced a witness who had talked with Sato at the office building in the morning and showed that the visitor's name had been recorded in the visitors' register of the office building. The prosecution also proved that the Hakodate meeting was late because Sato arrived only in the evening. (Incidentally, Sato failed to regain a seat in the 1976 election in which Kakuei Tanaka was re-elected in his constituency with the largest number of votes. Sato succeeded in his bid for election in 1979.)

Wakasa had heard from his predecessor that when ANA bought the B-727, Nissho-Iwai, Boeing's representative in Japan, sent suitable money donations to the politicians concerned. He was told, Wakasa said, that it was customary to make donations to politicians in the case of large transactions. Okubo had stated that he contacted Kotchian upon the request of ANA and asked for '30 units' to be distributed among six people: Hashimoto, Sato and four 'grey officials', Nikaido, Sasaki, Fukunaga and Kato. Matsui, a subordinate of Okubo, delivered and distributed the money as presents from ANA.

Judge Hanya accepted as creditable the testimony of Isao Soejima, former chief of Marubeni's secretariat, who said that he was entrusted by Okubo with the custody of ¥ 30 million and that on instruction by Ito, ¥ 2 million each were given to Sato and Kato, ¥ 3 million each to Sasaki and Fukunaga, and ¥ 10 million together to Nikaido and Hashimoto. The remaining ¥ 10 million were transmitted by Ito to Enomoto. Soejima testified that he had handed ¥ 2 million in cash to Sato at the Second Diet Members' Office building on the morning of 31 October 1972. Ito, Okubo and Soejima asserted that the amounts were determined by ANA and that Marubeni made no changes. But Wakasa and Fujihara contended that the initiative came from Marubeni, that Marubeni had emphasised that the politicians involved be given suitable donations and that the amounts were negotiated by Matsui, determining the recipients not by name but by title.

On 26 January 1982 Wakasa was sentenced to three years hard labour with five years of parole; all other defendants from ANA were found not guilty. The verdict on Hashimoto and Sato was announced on 8

June of the same year; Hashimoto's punishment was two and a half years hard labour with three years probation and forfeiture of ¥ 50 million; Sato's sentence was two years hard labour with three years probation and forfeiture of ¥ 20 million. Wakasa, Hashimoto and Sato appealed to the High Court.

The Tokyo High Court rejected Sato's appeal on 14 May 1986. Presiding Judge Yasuo Tokukuni stated that the appellant had failed to disprove the solicitation by Wakasa as well as the nature of the bribe of ¥ 2 million accepted by Sato. The judge upbraided Sato for showing no remorse for his misdeeds and continuing to serve in the Diet. Hashimoto's appeal was turned down on 16 May. Judge Tokikuni sustained the finding of the lower court that the ¥ 5 million was a bribe and maintained that no illegality was involved in taking the depositions of Kotchian and Clutter and that they were valid evidence. Wakasa's appeal was dismissed on 28 May. For all three defendants, the penalties imposed by the District Court remained the same.

All three appealed to the Supreme Court but in July 1986, Sato, who had been re-elected in the 'double election' on the 6th of that month, withdrew his appeal. He had asserted his innocence from the time of his indictment and in a fierce attack on the courts claimed that he could not expect a fair sentence. In February 1990, the Supreme Court discontinued the case of former Minister of Transport Tomisaburo Hashimoto who had died in January of that year.

Toshio Kodama, his secretary Norio Tachikawa and Kenji Osano were indicted on account of their involvement in the disbursement of the Lockheed funds for selling the TriStar. Kodama, who had concealed part of his income, was accused of tax fraud and violation of the Foreign Exchange Law. His secretary had been involved in the violation of the Foreign Exchange Law but he was also charged with extortion in a different case. Osano was accused of perjury because of his denial of any connection with Lockheed before the Diet. Because Kodama and Osano were sick, their trial was slow, even by Japanese standards. The procedure against Kodama was suspended because he was unable to understand the transactions and he died without having been sentenced. Tachikawa was found guilty of having violated the Foreign Exchange Law and was sentenced to four months hard labour with two years probation. Kenji Osano was convicted of perjury and received a sentence of one year hard labour. He appealed his sentence and on 27 April 1984, the Tokyo High Court dropped the charges against him connected with Lockheed's efforts to sell the P3C Orion anti-submarine aircraft to the Defence Agency and reduced his sentence to ten months hard labour with three years probation. Osano appealed to the Supreme Court but he died on 26 October 1986, before the court ruled on his appeal which was rejected on 12 November 1986.

An episode in the trial of Kenji Osano attracted much attention because of Judge Kyōichi Hanya's clever interpretation of a puzzling piece of evidence. In his deposition, Clutter related that he met Osano at the Los Angeles Airport on the afternoon of 3 November 1973, and handed him an attaché case containing $ 200,000. The money was part of Lockheed's payment to Kodama. Clutter volunteered this information without being asked by the American prosecutor. When asked about the room where this transaction took place, Clutter said that it was not the 'Red Carpet Room' on the mezzanine of the building but one of United Airlines' private rooms on the same level as the runway. Judge Hanya mentioned this detail to illustrate the credibility of the deposition. The prosecution later established that Osano had used the money to pay off part of a $ 1.5 million gambling debt of dietman Kōichi Hamada and his party of ten at a Las Vegas hotel. Osano had the debt reduced to $ 1.2 million and paid it off in installments. The $ 200,000 was the last installment.

The defence tried to disprove the evidence by producing an affidavit from the hotel management stating that Osano did not pay the money. The defence had also obtained Clutter's diary which, for the day in question, had the following entry: 'Saturday 11/3: 4.30 SGCC 9 holes'. SGCC meant the San Gabriel Country Club in Los Angeles and the defence argued that Clutter could not have met Osano at the Los Angeles Airport since it was established that Osano arrived at the airport at 4.18 pm and left for Las Vegas at 5 pm. The prosecution was stunned and argued, rather lamely, that Clutter must have been confused about the dates.

Judge Hanya surprised both defence and prosecution when he declared that the 4.30 had nothing to do with the time Clutter played golf. On that particular day, he explained, sunset in Los Angeles was 4.59 pm so it would have been impossible to start playing at 4.30 and finish nine holes. The juxtaposition of 4.30 and SGCC did not imply that these two entries were related. The meeting with Osano was the most important business for Clutter on that day on which he also intended to play golf at the country club. The prosecution obtained testimony from two employees at the country club who claimed that a bill sent to Clutter indicated that he did not play golf at the club on that day.

Many Japanese politicians, particularly those belonging to the Liberal-Democratic Party, have total contempt for public opinion. One of the most outrageous examples of the disregard of elementary decency was the appointment of Akira Hatano as Minister of Justice in the first Nakasone cabinet (1972). Hatano, an intimate friend of Tanaka, had been Superintendent-General of the Metropolitan Police. In an interview with the monthly *Bungei Shunjū*, Hatano declared that Tanaka's refusal to resign his Diet seat despite the guilty verdict was a matter for Tanaka to decide and nobody else's business. Seeking honesty in politicians in the conventional sense or blamelessness was like asking for fish at a greengrocer's. Politicians are lowly people, he said, and in view of the current political situation, they could not be regarded as unethical or lacking in morality.

Hatano had advised Tanaka on how to deal with the Lockheed trial. He severely criticised the prosecution for having indicted Tanaka and after the verdict of the District Court accused the opposition, some Liberal Democrats and the media of conducting a vendetta against Tanaka.

In a book published in 1984 entitled *What is Power?* Hatano condemned the prosecution for being 'self-righteous' and questioned the authority of the judiciary to judge the duties of the Prime Minister. Because his duties should be considered separately from those of other public servants, the powers of the Prime Minister did not come within the jurisdiction of the courts. He stressed that public prosecutors must obey orders of the Minister of Justice without commenting on their limitation. Hatano severely attacked the Supreme Court for agreeing on the prosecution's proposal to exempt the Lockheed executives from prosecution.

The first Nakasone cabinet comprised two former police officers besides Hatano. One of them was Masahara Gotoda, also a close friend of Tanaka. Gotoda was made Chief Cabinet Secretary and was generally believed to have been placed in this post by Tanaka (who actually decided on the make-up of the cabinet) in order to prevent Nakasone from betraying Tanaka. Mutsuki Kato, one of the 'grey officials', was made state minister in charge of the National Land Agency and the Hokkaido Development Agency. Another indication of the Liberal-Democratic Party's disdain of public opinion was the appointment of three politicians involved in bribery cases to the Disciplinary Committee of the House of Representatives in 1980. They were Kakuei Tanaka and Takayuki Sato, on trial in the Lockheed affair, and Raizō Matsuno, former Director-General of the Defence Agency, who had received ¥ 500 million from Nissho-Iwai in connection with the sale of the McDonnell-Douglas F-15 jet fighter to the Self-Defence Forces but denied that the money had been a bribe.

A professor at Harvard University Law School, Dr Jerome Cohen, was reported to have said that, according to rumours circulating in Tokyo, Prime Minister Kakuei Tanaka and two former prime ministers, Nobusuke Kishi and Eisaku Sato, had made fortunes from kickbacks given in return for Japanese aid to South Korea. The Foreign Ministry sent a letter to Professor Cohen saying that the statement was a serious insult to Japanese political leaders and that the persons concerned considered his remarks as slanderous allegations. 'I am directed from Tokyo', Mitsuhiko Harumi, press attaché at the Japanese Embassy in Washington wrote, 'that it is regrettable for a professor at one of the most prestigious universities in the United States to make such a false statement at a public forum and that an appropriate remedial measure on your part is in order.'

Professor Cohen angrily refused and charged that the letter amounted to an attempt to restrict free speech and that the Japanese government should rather investigate the rumours of the allegations of corruption.

Chief Cabinet Secretary Susume Nikaido called Professor Cohen's suggestion that the Japanese government should investigate the rumours an interference in Japan's internal affairs. In their comments, Japanese newspapers conceded that there were rumours and that the term 'Korea lobby' hinted at some kind of irregularity. 'Can there be smoke without a fire?' the newspaper *Mainichi* wrote. The Lockheed trial did not touch on kickbacks from Korea but it certainly confirmed that there was corruption at the highest levels of government.

THE PACHINKO AFFAIR

In the course of a vendetta against the Socialist Party (now officially named the Social Democratic Party of Japan) in general and Mrs Takako Doi (then Chairwoman of the party) in particular, *Shūkan Bunshun* (a weekly publication of Bungei Shunjū which publishes the monthly of the same name, the magazine instrumental in exposing the Lockheed scandal) in 1989, drew attention to the large political donations made by the National Federation of Entertainment Associations, the industrial organisation of pachinko parlours. Pachinko, a pinball game, is one of the most popular pastimes in Japan. The pinball machines are installed in large halls; pachinko parlours numbered 15,947 in 1990, with yearly revenues estimated of over ¥ 15 trillion. The industry is said to operate with large profit margins; according to rumours, the machines are arranged to yield a daily return of ¥ 10,000 per machine.

About 60 per cent of the pachinko parlour owners are Koreans, and some are controlled by North Korean agents or sympathisers to raise funds for the Pyongyang regime. In 1982, when President Kim Il Sung celebrated his 70th birthday, pro-Pyongyang residents in Japan were said to have sent ¥ 5 billion as a birthday present to Kim. Pachinko owners loyal to North Korea were rumoured to have opposed the introduction of the card system at the direction of Pyongyang because the system would invite police surveillance.

In addition to the general charge that Socialist politicians, including Mrs Doi, had received political donations from the pachinko federation or sold the federation party tickets, there were also allegations that two Socialist Diet members had received donations from North Korean residents which would be a violation of the Political Funds Control Law. The Socialist Party undertook its own investigation and as a result of this and other independent inquiries it became clear that from 1984 to 1987 the federation had spent a total of about ¥ 150 million on political donations and the purchase of party tickets. According to the information produced by the Socialist Party, Diet members belonging to the party had received a total of ¥ 8,020,000 from the federation. However, during the same period 81 members of the Liberal-Democratic Party had been given ¥ 124,825,000 by the federation, and 15 members of other parties ¥ 13.8 million. Eight members of the cabinet had received ¥ 4.97 million, including Prime Minister Kaifu

(¥ 450,000) and Foreign Minister Nakamura (¥ 1.06 million). The Communists were the only party which had received no donations from the pachinko federation. The Socialist Party denied that, contrary to the charges of *Shūkan Bunshun*, the donations had any connection with a revision of the Law Regulating Businesses Affecting Public Morals or the introduction of pre-paid cards for pachinko parlours.

Subsequently two other parties - Komeito and the Democratic Socialist Party - revealed that five members of both parties had been given a total of ¥ 2.75 million each. The Democratic Socialist Party also acknowledged that four of its members had received ¥ 190,000 from Korean residents. A press report quoted by a member of the Socialist party asserted that a former prime minister, Zenkō Suzuki, had received ¥ 3 million from a Korean pachinko owner in Iwate Prefecture and that another member of the LDP had been given ¥ 1 million by Mindan, the Korean Residents Union in Japan, an organisation of Korean nationals supporting South Korea. The LDP took the position that the donations received by its members did not involve any irregularities so that there was no need to make an investigation.

The pachinko federation raised the funds used for political donations by imposing special contributions on its members. It collected about ¥ 100 million in 1984 by levying a tax of ¥ 50 on each machine, over ¥ 100 million in 1985 and about ¥ 50 million in 1987 by collecting ¥ 20 per machine. The money raised in 1984 was returned to the prefectural organisations but the other funds were spent on lobbying.

Pak Chae Ro, Chairman of Chongryon (General Association of Korean Residents in Japan, affiliated with North Korea), denied *Shūkan Bunshun's* allegation that its Nagano chapter had made a political donation to Socialist dietman Yoshinao Kushihara but in the budget committee of the Lower House, Kōichi Hamada demanded that Ippei Koyama, a Socialist member of the Upper House, and Hiroshi Yamaguchi, a freelance journalist who had written the articles in *Shūkan Bunshun*, testified under oath on the alleged donations.

On 20 October 1989 Mrs Mayumi Moriyama, Chief Cabinet Secretary, announced that seven cabinet members, including Prime Minister Kaifu, had received a total of ¥ 3,170,000 from the pachinko industry, and Health and Welfare Minister Saburo Toida acknowledged that he had personally been given ¥ 1.8 million. It appeared that *Shūkan Bunshun's* attack on the Socialist Party had backfired badly yet Yamaguchi continued to write as if only the Socialists were involved. The Budget Committee of the Lower House wasted two days on charges and countercharges of who had received what from whom. After the debate the LDP published a list showing that it had received ¥ 118.38 million from the pachinko industry between 1977 and 1989. Together with the ¥ 4.97 million received by the cabinet, total pachinko funds given to the LDP amounted to ¥ 123.35 million. There were reports that a classified government document showed that the Socialist Party had been given ¥ 8.9 million by Chongryon but the Prime Minister, the Minister of Justice and the Minister of Home Affairs denied any knowledge of such a document.

THE RECRUIT SCANDAL

A new twist in bribery emerged in the so-called Recruit scandal. The Recruit Company was founded in 1960 by Hiromasa Ezoe, at that time still a student at the University of Tokyo (Tōdai), for handling advertisements in university newspapers. Three years later the company was renamed Recruit Centre and its business expanded to include information on the employment, housing and real estate markets. A real estate subsidiary called Recruit Cosmos was established in 1964 and the company's name changed back to Recruit Co. in 1984. Its core business was the publication of two magazines: *Recruit Book*, an employment information magazine for college students, and *Recruit Shingaku Book*,which provided information on colleges and universities for high school students. In the field of information, the company branched out into telecommunication networking. In 1986 and 1987 Recruit bought two of four supercomputers Nippon Telegraph and Telephone Public Corporation (NTT) had purchased from Cray Research and used them for computer time leasing.

In 1987 total sales of the Recruit group, which included 27 subsidiaries with 6,200 employees exceeded ¥ 350 billion. As of October 1986 Recruit Co. was the main stockholder of Recruit Cosmos Co., owning 11,191,000 shares, about 34 per cent of the total of 35 million shares representing the capital of the firm. Ezoe personally owned 4,558,000 shares; among the major stockholders were six of Japan's seven trust banks and 11 of the 13 city banks. Ezoe himself became a very wealthy man. In the list of leading taxpayers in 1987 published in May 1988, he ranked in 29th place with an income of ¥ 1.3 billion. He gained entry into the big business establishment and was named Councillor in the Federation of Economic Organisations (Keidanren), trustee of the Japan Association of Corporate Executives (Keizai Dōyūkai), and Managing Director of the Japan Federation of Employers' Associations (Nikkeiren).

Among the institutions with which Ezoe had connections was a foundation headed by former Vice-Minister of Education Isao Amagi, the Institute for Higher Education established in 1979. Recruit provided 60 per cent of the original capital of ¥ 35 million. Ezoe became Chief Director while Amagi was Chairman of the Board of Directors. Among the directors were Eiji Toyoda, President of Toyota Motor Co., Akio Morita, President of Sony Corporation, Takashi Makaibo, a former President of Tokyo University, and Sukenaga Murai, former President of Waseda University. Recruit supplied office space in Nihon Recruit Centre's Nishi Shimbashi Building. When the parent body of the institute, the Association for Democratic Education, was in financial difficulties, Ezoe offered to help. On the board of directors of the association were other leading personalities, Tadao Ishikawa, Deputy Chairman of the National Council on Educational Reform and Chairman of the Ad Hoc Committee on University Problems, Yasunori Nishijima, then President of Kyoto University, and Ichiro Kato, former President of Tokyo University.

For his business, Ezoe cultivated relations with three ministries, those of Education, Labour, and Telecommunications. He became a special member of the government's Tax Council and was appointed an associate member of the land policy discussion group of the New Government Reform Promotion Commission. Between 1984 and 1987, four Recruit executives, including Ezoe himself, were appointed members of eight committees connected with the Ministry of Education. Ezoe served on the Council for University Entrance Examinations, the Curriculum Council, the Council for the Establishment of a Second National Theatre and the University Council.

Recruit established contacts with high school teachers in charge of career counselling. The company's files contained the names of 30,110 teachers giving career guidance to second-year senior high school students and those of 29,783 teachers advising third-year students seeking enrollment in universities or vocational schools upon graduation. The information gathered through the nationwide intelligence network enabled Recruit to distribute questionnaires to students through guidance counsellors each autumn and send them free literature paid for by universities and other schools. These campaigns were made possible with the cooperation of the Ministry of Education and the local Boards of Education.

Recruit established subsidiaries in the US in order to handle the strong demand for foreign help by Japanese business. Two of its US subsidiaries were accused of 'blatant' employment discrimination based on race, sex, age and national origin, actions highly improper and often illegal in the States. Interplace-Transworld Recruit was said to have used a code in internal communications to indicate the preferences of its clients (Talk to Mary - Caucasian, Mariko - Japanese, Maria - hispanic, Maryanne - black, Adam - male, Eve - female, suite 20-30 - age 20-30 etc.).

The Recruit Scandal concerned the sale of shares of Recruit Cosmos Co., the property subsidiary of Recruit Co. In order to create goodwill towards his enterprise, Ezoe offered shares to a limited number of people before the shares were available publicly on the open market. When stock is offered for the first time to the public, the price is fixed by comparison with the stock prices of similar companies without taking into account the market potential. As a result, prices established by actual quotations after the stock goes public may be much higher.

Largely as a result of the Recruit affair, the government adopted new rules on insider trading in April 1989. The old rule had been that new shares should not be offered to 'specially interested parties' and that the authorities had to be notified when pre-flotation shares were sold to more than 50 people (50 investors are required for listing stock on the open market). Recruit had sold pre-flotation shares to a few people in October 1984 but in September 1986, Recruit Cosmos shares were sold to 159 politicians, government officials, businessmen and academics. The buyers included 17 members of the Diet (12 from the LDP and five from opposition parties). The price was ¥ 3,000 a share; all purchases were dated 30 September 1986, and First Finance Co. paid about ¥ 2 billion for the share transactions on behalf of all purchasers. As expected, the price went up sharply as soon as the stock became available on the market.

The case came to light as a result of two rather collateral incidents. In early 1984 the Kawasaki municipal government was looking for companies willing to join in an urban development project. One of the firms invited was Recruit. In December of that year, Masao Tatsumi, Director of Recruit's Building Business Department, called on Hideki Komatsu, then Deputy Mayor of Kawasaki, and offered him 30,000 shares in Recruit Cosmos. If needed, Tatsumi said, First Finance Co. would lend him the money to pay for the shares. In 1989 Tatsumi, who by then was no longer with Recruit, testified before a special investigation committee of the Kawasaki municipal assembly, that he acted on the explicit instructions of Ezoe and that the offer was not meant as a reward for Komatsu's assistance in the development project but because Recruit wanted to secure influential people as shareholders. Komatsu was not indicted.

The second incident involved the attempts to persuade dietman Yanosuke Narazaki not to press the investigation into the Recruit affair. Narazaki had the reputation of asking embarrassing questions when probing questionable cases. Several times in August and September 1988, Hiroshi Matsubara, then Chief of the Presidential Office of Recruit Cosmos, visited Narazaki and offered him ¥ 5 million. Narazaki videotaped the visit and filed a complaint accusing Matsubara of attempted bribery. In November 1988 the Tokyo District Public Prosecutor's Office indicted Matsubara. The Diet began an investigation to find out the truth behind rumours concerning the distribution of pre-flotation Recruit Cosmos shares but most of the witnesses appearing before the Diet's Special Committee denied any involvement.

One of the conjectures about the motive of Recruit's attempt to secure the backing of influential politicians and businessmen asserted that around 1984, Recruit encountered serious financial difficulties. In order to overcome the crisis, Ezoe contacted Ko Morita, President of the business daily *Nihon Keizai Shimbun*, and asked him to secure the support of influential public figures. His help must have given Recruit an enormous boost for the recipients of pre-flotation shares included not only all leading members of the LDP and some members of the opposition but also well-known business executives. Another conjecture was that sharp competitive pressure was partly responsible for Recruit's attempt to buy influence.

In October 1988 the Communist Party disclosed that besides politicians and high-ranking bureaucrats, the buyers of Recruit Cosmos shares included three executives of NTT, two professors at Tokyo University, and five executives of trust and banking companies or their relatives. Shares had also been sold to the executives of leading national newspapers, Kō Morita of *Nihon Keizai Shimbun*, Iwao Maruyama, Vice President of *Yomiuri Shimbun*, and Reizō Utagawa, Managing Editor of *Mainichi Shimbun*.

Kiichi Miyazawa, Finance Minister in the Takeshita cabinet (who later replaced Toshiki Kaifu as Prime Minister) was named as having bought 10,000 Recruit Cosmos shares in lists published in October 1988 by the Socialist and Communist parties. At first Miyazawa denied he had any connection with the purchase,explaining that his secretary had allowed his friend to use the minister's name. After changing this implausible story twice, Miyazawa admitted that he had indeed bought the shares himself. His resignation as Finance Minister was soon followed by that of other leading politicians; Takashi Hasegawa resigned as Minister of Justice after only four days in office, and Ken Harada stepped down as Director-General of the Economic Planning Agency after less than a month in office.

A list submitted to the Diet by Recruit Cosmos Co. in November 1988 showed that nine of the 12 members of the LDP involved in the stock purchases had been members of the Nakasone cabinet and four were members of the cabinet of Noboru Takeshita, Prime Minister when the affair came to light. In his testimony before the Diet, Hiromasa Ezoe declared that his sole objective had been to create good will for his enterprise group. He had personally selected more than half of the recipients: 'I chose people who were close to me. There was no promise of a reward and I had no intention of getting favours in return.' He regretted particularly that Kunio Takaishi, former Vice-Minister of Education, and Takashi Kato, former Vice-Minister of Labour, had become involved in the affair. 'They have been personal friends of mine for over ten years', he said. It is amazing how Ezoe, the president of a rather obscure company, managed to be accepted by leading figures of Japan's political and economic circles.

Altogether 77 people received pre-flotation Recruit Cosmos shares. Recruit executive Takeshi Ozawa stated that 39 politicians were targeted by Recruit Co. in testimony given to the Tokyo District Court in March 1990. Among the politicians named by Ozawa were cabinet secretary Misoji Sakamoto, who was Labour Minister in 1984, former Labour Minister Takeshi Kato, Lower House members Tatsuo Ozawa and Takashi Hamano of the LDP, and Seiichi Ikehata and Takanobu Nagai of the Socialist party and Upper House member Shōji Motooka of the same party.

The sale of pre-flotation shares was not the only way in which Ezoe had cultivated relations with politicians. Recruit made large political donations, paid membership fees to support organisations and bought tickets to fundraising parties. Kenzaburō Hara, who had been Minister of Labour and Speaker of the House of Representatives since 1986, received a total of ¥ 3 million in political donations from Recruit; the company paid ¥ 4 million in membership fees, bought 300 tickets priced at ¥ 30,000 each in October 1984 and 200 tickets in September 1985. The opposition demanded that Hara resign as Speaker but he refused maintaining that the ¥ 15 million had been returned to Recruit. However, he resigned on 1 June 1989.

Recruit shares had also been sold to members of the opposition parties. Takami Ueda of the Socialist party, Saburō Tsukamoto, Chairman of the Democratic Socialist Party, and Keishū Tanaka, a member of that party, had bought shares. Ueda gave up his Diet seat, and Tsukamoto resigned as party chairman. Katsuya Ikeda, a member of Komeito, who served on the Education Committee of the Lower House, was one of two Diet members indicted for accepting bribes. Recruit had purchased three tickets worth ¥ 90,000 for the inaugural party of Takako Doi as Chairwoman of the Socialist Party.

The most controversial figure in the Recruit affair was the former Prime Minister, Yasuhiro Nakasone. It appeared that one of his secretaries, Yasuo Tsuihiji, had bought 23,000 shares, another secretary, Yoshihiko Kamiwada, and an employee of Nakasone's support group Sannō Keizai Kenkyūkai, had also bought 3,000 shares each. After eight months of silence during which Nakasone refused to appear before the Budget Committee of the Lower House, he took part in a televised news conference in which he denied any involvement in the Recruit case. He admitted that his secretaries and an employee of his support organisation had purchased pre-flotation shares but he contended that he did not know why these individuals had been offered shares. The proceeds from the sale of these shares had been used to send seasonal gifts to acquaintances, to pay for business meetings and to offer cash gifts for funerals and weddings - expenditures which were unrelated to the personal affairs of the secretaries but obviously connected with Nakasone's political activities. It was not the first time that Nakasone's name had been mentioned in connection with dubious transactions. A Lockheed executive told a newspaper that Kodama had claimed that he had called Nakasone to secure a favourable government decision for the acquisition of P-3C and TriStar aircraft. Nakasone only admitted that he knew Kodama; Tsuneo Tachikawa, Kodama's secretary, had served as Nakasone's trainee secretary.

In 1973 Tamiyasu Tōgō, a high school classmate of Nakasone and former Chairman of Shokusan Jūtaku Sōgō, was arrested for income tax evasion. Tōgō alleged in a Tokyo District Court hearing that he had been asked by Nakasone to contribute ¥ 2.5 billion to enable him to run in the party's presidential election. Tōgō donated ¥ 560 million but Nakasone returned the money when a weekly magazine revealed the gift. In his 1977 Diet testimony, Nakasone denied Tōgō's account of the incident but Tōgō repeated his version when summoned before the Diet. In connection with the same 1972 election for the party presidency, the weekly *Shūkan Shinchō* quoted a party member as saying that Kakuei Tanaka paid Nakasone ¥ 700 million to gain the support of the Nakasone faction. Nakasone filed a libel suit against the magazine. The suit was later withdrawn although *Shūkan Shinchō* never printed a retraction or an apology.

Nakasone was said to have given support to Ezoe in connection with two events: Ezoe's appointment as a special member of the Tax Council in 1986 and Recruit's purchase of two Cray Research supercomputers in 1986 and 1987. In 1985, Nakasone, then Prime Minister, decided to enlarge the Tax Council in order, as he said, to better reflect public opinion. For appointments to this council, the Tax Affairs Bureau of the Ministry of Finance together with the Home Ministry jointly prepare a list of suitable candidates which must be submitted for final approval to the Prime Minister who has the legal authority to appoint the council members. Government sources indicated that Nakasone pushed vigorously for Ezoe's inclusion in the list but Takeshita who was Minister of Finance did not concur. Keizō Obuchi, Chief Cabinet Secretary in the Takeshita cabinet, said that Ezoe's appointment had been finally decided by Takao Fujinami (Chief Cabinet Secretary in the Nakasone cabinet) in accordance with the rules of the Prime Minister's Office.

Nakasone was also involved in Recruit's purchase of two Cray Research supercomputers from NTT (which was privatised in 1985). NTT concluded an agreement with the United States for the purchase of equipment in 1981 and altogether bought four supercomputers in April 1984, May 1986, and in March and June 1987. Ezoe met Hisashi Shinto, Chairman of NTT, to discuss the acquisition of computers on 3 September 1985, and on 12 September Shinto went to the US to negotiate the computer purchases. The second and fourth computer bought by NTT were resold to Recruit in December 1986 and December 1987. In addition to the two supercomputers, which were housed in buildings in Yokohama and Osaka belonging to NTT, Recruit owned two other computers and had leased circuits to about 1800 companies. According to NTT employees, Recruit's equipment was coded for fast repairs, a service not provided to other NTT customers. A label saying 'RCo' was attached to all items belonging to Recruit; the labelling had been arranged through negotiations between Ezoe and Shinto. Hisahiko Hasegawa, an NTT director in charge of computer business, left NTT and became the president of a Recruit subsidiary.

The role of Nakasone in the resale of the supercomputers to Recruit has remained ambiguous. During a news conference in a New York hotel on 25 October 1985, Nakasone said that as part of Japan's efforts to rectify the trade balance, NTT had bought or had definite plans to buy two Cray Research supercomputers and was going to buy a third. Reagan mentioned the NTT purchase at the 'Ron-Yasu' meeting in May 1988 and Nakasone observed tht NTT was going to buy another computer. At a news conference in Japan on 27 February 1989, Nakasone insisted that in his meeting with Reagan, he had referred to the third supercomputer bought by NTT and had relied on a newspaper report for this information. If this had been the case, he would have referred to the same computer he had mentioned in his New York press conference. Following the 1989 conference, Nakasone's office issued a statement saying that in his October 1989 press meeting in New York, he should have said that NTT had bought one computer. The point Nakasone wanted to make was that he had no previous knowledge of NTT's and Recruit's computer transaction. When asked in an interview whether Nakasone had approached NTT with the request to help Recruit acquire Cray Research supercomputers, Hisashi Shinto, then still Chairman of NTT, replied: 'I cannot make any comment.'

Nakasone testified as a sworn witness before the Budget Committee of the House of Representatives on 25 May 1989, when the prosecution had finished its investigation of the Recruit affair and it had become certain that nobody in the high command of the LDP would be indicted. As in his previous testimony, Nakasone denied any connection with the Recruit incident, asserting: 'I have done nothing questionable and I am innocent'. He said that he first heard of his secretaries' transaction in pre-flotation shares of Recruit Cosmos in December 1987, shortly after he was succeeded as Prime Minister by Takeshita. He was never asked for favours by Ezoe in connection with the acquisition of the two Cray Research computers and never discussed the matter with Hisashi Shinto, Chairman of NTT. He met Ezoe twice, he said, once in March 1985, when Ezoe called on him at the Prime Minister's official residence, and a second time when Ezoe paid him a visit in Karuizawa during the summer holidays. He also denied any knowledge of Recruit's efforts to establish an agreement regulating the recruiting of university graduates by business, commenting that this was a matter for the competent state minister. During Nakasone's tenure as Prime Minister, his organisation received a total of ¥ 25 million in political donations from Recruit, another ¥ 8.3 million in membership fees and ¥ 3 million for tickets to a fund-raising party in April 1988.

An Osaka group charged Nakasone with accepting pre-flotation shares in exchange for helping Recruit buy American computers. The Public Prosecutor's Office advised them to keep quiet since the charges had been investigated and no proof had been found. The group was warned that it would be prosecuted for malicious accusations if it repeated the charges. Nakasone withdrew from the LDP at the end of May 1989 and also resigned as leader of his faction, Supreme Adviser of the party and Chairman of the Policy Research Institute.

Hisashi Shinto, Chairman of NTT, and Kōzō Murata, his secretary, were arrested in March 1989 on suspicion of having accepted bribes from Recruit. (Because NTT was a public company, its employees were under the same restrictions as government employees.) According to the prosecution, Murata bought 10,000 Recruit Cosmos shares with a loan provided by First Finance Co. and sold the shares after their listing on the open market. The profit from the sale, about ¥ 21 million, was transferred to Murata's bank account but ¥ 9 million was later credited to Shinto's personal bank account and used to cover a deficit in his entertainment account. The balance, ¥ 12 million, was deposited in an account managed by the chief of NTT's presidential secretariat and used to finance relations with politicians. Although Murata's name appeared as buyer of the shares, they were actually sold to Shinto as payment, the prosecution claimed, for the favours rendered Recruit in connection with the purchase of the Cray Research supercomputers. Murata, therefore, was not indicted.

Besides Shinto, two NTT executives, Ei Shikiba and Hisahiko Hasegawa, were charged with having accepted bribes. In 1986 NTT imported modems and other communication equipment from the United States for Recruit who used them for subleasing large-capacity, high-speed circuits. Ei Shikiba was in charge of procuring equipment and of the resale of digital circuits. He had purchased 5,000 Recruit Cosmos shares; Hasegawa had bought 10,000 shares.

NTT was subsequently privatised but the government still holds 65 per cent of the capital. Although the enterprise is prohibited from making political donations the ban does not affect individual employees. Shinto donated ¥ 6 million from the sale of the Recruit shares to two members of the Upper House. An organisation called National Council to which about 70,000 NTT employees in management positions belonged donated about ¥ 100 million a year to LDP Diet members sympathetic to NTT. Members of the organisation contributed between ¥ 5,000 and ¥ 30,000 a year in fees.

Ei Shikiba was appointed to the Ad Hoc Committee on Education formed under Prime Minister Nakasone. Only two of the committee members were from the private sector, one of whom was Ezoe. When Recruit executives advised Shikiba to conceal his involvement with Recruit, he transferred the title of his shares to a friend in June 1988 when the Kawasaki affair became known. But in October when the opposition parties revealed the names of the purchasers of Recruit shares, he had the shares switched back to his own name. For its employment publications Recruit sought to build up close connections with the Ministry of Labour. The firm gave political donations to successive Ministers of Labour, paid membership fees to their support organisations and bought tickets to their fundraising parties. Recruit executives wined and dined ministry officials and invited them on all-expenses-paid golf trips.

The case which was investigated by the prosecution involved a revision of the Employment Security Law. There had been many complaints about incorrect information in employment magazines and exaggerated claims in advertisements, particularly in those of vocational schools. Other complaints concerned information on temporary workers. In 1983 the Employment Security Bureau of the Ministry of Labour compiled a draft for revising the Employment Security Law which would require reports to the authorities before publishing new employment information magazines. Ministry of Labour officials would be authorised to inspect publishers' offices and suspend publications giving incorrect information. The draft was leaked to the Association of Publishers of Employment Magazines and drew strong protest from the industry.

In June 1984 a new draft was prepared. Ezoe met with Takashi Kato, then chief of the Employment Security Bureau, two months later in a bar in the basement of the Recruit head office to discuss the proposed revision. Officials decided that it would be difficult to impose legal restrictions because of the constitutional guarantee of freedom of the press. Instead of government control, the publishers were to exercise self-restraint. Kato was promoted to Vice-Minister of Labour but resigned when the Recruit scandal became public and also gave up his post as head of the Japan Association for Employment of the Disabled. He had bought 3,000 Recruit Cosmos shares in September 1986 and made a profit of ¥ 6.9 million when he sold them in November. In his appearance before the Diet as a sworn witness, Kato denied that he had been involved in the work for revising the Employment Security Law although he had received a report of the draft of the revision in the summer of 1984. Kato was arrested on suspicion of having received bribes in August 1989 and later indicted. Also arrested was Shigeru Kano, Kato's predecessor as Chief of the Employment Security Bureau.

In March 1989 a Communist dietman charged that the Ministry of Labour had concealed evidence relating to the Recruit case. Shortly before the public prosecutors searched the ministry, papers concerning the recruitment of part-time workers had been removed, including documents on the negotiations between the ministry and Recruit on the request not to impose legal restrictions on magazines publishing job information. The Minister of Labour, Hyōsuke Niwa, denied the charges, explaining that the documents had been transferred because of lack of storage space.

Another matter involved in the Recruit case was the agreement of the business world not to start canvassing prospective college graduates before a certain date (20 August). Consultations between enterprises and placement officers usually started after the summer vacation but when the job market was tight or when enterprises were eager to secure the best students graduating from 'famous' universities, the quest for suitable employees began earlier and earlier. Nikkeiren (Japan Federation of Employers' Associations) had sponsored a gentlemen's agreement fixing a date after the summer vacation for the start of recruiting prospective graduates. After a few years, however, many enterprises ignored the agreement and the managing director of Nikkeiren called for its abolition. Had the agreement been scrapped, Recruit would have suffered serious damage to its business of publishing job information magazines. Ezoe instructed Masao Tatsumi, chief of

Recruit's secretariat, to urge Katsuya Ikeda, Deputy Secretary General of Komeito, serving on the Ad Hoc Council on Education, to argue in favour of the agreement. Tatsumi delivered to Ikeda's Diet apartment a list of questions to be asked in the Diet.

In June and August 1984 and in June 1985, Ikeda questioned government officials on alleged violations of the agreement by government agencies. On 26 June 1985 the Ad Hoc Council on Education submitted a report to the Prime Minister, Nakasone, calling for a new agreement to check excessive competition. Ikeda took up the issue in October and November 1985 and gained the support of Nakasone. A new agreement went into effect in March 1986. In September of that year, Ikeda's brother Yuzuru purchased 5,000 pre-flotation shares with a loan from First Finance Co. Ikeda sold the shares in October, making a profit of ¥ 10 million. He received a total of ¥ 14 million from Recruit in donations. Ikeda left Komeito after the Recruit affair was disclosed and stated that he would not seek re-election.

On 29 May 1989 Ikeda was arrested on suspicion of having accepted bribes. On the same day, Takao Fujinami, who had been Chief Cabinet Secretary under Nakasone, was arrested on the same charge. Fujinami had allegedly used his authority to counter employers' opposition to the new agreement. He was offered 10,000 pre-flotation shares and received ¥ 20 million in cheques, including ¥ 5 million at the Prime Minister's official residence on 26 June 1985, the day the Ad Hoc Council on Education submitted a report favourable to Recruit to Nakasone. Fujinami was also suspected of having used political funds for personal expenditure without reporting these funds as income. The prosecutor's suspicions were aroused when they discoverd that Fujinami had bought a house for ¥ 132 million in December 1986 without visible means to pay for this acquisition. According to the prosecutors' calculation, Fujinami may have received as much as ¥ 90 million from Recruit.

Also indicted was Kunio Takaishi who resigned as Vice-Minister of Education in June 1988. Takaishi had been Director of the Elementary Education Bureau when Ezoe was appointed to the Curriculum Council and Vice-Minister when Ezoe was nominated to the University Council. The prosecution charged that Takaishi had received 10,000 shares as remuneration for nominating Ezoe to the committees which enhanced Ezoe's social standing. Takaishi denied this, claiming that his wife had bought the shares. He acknowledged, however, that he had been offered the shares at a price of ¥ 3,000 a share while in office. When the scandal surfaced, he had sold 6,000 shares at a profit of ¥ 12 million. Takaishi had prevented stricter measures for regulating job and school placement magazines.

In January 1986 the Ministry of Education created a panel comprising 15 scholars and representatives of vocational schools to examine the exaggerated advertisements in vocational school guides. A year later, the ministry notified the industry that the matter would be left to its discretion. The panel was disbanded before its recommendations could be implemented. Following the submission of a final report to the government in August 1987, 20 members of the secretariat of the Education Reform Council, mostly from the Ministry of Education, were invited on a two-day golf trip to Morioka. Expenses, amounting to about ¥ 100,000 per person, were paid by Recruit.

Recruit sent representatives to the ministry's panels discussing educational guidance for senior high school students. Through this connection, Recruit secured the cooperation of high school teachers for surveys of students' job plans and could compile lists of graduating high school students. The guides published by Recruit were sent to students' homes which led to complaints about the way Recruit was conducting its business and charges of infringing on the students' privacy, involving teachers in business for profit and exaggerated advertising.

In October 1988 when the Recruit case had already aroused considerable public criticism, the Ministry of Education solicited a ¥ 10 million donation from Recruit for a fund to finance a Japanese opera performance in Warsaw under the sponsorship of the Japan Opera Foundation, an organisation affiliated to the Ministry of Education. The ministry's excuse for this lapse of propriety was that the project had been launched in May 1988, before the Recruit affair became known.

Among the politicians who greatly benefited from Ezoe's largesse was Noboru Takeshita, Prime Minister when the affair became public. Although Takeshita figured prominently in the list of share buyers, he denied any knowledge and defied the opposition's demand to resign. Ezoe had personally included Takeshita among the individuals to whom Recruit shares should be offered. Takeshita had been Minister of Finance in Ohira's cabinet and assumed the same portfolio in the first and second Nakasone cabinets. When Kiichi Miyazawa took over the Ministry of Finance in the third Nakasone cabinet, Takeshita was named Secretary-General of the LDP. He declared his candidacy for the party presidency in May 1987 and became party President and Prime Minister in November of that year. On paper, 2,000 Recruit shares were sold to Ihei Aoki, Takeshita's long-term secretary and confidant, and 10,000 shares were purchased by Katsuyuki Fukada, a relative of Takeshita. Ezoe had left it to the secretary which name would be used because he thought that a politician and his secretary shared the same safe. In an incident reminiscent of the Lockheed scandal, Aoki committed suicide after he had been questioned by the prosecution.

Takeshita persisted in his denial of having known of the stock deals. When the evidence of Recruit's financial support became overwhelming, he admitted that he had received a total of ¥ 151 million from Recruit. But further transactions came to light after this disclosure. When Takeshita campaigned to become Nakasone's successor as Prime Minister, Ezoe gave Aoki a loan of ¥ 50 million which was repaid in several instalments. It also transpired that Takeshita's support organisation had collected ¥ 30 million through a fundraising party in Morioka. Of this sum, which had not been reported as required by law, ¥ 20 million had been entrusted to Aoki.

On 25 April 1989 Takeshita promised to step down as Prime Minister after the fiscal 1989 budget had been passed by the Diet. The public was not impressed by this promise and press comments were generally negative. The opposition had urged the dissolution of the Lower House and new elections soon after the extent of the Recruit affair had become know. The public was particularly incensed by Takeshita's insistence on attending an ASEAN conference after having announced his resignation and his lavish promises of development aid. Junior members of the LDP accused the party leadership of attempting to cover up the scandal which, they charged, would hurt the party. Takeshita's proposals of political reform were branded by the opposition as tricks to deceive the people.

Shintaro Abe, then Secretary-General of the party and Takeshita's political mentor, admitted that Recruit had supported him by political donations and purchases of party tickets in April 1989; the total was said to have come to ¥ 100 million but Abe did not confirm these conjectures. For a period of two years and seven months, Recruit had paid Mrs Abe consultant fees of ¥ 500,000 a month, for a total of about ¥ 9 million. Profits from the 17,000 shares Abe was said to have bought were estimated at ¥ 88 million.

A final report on the investigation of the Recruit affair was submitted to the Budget Committee of the Lower House on 12 June 1989, by Justice Minister Takuo Tanikawa and the Director of the Criminal Affairs Bureau of the ministry, Yasuchika Negoro. According to this report, the investigation started on 8 September 1988 with the complaint of Yanosuke Narazaki and ended on 29 May 1989, stretching over 260 days. It involved the activities of 59 public prosecutors and 159 other officials and resulted in the criminal indictments of 13, summary orders against four and suspended indictments of another four suspects.

Hiromasa Ezoe and five other Recruit executives were indicted for bribery, three officials were indicted for accepting bribes, three executives of NTT were indicted for violation of the Nippon Telegraph and Telephone Public Corporation Law by accepting bribes, and Takao Fujinami and Katsuya Ikeda were indicted for accepting bribes with agreement to actions related to official duties. Kōzō Murata was indicted for violation of the Securities Exchange Law, the secretaries of Shintaro Abe, Kiichi Miyazawa and Mutsuki Kato for violation of the Political Funds Control Law. Hiroshi Matsubara, who had approached Yanosuke Narazaki, had already been sentenced for attempted bribery.

The report stated that three members of the Diet who had accepted shares a year and ten months prior to the listing of the shares were not involved in the case. In a passage which undoubtedly referred to Nakasone and Takeshita, Negoro said no connection could be established between the jurisdictional competence of state ministers and the purchase of Cray Research supercomputers, the legal regulation of employment magazines, the recruitment agreement and the development of a resort area by Appi Sōgō Kaihatsu Kaisha (a project in which Recruit was involved). The report did not name the members of the Diet who had received Recruit shares and Negoro refused to disclose the names of those the press referred to as 'grey politicians'. He could not reveal the names, he said, because investigative information on people who were not indicted could not be disclosed. The names of Nakasone, Takeshita, Miyazawa and Tsukamoto could be mentioned because they had already answered questions on these purchases in the Diet.

Negoro asserted that the questionable activities of the Recruit group were clearly outside the jurisdictional competence of members of the Diet and state ministers or were of such a nature that their relation was purely abstract. The opposition attacked the report as a whitewash of certain persons by concealing important facts of the case. It did not explain why the acquisition of shares by eleven politicians were not related to their office. They demanded the presentation of the information on which the prosecution based the conclusion that the jurisdictional competence of dietmen or state ministers was not involved.

THE RECRUIT FALLOUT

The Liberal-Democratic Party celebrated its 50th party congress on 31 January 1989. Among the guests invited to address the meeting was Ayako Sone, a well-known author. 'Frankly speaking', she said, 'the people harbour a deep mistrust of the present Liberal-Democratic Party. Possibly you may not have noticed it because the people who congregate around you ordinarily are fans of the LDP and people utter sweet words when they are face to face with people.... Concerning the Recruit case, politicians have taken the people to be fools. They have underestimated the seriousness of the situation thinking they could get away with this kind of explanation or justification. All actions lacking discretion or sincerity indicate arrogance.'

The following day, LDP Secretary-General Shintaro Abe defended the acceptance of Recruit money. 'Political donations', he stated, 'sustain the freedom of political activities and therefore are essential to maintaining dynamic democratic politics.... So long as they are clearly disposed of under the Political Funds Control Law and other relevant laws, they are legitimate financial assistance to politicians. Politicians should not be blamed one-sidedly.... The ethics of politicians are being questioned as a result of the Recruit scandal and the public is now demanding fairness, transparency, and a rigid distinction between public and personal affairs of political funds.... The party' the statement concluded, 'is determined to reform, in full cooperation with the government, political contributions, the national electoral system and political institutions.'

The statement fails on three counts. First, the Political Funds Control Law (which, of course, was enacted by the persons it is meant to control) requires reports on above-board political contributions but does not impose a requirement for an account of the purposes for which the funds are disbursed. Secondly, a substantial amount of the money spent is unrelated to public affairs but serves to consolidate the position of the politician and ensure his re-election. Thirdly, the extent and pattern of the political donations and share sales of Recruit indicated a scheme to influence government policies and decisions in favour of Recruit's business.

Among the proposals for reform were guidelines drafted by the Conference on Political Reform announced in April 1989. They included: 1. Disclosing the assets of cabinet ministers and parliamentary vice-ministers and their families upon nomination and resignation. 2. Discouraging cabinet ministers and vice-ministers from dealing in stocks. 3. Restricting fund-raising parties and purchases of tickets by corporations. 4. Imposing penalties for giving wedding presents and other gifts. 5. Returning the profits from Recruit share transactions to society. 6. Reducing the number of Diet seats. 7. Disclosing details on revenues and expenditures of political parties.

How seriously these reforms were meant can be gauged by Prime Minister Takeshita's proposal to reduce the number of Diet seats by one. A poll by Kyodo News Service in April 1989 found that public support for the Takeshita cabinet had dropped to 3.4 per cent while the rate of disapproval of the cabinet came to 87.6 per cent. No other cabinet in Japan's post-war history has experienced such a rejection by the people.

The prosecutors filed charges against eleven of the officials and politicians involved in the Recruit scandal. Hisashi Shinto, former Chairman of NTT, and Ei Shikiba, a former NTT executive, have been found guilty of accepting bribes, and so has Takashi Kato, former Vice-Minister of Labour.

RECENT SCANDALS

At the beginning of 1992 Japan's political establishment was rocked by two new scandals. The first involved Kyōwa Co., a steel-frame manufacturer which became the victim of the collapse of the 'bubble' economy. In its endeavour to expand its business, Kyōwa spent large sums in order to influence politicians. Fumio Abe, a former aide to Prime Minister Kiichi Miyazawa and state minister in charge of the Hokkaido and Okinawa development agencies was arrested and indicted for bribery in February 1992. He was charged with having accepted ¥ 50 million from Kyōwa for information on highway projects in Hokkaido. Goro Moriguchi, former President of Kyōwa Co., pleaded guilty of having given Abe ¥ 90 million in bribes. Former Prime Minister

Zenkō Suzuki was allegedly given ¥ 100 million for his agreement to become honorary chairman of a golf club Kyōwa intended to organise. Another politician implicated in the Kyōwa affair was Jun Shiozaki, also a member of the Miyazawa faction and former Director-General of the Management and Coordination Agency, who received ¥ 120 million from Kyōwa to buy a plot of land from the company.

A scandal which may rival the Recruit affair in scope involved one of the country's largest trucking concerns. Sagawa Kyubin comprised twelve regional companies of which Tokyo Sagawa Kyubin was the core member firm. The former President of the firm, Hiroyasu Watanabe, and a former executive, Jun Saotome, borrowed from banks and other financial institutions or guaranteed loans, thus raising a total of ¥ 528 billion. They channelled these funds to 58 companies and 26 individuals. Some of the companies were ineligible for bank loans, others were dummy corporations set up to circumvent the group's ban on stock speculation and some had ties with the Inagawa gangster organisation. Tokyo Sagawa Kyubin made political donations to about 130 members of the Diet. While Kyōwa limited its financial assistance to members of the Liberal-Democratic Party, Tokyo Sagawa Kyubin extended its financial largesse also to politicians of the opposition.

According to a TV news report allegedly based on statements of Hiroyasu Watanabe to the prosecutors, 12 politicians received a total of ¥ 2.23 billion in 1989 and 1991. Shin Kanemaru, Vice-President of the Liberal-Democratic Party, head of the Takeshita faction and chief power broker, admitted having received ¥ 500 million in unreported political donations from Watanabe. Other recipients included former Prime Ministers Noboru Takeshita and Yasuhiro Nakasone (¥ 200 million each), and former Prime Minister Sōsuke Uno (¥ 100 million). Also named were former LDP Secretary-General Ichirō Ozawa, former Chief Cabinet Secretary Takao Fujinami and Foreign Minister Michio Watanabe. The report also stated that the former head of an opposition party was given ¥ 200 million, a former cabinet member and a former head of an LDP faction each ¥ 300 million.

Another victim of the scandal was Kiyoshi Kanebo who was forced to resign as governor of Niigata Prefecture because his 1989 gubernatorial campaign had received ¥ 300 million in secret donations from Tokyo Sagawa Kyubin. In a front-page story, the *Mainichi Shimbun's* 1 September 1992 evening edition quoted 'informed sources' as saying that Transport Minister Keiwa Okuda had received ¥ 100 million in unreported donations from Tokyo Sagawa Kyubin over 1989 and 1990.

Shin Kanemaru tendered his resignation as Vice-President of the party and offered to quit as head of the Takeshita faction. As mentioned above, under Japan's bribery law, charges can only be brought against politicians who had government posts with direct authority over the briber when the money was given. Kanemaru was not serving in such a post at the time of receiving the donations.

Kanemaru was repeatedly summoned to appear before the Public Prosecutors for questioning but he refused. The Tokyo District Prosecutors' Office agreed to accept a written statement admitting that Kanemaru accepted ¥ 500 million in undeclared political donations from Tokyo Sagawa Kyubin Co. Based on this admission, the procurators will file a summary indictment for violation of the Political Fund Control Law and the case will end without a trial, Kanemaru only paying a fine.

The weekly *Shūkan Bunshun* published an article with the title 'Why is the prosecution so weak-kneed on Kanemaru?' which attributed the prosecution's retreat to political pressure. The prosecution's discussion of political donations in the initial statement in the trial of Hiroyasu Watanabe was reduced from several pages to a few lines and all names were omitted. According to the magazine, the main wirepuller influencing the prosecutors in favour of politicians is Yasuchika Negoro, Vice-Minister of Justice. That a politician can successfully defy the law shows that 'something is rotten in the state' of Japan.

Watanabe and Saotome have been arrested on suspicion of aggravated breach of trust. Also arrested was Yasuo Matsuyama, President of Heiwado Real Estate Co., who allegedly paid Watanabe 10 per cent of the loans guaranteed by Sagawa Kyubin. Losses suffered by Sagawa Kyubin from the liabilities incurred by the loan guarantees amounted to ¥ 64.5 billion. Unsubstantiated rumours denied by the government accuse Japanese politicians of accepting kick-backs from loans to South Korea and other development aid. *Japan Inc. in Asia*, a book published in the Philippines, alleges that Japanese firms paid kick-backs to former President Ferdinand Marcos. Official Development Aid (ODA) contracts required the hiring of Japanese consultants who received up to 350,000 pesos a month. Altogether, 24 Japanese consulting firms were paid ¥ 15 billion in connection with ODA contracts.

[See Appendix II]

An American newspaper claimed that Foreign Minister Michio Watanabe was linked to a consortium of companies building Asia's largest trade convention and amusement centre on the site of Jakarta's former Kemayoran Airport. The $ 220 million Jakarta Fair Project is partly financed by Japanese Official Development Aid and Japanese companies are said to pay huge sums to politicians who help them to participate in ODA projects. In reply to the newspaper allegation, the Foreign Ministry declared that Watanabe does not profit from the Indonesian project or any other project receiving ODA funds.

The search for a successor to Takeshita as party President and Prime Minister revealed the disarray into which the Recruit affair had thrown the LDP. Since the leading candidates for these posts prior to the scandal, Kiichi Miyazawa and Shintaro Abe, had become tainted with the stigma of money politics, even the LDP did not dare propose either for these posts. After much soul-searching, Abe asked Masayoshi Ito, chairman of the executive board of the party, to accept the positions. But Ito refused, citing as reasons his advanced age (75) and poor health (he suffers from diabetes). Actually, Ito was well aware that he was only to be used as a figurehead for a short period until the Recruit affair was out of the focus of public attention and politics was back to 'normal'. When Abe insisted, Ito, according to rumours, presented four conditions: first, Nakasone was to appear before the Diet and establish responsibility for the Recruit scandal; secondly, all party factions were to be dissolved; thirdly, important positions were to be given to younger party members; fourthly, senior politicians would have to resign from the Diet, including Nakasone, Takeshita, Abe, Miyazawa and Michio Watanabe. Ito himself would resign after elections for a new Diet. Watanabe was furious, and everybody found the demand of dissolving all factions unacceptable.

As it happened, Takeshita never asked Ito to become his successor in the end. Two party elders, Takeo Fukuda and Zenkō Suzuki, involved themselves in the talks. Fukuda declared himself willing to serve again as prime minister but both favoured Ganri Yamashita, a war veteran who had served as Director-General of the Defence Agency. Takeshita and the four party executives, however, chose Sōsuke Uno, a member of the Nakasone faction, who was Foreign Minister in the Takeshita cabinet. A party caucus which convened to ratify the choice was boycotted by 44 party members, including Fukuda and Suzuki. They were angry because the party rules which stipulate election by all party members in the Diet had again been disregarded, as in the nomination of Takeshita, and supplanted by backroom manoeuvring. There was an editorial in the London newspaper, *The Daily Telegraph* declaring that the Japanese did not deserve a ruling party whose sleazy habits were reminiscent more of the Third World than the advanced industrial state they had created since the war.

Uno was the first Prime Minister in the 34-year history of the LDP who was not backed by a faction of his own. In order to refurbish the party's blemished image, the Uno cabinet soon after its formation, published a number of guidelines. Cabinet ministers should refrain from accepting payments from private companies for lectures or other activities if amounts were 'socially unacceptable'. They should not buy unlisted shares or accept entertainment by executives whose business activities were under the jurisdiction of their respective agencies.

Four days after having taken over, the new team was embarrassed by the disclosure that Ryūtaro Hashimoto, appointed Secretary-General of the party, had failed to report ¥ 160 million collected by a fund-raising party in April 1985 for which Recruit had bought ¥ 400,000 worth of tickets. Uno was not rated as a leading politician (he was called 'a mediocrity among mediocrities') and he suffered a fatal blow when a weekly newspaper, the *Sunday Mainichi*, published allegations by a former geisha that Uno had paid her for sexual favours and that she had received ¥ 3 million for a five-month affair in 1985 and 1986. She appeared on television and produced the official envelope in which she had been given the money. Another geisha published an article in the magazine *Shūkan Shinchō* in which she described a ten-year relationship with Uno who came to her apartment every week for dinner and stayed overnight. A third geisha regaled the public with the revelation of her encounters with Uno. He refused to comment on these allegations claiming that his private affairs were no topic for public discussion. Since these disclosures came a few weeks before the Paris summit in July 1989, a rumour started that Uno would resign as Prime Minister but he denied any intention of stepping down.

Since the affair had received so much attention in the media, the LDP was frantically looking for a way to have somebody else rather than Uno to represent Japan at the summit but he insisted on carrying out his duties as Japan's highest official. The ordinary citizen was partly amused by the quandary into which the party had found themselves but even more angry that Japan's reputation was hurt by the irresponsible machinations of Takeshita and his cohorts. The press was unanimous in condemning Takeshita for failing to foresee the trouble. Because of the opposition within the party, Uno's casual remark that he was thinking of resigning was immediately leaked to the press and Uno was forced to deny that he was giving up his post. A newspaper poll in the middle of July found that only 14.5 per cent (men 19.6 per cent, women 10.8 per cent) supported the Uno cabinet while 50.0 per cent (men 54.4 per cent, women 46.9 per cent) were opposed to it.

The LDP, labouring under the triple handicap of the Recruit affair, the consumption tax and the liberalisation of agricultural imports, was further hurt by the battered image of Mr Uno. In an election to fill a vacant seat in the Upper House, the LDP candidate lost to a Socialist candidate, a housewife with no other political recommendation than the endorsement of the Socialist Party. This election, in Niigata Prefecture, the home province of Kakuei Tanaka and a traditional conservative stronghold, cast deep gloom on the party and boded ill for the elections in Tokyo and those of half the members of the Upper House scheduled for July 1989.

The elections to the Tokyo Municipal Assembly on 2 July 1989 confirmed the prognosis. The LDP lost 20 seats whereas the number of Socialist members increased three times. Particularly noteworthy was the increase in the number of women elected to the assembly which rose from 2 to 17. The wrath of women voters against the consumption tax and the sex scandal involving the Prime Minister surfaced in the large number of women voters (61.29 per cent of eligible voters) compared with men (56.16 per cent). The rate of successful women candidates was 51.5 per cent (17 out of 33) whereas it was 44.6 per cent (95 out of 213) for men. In 10 election districts, women candidates gained the highest number of votes.

The LDP seemed bent on self-destruction. Hisano Norinouchi, Minister of Agriculture, Forestry and Fisheries, was reported to have said in a meeting to support the local candidate for the Upper House election in Mie Prefecture: 'Women are useless in politics'. He attacked the chairwoman of the Socialist Party personally saying 'Chairwoman Doi is a fool. She does not have the ability to lead a government because the Socialist Party has spelled out an unrealistic agricultural policy!' Takako Doi would not be equal to the task of prime minister, he said, 'because she is not married and has no children'. It was doubtful, Norinouchi commented, whether the Socialist Party could take responsibility for the future of Japan because it placed 'Madonnas' in the political world (the media had dubbed the nomination of women candidates for the Upper House election 'Madonna strategy').

A few days later, Kurō Matsuda, an LDP Lower House member, infuriated farmers when he remarked on a television show that they were manual workers who would be incapable of finding other work if Japan's rice market were liberalised. 'Farmers are manual labourers. They have not received training for other work. If they become unemployed, they will have trouble finding work.' Matsuda, of course, was speaking in ignorance because Japanese farmers have traditionally taken up other work, particularly in the construction industry, during the winter months. The farm vote has kept the LDP in power and if the party loses the support of the farmers, it will not be able to maintain its position.

This was a contributing factor in the dismal showing of the LDP in the elections to half of the membership of the Upper House on 23 July 1989. For the first time since its formation in 1955 the LDP lost its majority. At stake were 126 of the 252 seats; 76 were contested in local constituencies, 50 were distributed on the basis of proportional representation by voting for the national lists drawn up by the parties. The LDP gained 21 seats in the local constituencies, down from the 50 seats it had held prior to the election. In the voting for the national lists, 15 of the party's candidates were elected, against 19 seats the party had held before the election. Altogether, the party gained 36 seats, down from 69 before the election. With the 73 seats not up for election, the party's strength decreased from 142 before the election to 109, insufficient for a majority in the 252-member House.

The Socialist Party emerged as the big winner from the loss of the LDP. It gained 26 seats in the local constituencies, up from 13, and 19 on the national list, up from nine. Together with the 20 seats not up for election, the party's strength rose to 66, a gain of 24 seats compared with the pre-election 42 seats. The party's victory was a personal triumph for Chairwoman Takako Doi,who had campaigned relentlessly from Hokkaido to Kyushu and succeeded in getting the party's candidates elected in some arch-conservative constituencies in rural Japan. Particularly noteworthy was the large increase in successful women candidates (21) which brought the number of women in the Upper House to 31.

Prime Minister Sōsuke Uno announced that he would step down as soon as a successor was named. How little some politicians had been affected by the anger of the people at the corruption in the LDP can be gauged from Motoharu Morishita's suggestion that Nakasone would be a suitable successor to Uno (Morishita belongs to the Nakasone faction). During the election, Ryūtaro Hashimoto, the party's Secretary-General, had become the public's favourite among the party leaders. But Takeshita feared that Hashimoto's popularity would become a threat to his leadership and the Abe faction wanted to safeguard Abe's chance of becoming prime minister. Takeshita, Abe and Nakasone agreed on making Toshiki Kaifu of the small Komoto faction Sōsuke Uno's successor. Kaifu was chosen not for solving the problems facing the party but because he could be used and discarded if the situation allowed a comeback of the old guard. The interests of the factional leaders, not those of the country or the party, were decisive.

On account of the strong criticism of the way in which Nakasone, Takeshita and Uno had been selected as Party President, it seemed desirable to have a pro forma election. Two other candidates ran in the election, Yoshiro Hayashi, a member of the Nikaido group, and Shintaro Ishihara who belongs to the Abe faction. He participated against the wishes of the faction's leadership and had great difficulty in finding 20 sponsors to back his candidacy. For the election, 47 representatives of the party's prefectural chapters were added to the party members of both houses. Kaifu received 279 votes, Hayashi 120 and Ishihara 48 (four votes were invalid). It was the first time in 17 years that a party caucus had elected the Party President.

On 9 August 1989 the Diet voted to nominate the Prime Minister. In the Upper House, none of the candidates gained a majority in the first ballot; in the second ballot, Takako Doi was nominated with 127 votes against Kaifu's 109. In the Lower House, where the LDP controls a solid majority, Kaifu was approved with 294 votes out of a total 487. In accordance to the Diet Law, a council of ten legislators from each house was formed to reconcile the divergent decisions of the two chambers. Since no agreement could be reached, the choice of the House of Representatives prevailed on the basis of Article 67 of the constitution.

Toshiki Kaifu's term of office ended on 30 October 1989 since he held office only for the unexpired rest of Uno's term. Kaifu's position was weak. A disciple of the late Takeo Miki, he lacked Miki's decisiveness in political convictions. In a TV appearance, Mrs Mutsuko Miki, Takeo Miki's widow, expressed regret that Kaifu let himself be used for factional politics. Although Kaifu succeeded in having two women nominated to cabinet posts (one, Mrs Sumiko Takahara, was the first non-politician to be appointed to a cabinet post) and resisted Takeshita's demand to retain some of Uno's crew, the line-up of the cabinet reflected the customary factional balance (Takeshita faction, five posts; Abe, Nakasone and Miyazawa factions, four each: Komoto faction, two). The three top party posts went to the Takeshita, Abe and Nakasone factions; the second largest faction led by Kiichi Miyazawa was left out. Kaifu, however, was able to strengthen his position, chiefly by avoiding making mistakes. When his term expired, the pachinko scandal dominated the political scene and the party could not afford to engage in an internecine struggle. Kaifu, therefore, was confirmed for a two-year term in his own right.

Eight members of Kaifu's first cabinet were reported to have received funds from Recruit amounting to ¥ 37.31 million. Kaifu defended himself and his colleagues by declaring that the money had been duly reported and that all contributions had been received prior to the disclosure of the scandal in 1988. In Kaifu's second cabinet, seven members had been given a total of ¥ 48.83 million. Kaifu told the Lower House that he had been given ¥ 14.4 million in the form of donations and purchases of party tickets between 1983 and 1987. When Kaifu formed his third cabinet, he successfully fought off attempts by factional leaders to include politicians tainted by the Lockheed and Recruit scandals. Some politicians, among them Nakasone, contended that their re-election in February 1990 had cleansed them of the stain of the scandal. Kaifu asserted that the funds he and six others in his cabinet had received were legitimate political contributions made before June 1988. But the media reported that a political organisation affiliated with Post and Telecommunications Minister Takashi Fukaya had received donations from Recruit Co. several months after the exposure of the scandal and Fukaya admitted the charge.

The cavalier attitude of many LDP politicians to the Recruit scandal was exemplified in a remark by Kazaya Ishibashi, Minister of Education in the first Kaifu cabinet. Commenting on the resignation of three high-ranking ministry officials who were forced to quit because they had accepted gifts from Recruit, Ishibashi said he would not have dismissed the officials as they had already been admonished which should have been sufficient. He added that the ministry had lost competent officials for whom he had not yet found suitable replacements. The National Tax Administration Agency decided that the profits from the sales of the Recruit shares were not liable to tax because they remained below the taxable minimum.

Only two weeks after the formation of the first Kaifu cabinet another extra-marital affair prompted the resignation of Chief Cabinet Secretary Tokuo Yamashita. He had had a three-year relationship with a young woman and when he was nominated to the cabinet post, he offered his ex-lover ¥ 3 million to buy her silence. The lady, offended by the politician's attempted bribe, told her story to a weekly.

With the appointment of Kiichi Miyazawa, who had been deeply involved in the Recruit scandal to succeed Toshiki Kaifu as Prime Minister, Japanese politics was back to business as usual.

Chapter 8

Education in Japan

PART 1: TEXTBOOK CENSORSHIP

POST-WAR EDUCATIONAL REFORMS

For a few years after the Second World War, the publication of schoolbooks was relatively free. The original Board of Education Law enumerated the determination of course content and the selection of textbooks among the rights of the Boards of Education (Art. 49, No. 3 & 4) and provided that the prefectural Boards of Education should examine textbooks for all schools in the prefecture 'following the standards of the Ministry of Education' (Art. 50, No. 3). But in the latter part of the 1950s, the trend to 'revise' the post-war educational system in conformity with Japan's 'national conditions' emerged.

In 1955 the Democratic Party (one of the predecessors of the Liberal-Democratic Party) attacked the 'bias' in textbooks which prompted the Ministry of Education to enforce stricter standards for the approval and selection of textbooks. In 1956 a bill incorporating the ministry's intention was submitted to the Diet but was not enacted, thanks to the determined opposition of teachers and educators. However, the new law regulating the Boards of Education deprived them of the right to examine and select textbooks and then Minister of Education Hirokichi Nadao declared that he would carry out a reform of the textbook system by administrative measures. With typical bureaucratic arbitrariness, he reorganised the Textbook Examination Council (*kyōkasho shingikai*)and without any legal foundation, created textbook examiners (*kyōkasho chōsakan*).

While the original text of the School Education Law (*Gakkō Kyōiku-hō*) had stipulated that textbooks to be used in elementary schools should have been examined or approved by the 'supervisory agency' (*kantoku-chō*) or should be textbooks for which the supervisory agency possessed the copyright (Art. 21, par. 1), the revised law provided that only textbooks approved by the Minister of Education or for which the ministry held the copyright could be used. This provision was also applied to junior (Art. 40) and senior high schools (Art. 51) for which no such restrictions existed in the original law. The revision did not change the provisions charging the 'supervisory agency' with determining the subjects to be taught in elementary (Art. 20), junior (Art. 38) and senior high schools (Art. 43) but since the Ministry of Education enforces its 'course of study', these provisions have lost all meaning. Paragraph 2 of Article 21 provides that 'Besides the textbooks mentioned in the preceding paragraph, books and other teaching materials which are useful and appropriate can be used'. But this provision only obscures the fact that in Japan's public school system, teaching has to conform to the thinking of the bureaucracy. That such a revision of the law could be enacted is a sign of a deplorable lack of understanding of the basic principles of democracy in the minds of the majority of Japanese law-makers.

The main effect of the Ministry of Education's censorship has been the suppression of everything the ministry does not like, including anything unfavourable to Japan. The situation has reverted to being very much the same as before SCAP's reforms of the educational system when the Ministry of Education actually compiled all textbooks. Another result has been the gradual reappearance of nationalistic tendencies and the slanting of history even to the extent of misrepresenting events. Fortunately, the ministry cannot control the thinking of teachers and the ideological sterilisation of textbooks has not been able to prevent the anti-establishment influence of living teachers.

Since the Ministry of Education has usurped the right to determine the curricula of Japan's school system, it naturally tries to adapt the textbooks to the curricula. The ministry's officials, who are always trying to improve the standards of the course of study, do not feel the burden imposed on the pupils. The members of the Examination Council are specialists who each think that their own field is of great importance and want to have things included the layman would consider superfluous but with which the teacher has to wrestle.

An Englishman who has helped Japanese professors write English textbooks for junior high schools declared that the stringent restrictions imposed by the ministry's guidelines on vocabulary and grammatical structures made it extremely difficult and sometimes impossible to create a natural and accurate text so that many awkward words and expressions had to be left in.

The Kishi cabinet (1957-1960) brought a shift to the right and the Minister of Education, Tō Matsunaga, unfurled the banner of 'racial reconstruction' (*minzoku saiken*). He ordered a revision of the curricula, including a revival of moral education, and had the Enforcement Regulations of the School Education Law amended. The 'Course of Study' (*Gakushū Shidō Yōryō*) was inserted in the official gazette in the form of a notification (*kokuji*) and later incorporated into the 'Examination Standard for Schoolbooks' which the Ministry of Education interpreted as having the force of law.

REVISIONISM

Based on the recommendations of the National Council on Education Reform re-established by Prime Minister Yasuhiro Nakasone in 1984, the Ministry of Education undertook a comprehensive revision of the courses of study for elementary, junior and senior high school. The most pronounced feature of the revised courses was the emphasis put on 'Japanese identity' and the strong nationalistic accents. Sixth-grade history classes comprise the study of 42 individuals prominent in Japan's history such as Queen Himiko, Prince Shōtoku, Emperor Shōmu, Murasaki Shikibu, Francis Xavier, Tokugawa Ieyasu, Motoori Norinaga, Commodore Perry, Emperor Meiji and Admiral Tōgō. In an attempt to instil respect for the Emperor, elementary school pupils are to be taught the 'matters of state carried out by the Emperor' which may attribute to these formal acts a significance at variance with their constitutional meaning.

The revised course of study reveals the ministry's obsession with the national flag and the national anthem. The course specifically orders teachers of elementary, junior and senior high schools to display the flag and to make students sing the *Kimi ga yo* at all school events such as entrance and graduation ceremonies. The revised ministerial ordinance ordains punishment for school principals disobeying the command to use flag and anthem at all school ceremonies. To my mind, the Ministry of Education has no legal authority to issue such an order.

In the description of civic studies for junior high schools, the phrase 'to make students aware of the historic significance of the enactment of the constitution which aims at the realisation of democracy' was dropped and replaced by the directive 'to make students think about the nation's security and defence'.

Although the post-war system remains more rational and less authoritarian than the pre-war order, there are still elements left over from the feudal era. The prevailing educational policies try to make the young generation loyal subjects of the Emperor rather than independent, thinking individuals. In the Meiji era the Emperor system was used to effect the country's modernisation; now it is used to maintain the existing social order. This policy can succeed because the Japanese are not critical of authority but rather tend to accept it without question.

Despite the post-war reforms, the present school system and the educational philosophy behind it are a direct continuation of the Meiji era. The system, called 'controlled education' (*kanri kyōiku*), makes the schools instruments of government policies. The central government makes the decisions about the right questions to be asked and the right way to answer them. Rather than encouraging students to think for themselves, the system makes sure that students passively accept what they are told. The mental regimentation is supported by external discipline. The school authorities tightly control the daily lives of the students with minute regulations concerning dress, hairstyle and activities after school. Although many teachers and parents regard these regulations as too strict and unnecessary, it seems unlikely that the system will be changed in the near future. Creativity is stifled and students often end up hating everything related to the school, but the ambition, if not of the students themselves, then of their parents of gaining admission to a 'good' university makes them endure the hardship of preparing for the entrance examination.

THE TEXTBOOK APPROVAL SYSTEM

The compilation and publication of textbooks has become a highly specialised field of publishing. The publishing companies act as mediators between the authors, the bureaucracy (Textbook Examination Section, Textbook Examination and Review Council) and the schools. Naturally, the examination and selection of textbooks are of great concern to the publishers, as usually the same books are chosen for all elementary schools in the prefecture. Textbooks for elementary, junior and senior high schools can only be published and sold by publishers approved by the Ministry of Education. With the exception of textbooks for universities, the constitutional guarantees of freedom of expression and academic freedom as well as the prohibition of censorship are a sham as far as textbooks are concerned.

In the old procedure for approval of textbooks, the author and/or publisher submitted the manuscript to the Ministry of Education, where it was first read by examiners (*kyōkasho chōsakan*) who wrote an opinion on it (*chōsa ikensho*) and sent it to the Examination and Review Council (*kyōka-yō tosho kentei chōsa shingi kai*). The council had the manuscript evaluated by experts (*chōsa-in*) who reported their opinions to the council (*hyōteisho*) which, on the basis of the two reports, decided whether it should be approved, disapproved or conditionally approved. The corrections imposed by the examiner could be demanded unconditionally (i.e., the author had to comply) or as proposals for improvement (which could be disregarded). About 95 per cent of all manuscripts were conditionally approved. If the passages found objectionable by the censors were corrected, the manuscript would be approved. The examination as to whether the correction had been made to the satisfaction of the censors constituted the second stage of the screening process referred to as private examination (*naietsu-hon shinsa*). At the third stage, a sample copy was submitted (*mihon-hon shinsa*) and binding, printing and other external aspects of the book were examined. The screening process also extended to the teaching materials for correspondence courses although there is no legal foundation for such an examination.

At the beginning of 1989 the Ministry of Education sent a proposal to the Textbook Authorisation Council under which the intermediate stage in the textbook review process would be eliminated. In the old system, if a textbook was conditionally approved the author submitted a second draft and negotiated with the examiners on the changes before submitting a final draft. This negotiating stage has been abolished. Under the new system, the council, not the examiner, directly instructs the author to make the changes deemed necessary. When the second draft is submitted, the council decides whether the textbook is acceptable. The new rules empower the Minister of Education to order publishing companies to make changes even after the textbooks have cleared screening.

The new screening standards require that textbooks deal with all items in the course of study. Moreover, a number of principles have to be observed. No unnecessary items should be added; there should be no inappropriate descriptions; items should not be described one-sidedly; rights or interests of particular individuals or organisations should not be infringed upon. In an attempt to obviate criticism of the screening system, the Ministry of Education announced in February 1991 that the original texts, summaries of the ministry's assessments and authorised versions of the textbooks would be made public. The textbooks for the school year starting April 1991 and the summaries of the reviews were displayed at the Textbook Research Centre Foundation in Koto Ward from 1 July to 30 September. The Japan Federation of Publishing Workers (Shuppan Rōren) demanded that the assessments should be made public in their entirety and that the deleted parts should also be disclosed.

VARNISHED HISTORY

The education division of the Liberal-Democratic Party had demanded that the history course for sixth-graders should include an account of Emperor Jimmu, Japan's first mythological Emperor. The ministry avoided mentioning this legendary figure directly, claiming that legend should not be confused with historical fact, but ordered that 'appropriate parts' of the *Kojiki* (*Records of Ancient Events*, compiled AD 711-712), *Nihon Shoki* (*Chronicles of Japan*, compiled AD 720) and *Fudoki* (*Reports on the Provinces*; only those on four provinces are extant; compilation ordered in 713) should be included. The ministry also commanded the 'Northern Territories' to be described as an integral part of Japan and the expression 'the World War involving Japan' instead of the 'Pacific War' to be used. The new regulations are apparently to make sure that textbooks contain nothing with which the ministry disagrees. If this is not censorship, I do not know what censorship is.

The officials of the Ministry of Education have been inclined to support a revisionist view of Japan's recent history, extenuating Imperialistic and militaristic excesses or even defending chauvinistic policies. Descriptions of Japan's penetration of China, the Sino-Japanese and Russo-Japanese wars and the annexation of Korea did not mention the injustices inflicted on the Chinese and Korean peoples by these aggressive actions. Particularly objectionable was the presentation of the Second World War and the attempts to play down or conceal the atrocities committed by the Japanese army, detailing the losses suffered by Japan (above all the horrors of Hiroshima and Nagasaki) without even mentioning the harm inflicted on the countries and regions victimised by the war. In particular, the ministry tried to suppress accounts of the Rape of Nanking in 1937. Over 140,000 civilians were killed in the orgy of rape and murder; altogether, 10 million Chinese were killed or died of starvation and disease as a result of Japan's invasion of China. Some authors were asked to use the expression 'Great East Asia War' when referring to Japan's part in the Second World War, a designation used by the government and the military to signify that the war was fought to liberate East Asia from Western domination.

In June 1990 the Japan Socialist Party demanded the abolition of the textbook screening system. In a statement signed by Chairwoman Takako Doi and presented to the Chief Cabinet Secretary, Misoji Sakamoto and the Minister of Education Kosuke Hori, the party said that the Ministry's 'unjust school textbook screening over the years has deleted and distorted historical truths'. Most textbooks, the party declared, did not discuss historical events related to Japan's colonisation of Korea or the massacre of Koreans in Japan during the Great Kanto Earthquake of 1923. Only two textbooks mentioned the draft of Koreans for forced labour in Japan.

Another episode the Ministry of Education has consistently tried to keep out of schoolbooks is the battle of Okinawa, the only major campaign of the Second World War fought on Japanese soil. The Japanese High Command regarded the battle not as a defence of Okinawa but as a delaying action, to slow down the American advance on Japan's mainland. It therefore anticipated that resistance would continue to the death of the last soldier (*gyokusai*). The total strength of the American forces deployed against Okinawa amounted to 548,000 men, higher than Okinawa's population of 450,000. Japanese combat troops numbered 110,000; they were reinforced by local regular forces, militiamen and boys and girls in their mid-teens drafted for auxiliary duty. They included the *Himeyuri butai* (Starlily Corps), a group of 223 field hospital nurses composed of girl students from Okinawa Normal School and No. 1 Women's High School and their teachers.

While the American losses came to 12,520 dead, Japanese casualties numbered about 66,000 regular soldiers, 84,000 local people who helped the army and 95,000 non-combatant civilians. Several hundred Okinawans were executed by the army as spies; women and children were robbed of their food or driven out of their shelters by Japanese soldiers and many died caught between the invading Americans and the defending Japanese. The carnage of the civilian population, and particularly the massacre of Okinawans by the Japanese army, has never been fully investigated and the accounts of this phase of the war have been deleted or embellished by the censors of the Ministry of Education.

The obliteration of the war from the collective memory of the nation (with the exception of the Hiroshima and Nagasaki bombings) has not been solely the work of the Ministry of Education. While the post-war ideology of peace and democracy together with the opposition to war and rearmament was very much alive in the student movement of the 1960s and early 1970s, the consumerism spawned by what was (erroneously) called the affluent society has pushed these issues out of the public consciousness. In 1988 the New York-based Chinese Alliance for Memorials and Justice organised a demonstration in front of the Japanese consulate to protest the attempts to conceal wartime events. The demonstrators displayed photos of war atrocities, carried placards decrying the massacre of civilians by Japanese forces in Nanking and called the Emperor the ultimate war criminal.

Foreigners have often blamed Japan for its failure to recognise its past and show remorse and compassion for the millions of people in China and South East Asia who were systematically starved, worked and tortured to death by Japanese forces. Former prisoners-of-war who survived the horrors of Japanese prison camps have been particularly bitter. Japan has not atoned for its war responsibilities nor given redress to those who suffered from the brutality and inhumanity of Japanese conduct during the war. Naturally the behaviour of Japanese soldiers was not universally bad, and there was much atrocity and inhumanity on the other side. But the attitude of the Ministry of Education and some Japanese politicians seems to say that there is nothing in Japan's war record for which it should be reproached.

The legacy of anti-Japanese feelings is not limited to the memories of physical and mental suffering caused by the war. There have been some effects seldom mentioned such as the enormous destruction of public and private property, the losses incurred by people forced to accept scrip (paper money denominated in yen issued by the Japanese military in occupied areas) or to buy German mark bonds which the Japanese government now refuses to redeem. The fiftieth anniversary of the attack on Pearl Harbor brought an avalanche of statements and ceremonies related to the war. Prime Minister Kiichi Miyazawa and Foreign Minister Michio Watanabe expressed remorse over Japan's aggression but the Diet refused to offer an apology for the war.

In 1982, when the Chinese protested against the attempts to whitewash Japan's wartime behaviour, Tokuma Utsunomiya, a politician who had contributed greatly to the normalisation of Japan's relations with China, expressed the opinion that the maturing of the generation born after the war and the sense of superiority stemming from Japan's economic strength has made the Japanese arrogant in their approach to foreign nations, particularly their Asian neighbours. Such arrogance, Utsunomiya said, was typified by the Ministry of Education's revisions of high school textbooks.

POLITICAL INDOCTRINATION

For the 1981 school year, the Ministry introduced a new course called 'Contemporary Society' (*gendai shakai*) to be taught in the first year of high school. The Liberal-Democratic Party and the ministry applied strong pressure to have right-wing views incorporated in the textbooks, such as the explicit statement that the Self-Defence Forces were constitutional. In the same year, the author of an elementary school textbook who had included a Russian fairy-tale was forced to omit the piece.

A social studies textbook stated that for the improvement of working conditions, working hours would have to be shortened. The ministry ordered the deletion of the reference to working hours and had the following sentence inserted: 'If women are to continue to work on equal terms with men, women's self-awakening is required in such fields as work morale and ethics'. Another textbook discussed the fingerprinting system under the Alien Registration Law and the opposition to it. The ministry ordered the omission of this section because it was a one-sided argument since the book did not state the law's purpose of clarifying the status of foreigners and confirming their identity - the government's argument for requiring fingerprinting. The ministry had the word 'fascism' deleted in a paragraph dealing with the forced labour of Koreans and Chinese and the massacre of Chinese in Shanghai and Nanking as a result of Japanese militarism. Demonstrating again the pig-headedness of Japanese bureaucrats, the ministry replaced 'aggression' by 'military advance' - a revision which had become a diplomatic issue in 1982 and was again denounced by the Chinese.

In September 1988 Sanseido Publishing Co. deleted a section dealing with atrocities committed by Japanese soldiers in the Second World War and replaced it with an essay on the musical *My Fair Lady*. The book, an English textbook for high schools, had already been approved by the Ministry of Education for use in second-year classes. Although the publisher denied that the change was made as a result of outside pressure, the section had been criticised by the Association of Comrades to Discuss the Nation's Basic Issues, a group of Liberal-Democratic dietmen headed by Shizuka Kamei, a representative from Hiroshima. There was not enough evidence, the group asserted, to substantiate such atrocities. The party's education affairs division likewise sent a protest to the Ministry of Education.

Reflecting its policy of making teaching conform to the tenets of the Liberal-Democratic Party, the ministry ordered the editors of social studies textbooks for junior high schools to include the assertion that Japan possesses the right to self-defence and intimated that textbooks not containing such a statement would not be approved. The textbooks for the 1993 school year, therefore, state that a sovereign country has the right to arm itself against aggression; only a single book mentions the views of the opposition. The new textbooks also express more positive views on the Self-Defence Forces than former editions.

A textbook entitled *Modern Social Studies* quoted from a novel by Michiko Ishimure to exemplify the impact of environmental pollution. Ishimure describes the feelings of a woman who lost her daughter due to the so-called Minamata disease, an organic mercury poisoning for which the pollution caused by the waste water discharged by Chisso Corporation into Minamata Bay was responsible. The ministry told the editor of the textbook that the novel was too depressing and that the book would not be approved unless the name of the company was omitted. The fact that Chisso Corporation was responsible for the pollution is a matter of judicial record because the company has been a defendant in numerous lawsuits for compensation. As the result of public protest, the ministry cancelled its prohibition and permitted the names of the companies involved in the four large pollution cases to be mentioned (the Minamata disease occurred also in Kumamoto and Niigata, the petrochemical complex in Yokkaichi caused asthma and the so-called *itai-itai* disease was caused by cadmium poisoning in Toyama).

Textbooks for the 1991-92 school year were examined under the new system which no longer allows conditional approval. Publishers, therefore, are under strong psychological pressure to conform to the ministry's guidelines. In the 67 new and 181 revised textbooks for senior high schools an average of 142 corrections were required per book. The consumption tax was mentioned in more than half of the 22 textbooks on 'Contemporary Society' but only a few touched on the Recruit scandal. The ministry instructed the publishers to tone down the people's opposition to the consumption tax and stress the positive features of the so-called tax reform, the reduction of income taxes and the implementation of welfare projects. The ministry objected to the discussion of the Recruit affair because the trials were still in progress. Publishers were also admonished to give a balanced presentation of nuclear power and to emphasise its safety if properly supervised and operated.

Primary school textbooks for the 1991-92 school year contain material on 42 historical figures as mentioned above chosen by the Ministry of Education as role models for strengthening moral education. Among them is Admiral Heihachiro Togo who annihilated Russia's Baltic Fleet in the 1905 battle of Tsushima during the Russo-Japanese War. South Korean newspapers and television stations promptly assailed the choice as a sign of Japanese chauvinism and one newspaper called Togo a 'hero of militarism'. As demanded by the ministry, the new textbooks also state that the *hi no maru* (Rising Sun) ensign is Japan's national flag and the *Kimi ga yo* the national anthem. They also assert that the four disputed islands of the Kurile chain have been Japanese territory since the Edo era and play down Japan's aggression in the Second World War.

The Japan Federation of Publishing Workers' Unions, Shuppan Rōren, compiled a number of reports on the Ministry of Education's control over the contents of textbooks. In an overall appraisal, the 1986 report said that the government had shifted from screening to require authors to omit what the government *did not like* to one requiring them to write what the government *wanted to be taught*. In a typical example, the censors issued detailed instructions concerning a discussion of the *Kojiki* and *Nihon Shoki*. These supposed chronicles of events from the age of the gods to the beginning of actual history were originally compiled to reinforce the legitimacy of the Japanese Emperors. The officials demanded that the textbooks state that the two compilations were 'books of history' and that an account of the birth of the Japanese nation be included. One textbook, therefore, inserted the following passage: 'According to these books, the Imperial family's ancestral deity is Amaterasu-Ō-Mikami, the goddess of the sun, and at her order, the Emperor started to rule the nation.'

RIGHT-WING PROPAGANDA

A recent case in which the approval of a textbook raised a storm of protest in China and Korea concerned a history book for senior high schools compiled by the National Council for the Defence of Japan. This group, headed by a former Ambassador to the UN, Toshikazu Kase, works for the revision of the constitution. It undertook the compilation of the textbook because it believed that most schoolbooks had been written by leftist scholars. The textbook, entitled *Shinpen. Nihonshi* (New Edition, Japanese History) and published by Hara Shobō, was compiled and edited by a team under the direction of Jirō Murao who served as textbook examiner from 1956 to 1975 and appeared as witness for the government in the suit filed by Professor Saburo Ienaga (discussed below).

The book shows the two tendencies typical of the recent revisionist interpretation of Japanese history: the denial or justification of the excesses of Japanese militarism and the cult of the Emperor. The restatement of the myths about the foundation of Japan in the textbook ignores the results of Japanese scholarship and the emphasis on the role of the Emperors in the description of Japanese history reflects the distortions called *kōkoku shikan* (Empire view of history). The compilers strongly resisted the attempts of the Ministry of Education to make them interpret the Imperial Rescript of January 1946 as the Emperor's renunciation of any claim to divinity. The book gives the impression that China and Korea were responsible for the Sino-Japanese War and the annexation of Korea by Japan and that Japan legitimately colonised Korea on the basis of agreements and treaties signed voluntarily by that country. It does not mention the attempts to assimilate Korea (forcing Koreans to adopt Japanese names and promoting the use of the Japanese language) nor the conscription of Koreans and Chinese for forced labour before and during the war.

The ministry approved the manuscript but wanted to have some 800 'inappropriate' expressions revised. The Foreign Ministry of the People's Republic of China accused Japan's Ministry of Education of failing to honour a 1982 promise to seriously self-examine the great harm Japan inflicted on the Chinese people during the 1937-1945 war. The Chinese news agency Xinhua charged that the textbook distorted history by describing Japan's aggression against China as necessary and glossing over the holocaust perpetrated by Japanese troops in Nanking in 1937. The book whitewashes the Pacific War as a Japanese effort to liberate Asia from the rule of the European and American powers and to build a greater East Asia Coprosperity Sphere. Similar protests came from North and South Korea, Hong Kong and the Philippines.

The group refused to comply with the instructions to correct some expressions three times but after the protests from abroad, Prime Minister Nakasone remarked that certain parts of the book should be re-examined and the group finally agreed to make some changes. Education Minister Toshiki Kaifu (who became Prime Minister in 1989) defended the approval of the book and said that the Japanese government would explain Japan's 'true intentions' to China. A private group calling itself the Takaoka Prefectural Education Council (affiliated to the National Council for the Defence of Japan) sent letters to high schools recommending the book, boasting that it had been very helpful to students for passing the university entrance examination and expressing the belief that the book had been used in the preparation of the examination tests. In the 1989-90 school year, 34 high schools used the book.

Naturally, conservatives are just as much entitled to present their view of Japanese history as 'progressives'. If there were no government censorship of textbooks, it would not constitute a problem if a political group produced a textbook. But government approval gives a textbook the image of authenticity and an implicit assurance that it is compatible with the principle of neutrality in public education. A book such as the *Japanese History* compiled by the National Council for the Defence of Japan should not have been passed by the screening process.

An indication of the politicisation of the Ministry of Education was the directive sent to prefectural boards of education and the heads of national schools instructing them to fly the national flag at half mast and have the students offer a silent prayer on 17 September 1987, the day the cabinet and the Liberal-Democratic Party planned a memorial service for Nobusuke Kishi. Kishi served as Minister of Commerce and Industry in the wartime cabinet of General Tōjō and played a leading role in the exploitation of Manchuria. He was arrested by the Occupation but not brought to trial and became one of the most influential members of the Liberal-Democratic Party. He served as Prime Minister from 1957 to 1960 and was a fervent advocate of a revision of the constitution.

Because of the strong opposition to its decision to reintroduce moral education into the curricula for elementary and junior high schools in 1956, the ministry decided not to prescribe special course books for this subject but allow teachers to use supplementary textbooks. Publishers, local Boards of Education and educational groups compiled over 100 books on the subject. The ministry was unhappy with most of them because, in its view, they were tainted with particular ideologies and failed to include certain virtues it wanted inculcated. In July 1988, therefore, the ministry inaugurated a 12-member council on supplementary textbooks for moral education in elementary and junior high schools which also worked out standards for the curricula. Obviously, the ministry was trying to control the values taught to children.

Despite the numerous attacks on the government's screening system and the control of textbooks, the National Council on Education (a body working out proposals for the reform of the educational system) decided in 1988 that the textbook authorisation system should be retained but that the screening process should be simplified to a one-stage system. Some committee members had proposed the abolition of the system and elimination of the minister's authority to approve or disapprove textbooks but the Liberal-Democratic Party mounted a strong campaign to make the council endorse the continuation of the screening system.

Censorship is not the only means of controlling textbooks. The actual choice of textbooks is subject to political pressure. In most districts, they are selected by specially appointed committees composed of teachers, headteachers, and the chiefs of the municipal Boards of Education. But the selection must then be approved by a prefectural committee which has the authority to reject the municipal committee's selection if they wish. A social studies textbook for elementary schools whose authors had come under attack by the Liberal-Democratic Party was recommended by teachers in Hokkaido, Saitama, Tokyo, Kyoto and Mie but rejected under instructions from the prefectural Boards of Education.

The Board of Education of the city of Iwaki prohibited the use of a supplementary textbook covering eight major problems which had emerged after the textbooks for 1989 had been published. The book which was intended to bring the textbook for civic studies for the third grade of junior high school up to date discussed the Recruit scandal, the introduction of the consumption tax and the resignation of the Takeshita cabinet. It had been distributed to about 2,000 high schools throughout Japan. After one of the members found the book inappropriate, the board asserted that the presentation of the Recruit case lacked neutrality because it included the names of politicians involved in the scandal. The schools retrieved the book from the students and gave them copies covering only the consumption tax.

PART II: PROFESSOR SABURO IENAGA VS. THE MINISTRY OF EDUCATION

Saburo Ienaga was a professor at the now defunct Tokyo University of Education. In his view, Japan's standardised system of education has failed to foster independent thinking and the restrictions imposed on students' behaviour by rigid school regulations denied individuality and favoured dogmatic moral education leading to ultranationalism. (An account of Professor Ienaga's early work can be found in Robert N. Bellah, 'Ienaga Saburo and the Search for Meaning in Modern Japan' in *Changing Japanese Attitudes Toward Modernisation*, ed Marius B. Jansen, Princeton University Press 1965.) He contributed to a history textbook called *Kuni no Ayumi* (Footsteps of the Nation) published under the auspices of SCAP's Civil Information and Education Section in 1946 and thereafter continued to write history textbooks.

The Ministry of Education approved a history textbook for senior high schools and it was published by Shiseido in 1953. Ienaga submitted the fifth revised edition of the book for approval in 1962 but was notified in 1965 that the book had not been approved because the censors had found 323 passages or expressions objectionable. If the censors disapprove a book, they do not state why certain corrections are required although in many cases the reasons are obvious.

Among the objections to Ienaga's book was his assertion that the *Kojiki* and *Nihon Shoki* were stories compiled to justify the claim of the Emperor to rule Japan. The ministry also criticised his failure to extol the virtues of being Japanese and his suggestion that the Imperial Rescript on Education and the Emperor's portrait were used as devices for manipulating national consciousness. The textbook was conditionally approved in 1964 after having been revised but the following year, Ienaga filed suit against the state (Ministry of Education) claiming that his right of freedom of expression had been violated (First Ienaga suit).

The textbook was again subjected to the screening process in 1966 and when Ienaga refused to alter six passages found objectionable by the censors it was disapproved the following year. Thereupon, Ienaga filed suit to have the disapproval rescinded (Second Ienaga suit). The two suits were processed in the Tokyo District Court. In 1968, presiding Judge Ogata (then in charge of the first suit) ordered the documents drawn up by the examiners (*chōsaikensho*) and the experts (*hyōteisho*) to be presented to the court. Ryōkichi Sugimoto, the presiding judge of the second suit, issued a similar order. The Ministry of Education, however, refused to present the documents and asked the Tokyo High Court to vacate the orders. In 1968 the High Court acceded to the ministry's demand. The documents, the court held, were internal data and the ordinance governing these data did not provide for making them public. It could not be said that without their disclosure, the supervisory administrative authority of the Diet could not maintain the fairness of the examination and there could be no assurance that their disclosure could not cause some damage to the public welfare. The ruling of the High Court is a typical example of bureaucratic quibbling and the tendency to keep administrative matters secret. The issue was taken to the Supreme Court which ordered the documents to be made available to the courts.

THE SUGIMOTO DECISION: EDUCATION, THE RIGHT OF THE PEOPLE

The Tokyo District Court announced its decision in the suit to have the disapproval of the textbook rescinded (Second Ienaga suit) in July 1970. In his ruling, Judge Sugimoto considered three points of contention: the role of the state in education; the textbook screening system and the freedom of textbook authors and teachers. The essence of the controversy concerned the interpretation of Article 26 of the constitution. Against the assertion of the Ministry of Education that 'the right to education belongs to the state', Judge Sugimoto declared 'the right to education belongs to the people'. Based on the consideration that education must be free from interference by the state, Sugimoto explained that following on Article 25 which guarantees the people's right to life, Article 26 guarantees education as the basis of culture. As far as the contents of education are concerned, the constitution guarantees everybody an equal right to education, and this guarantee applies particularly to children. The state has the duty of taking appropriate measures so that the people can make use of the right to education.

With regard to compulsory education provided for in paragraph 2 of Article 26, the decision stated that the duty to ensure that children received an education falls on the entire people, but particularly on the parents. To help the people fulfill this duty is principally the responsibility of the state. The performance of this responsibility does not necessarily require the intervention of the state in the contents of education but concerns the implementation of the conditions for promoting education. Interference in the contents of education is inadmissible. There are limits to the state's educational policy. Interpreting Article 10 of the Fundamental Law of Education, Judge Sugimoto described the role of the state as follows: 'The state's educational policy shoulders the obligation of providing the conditions for the external matters of education but with regard to the internal matters of education, apart from direction and advice, authoritative interference beyond determining the outline of the curriculum is not permitted and such interference must be interpreted as undue domination.'

On such premises, the decision stated that the screening of textbooks was not unconstitutional because it did not always turn into an examination of the ideological contents. But the limits of constitutionally admissible screening are much narrower than the usual practice of the Ministry of Education. In carrying out the screening, utmost care must be taken not to stray into an examination of the ideological content (including scientific views based on scientific research). The proper items of concern for the screening process are errors in writing, misprints and other objectively recognisable errors, the make-up of the book and other technical matters. The examination of the contents of the book has to be confined to ascertaining whether they are within the restrictions of the course of study.

Based on Article 21 of the constitution, Judge Sugimoto discussed the freedom of textbook authors and teachers. Freedom of expression is limited by the demands of the public welfare. With regard to education, these limitations must remain within the sphere of the duties the state must perform in accordance with Article 26 of the constitution. Academic freedom as guaranteed in Article 23 involves the freedom of education. It is, therefore, inappropriate if the state limits the participation of teachers by a unilateral selection of textbooks and constrains the teacher in the classroom by asserting the legally binding force of the course of study.

Applying the standards based on the interpretation of the constitution, Judge Sugimoto probed the reasons for which the six passages in Professor Ienaga's textbook were held inappropriate and concluded that each of the passages was declared inadmissible for reasons outside the screening standards. In short, the decision found that the textbook had been disapproved on account of its scientific contents which made the screening unconstitutional censorship and also constituted a violation of Article 10 of the Fundamental Law of Education. The decision, therefore, rescinded the disapproval. The years following Judge Sugimoto's decision have shown that the ministerial bureaucrats were not inclined to give up their quest for power and remain in the role of 'servants of the people' laid down in the constitution.

The educational reform after the war had dismantled the pre-war centralised system and tried to make education more democratic by entrusting its administration to prefectural and municipal Boards of Education. The Ministry of Education was to serve as the common research organ of the boards; its only administrative function was the management of the national universities. But the Boards of Education possessed little political power and were unable to beat back the attempts of the Ministry of Education, supported by conservative politicians, to regain its pre-war influence. Besides the screening of textbooks, the efficiency rating of teachers and the enforcement of its course of study marked the complete control of education by the ministry. In order to consolidate its domination, the ministry asserted a right to control the contents of education based on the 'state's right to education'.

Immediately after Judge Sugimoto's decision, the ministry issued a circular attacking the decision and claiming that in order to guarantee the people's right to education, educational administration had established standards for the curricula and screened textbooks. Trying to justify its textbook censorship, the ministry asserted: 'It is natural that the state's educational policy is carried out on the basis of laws enacted by the Diet based on the general will of the people to participate in the contents of education.' The argument has two flaws; first, the Diet has passed no law giving the ministry authority to censor textbooks; secondly, if the Diet were to enact such a law, it would be unconstitutional.

The ruling on the appeal of the state against the Sugimoto decision was announced by the Tokyo High Court (Judge Eiji Hanjō presiding) in December 1975. The court avoided touching on the constitutional question and vacated the disapproval on a different ground from the first instance. The measure taken as a result of the examination in the present case, the court said, turned the finding 'correction is desirable' of the examination three years earlier into 'disapproval'. It was an arbitrary measure, lacking in consistency in administrative action and stability, 'an illegal measure in which the Ministry of Education did not observe the rules it had fixed itself'. The court, therefore, upheld the vacation of the disapproval but the verdict was completely different from that of the court of first instance. Moreover, the court lashed out at Ienaga for making use of the screening system while assailing it as unconstitutional and accused him of 'inconsistency'. It also ordered him to pay the costs of the trial. There was a reason for the court's strange verdict. In May 1973 Ienaga's lawyers had filed a challenge to presiding Judge Michiyasu Toyonaga alleging that he had been snoring during the proceedings and on another occasion had apologised when counsel objected that his conduct of the trial was unfair. The challenge was rejected but soon after the judge retired for reasons of health and Judge Eiji Hanjō took over the trial.

The state took the case to the Supreme Court and in April 1982, the court quashed the verdict of the Tokyo High Court and remanded the case to the same court. The court kept silent on the question of the constitutionality of vetting textbooks and instructed the lower court to inquire into the usefulness of the lawsuit. On 27 June 1989 the Tokyo High Court announced its verdict on the remanded trial. Taking its cue from the Supreme Court's 1982 decision, the court ruled that Professor Ienaga's suit involved no benefit (*rieki*). The course of study of 1960 on which the screening guidelines were based was completely revised in 1978 and the guidelines for screening were changed correspondingly. Thus, Ienaga would not benefit from an annullment of the disqualification since his book could not be screened under the new guidelines. For good measure, presiding Judge Toru Tanno nullified the 1970 decision of Judge Sugimoto (an abomination to the Ministry of Education and the state supremacy crowd).

Technically, Professor Ienaga's complaint was treated as an administrative suit and his legal interest - the wrong inflicted on him by unconstitutional censorship - could be disregarded. The High Court assumed without the slightest reservation the constitutionality and legal binding power of the course of study and the screening process. This decision constituted a clear demonstration of the court's lack of neutrality and subservience to the powers that be.

THE TAKATSU DECISION: EDUCATION, THE RIGHT OF THE STATE

The Tokyo District Court (Judge Kan Takatsu presiding) made known its decision on Professor Ienaga's demand for damages (First suit) in July 1974. The decision asserted that in view of the nature of today's public education, the screening of textbooks was constitutional. 'In today's public education, the private nature of education is a mere abstraction. In changing this, the state must be interpreted to possess the authority to carry out public education from its own point of view at its own responsibility on the basis of the trust of the people.' Appealing to the 'principle of parliamentary democracy' as understood by the Ministry of Education, the judge declared: 'The system of screening textbooks itself is carried out on the basis of Article 21 (par. 1), Articles 40, 51 and 76 of the School Education Law which is directed towards the realisation of the people's right to receive an education laid down in Article 26, paragraph 1 of the constitution. Since the objective is to ensure equal opportunity of education, the maintenance and improvement of the standards of education and the neutrality of education, it is difficult to understand that it should violate the right of children to receive an education of Article 26, paragraph 1 of the constitution or the parent's right of education of paragraph 2.'

After discussing the teacher's freedom of education, the decision continued: '...on principle, educational administration is to be kept out of the method and contents of education at the place of public education, but as long as it remains with the determination of nationwide overall standards or direction and advice, the teacher's freedom of education and independence ought not to be exclusive and absolute. In order to fulfill its duty of education on the basis of Article 26 as a welfare state, the state has the obligation to establish and manage schools in accordance with law (School Education Law, Art. 2-4; Art. 106, par. 1). Because it has a duty to the entire people to pursue equal opportunity of education and the maintenance and improvement of the educational standards, it exercises its administrative right on the basis of lawfully ordained ordinances; although this might extend to the contents of education, it does not amount to so-called improper domination as long as these contents do not contravene the purpose of education laid down in the Fundamental Law of Education (Art. 2) and do not constitute an impropriety violating the essence of education and it is appropriate to interpret them as allowed.'

The decision asserts that the state has been given general authority over education on the basis of legislation: '...since the general will of the people through the Diet is reflected in legislation, it must be said that the state on the basis of law possesses the duty and authority to manage public education and, on the other side, only the state is in a position to assume responsibility towards the entire people.' It should be abundantly clear that the decision is based on the unqualified acceptance of the thesis that the state controls education. As mentioned above, Article 26 of the constitution does not give the state any right over education. Consequently, no legislation can give the state such a right. What the court calls 'lawful ordinances' contain provision for which the Ministry of Education has no legislative mandate. The court seems not to have the faintest idea that in a democracy, the state's responsibility towards the people is to let the people, not the bureaucracy, control education.

In view of the provisions in the Fundamental Law of Education that 'schools determined by law possess a public character' and that the state, local public bodies and school corporations can establish such schools (Art. 6, par. 1), the impression created by the decision that public education is necessarily related to the state is misleading. The assertion that the state has the duty to manage all schools is erroneous. The School Education Law provides that schools can only be established by the state, local public bodies and school corporations (Art. 2, par. 1); the law does not say that the state must establish schools.

The School Education Law does not give the ministry a general administrative right over education. According to Article 106, paragraph 2 of the law, the supervisory agencies of public elementary, junior and senior high schools are, 'for the time being', the prefectural Boards of Education. That the Takatsu decision accepted without qualification the claims of the ministry on the legitimacy of the screening process is hardly surprising. Although only books submitted for screening and passed by the censors can be published and selected as textbooks, Judge Takatsu said, there is complete freedom to publish them as ordinary books. Thought control is not the real objective of the screening system, therefore it does not violate the constitutional prohibition of censorship which means the previous suppression of publications chiefly for ideological reasons. The heart of the matter is that Judge Takatsu seems completely unaware of the danger to freedom if the state can determine the contents of education and ban anything not in conformity with its policies.

Nevertheless, Judge Takatsu found that the examiners had exceeded the limits of acceptable discretion in declaring 19 passages and expressions objectionable (11 out of 329 points declared unacceptable in the 1962 screening and 8 out of 290 points found improper in 1963) and ordered the government to pay Professor Ienaga ¥ 100,000 in damages. Ienaga appealed the decision.

THE SUZUKI DECISION: THE STATE'S AUTHORITY

In March 1986 (21 years after the beginning of the first suit and 12 years after the decision of the District Court) the Tokyo High Court (Judge Kiyoshi Suzuki presiding) turned down the appeal, pronounced the screening system constitutional and legal, ruled that the exceptions to the 19 expressions and passages did not constitute an abuse of power and disallowed the damages. Judge Suzuki's arguments were a repeat of the assertions of the ministry and the reasoning of the lower courts. With regard to the state's control over education, the Ministry of Education asserts that the state possesses the authority to determine, within necessary and proper limits, the contents of education. In a parliamentary democracy, the state acts for the entire people; the rights of parents and teachers are not opposed to those of the state. Educational administration is carried out in accordance with law, and as long as the control exercised by the state's administrative organs is not illegal and inappropriate, interference with the contents of education does not constitute 'improper domination' prohibited by the Fundamental Law of Education.

The Takatsu decision maintained that today's public education is the task of the state which transcends the parents' private right over the education of their children. Based on the mandate of the people, the state possesses the authority to carry out education as its own duty and on its own initiative. The implementation of the state's administrative authority on the basis of ordinances can also extend to the contents of education as long as it does not harm the essence of education. Judge Suzuki found that the state must ensure equal opportunity and a certain nationwide standard of education. To this end, it had the authority entrusted by the people to formulate and execute appropriate educational policies. Although the government must respect the autonomy of education, it could participate in education and intervene in its contents and methods within necessary and reasonable limits and measures taken to this effect do not constitute improper domination prohibited in Article 10 of the Fundamental Law of Education.

The Ministry of Education contended that the minister had the authority to determine the standards for the examination of textbooks and based on these standards could exercise suitable and reasonable discretion in approving or disapproving textbooks. In the case of Ienaga's textbook, the standards were applied fairly and impartially at every stage of the screening process and within the limits of permissible discretion. The District Court recognised the discretionary power of the minister within the limits of the screening standards. Beyond these limits, the measures become improper and illegal. The court found that the limits had been exceeded in 19 of the passages designated as objectionable. If the finding of the examination lacked a basis in fact and was improper in view of the generally accepted ideas of society, it constituted an illegal abuse of discretionary power and could be examined by the courts. However, Judge Suzuki concluded that no such abuse could be shown in the Ienaga case.

On the question of censorship, Judge Suzuki reasoned that the submission of textbooks to a preliminary examination was ordained by law and that the examination and determination whether these books should be given or denied the legal qualification to be suitable for use as textbooks in schools was an administrative decision. Even if, in the course of this examination, the ideological contents were reviewed, this was only from the point of view and within the limits of ensuring neutrality and fairness on account of their special character as textbooks. A book can be submitted for screening as a textbook even if it has already been published as an ordinary book, and a manuscript disapproved as a textbook can be published in the ordinary book market. The screening, therefore, lacked the distinctive features of censorship which consist of examining the contents of a publication or prohibiting publication. The ruling asserted that the screening system is meant to ensure that the subject-matter is presented in a way suitable to the immature minds of the children which makes a certain control necessary. Judge Suzuki admitted that the insertion of the Ministry of Education's course of study in the official gazette did not give it legally-binding force but that its inclusion in the examination standards made it legally binding - a completely gratuitous assertion.

Judge Suzuki wrote: 'Since the textbook examination has an important relation to freedom of expression, the rule of law requires not only that the exercise of the examination authority is substantially just but also an institutional guarantee of its procedural fairness' but then contented himself with asserting that the manner in which the screening process operated and the 'legal character of the examination' fulfill this requirement. The law requiring the 'approval' of the minister of education for textbooks (School Education Law, Art. 21, par. 1) uses the expression *kentei* which may involve an examination, but to infer from this expression that the strange screening system has been sanctioned by law is without any rational foundation.

THE KATO DECISION: THE VALUE OF STATE CENSORSHIP

Professor Ienaga brought a third suit in January 1984, demanding damages for having been forced to rewrite part of a revised edition of a Japanese history book he had submitted for approval in 1980. The book was conditionally approved in 1981 but the ministry instructed the author to correct several passages. Among the expressions found objectionable was 'Japanese aggression' for the invasion of China (the censors wanted to have it changed into 'armed advance') and the account of the Rape of Nanking. It was the demand for these alterations that prompted the first protest of the People's Republic of China and South Korea against the attempts of the Japanese government to cover up historical facts.

The Tokyo District Court announced its decision on the third Ienaga suit on 3 October 1989. Presiding Judge Kazuo Kato ruled that the censors were wrong in one case and ordered the government to pay Professor Ienaga ¥ 100,000 in compensation but that the other changes demanded by the ministry were justified. These included the reference of the rebellion of the Korean people against the Japanese army in 1894, the rape of Chinese women by Japanese soldiers in the Nanking massacre and the so-called '731 unit' said to have carried out experiments on several thousand Chinese. Judge Kato repeated the assertions advanced in the previous trials arguing that the screening of textbooks does not constitute censorship, that the state has the right to determine the contents of school curricula and to control education.

The Ministry of Education maintained its old position that the state could interfere in the contents of education and that the screening of textbooks served the preservation of the people's right to education. It required the consideration of educational policies and professional judgement. The minister of education, the ministry asserted, possessed wide discretion which justified the proposals for changes in textbooks which did not necessarily involve the screening of ideas but pointed out matters which had not yet been scientifically proven. The procedure also served to make expressions uniform.

In the opinion of the court, the screening of textbooks ensured correctness and neutrality and thereby promoted education. It was constitutional as long as the screening was carried out within appropriate limits. The exercise of the right to vet textbooks was within the discretion of the minister of education. The ministry's disapproval of the author's discussion of Nanking and the invasion of China and Okinawa was not illegal but the objections to the representation of the Sōmo-tai (a nineteenth-century incident) were unfounded.

Judge Kato's assertion that academic freedom does not apply to the publication of textbooks reveals the shallowness of the court's point of view. It is one thing to set and maintain curricula standards, but it is something altogether different to usurp the role of instruction that teachers should fulfill. Although textbooks are not scientific dissertations, they should contain an exposition of knowledge which relies on common sense and the traditional wisdom of the people and on the results of serious scholarship. The selection and presentation of the body of knowledge needed to equip young people for their part in society cannot be decided by bureaucratic fiat. Textbooks should enable the teacher to combine instruction with education and it is partly because of the ministry's lack of confidence in the capacity of schools and teachers to handle this task that it insists on screening textbooks.

Testifying before the Tokyo High Court in the third Ienaga trial, Chi Myong Kwan, Professor of Korean and Asian History at Tokyo's Women's Christian University, told the three judges hearing the case that the ministry had deleted accurate accounts of Japan's militaristic past as well as colonial and wartime atrocities from textbooks. Ienaga's book, Chi said, fulfilled the need of Japan to face up to its past and become more outward-looking. The book could be proudly presented to other Asian countries.

Chapter 9

Rearmament and the Interpretation of Article 9

DEMILITARISATION

At the beginning of the Occupation, the elimination of Japanese militarism constituted one of the paramount aims of the post-surrender policy. With the exception of the facilities used by the Occupation, whatever had been left of Japan's military installations was thoroughly demolished. In order to forestall the organisation of paramilitary forces, even the police force was broken up into 1605 small independent units. For localities without a police force, the so-called National Rural Police of 30,000 men was organised and put under the supervision of the National Public Safety Commission. In the early days of the Occupation, the idea that a neutralised Japan would serve as a buffer between the United States and the Soviet Union was frequently mentioned as America's basic policy towards Japan. In an interview with J. P. McEvoy, editor of the *Readers' Digest* Japanese edition published in the May 1950 issue, General MacArthur was quoted as having said that Japan should become the 'Switzerland of the Far East' and remain neutral in any future war.

Among the terms of surrender stated in the Potsdam Declaration were the destruction of Japan's war-making power and the complete disarmament of the Japanese military forces. The 'United States Initial Post-Surrender Policy for Japan', prepared jointly by the US Department of State, the War and Navy Departments and approved by President Truman on 6 September 1945, also listed 'complete disarmament and demilitarisation' among the principal means to achieve the objectives of the Occupation, together with 'the establishment of a peaceful and responsible government which will respect the rights of other states and will support the objectives of the United States as reflected in the ideals and principles of the charter of the United Nations.'

The document prohibited Japan from possessing land, sea or air forces, a secret police organisation and any kind of civilian aviation. This prohibition was incorporated into the 'Basic Post-Surrender Policy for Japan' of 19 June 1947, which added that Japan could not possess a military police but could have a suitable non-military police force. The American government directive known as SWNCC 228 stated that the civilian branch of government should control the military - which suggests that the American government did not expect a perpetually demilitarised Japan.

THE ORIGINS OF ARTICLE 9

The renunciation of war was one of the points expressly mentioned in General MacArthur's instructions to the Government Section for drafting the constitution (the original of these instructions has disappeared). Although he gave General Whitney full discretion, he insisted on three points to be incorporated in the draft. They were, according to General MacArthur's own notes: 'The Emperor is the head of state', 'War as a sovereign right of the nation is abolished', and 'The feudal system of Japan will cease'. Later, when the Korean War had broken out, the General declared that the idea of including the renunciation of war in the constitution had originally been proposed by Shidehara (Kijūrō Shidehara was Prime Minister from October 1945 to May 1946. He served as Foreign Minister in the Wakatsuki and Hamaguchi cabinets and was criticised by the military because he tried to improve relations with China), but he denied this.

General MacArthur upheld his version before the US Senate in 1951. Shidehara's former secretary, Kuramatsu Kishi, in his testimony before the Constitution Research Council on 20 November 1957, explained that Shidehara had been a confirmed pacifist throughout his diplomatic career and that the atomic bomb had strengthened his convictions. In a three-hour interview with General MacArthur on 24 January 1946, Shidehara had expressed to the General his view that, in future, Japan should renounce war. The General was visibly impressed by Shidehara's fervent pacifism, but when the Prime Minister saw the clause in the draft of the constitution, he was extremely surprised. So it may well be that the General got the idea from Shidehara but it was MacArthur who put it into the constitution. The second point in MacArthur's instructions to General Whitney read: 'War as a sovereign right of the nation is abolished. Japan renounces it as an instrument for settling its disputes and even for preserving its own security. It relies upon the higher ideals which are now stirring the world for its defence and its protection. No Japanese army, navy, or air force will ever be authorised and no rights of belligerency will ever be conferred upon any Japanese force.'

The Steering Committee in the Government Section organised in February 1946 thought that the war renunciation clause was to be inserted in the draft of the constitution in accordance with General MacArthur's directive. Frank Rizzo, who succeeded General Whitney as head of the Government Section, declared that General MacArthur was undoubtedly the author of the war renunciation clause.

The wording of Article 9 underwent some changes and part of General MacArthur's instructions reappeared in the preamble of the constitution. (SCAP's original wording of Article 9 was: 'War as a sovereign right of the nation, and the threat or use of force, is forever renounced as a means of settling disputes with other nations. The maintenance of land, sea and air forces, as well as other war potential, will never be authorised. The right of belligerency of the state will not be recognised.')

The personal notes of an officer on General Whitney's staff discovered in the Maryland Federal Record Centre confirm that General MacArthur was the originator of Article 9. Diplomatic documents published by Japan's Foreign Ministry show that the disputes concerning the position, powers and assets of the Emperor and the struggle of the Japanese government resisting attempts to change Japan's *kokutai* (national structure) were far fiercer than the question of the renunciation of war. Since Japan's demilitarisation was one of the basic objectives of the Occupation, it was difficult to assert that the country should have a military force for self-defence. Moreover, the barbaric excesses of the Imperial army during the conflict with China and the Pacific War were still fresh in the memories of politicians and bureaucrats and the prohibition of armed forces seemed to be an effective means of preventing the reappearance of militarism.

THE INTERPRETATION OF ARTICLE 9

The political problems created by Japan's decision to rearm for defensive purposes are far from being solved. The interpretation that Japan can possess armed forces for purely defensive purposes without contravening Article 9 of the constitution remains very controversial. The country's right to self-defence was acknowledged in General MacArthur's original instructions but was not included in the draft of the Government Section. Prime Minister Yoshida (who succeeded Shidehara in May 1946) asserted that military force was not to be used even in self-defence. In the debate on the government draft of the constitution in the 90th (Imperial) Diet, Prime Minister Yoshida stated: 'The provisions of this draft do not directly deny the right of self-defence, but as a result of the non-recognition of all military equipment and the country's right of belligerency in clause 2 of Article 9, war even as the activation of the right of self-defence and also the right of belligerency have been renounced.'

On another occasion, he said: 'War based on the state's right to legitimate self-defence may be justified but I think that it is harmful. It is a remarkable fact that many of the wars in recent times have been waged in the name of self-defence of the state. I think that the recognition of the right to legitimate self-defence has been the reason leading to foolish wars. I think that the recognition of the right to legitimate self-defence itself is harmful.' Thereafter, however, he maintained that the National Safety Force (*Hoan-tai*), the predecessor of the present Self-Defence Force (*Jiei-tai*, although it could be considered an army, constituted no war potential since no modern offensive war could be waged with such a force. Only land, sea and air forces which constituted war potential in a real sense were prohibited. He added, however, that Japanese forces could not be sent abroad.

In November 1947 the government asserted that Japan retained the right to self-defence under international law but that, by virtue of the second paragraph of Article 9, Japan could neither wage war not maintain an armed force even for the purpose of self-defence. At the same time, however, Yoshida stated as the unified view of the government that the constitution forbade only military forces which exceeded the minimum required for self-defence, not forces below this minimum. Prime Minister Yoshida's earlier interpretation (i.e., that any kind of armed forces was unconstitutional), the government declared, was prompted by political considerations and that later a more objective view prevailed. The distinction between armaments for defence and armaments which could be used for offensive purposes found its way into the 1951 Japan-US Security Treaty.

Every country has not only the right but also the duty to defend its people against outside aggression. This does not mean that in all cases military force has to be used nor does it mean that the use of military force is absolutely and intrinsically bad. A country choosing not to possess armed forces and renouncing the right to defend its people with arms is, to say the least, in a highly precarious position. Such a measure would presuppose general disarmament and creditable verification of the dismantling of military power. Throughout human history, eternal peace has remained an elusive goal and never has mankind even come close to this ideal. Today, we are still far away from a world without arms and military power.

Ichirō Hatoyama, who was leader of the opposition Democratic Party and became leader of the Liberal-Democratic Party when his party merged with Yoshida's Liberal Party, had attacked Yoshida's quibble as 'eyewash' and demanded a constitutional amendment which would allow rearmament for defensive purposes. Having become Prime Minister (1954-1956), he did not change his views but was unable to institute the constitutional reforms he considered desirable. Prime Minister Nobusuke Kishi (1957-1960) avoided committing himself on the issue as much as possible. Pressed by the opposition, he maintained that, in case of an attack on Japan, enemy bases would be a legitimate target of rockets and missiles (which, in his opinion, would be different from sending troops overseas - something considered unconstitutional). By the same token, Mr Kishi explained that, 'theoretically', Japan could possess small-scale nuclear arms for defensive purposes although he denied any present intention of introducing atomic weapons. This position was later endorsed by Eisaku Sato (Prime Minister from 1964 to 1972) and Kakuei Tanaka (Prime Minister from 1972 to 1974). In December 1965, Masami Takatsuji, then director-general of the Cabinet Legislative Bureau, maintained that Japan could possess nuclear and non-nuclear weapons for the purpose of defence against an armed attack by a foreign power. But, as Takako Doi pointed out in February 1978, the Nuclear Nonproliferation Treaty which Japan ratified in 1976, forbids the manufacture and possession even of defensive nuclear weapons.

In his interpretation of Article 9, Tokujiro Kanamori who, as State Minister in the first Yoshida cabinet, was in charge of the proceedings for enacting the constitution, declared that a defensive war would not be against the constitution. He stated that he was much annoyed when, in the Diet, Prime Minister Yoshida denied this. But Kanamori's assertion that any kind of 'war potential' was prohibited by the constitution was in turn contradicted by Hitoshi Ashida, one-time Prime Minister and Chairman of the Special Committee of the House of Representatives for drafting the constitution. Ashida explained that his committee inserted the phrase 'In order to accomplish the aim of the preceding paragraph' at the beginning of the second paragraph of Article 9 because they considered a defensive war compatible with the first paragraph and wanted to restrict the meaning of the second paragraph to a prohibition of military potential for an aggressive war. Since SCAP was much more concerned about the reaction abroad, even a defensive force would not have been acceptable to the Occupation authorities. So the constitution was worded in such a way (viz., by inserting the above phrase) that the organisation of some kind of self-defence would be possible. But Tatsuo Sato, former chief of the Legislative Bureau, stated that the cabinet held Kanamori's view and that he considered Ashida's interpretation erroneous.

Ashida's interpretation was supported by Professor Sōichi Sasaki who explained that the words 'the aim of the preceding paragraph' refer to 'justice and order... as a means of settling international disputes' in the first paragraph. The second paragraph forbids possession of war potential for wars of aggression and denies the right of belligerency for this purpose but does not deny war and the right of belligerency for self-defence. This view has also been maintained by Dr Masamichi Inoki, when he was president of the Research Institute for Peace and Security.

Grammatically, Ashida's construction is impossible but it has been argued that the formulation of Article 9 is not too different from the Kellogg Pact (Treaty for the Renunciation of War, 1928) which stated that the signatories 'condemned recourse to war for the solution of international controversies' and 'renounced war as an instrument of national policy'. The parties agreed that 'the settlement of all disputes or conflicts shall never be sought except by peaceful means'. The Kellogg Pact was never considered incompatible with the maintenance of armed forces or wars of self-defence but then, the Pact did not contain a prohibition of any kind of war potential.

Tatsuo Sato also related that a second paragraph was added to Article 66 of the constitution by the House of Peers which requires that the

Prime Minister and other ministers of state must be civilians. (A neologism, '*bunmin*', was created to translate 'civilian'.) According to Sato, this paragraph was added at the insistence of SCAP because of the change in Article 9 mentioned by Ashida. Actually, however, this stipulation is already contained in SWNCC 228, and it formed one of the 'basic principles' adopted by the Far Eastern Commission on 2 July 1946. Such a provision was prompted by Japan's pre-war arrangement under which only a general on active duty could serve as Minister of War and only an admiral as Navy Minister, so that the military could topple any cabinet opposed to its policies. The 'civilian' provision had not been expressed in the previous drafts for the obvious reason that the proposed constitution forebade any military establishment, but on 25 September 1946, the Far Eastern Commission reaffirmed its previous decision and SCAP urged an unwilling Japanese government to modify its draft.

REARMAMENT

The first discussions on an eventual rearmament may have been held as early as 1948, the year the Berlin blockade started. Hitoshi Ashida, who served as Foreign Minister in the Katayama cabinet, proposed that Japan should rely on American help against external aggression but should have its own forces for quelling internal disturbances. In December 1948 the Soviet Union asked the Far Eastern Commission about alleged plans by SCAP to rearm Japan. General Robert E. Eichelberger, commander of the Eighth Army, made speeches in the United States advocating eventual rebuilding of a Japanese army. A clear indication of a shift in the American attitude on Japan's rearmament came from General MacArthur himself. In his New Year message to the Japanese people on 1 January 1950, the General praised Japan's decision to remain unarmed but added: '...by no sophistry of reasoning can it be interpreted as complete negation of the inalienable right of self-defence against unprovoked attack....' In his New Year message the following year, referring to the renunciation of war as an instrument of national policy, he wrote: 'This self-imposed limitation has meticulously guided your thought and action on the problem of national security, even despite the menace of gathering storms. If, however, international lawlessness continues to threaten the peace and to exercise dominion over the lives of men, it is inherent that this ideal must give way to the overweening law of self-preservation and it will become your duty, within the principles of the United Nations, in concert with others who cherish freedom to mount force to repel force.'

This theme was taken up by Prime Minister Yoshida who, in his address on the state of the nation on 20 January 1950, emphasised that Japan had not lost its right of self-defence but would have to rely on Western protection for some time after the conclusion of peace. A few days later the government requested SCAP's permission to arm coastal patrol boats in order to prevent the seizure of Japanese fishing boats by Communist China, North Korea and the Soviet Union.

NATIONAL POLICE RESERVE

Japan's defence against Communist aggression became a matter of immediate concern with the outbreak of the Korean war on 25 June 1950. On 8 July General MacArthur authorised the creation of a National Police Reserve of 75,000 men to be trained in army-like fashion and capable of defending the country against Communist aggression. The government stressed that no purged army or navy personnel would be admitted to the new police force and denied any intention of lifting the ban on 'professional militarists'.

Senator Homer Capehart asked President Truman to have the UN Security Council approve the use of Japanese volunteers against North Korea. The Japanese government, however, was of the opinion that the participation of Japanese nationals in the Korean war was undesirable and Prime Minister Yoshida declared at a plenary session of the House of Representatives that the government had received no proposal or suggestion of organising a volunteer force. On the other hand, Senator Warren Magnuson introduced a bill which would have authorised the voluntary enlistment of Japanese in the US Forces.

In his consultations with John Foster Dulles, who had come to Japan at the end of January 1951 as special envoy to discuss the peace treaty, Prime Minister Yoshida opposed the demand that Japan should rearm asserting that Japan's first goal was to regain independence and rearmament would make economic independence impossible. The Japanese government ruled out a collective security system as well as a declaration of perpetual neutrality. But before Dulles left, he was given a document worked out by Yoshida and a few top officials of the Foreign Ministry entitled 'First Phase of Rearmament Programme'. The document stated: 'Simultaneously with the coming into force of the Peace Treaty and the Japanese-American Security Cooperation Agreement, it will be necessary for Japan to embark upon a programme of rearmament.' The measures proposed in the document comprised the creation of land and sea security forces totalling 50,000 men in addition to the National Police Reserve. These forces were to be better equipped than the police and put under a Ministry of National Security which would also control the National Police Reserve, the National Rural Police, the local police forces, the Maritime Safety Agency, the Fire Defence Board and the Immigration Control Agency. Officially, however, Yoshida stuck to the position that Japan would not rearm and that the National Police Force was not an army. He asked General MacArthur and Dulles not to mention Japan's rearmament in the peace treaty and not to divulge the rearmament plan to which both men agreed.

US-JAPAN SECURITY TREATY

The Peace Treaty of San Francisco, signed on 8 September 1952, recognised Japan's right of self-defence and laid down that Japan could voluntarily enter into collective security arrangements (Art. 5, C). The preamble of the US-Japan Security Treaty, signed the same day as the peace treaty, referred to the considerations which led to the conclusion: 'Japan has signed a treaty of peace with 49 Allied Powers. With the coming into force of that treaty, Japan will not have the effective means to exercise its inherent right of self-defence because it has been disarmed.

'There is danger to Japan in this situation because irresponsible militarism has not yet been driven from the world. Therefore, Japan desires a security treaty with the United States of America to come into force simultaneously with the treaty of peace between Japan and the United States of America.

'The treaty of peace recognises that Japan as a sovereign nation has the right to enter into collective security arrangements and, further, the Charter of the United Nations recognises that all nations possess the inherent right of individual and collective self-defence. In the exercise of these rights, Japan desires, as a provisional arrangement for its defence, that the United States of America should maintain armed forces of its own in and about Japan so as to deter armed attack upon Japan. The United States of America, in the interest of peace and security, is presently willing to maintain certain of its armed forces in and about Japan, in the expectation that Japan will itself increasingly assume responsibility for its own defence against direct and indirect aggression, always avoiding armament which would be an offensive threat or serve other than promote peace and security in accordance with the purposes and principles of the UN Charter.'

The substantive provisions of the Security Treaty, couched as the preamble in rather informal and undiplomatic language, only formulated the broad principles, leaving the details to administrative agreements. Article I stated that 'Japan grants, and the United States of America accepts, the right, upon the coming into force of the treaty of peace and of this treaty, to dispose US land, air and sea forces in and about Japan. Such forces may be utilised to contribute to the maintenance of international peace and security in the Far East and to the security of Japan against armed attack from without, including assistance given at the express request of the Japanese government to put down large-scale internal riots and disturbances in Japan, caused through instigation or intervention by an outside Power or Powers.'

In the second article Japan promises not to grant, without prior consent of the United States, bases or similar military facilities to any third power. The treaty was to remain in force until, in the opinion of the Japanese and the US governments, UN arrangements or other security dispositions provide for the maintenance of international peace and security in the Japan area. The Security Treaty was renewed in

1960 and extended automatically thereafter.

The text of the treaty indicated that its signatories expected Japan's future rearmament. Naturally, left-wingers who advocated a policy of unarmed neutrality opposed Japan's alignment with the United States and attacked this unconstitutional tendency as well as the right of the US to deploy its forces without prior consultation and to use these forces outside Japan. The indefinite duration of the treaty was also criticised as well as the provisions promising assistance in putting down large-scale internal riots and disturbances in Japan caused through instigation or intervention by an outside power or powers, which was objected to on the grounds that it gave the US the right to interfere in Japan's internal affairs, although the treaty stipulated that such assistance would be given at the express request of the Japanese government.

The treaty, it was charged, made Japan subservient to the US, was unilateral in giving the US rights without Japan receiving equivalent rights, and dangerous in exposing Japan to attack in case the US became involved in an armed conflict. It was disapproved of by some as 'unilateral' because the US had no legal obligation to come to Japan's assistance whereas others maintained that any legal obligation of the US forces to help Japan would make the treaty unconstitutional since in such a case the US forces would come under Japanese control and would constitute 'war potential' prohibited by the constitution. The attacks naturally grew stronger in times of international tension and the problem became more complicated by the progress in nuclear weaponry and the developments in the field of missiles.

NATIONAL SECURITY FORCE

Although the treaty does not say so, there can be no doubt that it was intended to obviate threats from Communism in general and the Soviet Union in particular and the same can be said of the subsequent moves towards rearmament. As mentioned above, a National Security Force (*Hoan-tai*) under the jurisdiction of the National Security Agency (*Hoan-chō*) was created in 1952. Officially, its purpose was the maintenance of peace and order inside Japan. The *Hoan-tai's* organisation was unquestionably military and so was its equipment which included tanks and artillery provided by the United States.

An opinion advanced in connection with Japan's admission to the United Nations (18 December 1956) held that Article 43 of the UN Charter obliged Japan to have armed forces. The text of Article 43 does not support such a conclusion. Although the article applies to 'all members', the contribution to the maintenance of peace and security involves not only armed forces but also 'assistance and facilities, including rights of passage'. The number and types of forces and the 'nature of facilities and assistance' to be provided are to be governed by agreements subject to ratification by the signatory states 'in accordance with their constitutional processes' (Art. 43, par. 2 & 3).

Prime Minister Yoshida and his Liberal Party asserted that the constitutional prohibition of war potential meant such military force as would be able to wage a modern war. To concerns raised in the Diet the government replied that the American security forces would repel 'direct aggression' but that Japan's security forces would only be used against 'indirect aggression'. The Progressives, the conservative opposition party, favoured open rearmament based on a constitutional amendment. The left wing and the 'neutrals', including a large section of the Protestants in Japan, opposed rearmament and called for the defence of the 'peace' constitution.

On an inspection tour of defence installations in Kyushu, Tokutaro Kimura, Director-General of the Defence Agency, disclosed in an interview on 8 June 1953, that the government had drawn up a five-year plan for the build-up of a defence establishment of around 200,000 men, composed of land, sea and air forces. At the same time he stated that he was sure the security force could quell any internal disturbance and he added that the forces to be created would naturally go into action if Japan were attacked by a foreign power. Kimura's statement aroused considerable controversy and the opposition parties demanded the disclosure of the plan. The government refused on the ground that, so far, no definite plan had been adopted and that the so-called plan was in fact just a preliminary study.

The rearmament issue entered a new phase when the United States proposed to include Japan in the Mutual Security Assistance (MSA) programme. Popular sentiment, which had consistently opposed rearmament, forced the government to move very cautiously and in the Diet the opposition parties did their utmost to thwart the agreement. Since the MSA programme made the extension of economic aid to a particular country conditional on that nation's contribution to the defence of the 'Free World' by a minimum build-up of military forces, Japan's inclusion in the programme presented a series of delicate problems.

Negotiations between the US and Japan for the conclusion of the MSA agreement began in July 1953. The Americans were unwilling to commit themselves to a specific amount of economic aid before knowing to what extent Japan would rearm whereas the Japanese stressed the constitutional, economic and political limitations making a rapid expansion of Japan's armed forces difficult. When negotiations dragged on, Prime Minister Yoshida sent Hayato Ikeda as his personal representative to Washington.

As a preliminary step, Ambassador John M. Allison and General Mark W. Clark met with the Foreign Minister, Katsuo Okazaki, and the Director-General of the Security Agency, Kimura, to discuss the problem. The Americans insisted on Japan contributing at least a ground force of ten divisions, meaning a total of 325,000 to 350,000 men; the Japanese foresaw a gradual increase of the ground forces to 210,000 men over five years which the Security Agency considered the maximum sustainable by a system of voluntary enlistment and payable without new taxes.

With the help of American aid, a navy of 140,000 tons and an air force of 1,350 planes was considered possible. In later Washington talks, the Japanese scaled their proposal down to a ground force of 180,000 men, basing their estimate on the 18,000-men strength of NATO divisions. An understanding was reached by negotiations between Assistant Secretary of State Walter S. Robertson and Hayato Ikeda and a joint declaration was issued at the end of October 1953.

The declaration led to a fierce clash between Yoshida and the opposition. Yoshida refused to divulge the contents of the talks between Robertson and Ikeda on the ground that Ikeda was his personal representative. After a meeting with Robertson, Japan's Ambassador, Eikichi Kimura, told Japanese reporters in Washington that, on instructions of the government, he had transmitted Japan's agreement with the joint declaration. When the news reached Tokyo, the opposition pressed its demand for full information but Foreign Minister Okazaki denied that the government had acknowledged its agreement and had only expressed its willingness to continue negotiations in Tokyo. In his address to the American-Japan Society in Tokyo on 19 November 1953, then Vice-President Richard M. Nixon stated that when the US insisted on Japanese disarmament in 1946, 'we made a mistake because we misjudged the intentions of the Soviet leaders'.

On 8 March 1954 Japan and the United States signed the MSA Agreement and three related pacts. Japan was to receive an unspecified amount of military equipment on a grant basis and orders for American off-shore procurement. Japan assumed the obligation to increase its defence capacity within the limits of its economic potential. In addition, Japan was to sell to the US such raw materials and semi-finished goods as the latter might want to purchase; collaborate in enforcing an embargo on trade with the Communist bloc; preserve secrecy regarding the commodities, services and information involved in US aid. The agreements were approved by the Diet and went into effect on 1 May 1954.

The only party which supported the rearmament policy, the Japan-US Security Treaty and the MSA programme has been the Liberal-Democratic Party. Because the party commanded a majority in the Diet since its formation in 1955, the opposition has been unable to stop the growth of Japan's remilitarisation. The Japan Communist Party has denounced every step the government has taken in its defence policy, from the interpretation of Article 9 and the defence treaties with the US to the budgetary appropriations for the Self-Defence Forces. It has persistently advocated unarmed neutrality. The Socialist Party has also rejected the government's interpretation of the constitution, opposed rearmament and favoured unarmed neutrality. The security treaty, the party maintains, runs counter to pacifism and internationalism and should be transformed into a treaty without a military alliance. But the party does not propose the unilateral scrapping of the treaty. Since the opposition gained a majority in the Upper House in 1989, the party has acknowledged that it would be impossible to abolish the Self-Defence Forces overnight. If the party were to join a coalition government, it would, for the time being, limit defence expenditures to 1 per cent of GNP and restrict the 'dangerous parts' of the Self-Defence Forces (the party did not make clear what it meant by 'dangerous parts').

In 1991 the party changed its official English name to Social Democratic Party of Japan (SDPJ) and reversed its long-standing policy of 'unarmed neutrality'. Although it continued to regard the Self-Defence Forces 'in their present form' as unconstitutional, it acquiesced in their existence and no longer opposed the Japan-US Security Treaty. The party stressed that the SDF should be strictly limited to the protection of Japanese territory and should not be armed with offensive weapons which could pose a threat to Japan's neighbours. The Democratic Socialist Party supports the Self-Defence Forces without reservations and maintains that Japan possesses the inherent right to self-defence. Komeito wants the capability of the self-defence forces strictly limited to defensive purposes.

SELF-DEFENCE FORCES

The government prepared the creation of the Self-Defence Forces by gaining the support of the conservative parties. Prime Minister Yoshida reached an understanding with the Progressive Party President, Mamoru Shigemitsu, on the transformation of the National Security Force into the Self-Defence Force. During the discussions, the Progressive Party insisted on the creation of a special organ which could ensure the proper control of the defence establishment. Hence, the Defence Agency Law provided for a consultative organ, called the National Defence Council, whose function would be to examine the fundamental defence policy, basic defence plans, industrial and other problems involved in the defence plans and the use of the defence forces.

The final draft of the bill regulating the Defence Council fixed its membership as follows: the Prime Minister (Chairman), Deputy Prime Minister, Director-General of the Defence Agency, Foreign Minister, Director of the Economic Council Board and members appointed by the cabinet and approved by the Diet. A revised version, which omitted members appointed by the cabinet, was enacted in 1956. The Defence Council has been reorganised as the Cabinet Security Office. Its members are the Prime Minister (Chairman), the Foreign Minister, Finance Minister, the Directors- General of the Defence Agency and the Economic Planning Agency, the Chief Cabinet Secretary and the Chairman of the Joint Chiefs of Staff.

In the debates on the bills the opposition attacked the Self-Defence Forces and the Defence Agency as unconstitutional. The Progressive

Party approved the bills but contended that the Self-Defence Forces should clearly be called an army and the constitution amended accordingly. This, however, was just wishful thinking since the government did not command the two-thirds majority in the Diet required for a constitutional amendment. Further controversy erupted on the hypothetical question of sending Self-Defence Force units abroad and on the civilian control of the forces. After much wrangling, the Self-Defence Forces Law (*Jieitai-hō*) and the Defence Agency Law (*Bōeichō Setchi-hō*) were passed in June 1954.

A measure necessitated by the MSA agreement was the enactment of an anti-espionage bill. Originally, the government intended to cover not only the American weapons and information given to Japan but also the secrecy of Japanese troop movements and domestically-produced weapons. But such a law would have been too reminiscent of similar pre-war measures and the final version applied only to American weaponry. Nevertheless, the bill drew criticism on account of its terminology and ill-defined prohibitions but was finally enacted as drafted by the government.

The Self-Defence Forces Law marked the transition from a force for maintaining peace and order within Japan to a force to counter outside aggression. The relevant passages in the laws read as follows: 'In order to provide a reserve force for the National Rural Police and the local police to the extent necessary for maintaining our country's peace and order and guarantee the public welfare, the Police Reserve is established (Police Reserve Ordinance, Art. 1). 'The Security Force will go into action in particularly necessary cases for maintaining our country's peace and order and protect human life and property' (Security Agency Law, Art. 4). 'The principal task of the Self-Defence Forces is to defend our country against direct and indirect aggression in order to guard our country's peace and security and preserve the security of the country but in response to necessity it also involves the maintenance of the public order' (Self-Defence Forces Law, Art. 3, par. 1). The transition from 'police' to 'army' is unmistakable.

At the end of 1956 the National Defence Council started its activities and, anticipating Prime Minister Kishi's visit to the United States, adopted a position paper called 'Basic National Defence Policy', which was followed by 'An outline of Potential Targets of National Defence'. The policy statement declared that Japan's defence aimed at stopping direct or indirect aggression, repelling any invasion attempts and protecting the independence and peace of the country. The declaration affirmed support of UN activities, international cooperation and world peace; efforts to stabilise the livelihood of the people, to heighten patriotism and to guarantee national safety; the gradual building of an efficient defence force within the limits required for self-defence in keeping with national strength and the national situation; to rely on the security arrangements with the US until the UN can effectively stop foreign aggression.

Numerically, Japan's armed forces are far below their pre-war level but they are by no means negligible. The successive defence programmes have expanded the strength of the Self-Defence Forces to about 250,000 men, not high compared with the military forces of other countries in the Far East but better equipped than any other force in this part of the world. An indication of the standard of Japan's military establishment is the organisation of joint manoeuvres of the Self-Defence Forces and American units. They comprise exercises of the single branches of the two services as well as integrated manoeuvres involving forces practising with real weapons. The Americans would hardly agree to this kind of cooperation if the Japanese forces were rank amateurs.

PARTICIPATION OF SELF-DEFENCE FORCES IN PEACEKEEPING OPERATIONS

Among the legal fictions invented by the government in connection with the organisation of armed forces was the assertion that the constitution prohibited Japan from sending troops abroad and taking part in collective defence arrangements. Japan used this hypocritical subterfuge to avoid participating in international peacekeeping activities such as in Namibia and the Middle East. Since Japan relies on imports from the Middle East for most of its oil requirements, the contribution of $ 4 billion to the cost of the Gulf crisis and the dispatch of a medical team was criticised as mere tokenism. The government first considered organising a non-military UN Peace Cooperation Corps. The rather negative response to this half-hearted measure prompted Prime Minister Kaifu and high government officials to change the interpretation of the constitution and to declare that, unlike collective defence arrangements, collective security measures were within the framework of the constitution and that the participation of SDF personnel in joint security activities based on the UN Charter and resolutions did not contravene the constitutional prohibitions.

Initially, the government and the Liberal-Democratic Party talked about the Peace Cooperation Corps as if it would be a special organisation but their real intention was to create a legal basis for sending SDF units abroad. The government had vindicated the violation of the constitutional ban on armed forces by appealing to the right of self-defence but by no stretch of imagination can the dispatch of troops abroad be justified as a self-defence measure.

Although the government's plan to send a 'peace corps' to the Gulf was defeated, the hawks in the Liberal-Democratic Party continued to press for the deployment of Self-Defence personnel there. In addition to promising a further $ 9 billion contribution to the cost of the war, the government focused on efforts to repatriate the refugees from Gulf states who had lost their jobs on account of the war and who were waiting in camps particularly in Jordan. There was no request from the International Organisation for Migration (IOM) responsible for the evacuation of the refugees for Japanese cooperation, but nevertheless the government decided to send five US-made C-130 Hercules transport planes to Amman. Proposals by the private sector, including the Catholic hierarchy, to help in the operation were turned down. An air force officer conceded that the aeroplanes were entirely unsuitable for the mission. The capacity of the C-130 is about 90 persons or 20 tons of cargo, only a fraction of that of modern jets, and the Japanese version of the plane can just cover the distance from Hokkaido to Okinawa.

A citizens' group asked the Kobe District Court to issue an injunction preventing the government from sending Self-Defence Force aeroplanes to the Persian Gulf but the court rejected the demand. Similar injunctions were requested by civic groups in Tokyo and Kitakyushu.

Since the hawks in the Liberal-Democratic Party had failed to involve the Self-Defence Forces in the Gulf War, they used another pretext for defying the supposedly constitutional ban on the overseas deployment of Japanese forces. The party decided to send minesweepers to the Gulf to help in the removal of the mines planted by Iraq. There had been no request for this action, neither by the Allies who had fought the Gulf War nor by Iraq which was legally responsible for clearing the mines. A squadron consisting of four minesweepers, a support vessel and a supply ship left Japan at the end of April 1991 on the 13,000 km voyage to the Gulf which took the slow vessels about a month with four port calls for fuel and water. The real purpose of the exercise was to create another precedent in the erosion of the constitutional prohibition of rearmament.

A bill submitted to the Diet in September 1991 would allow SDF personnel and other Japanese to participate in non-military UN peacekeeping operations, including the supervision of elections and transportation of war refugees. The soldiers would carry small arms for self-defence as well as the defence of Japanese nationals and other members of peacekeeping forces. The Cabinet Legislative Bureau declared that the use of weapons for the protection of life and limb of Self-Defence personnel and other Japanese in the area was a natural right and therefore not unconstitutional. Monitoring ceasefire agreements would be restricted to SDF personnel whose units would also be allowed to join UN forces separating opposing armies. Another bill would amend the law on international disaster relief and permit SDF units to join in such operations.

Academics and defence experts were critical of the bill. They claimed that volunteers possessing the required knowledge and skills would be better suited for such missions which were basically different from the tasks for which the military was trained. Not only the individual soldiers, but also the organisational pattern of the SDF would be unsuitable for peacekeeping assignments.

The government prepared a bill sanctioning the overseas dispatch of Self-Defence Forces personnel to participate in UN peacekeeping operations. The discussions in the House of Representatives' Ad Hoc

Committee on International Peace Cooperation revealed some odd ideas of individual lawmakers. Some insisted that the right to direct the troops taking part in the UN operations should remain with the Japanese government and not pass to the commander of the UN forces. Japanese participation should only be allowed if all parties directly involved in the conflict agreed to it. The bill provided that Diet approval would be required two years after the dispatch of the SDF personnel if the peacekeeping operations were extended for more than two years. The government, which opposed prior Diet approval, inserted this condition 'in order to maintain civilian control'.

The committee spent much time discussing the question whether sending SDF personnel abroad was constitutional, completely ignoring the unconstitutionality of the SDF as such. The large national dailies more or less parroted the government line although some tabloids and weeklies were highly critical of the government's efforts to rebuild Japan's military machine. There was even speculation that the legislation could be used for a revival of the draft. Since the SDF find it difficult to attract enough recruits, the government could invoke Japan's possible international obligations as a pretext for introducing conscription.

According to a magazine report, regimental commanders in the SDF are in favour of using their troops for peacekeeping missions but staff officers oppose it. They claim that peacekeeping operations are a difficult job and often have to be carried out under harsh conditions. Prolonged activities involve large costs, affect troop morale and often fail to achieve their purpose. In Cyprus alone, UN peacekeeping forces have suffered 150 casualties.

Komeito and the Democratic Socialist Party defected from the opposition (therefore now called 'centre' by the media) and voted for the so-called PKO Bill in both the Lower and the Upper Houses. (The defection of the two parties transferred the majority in the Upper House from the opposition to the government.) In order to gain the support of the two centre parties, the bill was amended to require the prior consent of the Diet for the dispatch of peacekeeping forces and to freeze for two years the participation of SDF units in armed operations for separating warring factions during a ceasefire.

One of the amendments to the bill called on the Diet to try to vote on the government's request for the dispatch of SDF members within seven days of the request being made. Some legislators objected to this provision because it infringes on the legislative authority of the Diet.

The approval of the PKO Bill by the committee was accompanied by a wild mêlée when the committee members opposed to the bill tried to prevent a vote by force. In the Lower House, the majority, made up of the Liberal-Democratic Party and Komeito, secured the passage of the bill but the Upper House failed to act on it despite an extension of the extraordinary Diet session.

In February 1992 a Liberal-Democratic Party panel headed by Ichirō Ozawa, former Secretary-General of the party, proposed to change the government's interpretation of Article 9 so as to allow the active participation of the Self-Defence Forces in peacekeeping operations sponsored by the United Nations as long as that participation was confined to non-military roles. The panel's draft report called for a change from passive to positive and active pacifism. Japan should cooperate with forces under UN command or become part of them. The UN Charter which permits the use of force for maintaining peace is compatible with the spirit of the constitution's preamble, the report asserted, and justifies the SDF's participation in the use of force abroad to help maintain international peace.

As with other measures for strengthening the country's military potential, the attempts to sanction Japan's participation in peacekeeping operations were viewed with dismay by Japan's Asian neighbours. Strangely enough, the Ministry of Foreign Affairs was one of the most active supporters of the legislation. The ministry was still smarting from the attacks on Japan on account of its refusal to send troops to the Persian Gulf and the almost complete disregard of the huge financial contribution Japan made to the war effort.

The bill authorising the dispatch of Self-Defence Forces abroad to participate in UN peacekeeping operations became law on 15 June 1992, when the bill, which had been amended in the Upper House, was passed again by the House of Representatives. The Liberal-Democratic Party, Komeito and the Democratic Socialist Party voted for, the Communist Party voted against the measure and the Social Democratic Party of Japan boycotted the session, its members having submitted their resignation to the Speaker of the House.

Although Japan's rearmament was a blatant violation of the constitution, the defence establishment has become a fixed part of the Japanese polity. With the exception of garrison towns, however, the Self-Defence Forces exist at the periphery of Japanese society. Their activities for disaster relief have earned them some public sympathy, but generally speaking, SDF personnel often encounter hostility. They have been denied resident registration when transferred to a new post, elementary schools have refused to accept their children and university students have forced the authorities to cancel the matriculation of members of the SDF. Not a single member of the SDF has combat experience, and the absence of real threats to Japan's security has made the maintenance of morale difficult.

The military nowadays has no political clout, unlike before the war, and generally does not engage in politics. Only one incident has surfaced in which SDF personnel was involved in a plot to overthrow the government. The scheme seems to have been hatched in 1980 but came to light only in 1983 when Representative Yanosuke Narazaki questioned the government about the incident. Thereafter, a daily and a weekly were given additional information on the case by unidentified SDF officers. The coup planners intended to seize the Prime Minister's official residence, the Diet Building, the Defence Agency, the

Metropolitan Police Department and two television stations, NHK and TBS. The Prime Minister and other members of the cabinet were to be arrested. The aim of the coup was the 'legitimisation' of the SDF, an appeal to the people to elect a new House of Representatives, and the installation of a 'man of probity' as Prime Minister.

The government and the Liberal-Democratic Party have never formulated a realistic defence policy. The four abstract principles announced in 1957 have not been made more definite. There has never been an official explanation of who the enemy is or what kind of attack the SDF should guard Japan against. Requests for more weapons and equipment, unrelated to any specific strategy and often on the insistence of the US government on purchasing military equipment from American manufacturers, take the place of a defence policy.

THE CONSTITUTIONALITY OF THE SELF-DEFENCE FORCES

With the expansion of military power and the progress in technology, the government's interpretation of what was permitted contrary to the text of Article 9 also increased. To justify the creation of the SDF, the government contended that since the state possessed the right of self-defence, forces which were purely for self-defence did not constitute war potential prohibited by the constitution. The use of armed force in a defensive war would not be based on the country's right to belligerency. But the question connected with Japan's Self-Defence Forces is not whether the country possesses the right of self-defence. As a sovereign nation, Japan obviously has this right and as a member of the United Nations, it has the right based on Article 51 of the United Nations Charter to possess armed forces and to defend the country against aggression.

These matters are completely irrelevant to the constitutional problem, which is not what Japan as a nation can do but what the government can do. Under the present constitution, neither the Diet nor the cabinet has the power to abrogate the constitutional prohibition of maintaining land, sea and air forces and other war potential, and the courts have no power to sanction such an abrogation. The Japanese people have the right to abolish Article 9 by amending the constitution and adopting a new constitutional provision allowing military establishment. Until such an amendment is adopted, all measures related to the Self-Defence Forces are unconstitutional.

The former West German chancellor, Helmut Schmidt, expressed concern over the impact of Japan's militarisation on international relations. Japan possesses the third largest navy in the world and the country's defence budget is the third highest. Self-Defence Forces has become a euphemism for a military establishment lacking a nuclear capability but otherwise constituting a modern fighting force.

THE SUNAKAWA CASE

A sensation was caused on 30 March 1959 when Akio Date, Chief Judge of the Tokyo District Court, handed down a verdict implying that the stationing of American troops in Japan was unconstitutional. The case was a result of the Sunakawa incident when demonstrators against the extension of Tachikawa Air Base broke down a fence and entered the base. The court acquitted seven demonstrators who had been indicted for violating Article 2 of the Special Criminal Law providing a prison term of not more than one year or a fine not exceeding ¥ 2,000 for trespassing on US military bases. Judge Date's opinion contended that Article 9 of the constitution had to be interpreted in connection with the preamble which makes it clear that war for self-defence and possession of war potential for that purpose are just as much prohibited as wars of aggression. Since the US Security Forces could be deployed outside Japan when the United States considered such action necessary not only for the defence of this country but also for world peace and security, Japan might get involved in a conflict which was of no direct concern to it.

From the point of view of international law, the US-Japan Security Treaty and the Administrative Agreement implementing it presented no difficulties, but under Japan's present constitution, the stationing of US Security Forces violated Article 9, paragraph 2 of the constitution. Consequently, there was no basis for the extraordinary protection afforded by the Special Criminal Law whose Article 2 imposes a severer penalty than that provided by Article 1, No. 32 of the Minor Offences Law for trespassing. Article 2 of the Special Criminal Law, therefore, violates Article 31 of the constitution requiring due process of law. In Judge Date's opinion, the government's consent to the stationing of American troops in Japan under the US-Japan Security Treaty was against the spirit of the constitution which expressed the people's resolve never again to be visited by the horrors of war through the action of government.

The prosecution appealed the case directly to the Supreme Court. Its contention was that, since Japan had no right of command over the US Security Forces stationed in Japan, these forces did not fall under the prohibition of war potential. It further asserted that the conclusion of the US-Japan Security Treaty was a problem of 'high politics' and that, being an 'act of state', the courts had no right to question its constitutionality. Concerning Article 31 of the constitution, the prosecution asserted that special protection of foreign troops stationed in Japan was a matter of course.

The decision of the Supreme Court, announced on 16 December 1959 reversed the verdict of the District Court and declared that US Forces stationed in Japan did not constitute 'war potential' in the sense of the constitution because Japan had no right to command these troops. The court avoided touching on the problem of Japan's Self-Defence

Forces. Going further than necessary for the decision, the court espoused the contention of the prosecution that the Security Treaty possessed a highly political nature and that the courts were incompetent to review it because it constituted an 'act of state' (*tōchi kōi*). Three of the fifteen justices took exception to the view that the courts could not review the Security Treaty, but agreed with the other justices that the stationing of American troops in Japan was not unconstitutional. The court likewise ruled that the constitutionality of the Special Criminal Law was no problem because the presence of American troops was in conformity with the constitution.

THE NAGANUMA CASE

A decision declaring the Self-Defence Forces unconstitutional was handed down by the Sapporo District Court on 7 September 1973. The facts of the case were as follows. Under the Third Defence Plan adopted by the government in March 1967, the government cancelled the designation of an area in Umaoiyama in Naganuma-machi (Yūbari-gun, Hokkaido) as a state-owned protected forest for catchment area conservation in order to build a site for Nike missiles. Demanding the retraction of the revocation, 271 residents of Naganuma-machi sued the government (Minister of Agriculture, Forestry and Fisheries).

Presiding Judge Shigeo Fukushima annulled the disposition revoking the designation as protected forest on the ground that the Self-Defence Forces were unconstitutional. He stated that the interpretation of the Forest Law would have to take into account not only the particular purposes of forest reserves enumerated in Article 25 of the Law, but also the general constitutional principles of democracy, respect for fundamental human rights and peace. If a disposition based on the Forest Law threatens the inhabitants' right to live in peace, they have a right to fight the disposition. In case of war, the radar site planned for the location would add a particular threat to the lives and property of the inhabitants. It would be too late when the threat became a reality; therefore, the inhabitants had the right to turn to the court for help before the threat materialised.

Regarding the question of the constitutionality of the Self-Defence Forces, i.e., whether the country can possess war potential for the protection of security, Judge Fukushima said that the preamble and Article 9 of the constitution had established a clear regulation; its meaning and interpretation had to be ascertained objectively and could not assume a second or third meaning with changes in the political system or in the international situation. The court, he said, did not intend to evaluate the international situation, decide whether the policy of possessing self-defence forces is correct or pass on the size, equipment or potential. It was up to the people to decide what policies the state should pursue for protecting security. The court had only to judge on the compatibility of the measures taken with the constitution.

The first paragraph of Article 9 renounces war, the second renounces war potential and all military equipment, including war potential for self-defence so as to remove completely the danger of war, and does not recognise the right of belligerency. The interpretation that the renunciation is limited to wars of aggression and that defensive wars are not foregone and permitted is erroneous. This recognition of war is incompatible with the renunciation of the right of belligerency. The constitution does not renounce the right of self-defence proper to a sovereign state but the use of armed forces is not the only means of self-defence. The choice of the exercise of the right of self-defence has to be left to the sovereign people.

The present size, equipment and potential of the land, sea and air forces make them an organisation with the material and human means for the purpose of engaging in physical combat with an external enemy: what is commonly understood by an army. They constitute land, sea and air forces in the sense of paragraph 2 of Article 9 and therefore are unconstitutional. The relevant legislation such as the Defence Agency Law and the Self-Defence Forces Law regulating the organisation, composition, equipment and activities of the Self-Defence Forces are unconstitutional and therefore, in accordance with Article 98 of the constitution, invalid.

The government argued that the defence of the country was a matter that had to be left to the discretion of the government and that judicial review did not extend to the constitutionality of the Self-Defence Forces. Judge Fukushima replied that the exercise of judicial review had to be carried out judiciously and with restraint, but if in the course of judicial proceedings it appeared that the state had exceeded the limits on its power set by the constitution and the suspicion arose that a serious violation had occurred and that the rights of the people had been infringed, then, aware that the cause of the suit could not be settled solely on other grounds - even if it might appear on the surface that the case might be solved formally, without offering any basic solution or vindication of the rights of the people - the court must exercise the right of judicial review. Otherwise, if there actually had been a use of state power beyond the framework of the constitution and the court connived at this, the violation would become even worse and it would become more difficult to protect the rule of law; and Article 99 of the constitution, which imposed the duty to observe the constitution on the judiciary and all public officials, would become a dead letter.

On appeal, the Sapporo High Court quashed the decision of the lower court on 5 August 1976. With regard to the right of peaceful existence, the court argued that it was a political declaration stating an ideal and containing no concrete provisions. The principle, therefore, cannot be interpreted to prescribe a certain policy or to find application on the basis of fundamental human rights. The court avoided ruling directly on the constitutionality of the Self-Defence Forces. Matters concerning the organisation and structure of the state and external relations relate to the fundamentals of guiding the state. Choosing the most appropriate policy requires a high degree of political judgement. Such essential state action does not lend itself to judicial judgement. The selection of such action must be decided and carried out exclusively by the competent agencies which have the political responsibility and are ultimately responsible to the people. Unless state acts related to governmental matters are patently unconstitutional and illegal, they are outside the sphere of judicial review. Judicial intervention would create chaos.

There are different interpretations of the second paragraph of Article 9; one sanctioning war potential, the other deeming it prohibited. It is impossible to decide which interpretation is correct since both are reasonable. In view of the actual international situation, the maintenance of war potential seems justified. The enactment of the Self-Defence Forces Law and the establishment and operation of Self-Defence Forces have as their principal objective the defence of the country and cannot be interpreted unequivocally and clearly as aggressive. The organisation, composition and equipment of the Self-Defence Forces have been fixed by law for a special purpose. A comparison with other countries shows that Japan could not sustain a war of aggression for which not only armaments but also other factors such as the economy, geography etc. would have to be considered. Such a difficult assessment cannot be made objectively which makes it impossible to decide whether armaments are for aggression or defence.

THE NAHA CITY CASE

In a suit by a municipal government against the central government, the city of Naha went to court to obtain the return of city facilities (port and airport) which the government had requisitioned for use by the US forces. The municipal government claimed that the Japan-US Security Treaty was invalid because it violated the preamble of the constitution (which guaranteed the people the right to a peaceful life) and Article 9. The city further argued that the requisitioning of the facilities offended against Article 29 of the constitution which stipulates that just compensation has to be given if private property is taken for public use.

In its decision, the Naha District Court (Judge Shigeki Inoue presiding) declared that the conclusion of the Security Treaty was an 'act of state' beyond the jurisdiction of the courts, agreeing with the argument of the state that as a 'highly political act', the treaty and the government's actions based on the treaty were outside the competence of the courts. The city government did not appeal the decision. 'I am not satisfied with the court decision,' Mayor Kosei Oyadomari said, 'but understand the serious situation surrounding the judiciary.' What the mayor called a 'serious situation' is of the courts' own making.

The mental acrobatics performed by judges who do not want to interpret Article 9 (and the preamble) in the way it is written are grotesque. That a war of self-defence waged against an outside aggressor should not be an international war is a piece of judicial semantics which defies common sense. It is perfectly correct that the constitution does not deny the right of self-defence but the assertion that this right justifies the organisation of self-defence forces is a *non sequitur*. As mentioned above, the problem is not what right the country as a whole has but the power which the government (Diet and cabinet) possesses under the constitution. Judge Fukushima pointed out that, as the constitution's preamble states, military force is not the only means of preserving peace and security. The renunciation of war is based on the premise that international cooperation will safeguard peace. If this assumption is not valid, the constitution should be changed: the unreality of this assumption does not justify the contorted interpretations used by the courts to accommodate the government's desire to disregard constitutional limitations because it is unable to change the constitution. The fact that the people have never given the Liberal-Democratic Party the two-thirds majority necessary to change the constitution may be an indication that the people do not want a change.

The justices of the Supreme Court are too intelligent not to know that they are evading the issue and shirking their duty. But they prefer sophistry to the unmanageable problem which would be created if they ruled that the so-called Self-Defence Forces were unconstitutional. This would force the government either to try to amend the constitution or to disband the armed forces. The conservatives have neglected to develop alternatives to retaining or abolishing Article 9.

The government's disregard of the constitution has encouraged the right wing to disparage the constitution openly. People upholding the constitution are derided as benighted and behind the times. Contempt of the constitution appeared in a number of articles. In the July 1991 issue of the monthly *Shinchō 45*, Takao Tokuoka called the Socialists Japan's second religious party (in addition to Komeito) which had made the constitution its Holy Writ. The party's faith in the constitution, the author claimed, had caused its loss of popular support. An article in the 4 July 1991 issue of the weekly *Shūkan Shinchō* heaped scorn on the constitution and praised the Liberal-Democratic Party's disregard of it as a wise policy. If put favourably, the article said, it was 'adult deception', if rated reprehensibly, it was 'deceitful shrewdness'.

Chapter 10

The Courts and the Judicial Ethos

DEMOCRACY AND THE JUDICIAL SYSTEM

Since the adoption of the constitution over 40 years ago, no judge has ever been removed from the bench on the basis of the constitutional provisions empowering the people to review the appointment of the justices of the Supreme Court. The system seems to be almost meaningless and the results disproportionate to the effort and expense involved. Serious doubts, however, on the fairness and impartiality of the judicial system have been raised by the acquittal of people condemned to death in retrials and the posthumous clearance of defendants found guilty mainly on the basis of forced confessions. It seems that the system relying exclusively on the judgement of professional jurists has an inherent bias against the accused.

Japan's constitution is not free from shortcomings but the irrationalities in its interpretation and application are more serious than the faults in the constitution itself. This touches on a basic problem. The constitution is not inherently bad but right from the start it has been without life or soul or any existential connection with the people. It has never been experienced as a living political reality but has remained a colourless enumeration of abstract principles and procedures. In the consciousness of the people, democracy has never been alive, neither as a conviction of democratic values nor as confidence in the soundness of democratic institutions. The decisions of the Supreme Court do not reflect a legal and political philosophy based on democratic principles. The constitution did not inspire a political value system guiding the life of the people in its political activities. It failed to exert a positive influence on popular thinking and the reality of the state.

As in other sectors of political life, the people have been kept out of the judiciary. In the Anglo-American tradition, the jury system was regarded as an integral part of a democratic polity. The grand jury summoned and returned by the sheriff to each session of the criminal courts receives complaints and accusations, hears the evidence and finds bills of indictment in cases where it is satisfied that a trial should be held. The petit jury determines by its verdict any question or issue of fact based on the evidence given in court.

In Japan the courts can only start a criminal case on the basis of an indictment by the Public Prosecutor. A Jury Law was enacted in 1928 which gave the accused the option to have a trial by jury. However, only males meeting a minimum income requirement were eligible as jurors and the presiding judge had the right to call for a new jury if he was unhappy with the decision. He could repeat the procedure until a verdict he found satisfactory was reached. Because of the qualification requirements, only prosperous gentlemen, usually of rather advanced age, served as jurors and the defendants choosing a jury trial had to pay court costs. The jury system was suspended in 1943 although the Jury Law has not been abolished.

In the present Japanese system of criminal justice, the Public Prosecutor decides whether to indict or not. Depending on the circumstances of the case, the prosecution can choose not to prosecute (Code of Criminal Procedure, Art. 248). The person harmed by the crime or his/her legal representative can bring suit (*ibid*. Art. 230-246); generally speaking, however, investigation and prosecution occur only if the Public Prosecutor pursues the case. This means that the courts cannot interfere unless the prosecution starts the proceedings. Since the Procurator's Office is part of the executive, the role of the judiciary as a check to the executive and the legislature is compromised. Moreover, the right of the Minister of Justice to issue directives to the prosecution (Public Prosecutor's Office Law, Art. 14) opens the door to undue political interference, as exemplified by the action of Takeru Inukai which saved Eisaku Sato from political obliteration in the famous shipbuilding scandal of 1954.

The 1948 Inquest of Prosecution Law (*Kensatsu Shingikai-hō*) provided for the formation of prosecution inquest commissions which decide whether the public prosecutor's decision not to indict in a given case was proper. At the end of 1990 there were 201 of these commissions at the locations of District Courts or their branches. They are composed of eleven citizens selected from registered voters, not connected with the judicial establishment or ineligible for various reasons. The commissions act upon the request of a party who filed a complaint or gave information to the Public Prosecutor's Office or of a party who suffered damage by the alleged crime if the public prosecutor did not pursue the case, and then submit a report stating the view of the majority to the chief of the District Public Prosecutor's Office.

Foreigners being tried in Japanese courts face considerable difficulties. All documents related to the trial, including indictment and ruling, are only available in Japanese (which is quite natural). Foreign defendants have to rely on verbal translations by interpreters employed by the court. In a case involving a Bangladeshi accused of murder, the defence lawyer asked the court for permission to have an interpreter employed by the defence present in the courtroom to check on the translation but the request was turned down. The defendant was found guilty. The presiding judge in charge of the appeal in the Tokyo High Court agreed to lend the defence a tape of the first hearing. In the police investigation, the suspect was questioned in English but the record was in Japanese and the defence complained of discrepancies between what the suspect thought he had said and the record.

American courts have often 'pierced the corporate veil' in order to base their decisions on the real relations of the parties. Japanese courts, it seems, prefer to respect the legal forms. In a suit which lasted 12 years and nine months, two farmers tried to regain ownership of 6,300 m^2 of land located in the former riverbed of the Shimano River. The land was part of 70 hectares in the Hasugata district which the firm Muromachi Sangyō purchased from about 300 farmers for a total of ¥ 412 million in 1964 and 1965 when Kakuei Tanaka was Minister of Finance.

Soon after the transaction, the Ministry of Construction started extensive projects in the area, including a new river embankment, a bypass for Route 8 linking the district directly with the central part of Nagaoka and the Nagaoka railway station, and a new bridge over the river. The value of the land, therefore, rose rapidly. The northern part was sold to Nagaoka City for about ¥ 800 million after the lawsuit was filed (1975), and at the time of the decision of the Nagaoka branch of the Niigata District Court, the value of the southern part was estimated at ¥ 30 billion.

The plaintiffs contended that Muromachi Sangyō acted on information obtained by Mr Tanaka in his official capacity, but which had been withheld from them. The transaction offended against public order and good custom and was, therefore, void (Civil Code, Art. 90). The plaintiffs further alleged that the contract should be declared void because it was based on error (*ibid.*, Art. 95) and that they had been deceived in the transaction (*ibid.*, Art. 96).

Muromachi Sangyō was the most important of the cluster of companies Mr Tanaka used for his deals; nobody doubted that he was in actual control of this and the other companies commonly known as the Tanaka family. However, the defence asserted that Muromachi Sangyō was an independent company and not related to Tanaka through capital or business activities. The President of the firm, Yasuhiro Kazamatsuri and other officers appeared as witnesses but the plaintiffs' efforts to have Kakuei Tanaka and Tomisaburo Hashimoto, Minister of Construction at the time of the transaction, called as witnesses were futile. Kakuei Tanaka suffered a stroke in February 1985 which precluded any further attempts to see him on the witness stand.

Judge Masao Araki decided that the plaintiffs had no case. Muromachi Sangyō and Kakuei Tanaka could not be considered as one entity, the sale did not involve error on the part of the plaintiffs or deceit on the part of the defendant, and Muromachi Sangyō did not reap exorbitant profits. There was no evidence, the court said, that Tanaka used information obtained on the basis of his position.

A newspaper's opinion: 'The Araki ruling stretches the limits of common sense.' I do not mean to imply that Japanese judges are remiss in the performance of their duties. In the innumerable everyday lawsuits and other legal procedures, the judiciary toils valiantly to contribute its share to the functioning of a democratic society. The delay in judicial procedures is a general complaint but this is largely due to the lack of rationalisation, the obsolescence of laws and procedures, the addition of new laws without a corresponding repeal of unnecessary laws and the insufficient number of judges and supporting staff.

EMOTIONAL JURISPRUDENCE

Western jurists studying Japan's administration of justice have found that the Japanese courts show a marked tendency to avoid a trial and persuade the parties to reach a compromise where possible. There certainly are many cases in which right or wrong is not unmistakably evident and the neat distinction between the black and white of the legal regulations is hard to apply. If disputes are settled through mediation, a clear-cut decision on who is right or wrong is usually avoided and an adjustment is made which saves the face of both parties. Modern law does not admit custom against the law but Japanese courts are reluctant to hold a situation or practice which has been in existence for some time illegal although it may be against the law. Although Japanese courts have never degenerated to the abyss of Nazi jurisprudence which considered the 'sound sentiment of the German people' the supreme norm, the courts try hard not to contravene the psychological climate peculiar to a case.

Before it developed into a precise system of justice with special rules administered by courts for a certain field of jurisdiction, equity, in the sense of equal and impartial justice, would adjust the conflicting rights or claims of the parties on the basis of a reasonable appreciation of the situation independent of positive law. What different people consider reasonable may vary considerably; character and upbringing, inclination and experience, sympathy and prejudice can all influence opinion. If a case involves strong emotional aspects, it is difficult to exclude the human element from the legal analysis. People will feel sorry for a frail or infirm defendant, for example, and an overly assertive plaintiff will make an unfavourable impression.

Actions by parents to claim damages for the loss of a child can hardly be free of emotional overtones. The premise that parents are entitled to damages because of their deep grief is obviously a *non sequitur*, yet this consideration seems to have been the basis of some decisions. A number of decisions have ruled on liability in cases in which children met accidental death. There seems to be some scope for evaluating the factors involved in these deaths. The Osaka District Court ordered the Neyagawa Municipal Government and Iwasaki Construction Co. to pay ¥ 5.7 million in damages to the parents of a three-year-old boy who fell into an irrigation canal while playing alone on an empty building site nearby. There had been a fence between the site and the canal but it had been torn down when the houses which had been on the site were removed. The parents contended that the construction company and the municipal government were responsible for the accident because they had neglected to put up a new fence but the presiding judge, Masaaki Kurokawa, noted that the parents were also responsible for the accident because they had failed to look after the boy.

In another drowning case, a two-year-old boy fell through a broken manhole cover into the sewer while playing in the garden of the Niigata Municipal Hospital where his mother was waiting for treatment. The Niigata District Court found that the hospital should have anticipated that children would play in the garden and have repaired the manhole cover but also held the mother partially responsible because she failed to keep an eye on her son.

In a fight between junior high school students during extra-curricular activities, a student was injured and became blind in one eye. The High Court had found the school authorities responsible but the Supreme Court reversed this verdict. A teacher who was appointed counsellor for extra-curricular activities had the general duty of supervising these affairs but was not obliged to be present at all activities. Originally, the extra-curricular activities were voluntary actions by the students and unless special circumstances indicated that something extraordinary might happen, the teacher was not obliged to be present, the court ruled.

The opposite position was taken by the Urawa District Court. A student at a prefectural senior high school, a member of the school's gymnastics club, fell from an iron bar while practising. He suffered a fractured neck and was paralysed from the waist down. He sued the prefecture alleging that the school was responsible for the accident because no teacher was present to give instructions and supervise the training. The court awarded him ¥ 46.9 million in damages. The accident, presiding Judge Ko Hashimoto said, was caused by the lack of suitable supervision over the extra-curricular activities on the part of the school authorities.

A decision of the Supreme Court announced on 2 February 1987 was noteworthy because it awarded the highest amount of damages in an accident suit up to that time and because it adopted the Ministry of Education's view that the educational activities of teachers at state schools constitute an exercise of state power. During diving practice, a junior high school student, Yoshihiko Imano, hit his head on the bottom of the pool and consequently became totally paralysed. The city of Yokohama paid compensation of ¥ 4 million and the Japan School Safety Association ¥ 15 million but the family felt that they would be unable to take care of the boy without further help and sued the city. The Yokohama District Court, however, turned down their demand for damages holding that the school was not at fault.

The Yokohama High Court reversed the verdict and the Supreme Court sustained the High Court decision awarding the parents ¥ 130 million in damages. Explaining why Article 1, paragraph 1 of the State Indemnification Law applied to the case, the court said that the law provided for the indemnification of injuries resulting from the exercise of public power and the accident occurred at a state school. The lawyer for the city found the decision of the Supreme Court unfair because it attributed the entire responsibility to the teacher. At the beginning of the exercise, the teacher had instructed the students that those who had no confidence in their diving ability should not dive, and Imano had attempted the dive of his own volition.

The families of children who had died or had become disabled by vaccination against whooping cough sued the state and the Nagoya District Court recognised the claims of 15 out of 24 families. The parents of an elementary school pupil bullied by classmates sued the parents of two pupils demanding ¥ 4.5 million in compensation. The Fukuoka District Court arranged an amicable settlement whereby each of the two families paid ¥ 500,000. This was the first time that parents had been held liable for bullying committed by their children.

COMPENSATION CLAIMS IN SUICIDE CASES

The courts are divided on the compensation for suicide. In June 1991 the Oita District Court overturned the decision of the Saiki Labour Standards Inspection Office which had rejected the application of the relatives of a 74-year-old man who had committed suicide because he was depressed over an occupational disease. The man had worked for many years in tunnelling and similar work and had contracted occupational pneumoconiosis (fibrous hardening of the lungs due to dust inhalation). He was diagnosed as suffering from the severest form of this disease in 1977 and committed suicide in 1978.

The deceased's widow applied for compensation under the Labour Accident Compensation Law but the labour office refused to recognise the suicide as an occupational accident. The Oita District Court, however, ruled that the worker's pneumoconiosis was the result of his work and had a causal relation to his suicide which should be regarded as death while on duty. The man's suicide, the court said, was the result of his depressed state brought about by anxiety and fear of death due to his incurable pneumoconiosis and hardening of the cerebral arteries. It is not clear what the financial situation of the worker's 82-year-old widow was but this may have been taken into consideration by the court.

The decisions ordering prefectural Boards of Education, schools or teachers to pay damages or compensation to parents whose children committed suicide are baffling. There is no direct physical connection between being scolded or punished at school, being teased or failing an examination and the act of taking one's own life. A child who is scolded or punished nevertheless commits suicide of his or her own free will. If this is denied, it would have to be proven that the psychic state resulting from the scolding or punishment necessarily produced the suicide. Behind the assertion that the school or the teacher was responsible lies the behaviouristic psychology which maintains that a criminal is the product of the environment and thus the environment is to be blamed for the crime. In a similar way, society, i.e. the school, is held responsible for the suicide of children. The question of what the parents did or did not do to deal with the situation in which the child took his or her own life remains unanswered.

A 17-year-old high school student hanged himself at home the day he was kept standing near the teacher's podium and later disciplined for reading some other textbook during a geography class. The parents sued the teacher and the Fukuoka prefectural government claiming that the illegal punishment had driven their son to commit suicide. The District Court found that there had been no cause and effect relationship between the punishment and the suicide but ruled that the punishment had been too severe and ordered the prefecture to pay compensation to the parents for their mental anguish. The Fukuoka High Court upheld the sentence and awarded the parents ¥ 600,000 compensation (they had asked for ¥ 18 million).

A Niigata court reached a different conclusion. A gang of rowdies had bullied a classmate, a 19-year-old high school student named Takaki during a school excursion, repeatedly extorted money from their fellow students and tortured them. Takaki told his parents who, in turn, informed the teacher in charge of the class of the misconduct. Thereupon the bullies tortured Takaki during the lunch recess and at 11 p.m. on the same day, Takaki hanged himslf in a room of the school.

The parents sued the prefecture alleging that the school had been negligent in curbing the violence and demanded ¥ 26 million in damages. The Niigata District Court, however, turned down their demand. Presiding Judge Hisashi Kakinuma observed that stricter supervision might possibly have stopped the violence but that suicide depended on the mind of the individual and that there had been no indication of Takaki's intention.

Another facet of the court decisions on children's suicide is the amount of damages paid. Generally, they amount to tens of millions of yen. The future earnings of a child are a matter of speculation and to what extent parents would have benefited from those earnings is even more conjectural.

SENTIMENTALITY IN JUVENILE CASES

The ascendancy of behaviouristic psychology has sometimes resulted in distortions of justice. The courts have been inclined to minimise the individual responsibility of criminals and stress the influence of an unfavourable environment, blaming family, school and society for the anti-social behaviour of individuals, above all of adolescents. A conspicuous example of this kind of judicial muddleheadedness was the punishment meted out to four minors who had kidnapped a teenage girl, kept her imprisoned and brutally assaulted her for 41 days, then put her corpse in a steel drum which they filled with concrete and threw into a landfill. The court treated the criminals as the victims of a hostile environment and minimised their atrocious torture of the real victim.

The prosecution claimed that the District Court had attributed too much weight to extenuating circumstances and the way of thinking incorporated in the Juvenile Law and appealed. The defence argued that the appeal should be dismissed and the case moved to the Family Court. Even in criminal cases, the defence contended, the Juvenile Law, with its emphasis on protection and rehabilitation, should prevail over the retributive justice of the criminal law. The Tokyo High Court, however, citing the brutality of the defendants' actions and the seriousness of their crimes, imposed stiffer sentences on three of the four defendants.

Another case of 'easy sentimentality' was the commutation of the death sentence to life imprisonment pronounced by the Tokyo High Court in August 1981. The Tokyo District Court had sentenced Norio Nagayama to death for four murders committed within one month in the autumn of 1968 at four different locations. Nagayama argued that he had become a criminal largely because he had grown up in poverty and ignorance for which he blamed the state and society. He shouted at the judge and three times abruptly dismissed his lawyer. Although Nagayama showed no repentance during the District Court trial, he impressed the High Court by the conversion he was believed to have experienced in prison, particularly after his marriage to a 26-year-old woman who had been greatly moved by his autobiography *Tears of Poverty* which sold 200,000 copies. Nagayama donated some of the royalties to two of his victims' families which the court considered a sign of contrition.

Judge Mitsuo Funada did not agree with the argument of the defence that the death penalty was unconstitutional 'cruel punishment' but he thought that the Juvenile Law which rules out capital punishment for 18-year-olds could also apply to Nagayama who could have been regarded as an 18-year-old in terms of mental maturity when he committed the crimes. Nevertheless, he rejected the argument of the defence that the penalty was unreasonable and that Nagayama was insane when he killed his victims. But Judge Funada argued that the state and society should have extended a helping hand to the defendant who had been raised in an inferior environment which, the judge said, was a consequence of the poverty of welfare policy.

The prosecution appealed to the Supreme Court, basing its appeal on Article 405, No. 3 of the Code of Criminal Procedure which sanctions recourse to the Supreme Court if a sentence is at variance with the precedents of the Supreme Court. The High Court's decision, the prosecution claimed, was emotional and its reasons unconvincing. A defendant convicted of theft, robbery and four murders, the prosecution contended, should be hanged. The five justices of the second Petit Bench of the Supreme Court unanimously quashed the sentence of the High Court and remanded the case. Presiding Justice Susumu Ohashi stated the position of the Supreme Court in general declaring that the death penalty was part of the legal system and a creditable option in serious cases. The ultimate punishment of taking human life should be applied with prudence but that it was justified when the criminal responsibility was truly serious. The crimes committed by the defendant were heinous and cruel and the High Court had erred in its appraisal of the facts and the measure of punishment. In the retrial, the Tokyo High Court imposed the death sentence on Nagayama but this time it was the defence that appealed to the Supreme Court.

Does the judicial system dispense equal justice? In May 1991 the Supreme Court rejected an appeal by five young men against a decision to send them to a reformatory for raping and murdering a 15-year-old girl in July 1985. The five, then aged between 13 and 15, were found guilty by the Urawa Family Court of raping a junior high school student from Soka, Saitama Prefecture, in a parked car and strangling her. The five denied the accusation. Under the Juvenile Law, appeals for a retrial are impossible. The law limits so-called complaints (***kōkoku***) to cases in which there has been a grave violation of the laws influencing the decision to commit the offender to a reformatory, a serious misunderstanding of the facts or a serious injustice. The complaint has to be filed within two weeks after the decision to commit the juvenile to an institution (Art. 32). If the complaint is rejected, another complaint is only allowed in case the rejection violates or misinterprets the constitution or conflicts with decisions of the Supreme Court or High Court decisions in appellate cases (Art. 35, par. 1).

After their release from the reformatory, the five applied to the Family Court to have the decision sending them to the reformatory rescinded without a trial. The court turned down their plea on the ground that they should have availed themselves of the procedure laid down in the Juvenile Law and that a cancellation would be pointless since they had already been released from the reformatory. When the Tokyo High Court upheld the ruling of the Family Court, the five appealed to the Supreme Court. The court agreed with the lower courts that a cancellation of the commitment would be useless and that a reversal in order to restore their good name was impossible. The court rejected the claim that the provisions of the Juvenile Law violated the constitutional guarantee of equality before the law and equal right to a fair trial without comment.

THE COURTS AND THE POWERS THAT BE

Generally, the decisions of the courts are fair and just but there are cases which, I think, do not measure up to the ideal of justice. To my mind, some decisions favour the authorities and in others, emotions have possibly influenced the evaluation of the case. Decisions in which I believe a bias is discernible comprise rulings of some High Courts and the Supreme Court in cases involving Article 9 of the constitution, in the decision of the Supreme Court and the Tokyo High Court on the dissolution of the House of Representatives, many decisions on the equality of votes and decisions involving foreigners. A former judge, Masamichi Hanada, asserted that the Supreme Court has been trying to influence the lower courts by using conferences to present the views of the Bureaux of Civil and Criminal Affairs as standards for deciding cases (Hanada used the expression *saibankan tōsei* - control of judges). The result has been a very conspicuous tendency in administrative suits to favour the government.

About six weeks prior to the Supreme Court's decision on the Daitō flood (1984) the General Secretariat of the Supreme Court (*Saikōsaibansho Jimu Sōkyoku*) assembled all High Court and District Court judges in charge of proceedings concerning damage claims for flooding against the state and gave them a statement containing the views of the civil affairs bureau announced in the Daitō decision. Following the Daitō ruling, the Tokyo and Nagoya High Courts overturned several District Court decisions awarding flood damages, but in the Tama River case, the Supreme Court, in 1990, quashed a decision of the Tokyo High Court which had overruled the Tokyo District Court's recognition of the state's liability for damages. A committee of the Japan Lawyers' Federation stated that in recent years, a number of prosecutors with trial experience have been appointed judges at lower courts handling cases of flooding; in all these cases, the state has been held not responsible for flood damage.

A recent decision of the Tokyo District Court illustrates a tendency to observe the letter of the law at the expense of justice. A convict serving an 18-year prison sentence for bomb attacks on businesses in the 1970s filed a lawsuit claiming that his human rights were violated while he was being held in a detention house. According to the complaint, the detention house authorities had prohibited the plaintiff from reading a book on Nietzsche. The book was in Japanese but an illustration showed a manuscript page in German. The detention house regulations state that detainees have to pay for translations if they want to read a book in a foreign language. Since the detainee and his associate refused to pay for the translation of the photograph, the authorities did not allow them to read the book. The plaintiff also claimed that parts of leaflets sent to him by supporters were blacked out. The Tokyo District Court rejected his complaint. The presiding judge, Norio Wakui, thought that the prohibition seemed too inflexible but that the detention house authorities were just following the rules and therefore had not violated the law.

In another attempt to discourage suits against the government, the courts increased legal fees. On 7 May 1991 the Tokyo District Court asked a group of 571 plaintiffs who sought an injunction against the government's payment of ¥ 90 billion in financial aid for the Gulf war to pay a filing fee totalling ¥ 3.4 trillion - the court, calculating the filing fee separately for each individual on the basis of the total amount of the value of the litigation, came up with a filing fee of ¥ 6 million for each plaintiff. The amount was later reduced. Similar action taken by the Osaka and Miyazaki District Courts drew sharp protests from anti-war and environmental groups claiming that the right to a fair trial was made illusory by the exorbitant filing fees.

In view of this trend, the method of appointing the justices of the Supreme Court as well as the appointment of other judges provided for in Article 40, paragraph 1 of the Court Organisation Law (*Saibanshōhō*) appear objectionable. There may be no intentional bias in the selection of judges but it may well be that the political neutrality of the judiciary does not exclude some kind of ideological orientation of jurists. There is also no guarantee that the desire for advancement will not be reflected in the handling of cases. The election of judges by the people, common in the United States, would encounter serious difficulties in Japan. However, a system in which the legal profession, including judges, prosecutors and lawyers, would play some role in the selection of candidates and the appointment of judges would seem to be feasible.

JUDICIAL SUPPORT OF THE DEMOCRATIC SYSTEM

The constitution provides that trials shall be conducted and judgment declared publicly (Art. 82, par. 1). Actually, however, publicity has been severely curtailed. There are no limitations on access to the visitors' gallery but space is limited and insufficient in sensational trials. Until December 1987 taking photos in courtrooms was prohibited. It is still very restricted: only one representative each of the pool of cameramen for still photos and for videocameras is allowed to take pictures and in criminal trials the defendant cannot be shown.

Only members of the court's press club used to be allowed to take notes during court proceedings. Otherwise, permission to take notes was left to the discretion of the presiding judge. An American lawyer, Lawrence Repeta, who first came to Japan in 1979 to study Japanese economic law, attended a series of hearings on tax evasion in stock speculation. He was stopped from taking notes by a court sergeant who informed him that he needed the judge's permission. Repeta repeatedly asked the judge to allow him to take notes but his requests were rejected.

Claiming that the prohibition violated his right to know, Repeta filed suit demanding ¥ 1.5 million in damages. While conceding that taking notes might help in understanding a trial, the Tokyo District Court turned down Repeta's claim on the ground that taking notes at a trial was not included among the human rights guaranteed in the constitution. On appeal, the Tokyo High Court upheld the District Court. Taking notes might interfere with the fairness of the court procedures and have adverse psychological effects on witnesses or the parties. There might be cases, the court admitted, in which the taking of notes would be necessary for the freedom of information, but since it might possibly interfere with the fairness of the trial, the prohibition was unavoidable. The refusal of the trial judge to let Repeta take notes was impolite, to say the least, but the court decisions were asinine. If reporters could take notes, there was no reason why other people should not do likewise.

Repeta appealed to the Supreme Court claiming that the prohibition of taking notes violated the freedom of information implied in Article 21 of the constitution and was incompatible with the public character of trials prescribed in Article 82, paragraph 1. On 8 March 1989 the grand bench of the Supreme Court recognised the right to take notes in open court proceedings. Taking notes was not included in the constitutional provision that trials should be conducted publicly and was not a right explicitly enumerated in the text of Article 21 but it conformed to the spirit of the constitutional guarantee of freedom of information. The judiciary, Chief Justice Kōichi Yaguchi declared, had not shown sufficient understanding of the meaning of freedom of information. The action of the presiding judge who had not allowed Repeta to take notes had lacked a rational foundation but it did not constitute an abuse of state power so Repeta was not entitled to damages. Chief Justice Yaguchi maintained that there might be circumstances under which the presiding judge would find it necessary to prohibit the taking of notes in order to ensure an orderly trial. The Supreme Court informed all courts in the country to remove notices prohibiting the taking of notes during open trials.

There have been a few cases in which members of the Young Jurists' Association (Seinen Hōritsuka Kyōkai) have not been appointed judges after completing the course at the Judicial Training Institute. Of 34 graduates who failed to receive appointments from 1970 to 1979, 23 were members of the association (in 1979, four out of five). In 1971 the rejection of the appointment of an assistant judge triggered a heated controversy on discrimination on ideological grounds, the appropriateness of the procedure for the reappointment of judges (judges of the lower courts are appointed for a term of ten years but can be reappointed - Court Organisation Law, Art. 40, par. 3), the standard for the reappointment and the guarantee of status. This problem is common to all democracies. Since the German Weimar Republic was taken over by the Nazis through legitimate democratic procedures and turned into a dictatorship, democracies have become apprehensive of the 'danger from within'. Although there have been excesses such as McCarthyism in the US, democracies have generally been too lax in protecting themselves against left- or right-wing extremists.

For a while Eurocommunism appeared to become a real threat in some countries. Eurocommunists professed to observe the rules of democracy but intended to build a Marxist state if they gained control of the government. In West Germany, the radical left, aided and abetted by the left wing of the Social-Democratic Party, adopted the strategy of taking over positions of influence in what was called 'the long march through the institutions'. In the 1960s, the educational system, from elementary school to university, was made an instrument of Marxist indoctrination. Leftists dominated the peace movement and the ecological movement, and doctrinaire Socialists occupied leading positions in the labour unions. In Hamburg, the Socialist city government, supported by the Free Democratic Party, refused to enforce the law against groups of anarchists occupying a section of the city.

Generally speaking, the Japanese have never fully understood the threat of Communism. For many years, a good many university professors, particularly professors of economics, were Marxists, and Marxist ideology was rampant among students. In many labour unions, the leaders were Marxists. There were people who supported Marxist policies without being Marxists or without being aware that the policies were Marxist. How can the attempt to keep people who advocate the overthrow of the democratic system by constitutional and lawful means out of public service jobs be reconciled with the constitutional guarantee of human rights? Article 99 provides that all public officials have the obligation to respect and uphold the constitution. The intention to use the provisions for the revision of the constitution to abolish it and do away with the democratic system is incompatible with the conscious and sincere affirmation which respect for the constitution demands. That the state requires a positive attitude toward the constitution and the public order based on it seems to form a reasonable condition for employment as a public servant and to insist on such a condition seems not only the right but also the duty of the state if it is to prevent its overthrow from within.

People who deny the state built on the present constitution and want a state other than a democracy are free not to become public officials and to pursue their political convictions. Naturally, to succeed in life without renouncing one's ideological preferences has been the traditional bourgeois ethos but the view that in the name of freedom of thought and freedom of choice of occupation, environmental conditions are to be shaped in accordance with every individual's wishes is utopian. No individual, however, should be forced to conform to environmental conditions. Instead of encouraging the self-contradictory expectation that somebody who rejects the constitution will faithfully support and apply the constitution and the laws, it would be more in the interest of the public welfare if measures were taken to prevent sabotage when public officials are hired.

IDEOLOGICAL CONFLICTS

There are a number of incidents in the judiciary related to ideology. One of them is the so-called Hiraga letter. On 14 August 1969 Kenta Hiraga, Chief Judge at the Sapporo District Court, sent a letter to Judge Shigeo Fukushima of the same court who was in charge of the Naganuma case (which involved the interpretation of Article 9 of the constitution) in which he counselled Judge Fukushima to be circumspect in handling the case. Hiraga's reason for this unusual step was the fact that Fukushima was a member of the Young Jurists' Association. Fukushima had made it clear that his thinking was in tune with the association's policy of protecting the constitution, democracy and peace. Hiraga's letter was obviously an attempt to use his position as Chief Judge to influence the trial and when Fukushima published the letter, a controversy on judicial independence, the ideology of judges and the freedom of association erupted. The Sapporo District Court and the Supreme Court reprimanded Hiraga and transferred him to the Tokyo High Court.

In April 1970 Seiichi Kishi, Director-General of the Supreme Court's Secretariat, stated that judges should refrain from becoming members of organisations with strong political connotations. A few days later, the Ministry of Justice, which was in charge of the defence in the Naganuma trial, challenged Fukushima, alleging that it was impossible to expect a fair trial from him because he was a member of the Young Jurists' Association. In a press conference on 2 May 1970, Kazuto Ishida, Chief Justice of the Supreme Court, declared that extreme militarists, anarchists and confirmed Communists were undesirable as judges (the Communist Party is legal in Japan and represented in the Diet). These occurrences stirred up fierce debates in Japan's legal circles questioning which organisations had strong political connotations, what kind of ideology was undesirable and who was to determine who or what was objectionable. The Young Jurists' Association protested asserting that the conservatives were attempting thought control of the judiciary. The 21st general meeting of the association established a special division exclusively for judges (with about 230-240 members) distinct from lawyers, scholars and students of the Judicial Research and Training Institute. A group of 29 scholars, clergymen and writers submitted a petition to the Impeachment Committee of the Diet calling for the dismissal of Chief Justice Ishida.

The challenge to Judge Fukushima was turned down by the District Court and the High Court and the ministry forwent an appeal to the Supreme Court. The Impeachment Committee decided not to take action against Judge Hiraga but decreed a suspended prosecution of Judge Fukushima on the ground that he had published the letter. Thereupon the Sapporo High Court called a meeting of judges and reprimanded Judge Fukushima for the same reason. In legal circles, both measures were criticised as politically inspired. Judge Fukushima declared that it was impossible to fulfill the duties of a judge and submitted his resignation which, however, he withdrew two days later.

In October 1979 it transpired that, because of a demand for prosecution, the Impeachment Committee had sent inquiries to 213 judges asking whether they belonged to the Young Jurists' Association. The judges who were members protested that it was an attempt at thought control and harassment of the organisation. At the same time, the members of the committee belonging to the opposition parties declared that they had not been informed of the mailing of the inquisitorial letters. At a meeting of the Chief Judges of the country's High Courts, Chief Justice Ishida remarked: 'The reprimand of Judge Fukushima was not a follow-up to the action of the Impeachment Committee. It is extremely regrettable that it is ineptly seen as a crisis in the judiciary.'

In 1987 a judge who had been on the bench for 30 years resigned rather than accept an appointment which would have been a demotion. He had served eight years at the Yokosuka branch of the Yokohama District Court when the time for the third renewal of his tenure came in April 1987. He was told that he would not be reappointed unless he accepted a transfer to the Shimoda branch of the Shizuoka District Court or the Ina branch of the Nagano District Court. The judge had refused the transfers before stating that these places were far from where he would like to be. Actually, most judges who had started their careers at the same time as him were holding much higher positions.

Bench assignments are handled by the Supreme Court. The judge in question had been a member of the Young Jurists' Association since his days as a student at the Legal Training and Research Institute and was active in a discussion group studying the role of courts and judges. His acquaintances thought that he was discriminated against because of his membership in the association. In an earlier case, Judge Yasuaki Miyamoto, Assistant Judge at the Kumamoto District Court, was refused reappointment at the end of his ten-year period. As in the refusal of the court to appoint some of the graduates of the Legal Training and Research Institute, the court remained silent on the reasons for these measures.

Behind such problems lies the ambiguity in Japan's political thinking. Neither the conservatives represented by the Liberal-Democratic Party nor the Marxists (who comprise the Communist Party and some Socialists) can be considered liberals. Attempts to interpret the constitution in conformity with democratic principles sometimes founder because true liberalism is confounded with socialism. The attitude of conservatives is frequently tainted by McCarthyism while other people fail to see that socialism cannot be reconciled with liberalism. The idea that the authorities are always right still lingers on in Japanese society and opposition to the government is looked upon as some kind of effrontery. Although rivalry is strong among officials and each agency jealously guards its own turf and tries to extend its influence, there is also a fundamental feeling of solidarity and a break of ranks is considered unethical.

In November 1991 the Supreme Court confirmed that Board of Audit investigations had discovered about 1,600 irregularities in the expense accounts of seven courts (the Tokyo, Fukuoka, Hiroshima, Utsunomiya and Mito District Courts and the Fukuoka and Utsunomiya Family Courts) amounting to almost ¥ 20 million. Judges were involved in about 100 of these cases. In most cases, officials who had received advance payments for business trip expenses failed to return the unused daily allowances and accommodation expenses if the trips were shorter than originally planned. All misappropriated funds had been returned, the Supreme Court said. The ¥ 20 million was only a small part of the ¥ 10.36 billion which, according to the Board of Audit, was wasted by government ministries, agencies and affiliated institutions in fiscal 1990.

Epilogue

In addition to the problems discussed in the foregoing pages, there are other numerous instances in which democratic principles and values have been disregarded or distorted in Japan's public life. Some of these issues involve the interpretation and application of the constitution, others the policies pursued by the government and the measures taken for their implementation. Japan's parliamentary system has been a disgrace. Not only has the Diet been unable to exercise democratic control, it has been the main cause of unbelievable waste and costly mistakes. Nobody has ever been brought to account for the incredible stupidity of locating Tokyo's international airport at Narita (although other sites were available) or for the enormous waste in the construction of the airport.

The decision to build a new airport for Tokyo was made in 1966; the airport was not opened until May 1978 after twelve years of construction costing ¥ 600 billion. It took two more years to build a fuel pipe-line. A direct rail link with the Tokyo metropolitan area was finally established in March 1991 when two railway lines, one operated by the East Japan Railway Co. and the other by Keisei Electric Railway were connected with the station under the terminal building which had been built with the airport but had remained unused while requiring huge maintenance expenses. Since there exists no direct access road to the airport, the drive from central Tokyo to the airport may take two to three hours.

Nobody has been held responsible either for the silliness of building three bridge systems to connect Honshu with Shikoku because politicians thought saving face more important than saving money. The domination of the public sector by unrestrained party politics is largely to blame for the inflation which has accompanied the country's economic growth and particularly the fantastic rise in land prices which has pushed the cost of housing in the large cities beyond what the ordinary wage earner can afford.

Fiscal policies, above all taxation policies, have persistently shown an outrageous disregard of the interests of the common people and a notorious bias in favour of big business and certain classes. The government's agricultural policy has been a dismal failure with its enormous subsidies to farmers, its army of superfluous officials and the ridiculously high price of rice (amounting to 6.5 times the international level). Another factor contributing to high food prices is the government's import policy. The government controls all grain imports and the increments in the prices of grain and flour provide part of the funds for subsidising the farmers. Prior to the liberalisation of beef imports on 1 April 1991, the Livestock Industry Promotion Corporation had a monopoly on beef imports which made beef retail prices four to ten times higher than the price paid to producers. The fund raised by the monopoly were partly used to subsidise Japanese beef producers. Premium beef was withheld from the general distribution system and channelled to hotels and restaurants. Import arrangements such as sole agents contribute to unjustified increases in the prices of imported goods.

Japan's health care ranks among the best in the world, yet hospitals and clinics are often crowded despite the fact that there are many competent doctors and excellent nurses. There is a certain danger of over-medication since hospitals have their own pharmacies and most doctors provide their patients directly with the medicines they prescribe.

Enormous sums of money are diverted to prestige projects while real problems remain unsolved. Not only the national, but also local governments have built splendid offices, grandiose international conference halls, museums and art galleries while problems such as housing, transportation and pollution have been neglected. The subway and commuter train systems are marvels of efficiency but overcrowding, particularly during rush hours, has been a problem for over thirty years and there is still no solution in sight.

Tokyo built a new city hall at a cost of ¥ 156.9 billion. Governor Shunichi Suzuki's office and related facilities occupy the entire seventh floor, with a floor space of over 1,000 *tsubo* (3,305 m^2), a seven-metre high ceiling, and floors and walls embellished with two-tone Italian marble. In a crowning display of ostentation, the buildings are illuminated at night, wasting additional millions of yen on top of the billions poured into the construction of the complex. Asked why the illumination was not suspended after the outbreak of the 1990 Middle East crisis, an official of the metropolitan government replied that since the most energy-efficient equipment had been installed, there was no need for saving. Yet the patience of staff and visitors is sorely tested by the inefficient elevator system. The monthly electricity consumption of the complex amounts to 6 million kilowatts which cost the city ¥ 110 million.

In addition to the new city hall, the metropolitan government sank ¥ 32 billion into a theatre complex containing four facilities for theatrical and other cultural performances. The largest theatre, with a seating capacity of 1,900, is equipped with a 50-ton organ. The instrument, designed by French organ builder Marc Garnier, actually comprises three organs, a Renaissance, a Baroque, and a modern organ, with a total of 126 stops and 8,286 pipes. It cost ¥ 387 million. Plans for the future envisage construction of a ¥ 96 billion International Forum and a ¥ 40 billion museum.

Tokyo residents have criticised the new facilities and other superfluous prestige projects as an unconscionable waste of the taxpayers' money. The overcrowding of hospitals, the insufficiency of homes for the aged and disabled and the lack of day-care centres for children of working mothers are some of the social welfare requirements which should be given priority over projects 'to improve the world's level of culture'. The city of Yokohama built a ¥ 100 million luxury yacht for entertaining guests. Under the pretext of reducing the foreign trade surplus, the government bought two jumbo jets for the exclusive use of the cabinet at a cost of ¥ 36 billion.

Prior to the privatisation of the Japan National Railways, the construction of new railway lines and the erection of new railway stations were favourite ploys of politicians to gain support in their constituencies. The politicians voted for the construction of new lines the management did not want because they would be unprofitable. When JNR was a government enterprise, only three lines were profitable: Tokyo's Yamanote line (the loop around the inner city), the *Shinkansen* (express train) from Tokyo to Osaka and the line from Ueno to Takasaki. The Japan Railways Construction Corporation, established under Kakuei Tanaka, built 35 railway lines all of which operated in the red. Even after privatisation, the construction of new railway lines remains tied to legislation to provide politicians with opportunities to woo their constituents.

The government has often expressed its dismay over the sharp increases in land prices but has taken no action to stop land speculation or to roll back the exorbitant real estate inflation. On the contrary, local governments avidly made the higher real estate values the basis of their real property taxes which greatly increased local revenues and provided the wherewithal to finance their extravagant prestige projects.

With the enormous increase in property values, inheritance taxes levied at pre-inflation rates on real estate assets have become confiscatory. For many middle-class families, the family home constitutes their only substantial asset. Although the amount of inheritance tax on the legal portion of the deceased's spouse is subtracted from the total tax liability, many families do not have the liquid assets necessary to pay the inheritance tax and have to sell at least part of the property to pay it. This is only one of the inequities of a tax system which, as in most developed countries, favours business. Individuals must pay tax on their income, whether they are solvent or not, while corporations only pay tax on their profits. The company, no matter how profligate in its spending, pays tax on what it declares as its net profit a couple of months after it closes its books. The 'salaryman' has his income tax withheld from his pay every payday and has to manage to live on what is left. His wife is charged a sales tax every time she makes a purchase.

The government's housing policy has been ineffective, to put it mildly. Housing built by public corporations has a bad reputation: rents are high (they are low for apartments for members of the Diet and high government officials), locations are inconvenient and the apartments are tiny. At the same time, the government built fine apartments for government employees with the taxpayers' money in first-class residential districts. Reacting to public criticism, some housing corporations went to the other extreme. The Osaka Prefectural Public Housing Corporation built nine new 'high tech' houses for sale in Senboku New Town (Sakai). All houses have two floors, four or five bedrooms, living room, kitchen and dining room; they stand on plots of 312 m^2. Some houses are equipped with saunas and the latest telecommunications system; some appliances can be controlled from outside by telephone. The prices of these units ranged from ¥ 49.9 million to ¥ 79.9 million, about 40 per cent higher than the usual public housing.

A three-bedroom apartment in a 37-floor, 458-unit building erected by the Tokyo Metropolitan Government, the Urban and Housing Public Corporation and other public organisations on reclaimed land in Tokyo Bay rents for ¥ 268,006 a month, plus a ¥ 8,000 service fee. The monthly rent is scheduled to reach ¥ 324,757 by April 1996. In 1990 the average industrial monthly wage (excluding overtime) was ¥ 227,700.

The Osaka branch of the Housing and Urban Development Public Corporation built an apartment which, the corporation said, was specifically designed for 'dinkies': double income, no kids families. The ¥ 51.6 million apartment forms the top floor of an eight-floor apartment building in Nishinomiya; it has a floor space of 87 m^2 with a 27.5-mat living room, large enough, the corporation commented, to hold parties. That a government-owned organisation can boast about the misuse of public funds for luxury projects is typical of the lack of social responsibility in government agencies. The construction of luxury dwellings financed by public funds is hardly in the public interest.

The Hyogo Prefectural Government built a housing project called Washington Village consisting of 55 American-style homes designed by American architects and furnished with fireplaces, jacuzzi and terraces for cookouts and barbecues. The project was undertaken in cooperation with the State of Washington. Not only the timber was imported from Washington State but doors, windows, mouldings, staircases and other finished and semi-finished materials were produced and provided by Washington State industry.

The houses were built on lots of 480 m^2, more than double the average 220 m^2 of Japanese housing lots. Prices range from ¥ 77 million to ¥ 104 million. The neighbourhood is free from through highways, power lines are buried underground and there are no fences, giving it a spacious ambience. By December 1991 the prefecture had received 650 applications, quite different from the tens of thousands of applications for low-cost public housing. Additional houses will be built in the future. The project would have been most appropriate if undertaken by private capital but is highly objectionable because financed by public funds.

The housing situation demonstrates the inequity of using public funds for luxury housing. Application rates for low-cost public housing in the Tokyo area far outnumber available homes. For flats in convenient locations the odds came to 250 : 1, although applicants in other regions have much better chances of buying a home in government projects. Conditions are more or less the same for tenants looking for low-cost subsidised housing. The chances of being allocated an apartment are about 20 : 1 in the Tokyo area although they are much better in other regions.

A company employee who wants to buy or build his own house relying on his salary and on the expectation that he will be able to work until his retirement may obtain a loan of, say, ¥ 30 million repayable in 20 or 30 years. The house may be a 30-minute bus ride from the nearest railway station and commuting time may be from one to two hours, which will require him to get up at six in the morning and return home at eleven at night. On his day off, he will sleep or play golf. His family life will be next to non-existant, as he will have no time for his wife and his children and be like a stranger in his own family. The housing situation provides an irrefutable argument for the proposition that, as far as the common people, the so-called middle class, are concerned, Japan's wealth is a fable.

Among unsolved social problems, the situation of the minorities described above, the indigenous Ainu and the *burakumin*, Koreans and Chinese is prominent. Also problematic is the plight of the newly-arrived refugees from South East Asia and the numerous foreigners coming to Japan to look for work, often without legal status. Another unresolved issue is the demand for sexual equality. Japan remains a male-oriented and male-dominated society. Japanese women are discriminated against in politics, in government service, in the economy and in social life. The Socialist and Communist parties have fielded many women candidates in national and local elections but very few women exercise any real influence. The handful of women in the Liberal-Democratic Party only have a token function as do the few women promoted to leading positions in the bureaucracy.

Although women make up about 40 per cent of the workforce, women's wages and salaries are invariably lower than those of men performing the same tasks. Women account for only 7.2 per cent of business executives and there are no women in leadership positions in the large business organisations: Keidanren - Federation of Economic Organisations, Nikkeiren - Japan Federation of Employers' Associations, Keizai Dōyūkai - Japanese Association of Corporate Executives, the Japan Chamber of Commerce and Industry, the industry associations such as the Federation of Bankers' Associations, or the large umbrella associations of trade unions such as Rengō.

In a move obviously made for its public relations effect, the Tokyo Chamber of Commerce and Industry appointed women to head two of its divisions. Hanae Mori, the noted designer, was put in charge of cultural activities and Kiyoko Koizumi, president of Suzunoya Inc, a kimono chain, was to direct the public welfare division. The appointments reflected the male notions of activities proper for women and the tendency to preclude women from exercising any real influence. There are many women in the medical profession but relatively few succeed in the main branches such as internal medicine or surgery while they are relatively more numerous in fields such as paediatrics, ophthalmology, otorhinolaryngology or dermatology. The ratio of women teachers decreases rapidly at the higher levels of education and is particularly tiny at state universities. However, compared with the situation before the war or even twenty years ago, the position of women has vastly improved. They usually run the household, educate the children and administer the family's finances. Many women have been successful in the entertainment world and a number of women have gained recognition as writers.

Bureaucrats reign supreme in most government agencies while ministers sometimes behave like simple robots. Since the Meiji era, the mission of the bureaucracy has been to further industry. Each ministry controls one or more public corporations which provide highly-paid sinecures and additional retirement allowances to retiring senior officials who are not furnished with executive posts in the industries which they controlled. The bureaucracy is generally competent although the bureaucrats seem to cherish the illusion that nothing can work properly unless it is regulated and subjected to administrative guidance. They jealously guard their own sphere of influence, are opinionated and sometimes pig-headed, and always biased in favour of their clientele. Bureaucratic control has been a serious obstacle to the development of a democratic mentality although it has greatly contributed to the stability of the public order.

Most bills are drafted by the bureaucracy and in many cases the laws passed by the Diet lay down only the basic rules and leave the details to administrative regulation (cabinet or ministerial orders, etc.). Since every government agency considers only its particular area, the sum of these ordainments imposes oppressive and sometimes even unjust burdens on the people. In many legal provisions, administrative convenience is given priority over fairness to the citizen and the cumulative effect of the measures ordained by the various agencies is beyond the understanding of legislators and bureaucrats.

In some cases, the actual impact on the people does not result from the law but from the enforcement ordinances or other administrative measures. To give an example: the rate of property tax is laid down in the Local Tax Law (*Chihō Zeihō*), Article 350, but the value of the real estate on which the tax is levied is assessed unilaterally by the Home Ministry every three years. The assessed value for inheritance and gift taxes is fixed by the National Tax Administration Agency. The property owner learns of the assessed value when he receives the documentation.

Commenting on Francis Fukugawa's essay 'The End of History', an editorial in the *New York Times* argued that Japan may look like a democracy similar to those in Western Europe but was actually a country ruled by bureaucrats and not by publicly-elected politicians. Under such a system, the individual has little say. Economic policies are not to further the common good, still less to protect the consumer, but to ensure profit for big business. The interests of the consumer has never been a bureaucratic concern. The reputation of Japan's financial system suffered a severe blow in the summer of 1991 when it transpired that over 20 securities companies had made secret payments to select customers to compensate them for losses resulting from the slump in stock prices in 1989 and 1990.

Japan's Official Development Aid (ODA which, in 1989, was the highest in the world ($ 8.96 billion; in 1990 it amounted to $ 9.07 billion, the second highest after the US) has often been criticised for its wastefulness and inefficiency. Japanese government representatives propose projects which will enhance their reputation and provide Japanese firms with opportunities to make a profit. The implementation of the projects sometimes inverses priorities; the execution of economic blueprints is considered more important than the usefulness of the projects to the people. According to press reports, President Daniel arap Moi of Kenya used Japanese ODA funds to give a Mercedes to every member of the legislature. The diversion of development funds for buying foreign products such as cars, whisky or cigarettes seems common in Africa, and in many African and Asian countries, foreign aid mostly benefits the ruling classes. The Japanese government does not check on the use of the economic aid it provides because the recipient governments consider any attempt at monitoring the use of development aid as an interference in domestic affairs. Foreign governments are unhappy with this situation and in the beginning of 1991, the Norwegian government decided to stop all aid to Kenya.

In their endeavour to portray Japan as a leading member of the international community, Japanese politicians travelling abroad promise huge sums of money wherever they go. They seem oblivious to the fact that Japan's own infrastructure is far from perfect and that the country's public debt which will amount to ¥ 174 trillion at the end of fiscal 1992 (March 1993) is one of the highest among the developed countries. Debt service is expected to require ¥ 18.5 trillion, 23.55 per cent of the provisional 1993 budget estimated at ¥ 78.55 trillion.

In agreement with other donor countries, Japan had suspended aid to Myanmar (formerly Burma) in protest at the violation of human rights and the continuation of the military dictatorship, but MITI and the Ministry of Finance resumed the aid payments in spite of the objections of the Foreign Ministry in order to prevent Myanmar's default on about $ 60 million in Japanese loans. Ecologists have criticised Japan's ODA because of disregard of the environmental impact shown in many of the projects financed by Japanese aid.

A constitutional ban the government has consistently violated is the prohibition laid down in Article 89 on spending public money or other property for the use, benefit or maintenance of educational enterprises not under the control of public authority. The subterfuge that all schools have to observe the pertinent legal regulations and the channelling of the funds through a special organisation, the Japan Private School Promotion Foundation, do not make the subsidies paid to private universities, junior and technical colleges (in fiscal 1990 ¥ 250.6 billion) constitutional. I think it would have been possible to pass a constitutional amendment abolishing this prohibition which reflects an American bias and does not suit conditions in Japan where, unlike the United States, there is no tradition of extensive private support of educational institutions.

It is a tribute to the native solidarity and good sense of the Japanese people that despite the dismal failure of the political leadership, Japan has remained an orderly society. Harmony is often mentioned as the basic value of Japanese society; its negative aspect of not causing trouble or dissent is deemed more essential than creating a sense of well being. Yehudi Menuhin observed that the Japanese grow up with two cultures, drawing on both the East and the West. Their commercial and technological success, Menuhin thinks, is entirely due to this cultural tradition. To the Japanese, the West was never an exotic wonderland or the site of a hidden Shangri-la - rather what they looked for in the West were not only science and technology but also art, music and literature. That is why the people living on a few islands on the fringe of Asia have been able to succeed so well in the world.

APPENDIX I

Extracts from

The Constitution of Japan

We, the Japanese people, acting through our duly elected representatives in the National Diet, determined that we shall secure for ourselves and our posterity the fruits of peaceful cooperation with all nations and the blessings of liberty throughout this land, and resolved that never again shall we be visited with the horrors of war through the action of government, do proclaim that sovereign power resides with the people and do firmly establish this Constitution. Government is a sacred trust of the people, the authority for which is derived from the people, the powers of which are exercised by the representatives of the people, and the benefits of which are enjoyed by the people. This is a universal principle of mankind upon which this Constitution is founded. We reject and revoke all constitutions, laws, ordinances, and rescripts in conflict herewith.

We, the Japanese people, desire peace for all time and are deeply conscious of the high ideals controlling human relationship, and we have determined to preserve our security and existence, trusting in the justice and faith of the peace-loving peoples of the world. We desire to occupy an honoured place in an international society striving for the preservation of peace, and the banishment of tyranny and slavery, oppression and intolerance for all time from the earth. We recognise that all peoples of the world have the right to live in peace, free from fear and want.

We believe that no nation is responsible to itself alone, but that laws of political morality are universal; and that obedience to such laws is incumbent upon all nations who would sustain their own sovereignty and justify their sovereign relationship with other nations.

We, the Japanese people, pledge our national honour to accomplish these high ideals and purposes with all our resources.

CHAPTER I. THE EMPEROR

Article 1. The Emperor shall be the symbol of the State and of the unity of the people, deriving his position from the will of the people with whom resides sovereign power.

Article 4. The Emperor shall perform only such acts in matters of state as are provided for in this Constitution and he shall not have powers related to government.

The Emperor may delegate the performance of his acts in matters of state as may be provided by law.

Article 7. The Emperor, with the advice and approval of the Cabinet, shall perform the following acts in matters of state on behalf of the people:

Promulgation of amendments of the Constitution, laws, cabinet orders and treaties.

Convocation of the Diet.

Dissolution of the House of Representatives.

Proclamation of general election of members of the Diet.

Attestation of the appointment and dismissal of Ministers of State and other officials as provided for by law, and of full powers and credentials of Ambassadors and Ministers.

Attestation of general and special amnesty, commutation of punishment, reprieve, and restoration of rights.

Awarding of honours.

Attestation of instruments of ratification and other diplomatic documents as provided for by law.

Receiving foreign ambassadors and ministers.

Performance of ceremonial functions.

CHAPTER II. RENUNCIATION OF WAR

Article 9. Aspiring sincerely to an international peace based on justice and order, the Japanese people forever renounce war as a sovereign right of the nation and the threat or use of force as means of settling international disputes.

In order to accomplish the aim of the preceding paragraph, land, sea, and air forces, as well as other war potential will never be maintained. The right of belligerency of the state will not be recognised.

CHAPTER III. RIGHTS AND DUTIES OF THE PEOPLE

Article 14. All of the people are equal under the law and there shall be no discrimination in political, economic or social relations because of race, creed, sex, social status or family origin.

Peers and peerage shall not be recognised.

No privilege shall accompany any award of honour, decoration or any distinction, nor shall any such award be valid beyond the lifetime of the individual who now holds or hereafter may receive it.

Article 19. Freedom of thought and conscience shall not be violated.

Article 20. Freedom of religion is guaranteed to all. No religious organisation shall receive any privileges from the State, nor exercise any political authority.

No person shall be compelled to take part in any religious act, celebration, rite or practice.

The State and its organs shall refrain from religious education or any other religious activity.

Article 21. Freedom of assembly and association as well as speech, press and all other forms of expression are guaranteed.

No censorship shall be maintained, nor shall the secrecy of any means of communication be violated.

Article 26. All people shall have the right to receive an equal education correspondent to their ability, as provided by law.

All people shall be obligated to have all boys and girls under their protection receive ordinary education as provided for by law. Such compulsory education shall be free.

Article 34. No person shall be arrested or detained without being at once informed of the charges against him or without the immediate privilege of counsel; nor shall he be detained without adequate cause and upon demand of any person such cause must be immediately shown in open court in his presence and the presence of his counsel.

Article 38. No person shall be compelled to testify against himself.

Confession made under compulsion, torture or threat, or after prolonged arrest or detention shall not be admitted in evidence.

No person shall be convicted or punished in cases where the only proof against him is his own confession.

CHAPTER V. THE CABINET

Article 69. If the House of Representatives passes a no-confidence resolution, or rejects a confidence resolution, the Cabinet shall resign *en masse*, unless the House of Representatives is dissolved within ten (10) days.

CHAPTER VI. JUDICIARY

Article 76. The whole judicial power is vested in a Supreme Court and in such inferior courts as are established by law.

No extraordinary tribunal shall be established, nor shall any organ or agency of the Executive be given final judicial power.

All judges shall be independent in the exercise of their conscience and shall be bound only by this Constitution and the laws.

Article 81. The Supreme Court is the court of last resort with power to determine the constitutionality of any law, order, regulation or official act.

CHAPTER VII. FINANCE

Article 89. No public money or other property shall be expended or appropriated for the use, benefit or maintenance of any religious institution or association, or for any charitable, educational or benevolent enterprises not under the control of public authority.

APPENDIX II

The Sagawa scandal – Update

[See Recent Scandals pages 189-190]

Having refused to submit to questioning by the public prosecutors and having escaped a formal indictment by the payment of a ¥ 200,000 fine, Shin Kanemaru, former Vice-President of the Liberal Democratic Party, intended to resume his role as the party's actual leader, when something unusual happened. Public anger exploded at the outrageous behaviour of the politicians and the connivance of the authorities. Rallies, petition drives, hunger strikes and resolutions of local assemblies protested the insolent challenge to the public order. In the afternoon of 15 October 1992, Shin Kanemaru announced that he would resign from the Diet to take responsibility for accepting illicit political donations. Public criticism also mounted against former Prime Minister Noboru Takeshita, blaming him particularly for relying on a mobster to protect his political interests.

The fight over the succession to Shin Kanemaru as chairman of the *Keiseikai* (statecraft association, the official name of the Takeshita faction) split the group. The faction had evolved from the Tanaka faction and counted 109 members. It was controlled by Shin Kanemaru, Noboru Takeshita and Ichirō Ozawa, former LDP Secretary General and protegé of Kanemaru. Kanemaru had become chairman because Takeshita was implicated in the Recruit scandal. Ozawa's attempt to take over the leadership of the faction was opposed by Keizō Obuchi, also a former Secretary General of the party, and Ryūtarō Hashimoto, former Minister of Transport, who had chafed under Ozawa's arrogance.

The collapse of the Takeshita faction may bring an end to the very undemocratic control of Japan's government by a small group of politicians. The 279 members of the LDP constitute 54.5% of the 512 members of the Lower House, and the 114 members of the LDP make up 45.2% of the 252 members of the Upper House. Altogether, the 392 members of the LDP account for 51.6% of all lawmakers. The Takeshita faction numbered 106 adherents (Lower House 69, Upper House 37), 26.9% of the LDP Diet members and 13.9% of all lawmakers. The other LDP factions, headed by Prime Minister Kiichi Miyazawa, Hiroshi Mitsuzuka, Michio Watanabe and Toshio Komoto, account for nearly 70% of the LDP Diet members but they cannot oppose the Takeshita faction because the support of the Takeshita faction controls the election of the party president (and thereby the prime minister). Until the split of the faction, it was under the control of a small group led by Shin Kanemaru and Ichirō Ozawa whose views dominated Japan's policies.

In the trial of Jun Saetomo, former managing director of Tokyo Sagawa Kyūbin, the deposition of Ryūmin Oshima, head of the rightist *Kōmintō* group, alleged that seven members of the Diet belonging to the LDP attempted to end the harassment of Takeshita in 1987 by *Kōmintō*. A proxy of Shin Kanemaru was said to have offered ¥ 3 billion and Yoshiro Mori, chairman of the LDP Policy Research Council, ¥ 2 billion, in exchange for stopping the group's harassment of Takeshita.

The prosecutors' reports also stated that Hiroyasu Watanabe, former President of Tokyo Sagawa Kyūbin, had contacted Kanemaru, Takeshita and Hideo Watanabe, Minister of Posts and Telecommunications in the Miyazawa cabinet, through Rekiji Kobari, Chairman of the Fukushima Kōtsū bus company, to obtain financial support from the Sanwa and Sumitomo banks. Kanemaru reportedly called on the President of Sumitomo Bank and asked for help.

Three of the politicians named in the depositions admitted contact with *Kōmintō* but four denied any involvement. All seven, however, seethed with rage and screamed that their human rights had been violated because their names had been disclosed. They threatened to sue the prosecutors for libel and demanded damages.

Tamisuke Watanuki, LDP Secretary General, complained that the prosecutors had neglected to confirm the facts with the politicians. The conduct of the prosecutors and the management of the court threatened to violate human rights and the independence of political parties. He told reporters that the LDP would bring an action for libel against Oshima and the prosecutors. Foreign Minister Michio Watanabe blamed the prosecutors for unilaterally divulging their names without first seeking their explanation.

Kōzō Watanabe, Minister of International Trade and Industry, made a similar statement. Seiroku Kajiyama, chairman of the party's Diet Affairs Committee, denied any involvement in the affair and termed the prosecutors' report totally groundless and 100 per cent wrong. The report defamed politicians, he said, and he was quoted as telling Prime Minister Miyazawa 'this is fascism by the prosecution'.

Actually, the furor of the politicians was groundless. According to Article 305 of the Code of Criminal Procedure, the presiding judge can, at the request of the defendant or his lawyer, but also at his own initiative, have the documents submitted by the prosecution read (the word used in the text of the article is *rōdoku*, meaning read aloud or recite) in court; the judge can also read the documents himself or have the assistant judges read them. As in all trials, the truth of the statements is established or denied by the court procedures.

A few days later, the plan of suing the prosecutors was dropped and Prime Minister Miyazawa ordered Cabinet Secretary Kōichi Kato to examine whether LDP members could lodge complaints by administrative procedures. The episode revealed how little some Japanese lawmakers understand democratic principles and procedures. Makoto Tanabe, chairman of the Social Democratic Party, remarked that the actions proposed by the LDP violated the constitutional separation of legislative, executive and judicial powers. Instead of accusing the prosecutors, the LDP should agree to have Takeshita and Kanemaru testify in the Diet.

INDEX

INDEX

INDEX

JUNIATA COLLEGE
2820 9100 011 846 2